Techniques of
Transport Planning

VOLUME ONE

Pricing and Project Evaluation

Books published under the Transport Research Program

Techniques of
Transport Planning

John R. Meyer, Editor

VOLUME ONE

Pricing and Project Evaluation

JOHN R. MEYER *and* MAHLON R. STRASZHEIM

*With special contributions by Benjamin I. Cohen,
Leon M. Cole, John F. Kain, Koichi Mera, Robert Mnookin,
Paul O. Roberts, & Martin Wohl*

The Brookings Institution
TRANSPORT RESEARCH PROGRAM
Washington, D.C.

THE BROOKINGS INSTITUTION is an independent organization devoted to nonpartisan research, education, and publication in economics, government, foreign policy, and the social sciences generally. Its principal purposes are to aid in the development of sound public policies and to promote public understanding of issues of national importance.

The Institution was founded on December 8, 1927, to merge the activities of the Institute for Government Research, founded in 1916, the Institute of Economics, founded in 1922, and the Robert Brookings Graduate School of Economics and Government, founded in 1924.

The general administration of the Institution is the responsibility of a Board of Trustees charged with maintaining the independence of the staff and fostering the most favorable conditions for creative research and education. The immediate direction of the policies, program, and staff of the Institution is vested in the President, assisted by an advisory committee of the officers and staff.

In publishing a study, the Institution presents it as a competent treatment of a subject worthy of public consideration. The interpretations and conclusions in such publications are those of the author or authors and do not necessarily reflect the views of the other staff members, officers, or trustees of the Brookings Institution.

Foreword

THE CLOSE CONNECTION between transportation and economic development has long been recognized but neither well defined nor fully understood, least of all in the underdeveloped countries. This paradox may stem from the widely held assumption that poor countries "need everything"—that the inadequacy of their transport facilities would seem to justify almost any additional investment in highways, railroads, or port facilities. But such an assumption may be ill founded. Although the total investment in poor countries may be inadequate, parts of their transport systems may in fact have excess capacity. Faulty analysis could lead to investment decisions that would waste scarce capital on unneeded projects, with adverse consequences for the location of industries, use of resources, and economic growth.

To shed light on planning problems and improve the quality of transport investment decisions in underdeveloped countries, the Brookings Institution has devoted much of its Transport Research Program to examining the interdependence of transport and development. The program has been supported by a grant from the U.S. Agency for International Development and directed by Wilfred Owen. It was conducted as part of the Brookings Economic Studies Program, headed by Joseph A. Pechman.

Some of the research was conducted at Harvard University under the direction of John R. Meyer. The Harvard program consisted of a series of working seminars and related research studies in transport planning and economic development. A fundamental premise of the Harvard program was that effective transport planning requires the systematic development and application of the principles of economic theory, engineering, decision theory, and systems analysis, in a format which takes into

vii

account the prevailing social, economic, and political environment. The interdisciplinary nature of the effort is shown in the academic background and experience of the participants, among whom were engineers, city planners, economists, and a lawyer. The integration of the principles of economic theory with techniques of systems analysis to define a transport planning framework has been the continuing challenge of the Harvard research.

The publication of *Techniques of Transport Planning* in two volumes completes the Harvard research and concludes the Brookings Transport Research Program. In this first volume, *Pricing and Project Evaluation*, the authors survey the principles of engineering design, price theory and welfare economics, capital budgeting, and decision theory as a basis for public policy decisions regarding transport investments. Using a single project as a frame of reference, they synthesize and extend the literature of conventional project evaluation, or cost-benefit analysis, as a tool for making those decisions. They thus lay the foundation for Volume 2, *Systems Analysis and Simulation Models,* which extends the analysis of transport planning to the transport system as a whole. Many transport projects affect the performance of entire transport systems and have a pervasive influence throughout the economy, as the authors illustrate by applying their model to the Colombian economy and transport system.

Volume 1 benefits from the contributions of several participants in the Harvard program, many chapters being the result of seminar papers and thesis research. The table of contents indicates the history of authorship. All the authors, especially the two principal ones, owe a substantial intellectual debt to the students, faculty, and visiting research associates who took part in the Harvard seminars. The authors also wish to thank the members of their reading committee—James R. Nelson, Robert Sadove, and George W. Wilson—for their comments; Ruth Westheimer for her editorial assistance; Irving Forman for drafting some of the more complex figures; and Marina Ochoa for her revision and typing of innumerable drafts.

As in all Brookings studies, the views expressed are solely those of the authors and should not be attributed to those who read and commented on the manuscript, to the Agency for International Development, or to the trustees, officers, or other staff members of the Brookings Institution.

KERMIT GORDON
President

June 1970
Washington, D.C.

Contents

TEXT TABLES

CHAPTER ONE

The Transportation Planning Problem

THE SPECIFICATION of a transportation planning system and the description and evaluation of its performance is a complex undertaking. Transportation systems produce outputs of many dimensions: both freight and passenger services are involved, and their description involves travel time, costs, comfort, convenience, and a host of other considerations. Transport technology is, similarly, multifaceted and proliferating rapidly.

The economic environment also has an important bearing on any transport planning problem. A variety of market structures exists in the transportation sector, including many that are not perfectly competitive. Both governments and private decision makers commonly are involved, so that planning the appropriate system usually requires an examination of the role of the public sector. Among the questions to be answered are what the proper mix of public and private ownership and public regulation is, and to what extent recourse is to be made to market pricing in decision making.

Decisions regarding a transportation system also influence development elsewhere in the economy of which it is a part. The static effects of transport policies on efficient allocation of resources have often been discussed, but the dynamic and social effects of such policies on the distribution of income, on the level and rate of saving, on the development of entrepreneurial and labor skills, and on location decisions may be of even greater significance. Indeed, static efficiency in the allocation of already recognized resources may be less important than the promotion of growth in technology, industry, and capital stock.

A solution to these questions requires specification of the mix of public and private ownership; a description, wherever relevant, of the regulatory environment for the private sector, including safety and service levels, pricing standards, and rates of return on capital; and criteria for system design, pricing, and investment decisions for the public sector. Formulation of a plan will require an objective function of considerable scope if even a part of these economic and social consequences is to be encompassed.

Systems versus Project Analysis

Systems analysis has been described as a process in which "means and ends are continuously played off against one another. New objectives are defined and new assumptions made, new models constructed until a creative amalgam appears, a solution that is better than others even if it is not optimal in any sense."[1] With this emphasis on the interplay between means and ends, a systems analysis makes it possible to consider and evaluate a broad range of economic and social effects. While systems analysis is no substitute for the political process (for example, in evaluating the relative weights to be attached to diverse objectives), when properly done, it provides a basis for projecting the probable social and dynamic effects of alternative transport decisions or operating procedures. A systems approach is particularly amenable to sensitivity analysis, which permits testing of a range of different assumptions and contingencies, without recourse to the discomforts or costs of learning from experience exclusively.

The description of a transport system and the tracing of its ramifications are the usual problems to which transportation systems analysis is directed. Transport technology can be represented as a series of particular modes which represent certain combinations of available technologies, often described in the form of prescribed design standards. Implied in these descriptions, however, are significant trade-offs—between vehicle size and weight, pavement structure, control procedures, and performance characteristics such as speed, safety, and schedule frequency. Frequency of service,

---

1. Aaron Wildavsky [F46], p. 36. Throughout this volume, citations are keyed to the bibliography, pp. 317–36.

vehicle and crew scheduling, type of vehicle, length of train, one- or two-way service, controlled access, signaling procedures, and control of right of way can be most important in determining capabilities, costs, and economic effectiveness. By contrast, indiscriminate application of accepted engineering standards in these matters may produce unfortunate consequences.

The demand side of a transport system is as complex as the supply side. Demand will be responsive to a wide variety of pricing and service standards that must be defined over the entire trip contemplated, reflecting line-haul, waiting-time, collection, and distribution costs. Transport demand will, in the long run, respond to new locational decisions, which in turn are made in response to transport availability. Similarly, other changes in the economy, such as changes in consumer demand or plant technology, will influence and be influenced by transport development.

A good systems analysis normally involves description of the transport system itself, its technology, its use, and its interaction with the economy. The possible configurations that might be evaluated are numerous indeed. Such an approach to transport planning is explored in Volume 2 of this study. A computer-oriented simulation model is described there which models the transport system and its performance in detail and superimposes this system onto a simulation of an economy disaggregated by regions.

Ceteris paribus, a systems approach would appear to be the recommended planning procedure. In long-range transportation planning where the technology and location decisions can be varied, considerable gains appear possible from a systems planning approach. The result of a systems approach will depend not only on the model structure and its ability to represent the important system interdependencies, but also on data inputs, the specification of appropriate objective functions, and the pricing, investment, and regulatory criteria that are included.

Despite these compelling arguments for a systems approach, governments and financial agencies are presently project oriented in their decision and policy processes. One reason is that a systems analysis can be a considerable task. Furthermore, the data required for a complete systems analysis are often difficult and expensive to obtain or to analyze. In many cases, given a relatively short planning period, the decisions to be made may not involve interdependencies of sufficient consequence to justify a systems approach. The most important decision in some projects may be their timing; for example, the determination of the point in time when traffic demand warrants that a road be straightened or widened or that a narrow bridge be replaced. This is, in essence, a relatively conventional capital budgeting problem, which is susceptible to a reasonably straightforward treatment on a project basis.

Project analysis may also provide useful insights about alternative pricing, investment, or design standards. By limiting attention to one particular project, more effort can be expended in examining cost and demand responses to a variety of design and pricing possibilities. A complete systems analysis, which stresses interdependencies of projects and the feedback of the transport system on the economy, will not be as useful for this detail work. Fundamentally, the two approaches are complementary: information learned from a detailed examination and planning of projects on a disaggregated basis is, at a minimum, an indispensable input to a broader systems approach.

Planning in a Project Context

Several simplifications are required for proper application of a project planning approach. One lies in the nature of the technology, which must lend itself to disaggregation in such a way that meaningful measures of cost and performance can be ascertained. In particular, the users of a transport project must be identifiable. In truth, there is probably no fully satisfactory way to divide a transport system into projects without encountering important interdependencies, especially in determining net benefits over a long period of time. The use of a facility is not always easily explained by the physical or economic characteristics of a particular link or project in question. Similarly, shippers' decisions are sensitive to the effects of the entire trip, from origin to destination.

Another difficulty in a project approach is that of estimating the demand consequences of location changes induced by transport investments. These are extremely complex and are neither widely understood nor easily quantifiable. Thus, while the project planning discussed in this book is based on the customary "link addition" concept of a project, assessing the demand consequences is a formidable task—formidable enough to imply that long-range demand forecasting, short of a more complete systems analysis, will yield estimates good only to a first approximation.

An outline of a recommended project planning format is illustrated in the flow diagram of Figure 1-1. The interdependencies among costing, pricing, project design, and demand are represented in the top half of the

FIGURE 1-1. *Transport Project Planning Format*

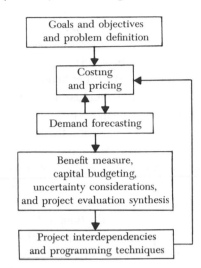

flow diagram by two-directional arrows. While the discussion in this volume more or less follows the sequence shown in Figure 1-1, planning practice will normally entail at least a few simple iterative procedures. For example, given preliminary estimates of demand (based on both aggregate and regional economic variables and a first approximation of feasible transport service and pricing principles), iterations will be required to determine better project designs, pricing practices, and hence net benefits of candidate projects. Project proposals that emerge from these initial design and selection activities then become inputs to the capital budgeting decision.

Estimation of pricing and cost characteristics is discussed in Part 1 of this book. Transport pricing decisions involve an examination of the nature of market pricing elsewhere in the economy and include questions of the distribution of income, dynamic effects of pricing policies on savings rates, and so on. A major conclusion of the pricing discussion in Part 1 is that there is not likely to be a single optimal pricing strategy applicable in all circumstances. Long-run marginal and average cost pricing both have advantages. Similarly, pricing based on short-run marginal, average, or out-of-pocket costs may be appropriate in particular applications.

Some of the most complex pricing questions are posed when setting charges for facilities subject to peak periods of congestion. The customary recommendation is that congestion tolls should be imposed on travelers who, by their presence in the peak period, add more to marginal social cost, through congestion, than their perceived private costs. Aside from the economic costs of imposing such toll schemes, serious efficiency and redistribution questions must be addressed. For example, those forced off a facility by tolls may use alternative routes, thus producing system effects on these alternatives. Tolls may also be regressive and therefore unacceptable on equity or political grounds. On the other hand, they may raise important revenues, which can serve both as an indication of the need and as a means for financing further additions to capacity.

The widespread existence of market imperfections also raises the question of whether transport pricing policies might be altered systematically to offset these imperfections. So-called second-best pricing can be shown to offset certain kinds of market imperfections and leave everyone better off in terms of efficient allocation of resources. But to implement such a procedure involves considerable data collection, analysis, and administration, which may be neither cheap nor easy to accomplish.

Demand estimation is the subject of Part 2. Among other problems encountered when estimating the demand for a particular transport project is, for example, that there may be no established market for transport service, or, if a market exists, there may be no available user pricing mechanism which is both feasible and sensitive. Gasoline user taxes, which are unrelated to the time of day a road or airport or marine facility is used and which are often poorly correlated to the costs imposed by the marginal users, are one such example—and by no means the worst of the types of user prices in existence. It therefore is often no mean task to infer demand responses to alternative prices, travel times, or service standards from the sort of market information available.

Procedures for evaluating proposed transport projects are discussed in Part 3. This involves assessing net benefits, which depend both on a proposed project's ability to serve demand in a static sense and on a variety of macro and system-wide effects. The implications for the decision to accept or reject any project will depend, in turn, on the pricing policies used and on the capital budgeting criteria adopted for public projects.

Several capital budgeting criteria are reviewed in Part 3, and the maximization of net present value is suggested as the best decision criterion of those conventionally employed for capital budgeting purposes. Application of capital budgeting procedures to public investment decisions requires some modification of those criteria developed in the economic theory of the firm for evaluating private investment decisions in perfect capital markets. The most important such modification is the choice of an appropriate interest rate. Governments may not be able to borrow and lend any desired amount at prevailing market rates of interest; market interest rates, therefore, may not reflect the marginal terms at which the government should value costs or benefits over time.

A decision criterion for project evaluation must simultaneously consider pricing decisions and capital budgeting questions. Pricing procedures may be designed to recover a small or large share of the net benefits which accrue, depending on policy objectives. Furthermore, decisions on transport pricing may have implications throughout the economy. For example, the use of price discrimination or subsidies in one sector of an economy and not in others raises questions about the static efficiency and dynamic effects on investment allocation. In Part 3, a sequential procedure is developed for simultaneously considering the interdependencies of benefit measures, pricing, and financial viability in deciding whether to accept or reject a project.

Project evaluation must be based on an assessment of future demand and technology, both of which are uncertain. Customary adjustments for risk, such as adjusting the benefit–cost ratio or the interest rate, represent rather gross methods for handling such problems. A decision theory approach to the treatment of uncertainty, in which probability concepts are applied, is also outlined in Part 3.

As suggested earlier, an individual project orientation may lead to neglect of many system interdependencies. Two relationships especially relevant in transport project planning which may be unevaluated in a project-by-project approach are those of network dependencies and financial dependencies arising from budget constraints. These are considered in Part 4. Both are amenable to fairly simple programming formulations. As such, they foreshadow the sort of system effects considered more systematically in Volume 2. The particular subclass of network problems addressed in Part 4 is the simple staging question of when to add new links. A recursive programming model can handle this problem essentially by mapping out a staging schedule for new projects to meet demands expected during the period under consideration, subject to a given total budget.

As for financial dependencies, much public and private investment planning is done in the context of budget constraints. In a broader context, imperfections in capital markets, especially with the government as a participant, are such that no single rate of interest may be relevant for discounting benefits and costs. Moreover, since projects are not always independent, it may not be feasible to choose them on the basis of discounted net benefits, using prescribed rates of interest.

A programming approach to capital budgeting, as outlined in Part 4, provides a means of handling many of these problems. Proposed transport projects can be used as inputs in a programming format in which planners choose the preferred set of projects subject to budget constraints. The so-called dual of the programming solution provides a measure, moreover, of project profitability to be compared with other public and private investment projects and thus provides a focal point for coordinating transport policy with broader government objectives. Programming also permits a more explicit treatment of risk.

Again, various aspects of project planning are invariably interdependent, and hence there is no unique organization of the planning problem. The sequence outlined in Figure 1-1 and around which this volume is organized permits an analysis of the components of the planning problem so as to minimize the extent and importance of interdependencies that might otherwise be ignored. In general, the proposed approach to project planning is only a first approximation to planning in a systems context—an approximation which will be more or less useful depending on the nature of the problem. Moreover, even if the systems approach is conceptually more satisfying, it may be prohibitively expensive to apply. Thus simple improvements in project planning, as outlined in this volume, can be of immediate interest even if one accepts the argument that systems analysis, as outlined in Volume 2, represents a fundamentally better overall approach to transport planning.

PART ONE

Pricing Principles and Their Implications

CHAPTER TWO

Alternative Pricing Strategies

Pricing policy, particularly as it pertains to public facilities, can be established with many purposes in mind. Transport tariffs can assist in the proper allocation of resources by signaling effective demand for transport. They can provide revenues for operating, maintaining, and financing a facility, or aid the rational allocation of capital among competing modes. They are a possible means to redistribute income or promote growth of particular regions or industries and may help to control congestion.

Transport prices may be set so as to maximize economic growth over a stipulated planning horizon or time period. They often affect savings and investment rates within a society and the rate at which certain kinds of economic resources are developed and brought into a market economy, domestic or international.

As a means of effecting redistribution of income between regions or special groups (for example, school children, farmers living in remote areas, or disabled war veterans) the pricing decision may be independent of growth objectives. Normally, redistributive goals through transport policy are closely tied to such social goals as creating more national unity, developing better national defenses, or promoting the development of underdeveloped or underprivileged regions or sectors of the economy.

Similarly, pricing policy and transport regulation, particularly in North America and Europe, often have assumed the objective of maintaining the existing pattern of modal shares among common carriers or between common and private carriers. Indeed, the United States Interstate Commerce Commission (ICC) has at times seemed to consider maintenance of the status quo in traffic allocation as virtually a legislative fiat—and not without basis.

Maintenance of the status quo is often closely related to providing the financial means to underwrite the losses of certain kinds of unprofitable "social services" provided by transport systems. Thus, in many parts of the world, earnings on rail freight traffic have long financed losses on passenger services, and earnings on large volume shipments have been used to offset losses on small volume shipments.

Indeed, a common constraint on transport pricing policy can be the objective of financial integrity—total revenues of a particular transport operation being sufficient to cover total costs. For present purposes, the most important consequence of this constraint is that in some circumstances it can force a choice between abandoning marginal cost pricing (which is generally deemed to have certain efficiency advantages) or subsidizing the transport undertaking from external sources.[1] Views on the advisability of these two courses differ sharply; thus, some who accept the desirability of marginal cost pricing as a concept feel that the constraint of total revenue equaling total cost is needed to discipline managements to seek minimum cost solutions to production problems.[2]

In general, because of problems of cost estimation, imperfect markets, and multiple and conflicting objectives, suggested strategies for pricing transport facilities and services have differed widely. Some of these strategies have arisen from experience and pragmatic adaptation to observed circumstances. Others represent concepts derived from theoretical analyses. In general, the most fundamental difference between alternative pricing strategies for transport probably is the degree to which a particular price is demand (or profit) as opposed to cost oriented, although the distinction is not always clear-cut.

Needless to say, transport charges have not always achieved stipulated purposes. Major conceptual and practical difficulties have accompanied attempts to set charges which would pay for, as well as efficiently ration,

1. For the controversy over the welfare implications of marginal pricing, see two articles by Nancy Ruggles [B27, pp. 29–46, and B28, pp. 107–26]. In one she traces the concept of marginal cost from Marshall through the socialist writers of the 1930s, and in the other she discusses Hotelling's article, "The General Welfare in Relation to Problems of Taxation and of Railway and Utility Rates," *Econometrica*, Vol. 6 (July 1938), pp. 242–69.

2. See Maurice Allais [B2], pp. 212–71.

a fixed investment or capital commitment. The difficult questions, in fact, are almost invariably the same: How much investment should be undertaken? How is the cost associated with an investment to be shared among different classes of users in different periods and with different needs?

Conventional Practice: Monopolistic Price Discrimination and Average Cost Pricing

Whenever a service is involved, as in transportation, and particularly when that service is sold in markets that are less than perfectly competitive, price discrimination or differentiation, even where costs may not differ, becomes a possibility.[3] Three general types of such price differentiation can be identified: (1) *cyclic* recurrent price discrimination or differentiation applicable where very sharp seasonal, daily, or other variations occur in the rate at which the service is consumed;[4] (2) *interpersonal* price discrimination, which involves different price levels (within any single time interval) for different categories of consumers; and (3) *intertemporal* or *secular* discrimination in which the basic price level rises or declines over time.

One of the most popular transport pricing strategies has been to discriminate between users according to value of service, that is, essentially to ignore costs and charge what the traffic will bear. In unsophisticated usage, gross revenue maximization may even be the objective. In sophisticated applications, the goal is profit maximization, to be achieved by monopolistic price discrimination. Technically, this would mean setting prices that would equate marginal revenues to marginal costs for separate classes of users. Multiple-price strategies of this type are the most prevalent approach to establishing railroad, airline, and truck tariffs in the world today. They are practiced both by carrier management and, in many circumstances, by the regulatory authorities that establish or sanction rates. The influence of such pricing can also be seen in many highway, airway, and waterway user charges.

3. For elaboration of the role of these characteristics, see James R. Nelson [B22], pp. 414–81; Yale Brozen [B7], pp. 67–75.

4. Jack Hirshleifer claimed a fundamental distinction between discrimination and differentiation if social marginal costs are defined in the opportunity sense. Given such a definition, no discrimination exists in the case of different charges for peak and off-peak consumers because the relevant social marginal costs of service also differ. Such a definition stirs up definitional problems of marginal costs, however. The preferred use here is the term "discrimination" in its usual looser sense. See [B13], pp. 451–62.

The railroads, in particular, have long practiced value-of-service price discrimination as a means of recouping overhead costs not directly traceable to carrying any particular commodity. The ICC has implicitly accepted this procedure. By lowering the rate paid by shippers of commodities with an elastic demand, such price discrimination may induce a higher utilization of fixed rail investment. However, such discriminatory prices have important secondary effects on the allocation of traffic among carriers and ultimately on relative prices of all intermediate and final products.[5]

In practice, systematic or thorough estimates of the marginal costs or revenues needed for implementing a value-of-service pricing scheme are seldom made. At best, demand elasticities, and thus marginal revenue, are generally assumed to be roughly inverse to the value of the product or service being rendered. Even in simple cases, these pricing procedures are not likely to be easy to administer. Markets must be identified and segregated and the price structure established and maintained. These may be difficult to accomplish if the structure is complex, and especially if maintained over a long period. Over time, the likelihood increases that the demand elasticities for various products will change, as the competitive threat of new or other transport modes appears.[6]

The fewer the number of prices, the easier any rate system will be to administer or manage. The extreme is single-price profit maximization. This would be the practice of manufacturers who possessed market power but who were dealing in homogeneous industrial products. Because of the inherent geographical, service, and commodity heterogeneity of transport, single-price profit maximization has rarely, if ever, been applied. To do so would involve potential profit losses in some submarkets.

Complex multiple-price systems have thus dominated the private sectors of transport. By contrast, simple average cost pricing, in various modified forms, has characterized the approach of many public agencies to establishing tolls or user charges for highways, airports, airways, bridges, and similar facilities. Average cost pricing in application has differed somewhat in the definitions used to determine costs and output. Normally, the relevant costs are defined as those of operating and amortizing a facility, while output is some measure of the use made of that facility. In the United States, however, the federal government's highway program uses a price based on the cost of constructing *new* facilities, and output is taken as the use

5. See John R. Meyer and others [A7], Chap. 7. The consequences of the U.S. railroads' practice of value-of-service discrimination are discussed on pp. 170–88.
6. Merrill J. Roberts [B25].

of *all* highways, old and new. There is also considerable disagreement as to the proper measure of output. Ton-miles, vehicle-miles, and axle-ton-miles have all been recommended. In practice, the usual measures have been gallons of fuel and pounds of rubber consumed since these are easier units on which to administer an excise tax.

The cost of a facility might be expected to be a function of the volume of services provided or demanded, and these in turn would normally be sensitive to price. Thus, under an average cost pricing scheme, price itself is a function of cost and a certain simultaneity or interdependency is introduced into the pricing and capital budgeting procedure. To a first approximation, with average cost pricing, only one price or a few prices common to all users will be charged. Accordingly, an average cost pricing scheme, like other single-price schemes, is relatively simple to administer.

Marginal Cost Pricing

Application of marginal cost pricing to transportation has been advocated in several forms. As in any sector of the economy, its usual justification is to improve the use of resources.

Full implementation of marginal cost pricing implies a capital budgeting as well as a pricing regime. Under strict marginal cost pricing, "an investment must be undertaken if the total revenue, derived from the stream of output added to the network and sold throughout the year at the variously prevailing [short-run] marginal cost prices, exceeds the cost for the year of using the additional capacity: the cost of the capital (interest and 'true' depreciation) plus the sum of the additions to the stream of variable costs incurred throughout the year in its utilization."[7]

Administrative and other practical difficulties can arise if the "variously prevailing marginal cost prices" are different at different periods of time or for different classes of users or if homogeneous classes, by time or user, are not easily identified or segregated. In transport, the short-run costs generally pertain to conditions at only one or a few points in the operating cycle. The long-run costs relate to the aggregate effect throughout the complete operating cycle. This means that equality between short- and long-run costs can generally be met only by aggregation (as stated in the above quotation), even with an optimum facility.

7. Fred M. Westfield [B34], p. 68.

The application of short-run marginal cost pricing principles has been widely advocated for transport in circumstances where congestion creates a divergence between private costs and the marginal social costs of using a facility. The usual proposal is to set tolls so that the total price perceived by users is equal to the short-run marginal cost of using the facility. The increments in cost to which prices are adjusted are normally attributed to increased congestion created by more intensive use of the facility at certain times. Since the incremental level of social or congestion cost would be a function of facility design and capacity, an interdependence exists between the solution to the normal supply and demand problem and the capital budgeting process. This, however, is sometimes overlooked in congestion cost pricing proposals since the objective is not so much to recoup the investment as to induce better or optimal use of the existing facility by prohibiting use in circumstances where the price paid or perceived falls short of the marginal costs of such use.[8]

Short-run marginal cost pricing can be expected to produce a profit or surplus when capacity is in short supply. These profits obtained from a short-run marginal social cost pricing solution are analogous to scarcity or quasi-monopoly profits. Such rents would be expected to be largely eliminated, that is, temporary, if the transport facility were provided within the private sector of a market economy and if entry were relatively easy.[9] It has therefore been suggested that profits obtained by a public agency from following a short-run marginal social cost pricing scheme might be invested in expansion. Without further consideration of how the financing is done, expansion of facilities yielding such surpluses will generally be consistent with a fully implemented marginal cost pricing scheme.[10]

Whether the pursuit of a marginal cost pricing scheme would result in a profit or loss in long-run equilibrium would depend on whether the additional units of capacity were subject to increasing, decreasing, or constant returns to scale. Specifically, only in the case of constant returns to scale will the long-run equilibrium obtained from a marginal cost pricing

8. One critic, Alan A. Walters, has stated: "The costs of providing the [highway] network are irrelevant for optimal utilization" [B33], p. 685; and James C. Nelson has stated: "The rule of self-liquidation as a general guide to efficient investment is thrust aside as unnecessary and as a substantial hindrance to efficient utilization of existing highways" [B21], p. 426.

9. Such profits would not be the same as conventional monopoly profits because quantity would be determined by the intersection of average revenue and marginal cost rather than marginal revenue and marginal cost as in the monopoly case.

10. Herbert Mohring [B20], pp. 1–13; Robert Dorfman, ed. [F4], pp. 231–91.

scheme yield revenues exactly equal to those required to finance the equilibrium level of plant or capacity; and even then, only if an aggregation scheme is found to make the short-run subclass solutions over the operating cycle consistent with the long-run solution.

With conventional average rather than marginal cost pricing, of course, the facility would always be just self-sufficient. That is, a loss would not appear even if increasing returns prevailed. Whether average cost pricing is to be considered superior to marginal cost pricing is an old problem that has figured prominently in the economics and transportation literature for many years. One proposed solution to the budgetary problem when increasing returns to scale exist is to assign facility costs in proportion to short-run marginal costs, the size of the markup being subject to the break-even constraint.

Another marginal cost pricing rule that is sometimes advocated is longer run in character. This is to set tariffs, even if the facility is not at an equilibrium capacity, at a level equal to what is needed to cover the incremental cost of the last additional unit of capacity needed to achieve equilibrium. Long-run equilibrium marginal cost pricing of this type assumes that increments of capacity should be made available as long as people are willing to pay the incremental cost of supplying them. This rule, which implies stable prices over time, is to be contrasted with the more strictly conventional marginal cost pricing alternative of setting charges to the short-run marginal cost and continuously varying the price as marginal cost changes over time.

In general, a marginal cost pricing criterion for transport services is theoretically sound only if all other services and enterprises in other sectors of the economy are also selling output at marginal costs. As will be pointed out in Chapter 5, applying marginal cost pricing principles in transport while other sectors pursue other types of pricing policies might induce distortions or inefficiencies as serious as those to be overcome. In fact, systematic deviations from marginal cost pricing will usually be required for optimal resource allocation because of the need for the economy in aggregate to balance the deficits and surpluses of individual activities.

Prices Based on User-Cost Estimates

A natural and widely advocated extension of the long-run marginal cost approach in transport pricing is to separate facility costs into categories associated with incremental additions needed to serve different classes of users. Charges equal (as in average cost pricing) to the quotient of these categories divided by the units of use attributable to each category are then set.

It is this approach that underlies much highway costing and taxation within the United States today. That is, highway costs are assigned to different vehicular classes according to the extent to which they require special or particular facilities. The usual procedure is to define those additional costs that seem necessary to meet the demands of a particular class of users and to assign to those users both these costs and a portion of basic facility costs as well. The basic facility might be defined as that needed to meet light vehicle traffic or to permit minimum required access to abutting property. The premise is that heavy vehicles need the fundamental facility as well as all the engineering specifications added to meet their special needs. The heaviest vehicles using a road would bear a proportion of the increments needed to create the basic facility as well as the cost of specially heavy pavement, specially wide shoulders, passing lanes in hilly terrain, and so on, which would be needed for their purposes only.[11]

The underlying rationale is the usual efficiency argument that prices for resources used should be closely correlated with the marginal opportunity costs of those resources. Practical applicability obviously depends on the ability to identify costs in some sense with particular segments of usage.[12] Other problems can also arise. For example, it can be argued that if heavy highway vehicles do not need more than one lane of a multilane facility at any time, they should be required to pay only the additional structural costs of that one lane. To the extent, however, that the heavy vehicles are the marginal users of the facility, and with the assumption that it would not pay to provide a separate facility for them alone, allocation of some basic construction costs as well as all heavy structural costs to heavy vehicles seems appropriate. In essence, the cost allocation problems arise because economies of scale make it advantageous to consolidate different types of uses on one facility.

Long-run marginal cost pricing of this approximate sort, which is differentiated by different categories of users, has been applied primarily where flat or invariant charges, such as a combination of fuel taxes and license

11. These cost assignments and procedures are discussed in Meyer and others [A7], pp. 65–85.
12. John R. Meyer and Gerald Kraft [A6], pp. 313–34; Meyer [A4], pp. 209–22; and Allen R. Ferguson [A2], pp. 223–34.

fees, are applied to broad categories of users to recoup facility costs. In such instances, estimation of the average incremental cost also may provide a rough check on the equity of the user charges. Such comparisons have been used to indicate whether an existing scheme of user taxes results in any disproportionate burden being assigned to one class of users and whether this disproportion is sufficient to suggest that major distortions affecting the choice of transport modes may be introduced.[13]

A similar long-run incremental cost principle applied to peak and off-peak users could have the result that peak-hour users would be assigned all the costs of extra length or extra capacity needed for their use alone plus a proportion of the base road or capacity that is needed for other hours of the day.[14] Under a strict marginal cost doctrine, of course, *all* costs would be assigned to peak users (or the marginal class of users where classes are defined, as above, by size or weight of vehicle), except to the extent that this practice produced shifting peaks.[15] Since shifting peaks might be the rule rather than the exception if heavy capacity charges were assigned to a narrowly defined peak period or class of users, it is not clear that the cost assignments based on a practical and stable peak-period marginal cost pricing scheme would differ markedly from those of the cruder incremental cost approach just described. It is clear, though, that the cost information required for the "approximate incremental" approach is usually more available than the extensive demand information necessary to implement a more complete or thorough marginal cost approach.

In general, public agencies have often been reluctant to assign all the costs of a fully developed or expanded capacity to *only* the marginal users or those requiring the most complex facilities. This reluctance may derive from a feeling of what is equitable, and it is therefore essentially antimarginalist in character. Or it may reflect some intuitive notion of what is practical, because of possibilities for shifting peaks or difficulties in administering more complex schemes. In this case, the approach may or may not be conceptually consistent with marginalist doctrine. If there is some presumption, as often appears to be the case, that only by combining the demands of different users can one justify the financing of a more

13. Meyer and others [A7]; John R. Meyer, John F. Kain, and Martin Wohl [A5].

14. Allocation problems for urban highway facilities are discussed at length in ibid., pp. 69–74.

15. A shifting peak is one where a strict marginal cost approach gives rise to unstable or ill-defined demands for basic capacity. This problem and suggested solutions to it are discussed in the next section.

elaborate facility that benefits all, this suggests, in turn, that total costs must be apportioned in some measure to all users.

Allocations that reflect benefits received are often suggested in situations where different levels of capacity tend to have a great deal of complementarity or interdependence for different classes of users. For example, the provision of a six-lane instead of a four-lane highway normally confers benefits on highway users during off-peak periods as well as peak periods by permitting higher travel speeds and a somewhat safer trip, everything else being equal, during the off peak. Similarly, providing twelve-foot rather than nine- or ten-foot lanes on a highway because truck and heavy vehicles are expected would normally result in a better level of service for automobiles at most times of the day and in most circumstances. It is therefore not surprising that a blend of long-run marginal cost and benefit-oriented prices does, in fact, characterize the setting of user fees on many public facilities. In such circumstances, the user fees, even if oriented to long-run marginal costs, can acquire, for better or worse, some of the appearances and characteristics of value-of-service or similar demand-oriented tariffs.

Complex Differentiated Pricing Schemes

Problems of rationing peak demand and providing for financial viability and simple concepts of what is equitable or just in redistributing the burden of financing transportation facilities, particularly where there are common costs to be allocated, have led to several proposals of complex, differentiated, or discriminatory pricing schemes for such facilities.

Probably the most basic of these is one borrowed from public utility pricing. In this scheme, prices would be used as a means of equilibrating facility use in different periods of time. The basic notion is simple enough; use of the facility should be maximized subject to the constraints that users pay the incremental costs directly assignable to their consumption and that total revenues equal total costs. Thus, if peak-period total demand is so much greater than off-peak total demand that an off-peak charge that just covers direct operating costs is insufficient to generate off-peak demand in excess of peak-period demand, all costs of providing the basic facility should be charged to peak-period users.

Complications arise if a shifting peak occurs, that is, a situation in which the off-peak demand exceeds the peak-period demand at an off-peak price equal to direct operating costs. The usual solution suggested for this case is rather simple: charges should be set during the peak and off-peak periods so as to equilibrate demand in the two different periods, usually subject to the constraint of covering at least the long-run marginal costs. Determination of the appropriate charges in the shifting-peak case is greatly facilitated if interpersonal price differentiation is ruled out and only cyclic price differentiation is considered.[16] Another practical problem in implementing peak and off-peak pricing schemes is that of defining the relevant time periods. Not only is the existence or nonexistence of a shifting peak sensitive to such definitions, but the prices charged to different consumer groups can vary with these definitions.

Another suggested multiple price policy represents a modification of the short-run marginal cost approach discussed previously. Instead of setting the charge directly equal to the marginal cost, the privately perceived discrepancy between marginal social costs and average costs would be used as a means of determining the proportional allocations of a facility's total cost.[17] This policy has been suggested, for example, where cyclic variations in demand and therefore in congestion occur. The suggestion is that the cost of the basic facility be allocated to the users of each time period according to that period's percentage of the total congestion incurred over a total operating cycle.[18] (Thus, the denominator of the allocation ratio would represent the sum of congestion costs incurred during a complete operating cycle, while the numerator would represent the proportion of these costs attributable to a specific group of users associated with one specified period of the cycle.)

This congestion-cost proportionality results in an allocation roughly proportional to benefits, net of any consumer surplus received by different classes of users. Furthermore, these prices would normally have essentially the same proportional relationships as the short-run marginal costs. Thus, if different subclasses of users had approximately the same cross elasticities with other sectors of demand, about the same choices might be expected between subclasses.

It is important to note that this procedure is not the equivalent of a short-run marginal cost pricing procedure, in which prices equal to the intersection points of peak and off-peak demand curves with short-run marginal costs are set. The proportional use procedure derives the alloca-

16. James M. Buchanan [B8], pp. 463–71.
17. William Vickrey [B32], pp. 275–96.
18. Lyle C. Fitch and Associates [D13], p. 1.

tion of costs from the present facility's use, without reference to how it is priced. Prevailing costs are a function of facility design and utilization (and hence prices), so that the charges created by a proportionality approach could differ significantly from the long-run equilibrium relationships if capacity were in either short supply or oversupply. If capacity is badly underbuilt, for example, the share of facility costs to the peak users will be very high.

Thus, the implications of the procedure are different from a full marginal cost pricing and capital budgeting solution. As suggested above, and anticipating the discussion of congestion cost pricing in Chapter 4, the long-run equilibrium under a short-run marginal cost pricing scheme treats toll receipts as a measure of facility benefits, which are properly compared to the marginal costs of adding capacity. This suggests, however, that the investment costs should be allocated on the basis of the congestion costs which were eliminated by construction rather than those which occurred after construction. This distinction can become significant when there are indivisibilities in project construction, as, for example, adding one more lane. The relevant question in this latter instance is the effect on peak and off-peak users of that additional lane, which may be quite different from the allocations derived from previous available capacity. Constructing additional capacity, for example, could eliminate all congestion during the off peak, which, under the proportional use allocation, would result in a zero cost allocation to the off peak, yet the amount of cost savings to off-peak users resulting from the project could be considerable.

As noted previously, a somewhat similar procedure, that of specifically assigning facility costs in proportion to short-run marginal costs subject to a break-even constraint, has also been suggested as a solution to the budgetary problem when increasing returns to scale exist.[19] Not only might such a pricing policy improve resource allocation, but also many of those advocating proportional markups of this type often do so for practical reasons. For example, the break-even constraint may be introduced because it creates incentives for management to achieve minimum production costs.

In general, arguments in favor of pricing rules that are oriented to costs, and thereby possibly deviate from profit maximization, are strengthened if the operating costs of a particular transport facility are the same regardless of the rule by which management is compensated. In many circumstances, this is probably an unrealistic assumption. Management's efforts

19. Allais [B2].

to minimize transport operating costs, thereby freeing resources to be used elsewhere in the economy, may well depend on whether it is rewarded for reducing costs. Rewarding management for reducing operating costs is equivalent (if receipts are independent of costs) to rewarding it for increased profits. A transport facility's profits are determined by management's joint decisions on investment, price, and operating costs. It is doubtful whether any board of directors, public or private, would have enough information to isolate the effects of pricing decisions on profits from the effects of the other factors. In addition, it is often administratively simpler if management compensation is based on one rule which applies to all decisions.

The problem of determining an appropriate set of prices when strict marginal cost prices are ruled out by the necessity of meeting a budget constraint can also be investigated in the context of a second-best situation, where part of the economy is characterized by the normal competitive processes and part is not. In this approach, prices are set, after stipulated market imperfections have been taken into account, so as to achieve as much social welfare as possible. Almost by definition, prices determined in this fashion would be conceptually superior, at least in a static framework, to those determined by any of the cruder pricing rules discussed previously. On the other hand, determination of these second-best prices would also require considerable information. This point will be elaborated in Chapter 5.

Options, Superpeaks, and Eclectic Pricing Strategies

Another suggestion for recouping some of the costs of transport facilities is implicit in what one might call the option approach to the pricing of public services.[20] In its most dramatic form, it relates to the "unexercised option." The argument is that in many cases people would be willing to pay a price for the possibility of someday using a facility. Commonly cited examples of such items outside of transportation are national parks and hospitals. An analogous situation might occur in transport when occasional or random additions to transport peaks are created. Some urban commuters, for example, may never want to use transit regularly but desire enough

20. Jacques H. Drèze [B10], pp. 1–64.

transit capacity available for their occasional use if needed, say, in bad weather.

In a strict sense, it is these extra random or irregular demands at peak periods to which the option seems to apply best. To the extent that these demands create occasional superpeaks which require services or system outputs above those normally required, the question arises as to what pricing scheme might recover any additional costs created, assuming subsidies are infeasible.[21]

The impact of the optional users should be distinguished from that created by uncertainty attached to the demand of regular users. An uncertain or stochastic demand situation can be extremely troublesome for public utilities because of sharply rising marginal costs at or beyond capacity. Such problems have therefore been analyzed for public utilities with the use of operations research techniques closely analogous to those used in some inventory analyses.[22] The major outcome of the analysis has been the discovery that, on statistical principles, if the demands of different users are imperfectly correlated, the overall standard deviation applicable to all demands will be less than the sum of the standard deviations of the individual demands. Thus, as in the inventory case where holding costs are linearly and homogeneously related to the size of the inventory, the concentration of many individuals' demand at one facility will create increasing returns to scale, even though the basic cost of the services without uncertainty is subject to constant returns.[23]

Stochastic demand variation attributable to regular users of a transport system has not been a major concern of transport analysts or policy makers. The most costly consequences of insufficient transport capacity are likely to be associated with passenger transport for which demand is thought to be binary or discontinuous in character. That is, a person is assumed either to demand or not to demand passenger transport facilities. In transport, therefore, the usual procedure is to analyze the impact of variations in passenger demand in terms of congestion cost. Freight demands register, of course, along a continuum, and regular users can, on occasion, evidence considerable variability in their demands. However, if the probability of

21. For a discussion of using subsidy for this purpose, see Meyer, Kain, and Wohl [A5], pp. 347–48.

22. Edwin S. Mills [B19] provides a summary of the underlying inventory theory applied to a broad context of circumstances.

23. For an application to public utility pricing, see Marcel Boiteux [B5].

not being served within a given period of time is not large, the cost associated with temporarily insufficient capacity for freight demands will probably be expressed in a short delay, which in turn is not likely to be very costly. Furthermore, since the need for prompt and reliable freight services is likely to be greater for some commodities than for others, with minimal organizational control the commodities with the high priority can normally be accommodated with reasonable promptness. Specifically, for many low-cost bulk commodities, such as coal, grains, ores, and lumber, relatively slow service is often quite acceptable, sometimes even preferred, by shippers seeking to reduce storage costs.

The occasional users of transport, by contrast, will often exercise either an explicit or an implicit option for excess capacity during a particular period. Structuring a pricing policy which retrieves some of the value of these options from the holders, in order to cover the costs of the requisite standby capacity, could aid in a rational allocation of resources. The strict marginalist solution would be to charge all capacity costs, both regular and standby, to superpeak users on a uniform basis. This scheme might be hard to administer because of the difficulty of predicting when the random events might occur and how long they might last, although this could probably be solved as experience accumulated. More difficult still is the possible intensification of the shifting peak and the attendant empirical estimation problems. To the extent that the burden of capacity costs was placed on the superpeak users, regular users could expect lower charges for use of the facility.

If instead of the strict marginalist approach an attempt were made to segregate the special costs associated with the superpeak and to charge these costs to the superpeak users, difficult problems of identification could arise. Indeed, those who value an option for standby capacity, yet never have an occasion to use it, could avoid most plans for assessing user charges. For such people, some method of taxation to finance a subsidy might be appropriate. Still, the implication appears to be that occasional or latent users, *if identifiable,* should be charged most or all of the costs of any specialized additional capacity to meet their special needs. This would, of course, occur in the strict marginalist case as well.

One possibility would be a set of surcharges over and beyond the basic and peak-period charges assigned to other users in the system. For example, a tripartite tariff might be established for urban systems, with off-peak users paying the lowest fare, regular peak-hour users a somewhat higher tariff, and occasional peak-hour users the highest rate.[24] This tripartite tariff would seem to be relatively more attractive if the excess capacity is truly excess or standby, that is, if it is not used except during superpeak periods. An example might be old surplus buses parked in a vacant lot and used only in periods of exceptional demand.

If, however, the technology of the extra superpeak capacity is such that it is fixed or is subject to joint use by both optional, occasional users and regular patrons, the allocation of the incremental capacity costs might become somewhat more involved. A commonly held view, for example, is that if additional capacity to serve superpeak users also improves the quality of service to regular users, the regular user should in turn expect to pay some of the cost of the additional capacity.

Referring back to the discussion of peak-period pricing, it could be argued that if the superpeak demand supplied by joint use of a fixed capacity is then nonshifting, relative to the regular peak, the superpeak users should be charged all the costs of the extra capacity. If, however, a shifting peak exists between regular and superpeak users, which seems more likely, prices must be computed according to the demand and cost parameters of the particular case in order to equalize use in different periods. Thus, if the situation is one with a firm or nonshifting peak, capacity charges are assessed to the superpeak users, following strict marginalist doctrine. Regular users would be charged only for direct operating costs. If a shifting peak exists, a portion of the capacity cost is charged to more than one class of user, the exact proportion varying with the particular parameters of the specific case. As before, the scheme would be to maximize use of the particular facility, subject to the constraints that direct costs and total costs be covered by prices charged. In such circumstances, no capacity charges need be retrieved as such. Still, it may be desirable to charge the optional users to reflect the extra costs they impose on the regular users. Short-run marginal congestion cost pricing has an obvious and intuitive appeal in such a case. Schemes for charging consumers of transport services according to each user's proportional contribution to total congestion cost might also be deemed appropriate. The result would be higher prices to all users during superpeaks and, possibly, lower rates for the regular peak periods, for example, if the "profits" generated by the congestion prices were used to reduce the basic cost burden of the regular peak-period users.

24. Boiteux [B5] has made some suggestions for treating the public utility stochastic demand problem in terms that are somewhat analogous to those applied to congestion cost situations in transport.

Summary

Strategy in transport pricing varies, but the total number of pure strategies is reasonably limited. Option pricing, for example, involves no new concepts in a strict sense; rather, it is a synthesis of other basic pricing strategies applied to particular circumstances. Similarly, the several manifestations of long-run marginal cost pricing involve no new concepts beyond the one inherent in all long-run marginal cost pricing strategies, namely, that price should be set equal to the long-run equilibrium position at which the demand curve and long-run marginal cost curve intersect.

This is not to say that these derivative pricing schemes may not be worthy of careful consideration in many circumstances. For example, proportional markups of either short- or long-run marginal cost prices might be worthy of investigation where financial integrity and maintenance of managerial incentives for efficiency are deemed necessary. When demands fluctuate widely over time, peak and off-peak price differentiation schemes that optimize capacity use should be useful. However, both proportional markups and peak and off-peak pricing are basically derivative from marginal cost pricing principles.

Profit maximization without price discrimination can also be construed as a derivative strategy in the sense that it is monopolistic practice constrained to only one price to be charged for a reasonably homogeneous service. As noted, transport markets tend to present many opportunities for market segregation and differentiation, so that profit maximization pursued without price discrimination tends to suggest some form of constraint on normal monopolistic urges.

Of the pure strategies, the two most common are simple average cost and value-of-service pricing. Value-of-service pricing, as noted, is similar to price-discriminatory, monopolistic pricing, and its economic implications are best understood in terms of the corresponding conceptual model. Value-of-service pricing rarely appears, however, in pure profit-maximizing form. Indeed, it is probably best analyzed as constrained, price-discriminatory, monopolistic pricing. It derives much of its historical popularity from the fact that it lends itself well to the financing of noneconomic transport goals, particularly in a context of government control. Typically, the monopoly profit derived from large markups on certain transport markets has been used to finance losses on other transport activities serving social or political goals. In short, constraints are placed on prices in the unprofitable, social service sectors. Thus where private transportation companies operate under government regulation, as in the United States, the regulatory authorities often cooperate with the private transportation companies in achieving high markups and profits in some sectors of transportation to finance losses imposed by pricing constraints in other sectors. In much the same vein, simple average cost pricing can be modified to achieve certain noneconomic goals of public policy. As a rule, these modifications tend to create a price structure roughly consistent with a value-of-service tariff schedule.

The two transport pricing strategies most often advocated by economists in recent years have tended to be either short- or long-run marginal cost pricing. The choice between these two depends on practical considerations. If one can hypothesize flexible adjustment of prices to changes in cost, perfect competition, and the institution of policies or reforms to ensure that changes in prices are well understood and forecast by those consuming transport services, it is difficult to argue against short-run marginal cost pricing or an approximation thereto. Assuming that competition is reasonably well approximated on a consistent basis across the entire economy, short-run marginal cost prices tend to have favorable resource allocation implications and provide good guides for investment decisions over time.

The argument for long-run marginal cost pricing is that tariff schedules do not adapt with the flexibility or speed required to derive maximum benefits from short-run marginal cost pricing. The empirical argument for the existence of some lethargy in transport market adjustments would seem to be strong, given that transport usually operates under direct government ownership or regulation. The process of adjusting transport prices to other objectives of political or public policy takes time. Moreover, there are reasons for doubting that the consumers of transport services have perfect foresight in predicting potential changes in prices under a short-run marginal cost pricing regime. Accordingly, it is possible that derivative locational and other decisions could be wrong.

On conceptual grounds, the only alternative preferable to short- or long-run marginal cost pricing would be optimal second-best pricing; that is, a system of prices which, when applied to transportation, would maximize total society welfare accounting for systematic differences between marginal costs and prices elsewhere in the economy, including those induced by market imperfections, excise or income taxes, or any other source. Marginal cost pricing principles derive their optimality properties on the premise that they are essentially universally observed. Such an assumption is obviously heroic; it may not be satisfied within most modern industrial economies. It seems even less likely to be correct for most of the less developed economies. The important empirical questions are, of course, whether the extra information needed to implement optimal second-best pricing is ever really available and whether the imperfections in the rest of the economy are sufficiently extensive to create significant losses if marginal cost pricing within transport is pursued. These questions are explored further in Chapter 5.

In general, the choice of a pricing strategy depends, at least to some extent, on subjective preferences and objectives of public policy. This is true even within a relatively limited and static view of technologies and demand structures. Among the range of issues to be considered are development objectives, administrative questions, and welfare issues. In short, any viable generalization about what constitutes an optimal pricing strategy is likely to be difficult, if not impossible, to obtain. Accordingly, an effort to improve the process of identifying goals and their relationship to alternative pricing strategies seems worthwhile.

CHAPTER THREE

Cost Concepts

COSTS AND COST CONCEPTS have always played an important role in transportation economics and policy discussions. Indeed, as a result of the diversity and complexity of transportation operations and the history of public participation in the transportation industry, the industry has pioneered many cost accounting techniques. Furthermore, policy decisions on and applications of cost concepts in the transportation industry have clarified cost concepts in general use in economics. As for the relevance of these cost concepts, it seems reasonable to say, as it was once said in the context of evaluating important contributions to public utility pricing, that "success . . . in solving difficult practical [pricing] problems . . . rests ultimately upon a sound and sometimes subtle understanding of the classical marginal cost concepts."[1]

Costing procedures and concepts involve many special terms and, indeed, even a special jargon. Subtle and difficult distinctions are often needed in costing discussions; hence the proliferation in terminology can perhaps be justified. Nevertheless, interaction between the accounting and economics professions, with their different traditions and terminologies, has led to confusion and ambiguity. Moreover, cost information ideal for the problem at hand is rarely available. Considerable judgment is required in defining what sort of cost information is necessary and in making and interpreting the estimates. An unfortunate byproduct of existing transport regulation is that management is often tempted to use cost concepts designed for regulatory decisions for systems design and managerial guidance rather than

1. Jacques H. Drèze [B10], p. 8.

cost information created de novo for these purposes. At the same time, it is often difficult to determine from the accounting information available costs that are relevant to the regulation of prices, rates of return, or other public policy decisions.

Of the cost categories used in economic analyses, the most basic terminological distinctions are those relating to total, average, and marginal cost. As suggested earlier, these concepts are complicated by the necessity to differentiate operationally among the many services offered by time of day, geographical location, type of route, and so on, and by the existence of many common costs. The other cost distinction important to economists is the temporal difference between the short run and the long run. This distinction is often blurred or imprecisely made. Because temporal distinctions are a matter of degree, the short run must obviously shade into the long run and vice versa. The distinction between short-run and long-run costs depends on the fixity of certain categories of costs and on the time required to modify certain cost commitments.

The Structure of Accounting Costs

One of the first problems in most transportation costing exercises is to relate the accounting costs available to the more fundamental economic cost concepts. The accounting definitions used in transportation can and often do differ from those used elsewhere in business. Moreover, some special terminology has evolved for each mode. Nevertheless, seven standard categories of cost can be discerned in most transportation accounting reports.

The most fundamental, for basic operating purposes, is what the accountant might call the cost of creating the transportation. In railroading, these will be called train costs; in airlines, flight costs; in trucking, over-the-road or truck operating costs. They will be the costs of moving the vehicles and include the direct operating labor costs, costs of fuel and other supplies needed for maintaining operations, and miscellaneous costs associated with insurance and compensation for damage claims.

A second accounting category is comprised of terminal or station operation and, in the case of railroads, yard costs as well. Such costs can be further classified under three headings. First, there are the costs of dispatching and organizing the shipments, which include that of classifying the shipments by destination points. Second, there are what might broadly be termed handling costs. These can vary widely with different operations. Obviously, they are not the same for passengers as for freight or for small package freight as for freight moving in volume. Third, there are costs associated with meeting the public, receiving packages or baggage, and so on.

A third category, of great importance in the structuring of transportation costs, is accounts that deal with the maintenance of way and of equipment used by the transportation mode. These include the normal costs of repair and other services related to such maintenance. An important difference occurs between the modes that use publicly owned ways and those that use their own, or privately owned, ways. For the privately owned, the maintenance of way account will be an integral part of the accounts for individual firms in the industry. For those operating over public ways—airlines, trucks, and ships—maintenance of way will be by a public agency which also keeps the accounts on these particular activities, the costs of which, however, can be reflected in the private firm accounts as additional tolls or taxes paid directly or indirectly.

A fourth category of costs generally included in accounting reports relates to the overhead costs associated with administration. These are often, as in the case of railroads, called general expenses. Included in this category are salaries for officers, their clerical help, and other superintendence.

A fifth accounting category that can be of considerable importance but has received little attention in engineering, economic, or other analyses of transport operations is marketing or advertising expenses. These are often lumped together under the label "traffic expense." In addition to costs that might be more strictly associated with the selling or marketing function, traffic expense can include routine costs of processing bills or invoices.

Accountants also typically report what might be called capital costs or expenses. From an economic standpoint, the appropriate economic charge for capital goods is the item's opportunity cost—the return or worth of the item which is forgone in its next best alternative employment. In accounting practice, costs for capital investments are represented by interest charges and an allowance—the so-called depreciation expense—which divides a large expenditure of resources in one time period into several smaller allotments in many time periods. Techniques for estimating depreciation allowances in transportation are perhaps no better or worse than in other industries, but they do leave much to be desired in the extent to which they reflect real opportunity costs relevant to public policy decisions or management planning.[2]

2. For an illustrative case history of how depreciation expenses have yielded both underestimates and overestimates of true economic costs in the airline industry, see Mahlon R. Straszheim [A11], pp. 67–69.

A special case of interest in depreciation accounting in transport is when the alternative returns are considered to be zero or near zero. In such circumstances, the costs of the invested capital are assumed to be sunk costs and therefore can be ignored in arriving at rational decisions in the future. In reality, however, many costs listed as sunk have alternatives. For example, real estate committed to many transport undertakings often has a high alternative value for other uses. This fact is frequently overlooked. In general, caution should be used before assigning a zero alternative opportunity cost to almost any transport investment.

Conventional interest charges as carried in accounting reports can also be deceptive. The ownership of transport facilities or operating carriers is often a mix of public and private ownership financed by a variety of special forms such as interest-free loans or grants. Hence the accounting records may bear little relationship to the true economic costs. Determining what the real equity or investment in the facility is can be complex. What is usually desired is the interest charge in an opportunity sense of the enterprise as a going concern, abstracting from the ownership which will be created by or result from the particular institutional circumstances.

A final, and most complex, accounting cost category relates to taxes. The complexity arises mainly from the fact that in transportation the way can either be privately or publicly owned; and different practices with regard to property taxation can be encountered under the different forms of ownership. Specifically, there is some tendency for privately owned transportation ways to be overtaxed. These are among the most immobile of business properties and are therefore an easy target for the assessor. By contrast, publicly owned ways are often carried on the books on a tax-free basis. Unless there is some offset made in the form of other payments to government, this tax-free status of public ways implies that they occupy a privileged position relative to privately owned facilities. It should be stressed, however, that in certain cases some of these alleged or actual biases may be redressed through extra excise taxes, that is, in excess of assignable costs, on particular modes using public ways. At any rate, property taxes can be an important item in privately owned railroad and pipeline accounts and be relatively limited for trucks, airlines, and waterborne carriers, applying only to some terminals and similar structures, and even these are often publicly owned.

Treatment between carriers is more symmetrical in the other major categories of taxes, those on income and employment. With the exception of some special replacement reserve allowances provided for international shipping concerns, the tax treatment of income and employment for transportation companies in the United States, for example, is essentially the same as that accorded to other private industries.

Problems Associated with Common Costs

Several difficult applied problems in transportation concern the interpretation of common costs. Common costs pertain to cost categories relating to a set of different outputs.[3] In transportation, for example, expenditures on maintenance of way serve both rail freight and passenger operations and are often considered a common cost of both services.

Common costs are usually defined for practical purposes in terms of their opposite, traceable costs. Specifically, a traceable cost is a cost whose cause can be determined by observing, either experimentally or statistically, changes in output in multiple product situations.[4] Common costs, then, are by elimination the costs in such situations which cannot be so traced. Obviously, if the variations of the proportions in which the final products are produced are limited, that is, in circumstances of joint production, it is difficult or even impossible to trace output cause to a cost effect.

The problem is particularly acute when attempting to assess the cost relationships for maintenance of way, because a common facility meets the needs of several transportation services simultaneously. It is a problem, moreover, common to almost all forms of transportation. The complexity of assigning maintenance of railroad way to different classes of freight and passenger services is matched in the highway sector by the problem of allocating highway maintenance costs to different classes of traffic, such as private automobiles, light trucks, and heavy trucks. Similarly, a major costing problem in civil aviation is that of determining an appropriate allocation of federal airway costs to commercial airlines, military aviation, and general aviation.

---

3. Costing terminology that refers to "joint" versus "common" costs is sometimes confusing. Joint costs are a special kind of common costs. They refer to situations in which two products are produced in more or less fixed or rigid proportions. The classic example of joint costs is joint production of mutton and wool. It has been argued with considerable validity that if a reasonably long time horizon is adopted, the rigidity in most joint production or cost situations disappears. For example, over a period of time lambs might be bred that had extremely heavy coats and virtually no meat and vice versa. In general, the distinction between joint costs and common costs is not a particularly productive one.

4. John R. Meyer [A4], pp. 209–22.

An interesting phenomenon of costing procedures, and one especially important in understanding pricing procedures, is that accountants of transportation operating companies often attempt to make complete allocations of all costs to particular services. That is, they construct what they call fully distributed costs by arbitrarily allocating common or nontraceable costs. In defense of these accounting procedures, the distinction between traceability and nontraceability may be difficult to determine. The accountant may be working on the presumption that if better experimental or statistical procedures were available cause and effect relationships between cost and output which are not now observable could be observed. These observations, in effect, would tend to reduce the segment of cost classified as common or nontraceable. In such circumstances, prudence might suggest (particularly for private managements) that care be exercised not to set prices at a level that might prove to be noncompensatory. Clearly, the length of the time horizon employed in the analysis can also affect the degree to which costs are likely to be defined as traceable or nontraceable. The accountants' attempt to fully distribute all costs tends to place an implicit emphasis on taking a longer view, since it seems likely that more costs will vary with output in the long run than in the short run.

In short, the accountant's emphasis on fully distributed costs tends to build a certain conservatism into pricing policies which limits, inhibits, or prohibits prices that would fall beneath avoidable or incremental costs. If some costs are not traceable to particular outputs, the economist would recommend that pricing policy be directed toward recovering these non-traceable or common costs (to the extent this is considered desirable) through consideration of demand characteristics.

Defining Marginal and Fixed Costs

For economists, much significance is attached to marginal costs, and in many cases to the distinction between the short and the long run. For regulatory procedures, the cost concepts usually of concern are either typical long-run marginal costs or typical fully distributed costs.[5]

5. See William J. Baumol and others [B3], pp. 357–66; Joseph R. Rose [B26], pp. 336–37; J. W. Hershey [B12], pp. 338–40; James R. Nelson [B23]; George W. Wilson [B35], Chap. 5. Exceptions to typical costs have occurred when a low-cost firm within a specific branch of the transportation industry has attempted to substitute its own "efficient" long-run marginal costs for typical costs, the objective being to transfer business away from other modes or firms.

These two concepts are accepted in most cases as measures of the long-run goals or limits against which the validity of regulated rates must be tested. Aside from the wisdom of the regulatory criteria, the measurement and interpretation of these costing standards poses some important problems.

The accountant's out-of-pocket costs are, for example, often considered rough estimates of the lower bounds of any potentially compensatory rate, that is, of an acceptable minimum rate for the short run. Out-of-pocket costs are neither what the economist conventionally calls marginal costs nor what he calls variable costs, but they are close enough to these concepts in particular applications that a confusion of out-of-pocket and marginal or variable costs is common. If computed by an accountant for a specific piece of additional business, out-of-pocket costs are akin but not identical to an economist's short-run marginal costs. Economists usually have in mind a small incremental change in output, whereas accountants will define out-of-pocket costs for large, discrete changes in output.[6] Normally, out-of-pocket costs are what the accountant identifies as expenses for which payment must be made almost immediately on incurrence, that is, wages, payments for supplies, and so forth. They are useful to the accountant or to a financial officer because they help in gauging the amount of liquid funds the firm must keep on hand for day-to-day operations. They also may be helpful, if carefully used, in establishing a lower bound for prices or rates. In transportation, the most important out-of-pocket costs are usually operators' wages, fuel, and expenditures for other operating supplies.[7]

Transport managements have increasingly displayed a tendency to use the direct increment in out-of-pocket costs as the basis for establishing rates on empty backhauls. This has been particularly prevalent where the commodities available for the backhaul have not been under regulation. Agricultural and bulk commodities in the United States are examples. They are largely exempted from regulation when carried by trucks or barges.[8]

6. Wilson points out the difficulties in relating marginal to average variable cost which arise because of the ambiguities in defining output [B35], pp. 32–42.

7. Closely related to out-of-pocket costs is a transportation category known as "wheel-up costs." These pertain to costs directly incurred in operating the vehicles of the transportation system, literally for all operations above the roadbed or right-of-way. They have occasionally been used by transportation economists as a crude estimate of short-run avoidable or incremental costs. This concept is most useful where, as in the case of highways, there is separation of ownership between the roadbed or right-of-way and the rolling stock or vehicle. Generally speaking, wheel-up costs would not appear to be of much analytical value.

8. For a different point of view on these matters (that is, suggesting an allocation of total costs for empty backhauls), see Alan A. Walters [A12], pp. 419–32.

An accounting category roughly the antithesis of out-of-pocket costs is that of book charges. The classic and by far the most important example is depreciation expense. The amortization of goodwill and investments in natural resources, like forests or oil wells, are also book charges. These charges are obviously not necessarily equal to fixed costs. The economist often makes a distinction between what he calls use-related and time-related depreciation of productive facilities. The accountant will conventionally lump all categories of depreciation into one category and call it book charges. To the economist, the distinction between the use-related and time-related depreciation is important and corresponds to the distinction between variable and fixed costs at different levels of output. On the other hand, an economist might regard certain expenditures on administrative overhead as fixed, at least in the short run. The accountant would not regard these as book charges because they involve a specific outlay of cash within most relevant accounting time periods.[9]

In estimating long-run marginal costs, a distinction, borrowed from public utility studies, between so-called capacity costs and operating costs is widely used. Capacity costs usually refer to costs associated with creating an addition to productive capacity at a certain point in time. Operating costs, as costs of making a given capacity functional, can usually be equated to short-run variable costs. The capacity costs can be interpreted on a marginal or incremental basis as plant development costs—the expenditure required to increase plant capacity by some designated unit of productive output. As such, these costs become an important component in estimating long-run marginal costs. Under conditions of constant returns to scale and rigidly fixed capacity limits, long-run marginal costs will equal plant development costs plus short-run marginal costs. Even if these conditions are not met, plant development costs plus average variable costs will usually provide a fair approximation to long-run marginal costs. They are, of course, only an approximation. Capacity costs are obviously not necessarily equal

9. Reference commonly is made to "threshold costs." They refer primarily to the level of total cost that must be achieved before a specific function can be executed with reasonable efficiency or even at all. For example, threshold costs sometimes are defined in relation to the point at which long-run marginal costs in a production process reach a minimal level (at which, moreover, it is usually assumed that they remain over a considerable range). It is not uncommon for marginal costs to be very high at very low levels of output, to taper slowly downward as output rises, and finally to reach a constant and roughly minimal level. The term threshold costs is often used to refer to the total cost incurred at the point at which this minimal incremental cost is achieved. While threshold costs and fixed costs are not necessarily synonymous, they are often confused.

to fixed costs, nor are operating costs necessarily the same as marginal or average variable costs.

As noted, long-run marginal costs are considered to be a good first approximation for testing the profitability, or sometimes even the propriety, of transportation rates, especially in an atmosphere of public regulation. When using long-run marginal costs, the recent trend has been to distinguish between avoidable long-run marginal cost of a decline in output and the incremental long-run marginal cost of an increase. Avoidable costs are sometimes called contraction or regression costs, while positive incremental costs can be designated as expansion or development costs. The usefulness of the distinction obviously depends on whether there is an asymmetrical relation between the marginal costs of expanding and contracting output. In many transportation circumstances, particularly those of railroading, cost asymmetry may be significant, especially in the short run. The marginal costs of eliminating certain railroad services often differ sharply from those for increasing the same services, again with particular emphasis on the short run. The introduction of avoidable and incremental concepts as a practical refinement in marginal cost definitions has been accompanied by some reduction in emphasis on fully distributed costs as a basis for regulatory decisions.

Short-run marginal or average costs as a basis for rate setting are commonly advocated in situations where: productive capacity is not in short supply; equipment has a very long life, so that financing replacement is not an immediate problem; or physical capital is not expected to be replaced when worn out. Short-run costs represent a lower floor for rates that often will be considered tolerable, though only in the short run, by private managements. In some railroad circles, there used to be considerable support, particularly in the pricing of passenger operations, for using short-run marginal costs in establishing rates. Such a practice can be sensible if the short-run marginal cost pricing is part of a process of phasing out a specific undertaking. The major danger is that the short-run marginal cost rates may become an ineradicable part of the price structure.

Defining the relevant time horizon for performing the analysis raises the old economic questions, How short is the short run? How long is the long run? The concept of fixity of costs normally is closely related to the definition of productive capacity. The definition of variable costs as those that can be changed without a basic modification of the productive capacity of a plant is less than precise in most practical applications. In most plants, a number of marginal adaptations in capacity can be made, with differing amounts of time required to make the modifications. Accordingly, a workable distinction can be made between variable and fixed costs only if a time period for making adjustments in productive relationships is well defined. A determination often requires consideration of the relationship between the objectives or policy decisions for which the cost estimates are sought and the particular costing procedures used.

The question of defining the relevant time dimension arises in another policy area, that of regulating what is a fair rate of return on capital. Fair returns are calculated as a specified percentage on estimated capital costs. The latter can be estimated by present market values of the assets— replacement cost—or by historical costs. Replacement cost is defined as what it would cost to replace the capital now being used at present price levels, whereas historical costs refer to the costs incurred to create the present productive plant at the time it was installed.

The distinction between historical and replacement costs has played a very important role in regulatory discussions.[10] The choice can make a considerable difference under conditions of general price inflation. Present market values are probably more relevant for most purposes than historical purchase prices and associated, random write-offs. However, the calculation of replacement costs can often be an arbitrary and difficult exercise, since, for example, technological changes over time can make replacement of the present capital stock or plant meaningless. Indeed, these technological changes may be so dramatic that the original capital stock in question is not sold on the market at a subsequent time, and hence the usual market standards for performing needed cost evaluations disappear. Positing market values in such circumstances can be hazardous.

Cost Concepts and Statistical Estimation

The basic cost relationship in economic theory is between a stipulated level of output and the minimum dollar outlay needed to achieve that output. The relationship itself can be derived from the technological production function and prevailing factor prices. Because of the number of factors involved in modern production processes, it is usually easier to work with cost than with production or technological relationships. The cost function is, in many ways, a shorthand way of summarizing these basic technological and economic relationships.

10. Merton J. Peck and John R. Meyer [B24], pp. 199–239.

A crucial procedural question in many cost analyses is when and if to use statistical techniques to estimate these relationships. In statistical cost estimation, cross-section or time-series sample data are observed over a range of operating circumstances, with these data serving as the basis for defining a function which best suits the sample experience. The sample data may be supplemented by other information, which can be used in helping to specify the form of the functions or their parameters.[11] The alternative is engineering costing, in which analytic models are developed, usually premised on basic engineering or production relationships of a causal nature between inputs and outputs. Engineering costing is usually conducted at a more disaggregated level and often involves systems of equations. These may be solved analytically or numerically, perhaps in the context of a computer simulation.

The choice of techniques hinges on a variety of factors—the objective of the costing, the data available, the knowledge of underlying engineering relationships, and the analytic and numerical computational aids at hand.[12] Relevant considerations are whether the production process under observation produces a single product or many products, and the extent to which cause and effect relationships between output and cost can be determined by direct observation of actual operations or, alternatively, experimentally controlled operations. Where causation is obvious and experiments can be conducted, engineering cost procedures will be relevant. Conversely, when several simultaneous relationships between output, capacity, and input variables exist, and where observation of historical operating experience is the only source of data, statistical costing procedures may be necessary.

In statistical costing, time-series and cross-section data present their own particular problems. A special difficulty with time-series data is that of technological change. Statistical cost analyses are normally based on the assumption that the observations are generated by the same underlying production structure. Technological change over time obviously undermines this assumption. Accordingly, the cost analyst using time-series data often faces the dilemma of having to choose between restricting his sample to an inefficiently small size or incorporating into one sample observations from several time periods that he suspects are less than fully homogeneous in terms of technological characteristics. The usual solution is to attempt to control for the technological change. The easiest control is the inclusion

11. There are several good survey discussions on the problems of estimating costs; see John Johnston [A3], Chap. 6, and Alan A. Walters [A13], pp. 1–66.

12. For a discussion of the issues important in this choice, see Meyer [A4], pp. 209–22.

of some simple trend variable in the statistical cost function. Another alternative, which is particularly attractive if the technological change occurs abruptly and at well-defined points in time, is to use dummy variables in the cost function in an attempt to capture the major cost differences between the technologically different periods. Both methods leave much to be desired. The simple trend variable approach is based on the assumption that technological change occurs in a more or less continuous fashion over time. The use of dummy variables requires that the effect of the technological change can be captured by more or less additive once-and-for-all effects on the overall cost level.

A problem closely related to technological change is that of changes occurring in factor prices. Over a fairly long time series, these may have considerable impact on observed costs. Furthermore, changes in the relative prices paid by producers for labor, capital, and other important inputs will induce factor substitutions. If the factor price changes are substantial enough to induce a modification of operating procedures, the net effect will be very much like that of a change in technology. These effects are difficult to disentangle, when using time-series data. Indeed, an analyst is well advised, when analyzing data that have been subject to sharply changing factor prices, to turn to cross-section analysis if at all possible.

Cross-section data are subject to their own problems, however. The most important is the necessity to control for different levels of capacity utilization by different firms or plants in the sample. This problem will be particularly acute if the objective of the cross-section analysis is (as it often will be for costing undertaken as part of a regulatory proceeding) the estimation of long-run marginal cost.[13] The difficulty when different levels of capacity utilization occur is that the estimate of long-run marginal cost is likely to be biased. Indeed, even if each firm or plant in the cross section were operating at the same percentage above or below full-capacity utilization, biased estimates of long-run marginal costs would be obtained from a conventional cross-section analysis. This is a well-known phenomenon in statistical regression applications.[14] In fact, under most plausible assumptions, if the usual least squares statistical procedures are applied to cross-section data, long-run marginal cost will tend to be overestimated.

One common way of attempting to control for different levels of capacity utilization in cross-section cost analyses is to include in the cost equations

13. An explanation of this point can be found in John R. Meyer and others [A7].
14. For a good summary discussion of this problem, see Johnston [A3], Chap. 6.

a measure of capital stock or capacity for the different firms or units observed. As suggested earlier, one difficulty with this procedure is finding an adequate measure of capacity. Furthermore, introducing a capacity variable into a cross-section analysis will tend to yield parameters (associated with the output variables) that are probably more nearly estimates of short-run marginal costs than estimates of long-run marginal costs. Moreover, basic technological differences may be reflected in both cross-section and time-series data. The observations contained in a cross-section sample are often obtained from widely different geographic circumstances. If sufficiently differentiated, different wage, interest, or other factor prices may dictate different technological choices.[15]

Perhaps the most troublesome problem of transportation costing is that of extrapolating from limited historical or experimental information to future or actual world conditions. In most circumstances, the cost analyst has no alternative but to make such extrapolations. However, extrapolations necessarily rest on the assumption that the world of the future will be more or less like the world which generated the information used for the analysis. In some circumstances, this will obviously not be true, as when consideration is directed to the potential costs of fundamentally new technologies. A current example of such a problem would be an attempt to estimate the operating and other costs associated with supersonic transport or with a very high speed (over 150 miles per hour) railroad. In such circumstances, or even in less dramatic situations of technological change, the analyst must build correction factors into his estimating procedures in order to reflect or anticipate as many of the altered circumstances as possible.

One other methodological question may be important in certain circumstances—the treatment of errors in fitting the sample data. Most statistical relationships between costs and outputs are determined by a least squares estimate. The line or curve relating costs to output is fitted by placing it at the (conditional) mean of existing cost–output relationships. In many circumstances, especially in regulatory proceedings, the distinction between an efficiency norm and a typical cost is important. The norm might be more appropriately determined by empirically fitting an envelope curve to the sample cost data, so that the function lies on or below all existing

---

15. These problems of different factor prices and different management and operating procedures are discussed in the context of fitting a cost function for international air operations, where substantial differences existed in a single cross-section sample. See Straszheim [A11], Apps. A and B.

cost–output relationships. The fitting procedure would then be one in which no negative errors were permitted.[16]

Summary

Transport costing, like most empirical costing exercises, is not an exact science. The estimates normally will bracket a range of possibilities. The degree of approximation will also depend on the particular figures sought. Unfortunately, the simplest figures to obtain are usually the least useful analytically. The most pertinent to developing an economically rational approach to transport pricing policy are the most difficult to estimate. In general, the solution to the costing problem necessitates a clear delineation of objectives and specification of the cost concepts required for particular decisions. The actual estimates obtained may only approximate the desired concepts, but the very act of definition and attempted quantification usually helps clarify the alternatives available to decision makers.

16. John R. Meyer and Gerald Kraft [A6], pp. 313–34.

CHAPTER FOUR

Congestion Cost and Transport Pricing

CONGESTION IN TRANSPORTATION can be viewed as a cost effect analogous to overcapacity use of any productive plant and to any situation that leads to an increase in short-run costs as volume increases with a fixed level of plant capacity. Thus, for transport as for most other production, the influence of congestion can be represented by a rising short-run marginal cost curve (short-run in the sense that the marginal cost curve applies to a fixed level of productive capacity) and by an eventual rise in the short-run average variable cost per unit of output as well.[1] A divergence between short-run marginal and average cost can therefore occur; this in turn can lead to a potential misuse of resources if privately perceived costs deviate from marginal social costs.

This is not to say that travelers or shippers are unaware of congestion. But the decentralization or segregation of decision making, so common in transport, adds a new dimension which does not occur in most other activities.[2] A public agency often provides much of the needed capital or productive plant in transportation, and individuals or private business

1. The suggestion has been made that congestion be treated as a demand rather than as a cost effect. Such treatment, however, reduces the comparability of transport analyses with those of other economic situations. The distinction is arbitrary and a matter of degree. For example, Robert H. Strotz ([B31], pp. 127–69), in a comprehensive analysis of road congestion tolls, treats congestion as a disutility.

2. The importance of separation of decision responsibility in congestion cost toll arguments was recognized by Frank H. Knight [F20], pp. 582–606.

organizations complete the activity in ways that suit their individual needs. This description would fit most highway, water, and air transport. Thus, for these modes, whether of a public or private character or by common or contract carriage, a bifurcation of the decision processes occurs by which assembly of needed productive factors is effected.

Short-Run Allocative Costs

Three cost categories are identified in transport congestion analyses: (1) facility costs (including interest, amortization, and maintenance); (2) vehicle operating and ownership costs; and (3) time costs, that is, the value of the time spent in transit. The congestion problem focuses on the ways in which congestion can induce a discrepancy between the privately perceived average level of operating and time costs and the marginal level of those costs. One proposal for doing away with this discrepancy is to set the facility charge, that is, congestion toll, at an appropriate level to close the gap as circumstances warrant.

By contrast, most airway and highway systems are operated today with a uniform user charge levied throughout the system at all times and in all circumstances. Similar practices characterize waterway facility charges. Congestion tolls have been recommended as special surcharges to close the gap between average and marginal costs, even when uniform user charges exist. Unless the cost categories are carefully defined and well understood, the economics are different in the two cases. In one case, the facility toll is determined strictly by congestion. In the other, it is composed of two parts, a basic uniform facility charge plus a congestion toll.

Vehicle, plane, or vessel ownership and operating costs that are applicable in the short run normally can be considered as a reasonably uniform or constant function of volume. On the assumption that all individuals using a particular facility on any specific occasion will experience roughly the same travel conditions and thus time and congestion costs,[3] the total of all short-run transport costs for a fixed level of capacity for water, air, and highway modes can be characterized by one average cost function of the type indicated by the curve C in Figure 4-1. If the uniform facility user

---

3. This presumes homogeneity of the utility functions and time and congestion values and costs for all users. Though available travel data do not appear to support this assumption, the analysis is simplified by their introduction. Alan A. Walters ([B33], pp. 677–99), makes substantially this assumption. It is also made by Strotz [B31].

FIGURE 4-1. *Short-Run Average and Marginal Travel Cost Curves*

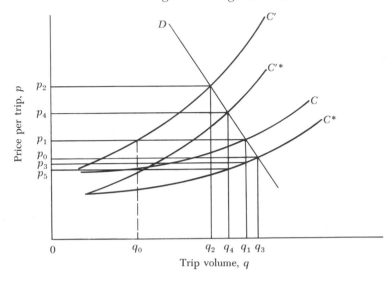

C = average total travel cost inclusive of a uniform facility user charge
C* = average travel cost exclusive of a uniform facility user charge
C',C'* = marginal travel costs
DD = demand schedule

charge is subtracted, the perceived average cost curve would be C^*. To each of these average cost curves, corresponding marginal cost curves, C' and C'^* respectively, can be specified.

These average and marginal cost relationships are presumed to include only those short-run travel costs that the user takes into account in deciding whether or not to transport, when and how to do so, which route to use, and so forth. Those costs paid by the user but considered by him only on some longer-run basis are not included.

In the conventional or more common case where uniform user charges are applied, as in the form of gasoline taxes, and utilizing the demand schedule indicated in Figure 4-1, the demand and unit price would be expected to stabilize at volume q_1 and price p_1.[4] If the uniform user charge happens to be just sufficient to equate total revenue to total cost, this solution corresponds to conventional pricing practice in which facility use would be maximized while total costs and payments are kept in balance.

4. In reality, the flow will vary around this stability point because everyone in the flow will not value time equally, the users making up the flow on successive days will vary (as will their values), and travelers will misjudge when they guess in advance what the equilibrium point and thus the price will be if they make the trip.

Superficially, it also appears that each increase in the flow rate above q_0 will contribute a marginal cost that is larger than the average cost price, p_1, paid by each additional user. A marginal cost pricing rule seems to suggest a volume of q_2 and a price of p_2. To achieve a volume level of q_2, the unit price would have to be raised to p_2 by imposing a congestion toll charge of p_2 minus p_0. This would represent a situation where the congestion toll is superimposed on an existing user charge.

Such a procedure, however, would clearly be incompatible with conventional marginal cost pricing principles. In essence, the congestion toll is a facility charge. By ignoring the existing uniform user charge, it places the toll too high and reduces demand too much. Incidentally, it would inevitably create a profit or surplus whose disposal or use would raise difficult questions of income redistribution or taxation.

The correct curve for evaluating marginal cost congestion tolls is C'^*, that is, the curve marginal to travel costs exclusive of facility charges since, again, the point of the marginal cost pricing exercises is to set the facility charges. The relevant total charge would be p_4 and the corresponding volume, q_4. The facility charge or congestion toll that would achieve this objective would be $p_4 - p_5$. In the particular case diagramed in Figure 4-1, the congestion charge for use of the facility would yield total revenues greater than total facility costs. This result is by no means the general consequence. Whether a profit or loss results from marginal cost tolls depends on the particular circumstances.

Several important observations can be made about the measures used to evaluate the costs of increased travel time. Consider a case where 3,000 vehicles are using a facility for one hour, and each would have two seconds added to a fifteen-minute travel time if the total hourly flow were increased to 3,001 vehicles per hour. The relevant measure of time value or cost would be what the 3,000 initial operators, all assumed to be identical in their preferences, would willingly accept from the 3,001st vehicle to compensate for the additional two seconds added to travel time for the original users.[5] While one hundred minutes extra may be experienced collectively

5. The driver or vehicle at the cost margin can be detected only by observing his willingness to pay for travel. However, there is not necessarily any relationship between the last vehicle willing to pay the price p_2 and the vehicle that imposed the marginal costs at that level. In fact, for the highway case, every vehicle in the flow q_2 is equally responsible for increasing the sustained hourly rate from $q_2 - 1$ to q_2 and thus is unidentifiable with respect to determining responsibility for the marginal cost (q_2) at that volume level. And each vehicle in the flow contributes as much as any other to the total overall cost; thus each is unidentifiable with respect to allocating the total costs.

by the 3,000, from the standpoint of determining cost the real impact or effect of the extra vehicle and extra travel time is felt only in terms of the two seconds that are added to individual travel time. In short, travelers can only evaluate differences in individual average travel time and not differences in travel time experienced collectively. This distinction between individual and aggregate time losses will be particularly important if the individual relationships between cost and time loss on a trip are not linear. For example, the cost or disutility of a five-minute delay on a trip as compared with a one-minute delay may be considerably more (or less) than proportional to individual users.

Certain additional complications are introduced if the assumed homogeneity of the cost characteristics for the user group is modified. In fact, a major justification for congestion tolls in many cases would be to encourage more use by those vehicles experiencing the greatest cost savings from congestion reduction. For example, in urban areas buses might be expected to incur a higher cost per unit of time delayed than most other vehicles. The bus would derive considerable operating saving from higher speed and would consolidate the time savings of fifty or so persons on a highway space equal to that required for about 1.5 to 2.5 private automobiles, and therefore approximately two to five persons at typical urban automobile load factors in the United States.

Extending the analysis to heterogeneous uses—buses, automobiles, and trucks on the same highway—is not difficult. To begin, demand functions must be defined for each use. The quantity variables for all uses must be entered as arguments in the cost functions for each use, since the different uses compete for the limited capacity. The condition that price equals marginal cost would, of course, be retained. In addition, the tolls charged to the different users should be proportional to their capacity requirements: if one bus requires twice as much capacity as one car, the bus tolls should be twice the car tolls.

The basic analytical problems created by differentiated users can also be evaluated from the perspective of the two-road case.[6] This case also has some special significance in and of itself. It illustrates a situation in which a pure Paretian gain might be effectuated—everyone made better off and no one made worse off—by instituting a marginal cost pricing scheme. The circumstance is that of two roads, or two transport facilities,

6. This case is generally attributed to Arthur C. Pigou [F38].

FIGURE 4-2. *Average and Marginal Cost Curves for Alternative Transport Facilities*

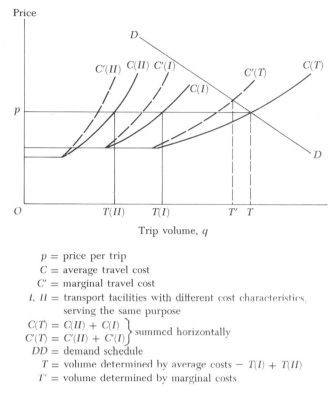

p = price per trip
C = average travel cost
C' = marginal travel cost
I, II = transport facilities with different cost characteristics, serving the same purpose
$C(T) = C(II) + C(I)$ ⎫
$C'(T) = C'(II) + C'(I)$ ⎬ summed horizontally
⎭
DD = demand schedule
T = volume determined by average costs − $T(I) + T(II)$
T' = volume determined by marginal costs

with unequal cost characteristics, both serving the same basic purpose—running between the same two geographic points.[7]

If facility costs are ignored, the pertinent cost information on these two roads could be expressed in terms of average variable and marginal cost curves as before (C^* and C'^* in Figure 4-1). The low-cost road must be characterized by average variable and marginal cost curves lying below those of the high-cost facility for initial or normal design volumes. The cost levels could be expected, however, to intersect or overlap at some of the higher volumes at which congestion becomes significant. The situation might be as diagramed in Figure 4-2. The C curves indicate the privately perceived (average) costs, and the C' curves the marginal social costs

7. Strotz [B31] extends this argument to the case where the two roads or facilities do not serve the same two points.

exclusive of any facility charges; the $C(T)$ and $C'(T)$ curves represent the horizontal sums respectively of $C(I)$ with $C(II)$ and $C'(I)$ with $C'(II)$.

As before, individual users would ignore marginal costs and react instead to the average variable costs they individually perceive. Accordingly, when total demand is at a level which could not be accommodated on the low-cost facility at a lower average variable cost, the use of the two facilities would stabilize at levels for which average variable costs were equal, say, $T(I)$ and $T(II)$ respectively. However, at this point, marginal costs would normally be unequal. In Figure 4-2, $C'(II)$ would be greater than $C'(I)$ at volumes $T(II)$ and $T(I)$. The total cost of transport between the two points could be reduced by reallocating traffic between the two facilities as long as the marginal costs on the two facilities were unequal.

Such a reallocation is shown in Figure 4-3 for two facilities with cost curves $C(I)$, $C'(I)$, $C(II)$, and $C'(II)$ and a fixed demand of OT equal to $T(I)$ plus $T(II)$. The cost curves in Figure 4-3 have been deliberately drawn differently from those in Figure 4-2. The optimal or marginal social-cost traffic allocations, $T^*(I)$ and $T^*(II)$, are to be compared with the private or original allocations, $T(I)$ and $T(II)$. (Note that one obvious difficulty with this analysis is the doubtful validity of the assumption that demand is not influenced by the particular, and in most practical situations different, qualities of the two facilities.)

If one individual or organization were in control of transportation between the two points, self-interest would dictate the lowest total cost solution for a given volume. In the absence of such control, a suggested solution is to apply tolls so that the adjustment to average costs by individual users results in the same output distribution as would be achieved if marginal costs had been directly perceived. Analogous to the case of congestion on the single road, the tolls would have to be equal to the difference between average and marginal costs at the volume levels corresponding to the optimal distribution of traffic between the two facilities; that is, at a traffic division that would equalize marginal costs. In Figure 4-3, this would mean a toll of Ep^* for facility (I) and Fp^* for (II).

To achieve a pure gain in the Paretian sense, even without recourse to compensating payments, the sufficient condition in the two-road case would be that the total traffic between the two points is below a volume that can be handled simultaneously on the two facilities without marginal costs exceeding average costs on the inferior (higher average cost) facility. If costs were defined to behave as illustrated in Figure 4-1 or 4-3, this condi-

FIGURE 4-3. *Allocation of a Fixed Demand to High-Cost and Low-Cost Transport Facilities with and without Marginal Cost Tolls*

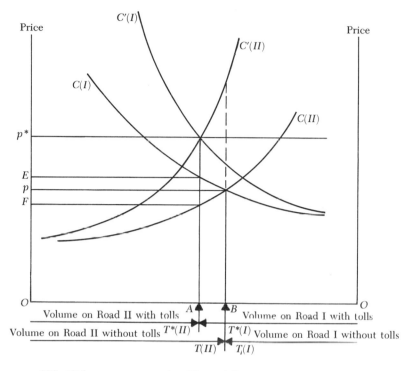

C(I), C(II) — average costs (see Figure 4-2)
C'(I), C'(II) = marginal costs (see Figure 4-2)
E − F = toll to be placed on Road II
T(I), T(II) = original traffic allocations
T*(I), T*(II) = marginal cost traffic allocations
p = price or costs determined by equalization of average costs
p* = level at which marginal costs are equal

tion could never be met. If, however, demand intersected the combined cost curve C(T) in Figure 4-2 somewhere along its flat portion, where C'(T) is identical with C(T), then a toll system could be beneficial, or not harmful, to all. As a practical matter, moreover, some transfer of traffic to a relatively underutilized facility might take place in some instances without markedly raising marginal (social) as compared with average (private) costs.

Similar conclusions apply when a single facility is employed by users with very different cost characteristics (that is, potentialities for reducing costs by reductions in travel times). Return, for example, to the case of the buses and private automobiles using a congested urban road. At the private choice equilibrium where average costs were equal, marginal costs might be quite different. Again on the assumption that the two facilities meet the same basic needs or demands, total costs of meeting the demand would be minimized by reallocating facility capacity until the marginal costs of going by the two modes were the same. To achieve this, special tolls could be set on the buses and automobiles so that their average costs would intersect at the same volume point as their marginal costs exclusive of any facility charges—such as $T^*(I)$ and $T^*(II)$ represent in the two-road case of Figure 4-3. Moreover, if the marginal costs after the reallocation were not above average costs on the facility receiving the additional use, the reallocation could be accomplished without harm to any users, always retaining the assumption that the two services are indeed equivalent.

This assumption, of course, will not as a rule be even a good approximation to reality. Furthermore, cost relationships are more apt to be like those of Figure 4-1 or 4-3 than like those of Figure 4-2, and distribution questions cannot be avoided. Similarly, when capacity is in short supply, profits can accrue to the toll-collecting agency so that additional distribution questions arise. In addition, with tolls, extra collection costs and delays (should it be necessary to stop users to collect the toll fee) would commonly be incurred. Such costs can be far from negligible, particularly when related to short urban trips. By virtue, therefore, of adhering to a short-run marginal cost pricing policy, it is conceivable that all groups of users could suffer a loss relative to the situation in which a uniform average cost or a similarly simple pricing policy were adopted.

Consumer Choice and Effects on Income Distribution

To return to resource allocation questions narrowly construed, when other than the pure gain case is encountered, some travelers will be rationed off by a toll and will make new consumption choices. On the assumption that road capacity is fixed in the short run, the operating costs saved by displaced travelers reflect the real resources available for other uses, such as a different form of transport. The other important real resource that will be allocated differently is time, since the travel time charges on this and other transport facilities resulting from the tolls will influence consumers' choices between income and leisure. The immediate direct effect of imposing a toll, therefore, will normally be to leave some people worse off, on the presumption that they had been maximizing before. The existence of the toll receipts, however, is a claim on real resources. The nature of the distribution of this claim will affect both resource allocation and income distribution—there may even be a toll distribution that can make everyone better off.

One possible distribution of toll receipts would be to return the toll revenues to those users from whom the tolls were originally collected—let us say, on an annual lump-sum basis. The net effect of such a reimbursement would vary according to the way in which it was manifested with respect to the demand schedule. To return to Figure 4-1, in a case where users saw no relationship among transport costs, toll charges, and annual reimbursement, the consequence might logically be to stabilize flow at volume q_4 as intended and with a price of p_4. However, if the annual reimbursement were to be considered by users in their personal assessment of trip costs, the eventual result might be to return to the average total cost price of p_3 and its related volume of q_3. There might, however, be an upward adjustment in p_3 and a decline in q_3 to reflect the contingency that toll collection charges are netted out of revenues before reimbursement.

Another suggestion is to use toll revenues to compensate users forced off a facility by the imposition of a toll. Conceptually, it should be possible to determine that sum of money which, if transferred to these individuals, would restore them to the level of utility or satisfaction experienced before the toll imposition. Furthermore, under most plausible assumptions about the nature of the underlying utility functions for the different classes and groups of users, the revenues from the tolls should be more than sufficient to achieve this objective. From a practical standpoint, however, identification of different users and establishment of an administrative mechanism for effectuating the compensatory income transfers would not be easy.[8] A somewhat more practical solution, therefore, might be to use the toll revenues to finance an expansion of the transportation system, so long as the long-run expansion costs are less than the short-run congestion costs.

8. This is not to deny the possibility that these transfers could be incorporated into a more general scheme for effectuating income transfers considered desirable on other grounds.

In almost any realistic circumstance, a congestion toll will introduce some income transfers. Without the toll, congested passenger transport facilities tend to be rationed by reductions in time available for other purposes, such as leisure or work. In urban situations, for example, there may be some presumption that most of the extra time spent on congested commuter transport facilities comes from a reduction in available leisure.

Since wages and salaries are not the only source of money income and other market imperfections exist, there may be a less than perfect adjustment between the marginal utility of leisure time and that of income. If, in these circumstances, low income groups find that leisure has a much lower marginal utility to them than money, a shift to a money toll for rationing transport facilities may tend to be regressive. Also, if the higher income groups can adjust their work schedules on a personal basis while the lower income groups cannot (so that the elasticity of demand for transport services during peak hours may be different for the two groups), the net social effect of shifting from congestion or leisure time tolls to money may not be an obvious improvement in the general welfare.

Of course, toll revenues might well be used to help groups other than the specific users of the facility. In circumstances of imperfect fiscal and tax institutions, for example, congestion tolls might constitute a useful source of additional government revenue, available for investment or other purposes. To the extent that any toll revenues are used for general government purposes, however, the policy is probably best defended on the grounds of achieving desired income redistributions or development objectives.

Indeed, promoting further use of a highly congested transport facility might well serve development needs or objectives, particularly if the development goals include some that are not immediately related to static economic efficiency. Such goals might be national defense, employment maximization, or a redistribution of regional economic activities so as to equalize (or reduce) differences in income in geographic regions of the economy. However, in a developing situation the potentially harmful effect of transitory short-run marginal cost prices on location decisions of households and firms must also be taken into account. Specifically, care should be exercised to ensure that locational choices are not too inconsistent with those that would be optimal if a full long-run equilibrium in the provision of transport facilities were to be achieved. At a minimum, short-run marginal cost prices are best implemented if transport consumers have some understanding of how long specific short-run pricing schedules can be expected to endure.[9]

Finally, it is worthwhile to repeat the caution that marginal cost pricing (particularly in an economy in which only an imperfect approximation to such pricing may be achieved in other sectors) could produce potentially undesirable system effects that should be taken into account in any complete analysis. For instance, if users are forced off one facility onto another or onto other modes of transport, congestion may be manifested on the alternative facility or mode, which may or may not be under a marginal congestion cost toll regime. Consequently, an evaluation of a marginal cost pricing scheme for a particular facility should include any increased costs imposed on individuals who use other facilities. In the case of highways, these could be reflected as added vehicular flow on other highways, and thus higher congestion and travel times; or, more subtly, as increased car pooling and inconvenience or increased crowding and congestion within the vehicles themselves (as would probably be the case with transit systems).[10] Moreover, there is the additional constraint that in the aggregate total resource requirements must be in balance, a condition that does not automatically follow from universal application of marginal cost pricing.

Adjustments to Congestion in the Long Run

For transport, as for other productive activities, long-run cost curves can be defined by an envelope containing the most advantageous production points of a series of short-run curves—for example, the lowest total or

9. If demand in the short run greatly exceeds available capacity, and if use of congestion tolls is deemed unwise, an alternative rationing scheme could be useful, at least temporarily. In general, physical controls can be viewed as an alternative, but somewhat gross, means of coordinating decentralized or individualistic decisions to restrict demand to a level more consistent with marginal cost pricing or other goals. The need for such controls would seem to be undeniable if the level of demand generated by existing prices went so far beyond the available capacity as to lead to a backward bending supply curve or, more properly, to shock wave effects that resulted in a reduction in the effective capacity of the facility during peak congestion periods.

10. Obviously, congestion or crowding could be avoided on transit systems, though not without increased costs. More rolling stock could be purchased and more operators hired when necessary to handle the extra peak-hour travelers. The increased schedule frequency might produce offsetting service benefits, of course. Since highways generally have less peaking than transit systems, marginal cost pricing for highways might intensify the imbalance in peaking between highways and transit systems.

average cost points from individual plant curves. The long-run marginal cost curve can be obtained from the first derivatives of the long-run total cost function defined by the envelope. The long-run marginal and average cost curves will be identical if highly refined or continuous adaptations can be made in the cost–output relationships, and if the expansion of output is not marked by increasing or decreasing costs. Such a situation is shown in Figure 4-4 with two plants or capacity levels indicated. In discussing longer-run adjustments, all gasoline or other excise taxes that might be deemed payments to amortize the sunk costs of a facility are excluded. Thus functions C^* and C'^* in Figure 4-4 can be interpreted as being of the same type as the similarly labeled functions in Figure 4-1. If average cost increased as volume expanded, the long-run marginal cost curve

FIGURE 4-4. *Long-Run Average and Marginal Travel Cost Curves*

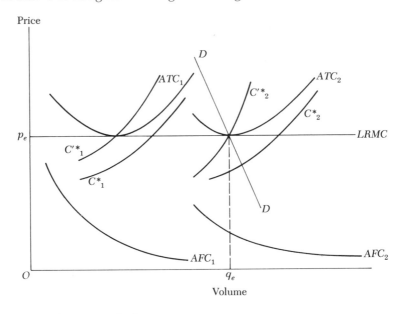

AFC = average fixed cost
$ATC = C^* + AFC$ = average total cost (including cost of the facility)
C^* = average travel cost
C'^* = marginal travel cost
DD = demand schedule
$LRMC$ = long-run marginal cost
1, 2 = two transport facilities
p_e = equilibrium price per trip
q_e = equilibrium trip volume

would lie above the long-run average cost curve. Conversely, if average costs declined as volume increased, the long-run marginal cost curve would lie beneath the long-run average cost curve.

These basic short- and long-run relationships are much the same for transport as for other economic activities.[11] Transport services normally require an investment in fixed capacity. That investment, moreover, conventionally implies a short-run average and a short-run marginal cost relationship. A full economic adjustment in transport, therefore, as in other activities, implies that the relationships between demand and the long-run cost relationships be established. Indeed, in a competitive market, anything other than the long-run equilibrium position would be subject to change. For example, if capacity is in short supply and therefore priced in excess of average cost, the normal competitive expectation would be that the profits implied by this situation would induce entry and increase supply until the price is brought into rough equilibrium with long-run average cost. For example, a long-run solution for the demand curve DD in Figure 4-4 would be at the price p_e and quantity q_e.[12] The proper congestion toll would still be defined by the difference between average variable cost and marginal cost at this volume level (q_e). This toll, however, would now be exactly equal to that required to cover average fixed or facility costs (AFC), so no profit inducement or justification for further expansion would exist.

The equilibrium depicted in Figure 4-4 is highly simplified. In the real world, most transport facilities would be subject to several classes of demand at one point in time and to significantly different levels of demand at various times of the day or in different seasons. These differences create aggregation and other analytical complications, but they do not basically change the underlying conclusions.

More important, the constant returns (that is, long-run average costs equal to long-run marginal costs) embodied in Figure 4-4 may or may not be a good representation of transport realities. The evidence is somewhat conflicting, though constant returns in the long run would not seem to be too poor an approximation for most water, air, and highway transport. If, however, decreasing returns prevailed, so that long-run marginal costs grew more rapidly than long-run average costs, the final equilibrium would result in total revenues exceeding total costs. If, by contrast, increasing returns

11. A standard illustration of these cost relationships is in Edward H. Chamberlin [B9], App. B.

12. For an algebraic and empirical development of this argument, see Herbert Mohring [B20]; see also Strotz [B31].

prevailed, the final equilibrium would result in total revenues lower than total costs.

Head taxes or lump-sum transfers have been suggested as means of either eliminating the profits in the decreasing returns case or subsidizing the losses in the increasing returns case in order to achieve an optimum. However, in most realistic circumstances, price-neutral taxes are not easily instituted. When this is the case, strict marginal cost pricing will not be consistent with optimal resource allocation.

Summary

In situations where demand is high enough to cause congestion in the short run, many argue for the use of congestion tolls. Specifically, some users of congested facilities may not be willing to pay for all the congestion costs they impose on others. Under existing procedures, users normally perceive and react to some concept of average costs rather than of marginal costs of facility use. In such circumstances, an improvement in resource allocation might be achieved by assessing a congestion cost toll that makes the choices based on perceived average costs the same as those that would be made if users reacted directly to marginal costs.

The imposition of congestion tolls, however, may cause losses to both those unwilling and those willing to pay the tolls. This can be obviated only if the toll revenues are distributed so that users are compensated for their losses. As a practical matter, such compensations will be difficult to implement. Also, users of other facilities can be disadvantaged as a result of diverted travelers in situations where marginal cost pricing is not applied universally.

Two-road or two-facility cases may exist, however, where someone can be made better off without making anyone worse off. In such circumstances, the argument for congestion tolls is quite persuasive. In addition, wherever heterogeneous uses are made of a facility and considerable gain might be achieved by better allocating the use of the facility among different users (fairly typical with airways, ports, and highways), some congestion-oriented tolls should be useful.

In general, the economic principles and cost relationships pertinent to the evaluation of transport congestion are essentially the same as those conventionally employed for analysis of other economic activities in the economy. As one consequence of this, it is not particularly useful to be concerned solely with short-run costs and effects, or to treat only the circumstances of costing and pricing the use of existing facilities of fixed capacity. The obvious and important long-run possibility of reducing congestion and short-run costs by expanding capacity is usually relevant. In short, if congestion is really intolerable, users may be willing to pay for its reduction. Thus, facility expansion as a means of reducing or eliminating congestion is clearly worthy of consideration, at least in the long run.

CHAPTER FIVE

Problems of Resource Allocation in a Context of Second Best

THE UNDERLYING RATIONALE for most transport pricing strategies recommended by economists is the achievement of a more efficient use of resources. Generally speaking, the advantages of the prescribed pricing policies are based on deductions from economic models in which competition is considered pervasive and constant returns to scale are assumed. These are necessary conditions if market prices and decisions are to fulfill the familiar marginal conditions required for efficient allocation of resources.

When analyzing the efficiency or resource allocation implications of transport prices, however, one is usually operating in a less than fully competitive environment. This has been labeled a second-best situation since the existence of market imperfections means that the optimal level of welfare cannot be achieved. The general theory of second best addresses itself to welfare optimization given constraints which cause a deviation from some of the marginal conditions necessary to reach an unconstrained optimum. The primary thrust of the theory is that all of the traditional marginal conditions and the associated implications for pricing must be modified. In particular, the violation of some marginal conditions may be advisable in order to offset, in a certain sense, existing market imperfections. For example, if price is held unequal to marginal cost in one sector, welfare optimization given this constraint may require that such an inequality be pursued in other product markets as well. To take another example, in the context of international trade, a tariff barrier or some other trade restriction in one country may imply that less than a complete free-trade environment among all other countries may be necessary to achieve a second-best optimum.[1]

Given the significance of imperfect markets in many applied circumstances, the fact that finding a second-best solution may involve a recalculation of all the marginal welfare conditions is an important result. The size and complexity of such a problem can clearly be considerable.

In this chapter, a simple two-sector model is used to test the (static) allocative aspects of different transport pricing policies in a second-best context. The example illustrates the general theory of second best, and how transport price as an input price might be altered in such a way as to achieve maximum welfare, given various imperfections in product or factor markets. Transport prices are available as a tool for such a purpose in many circumstances, especially in the less developed countries where transport markets are not well developed and only a few alternatives are typically available to shippers. The underdeveloped countries are also the most likely candidates for a second-best pricing strategy, since market imperfections are likely to be more dramatic than in the well-developed economics. Also, the less developed economies tend to be less complex, and their markets lend themselves better to identification and disaggregation, for example, by geography. This obviously facilitates analysis and the chances for public intervention through special pricing means. While simplified, the model suggests the kinds of issues raised in implementing a second-best solution, not the least of which is that of assembling the requisite amount of information and administering a solution.

A Basic Model of Welfare Maximization in a Static Context

Let a simple two-sector model be postulated.[2] Each sector is represented by an aggregate production function which relates how three inputs—labor,

1. R. G. Lipsey and Kelvin Lancaster [B16], pp. 11–32.

2. This model owes its structural inspiration to Albert Fishlow and Paul A. David [B11], pp. 529–46. It is, however, also similar to a model developed by Marcel Boiteux, "Sur la gestion des Monopoles Publics astreints à l'équilibre budgétaire," *Econometrica*, Vol. 24 (January 1956), pp. 22–40.

capital, and transport—are technologically related to outputs (equation [1]). The output of one sector is denoted by M, that of the other by D;[3] thus,

$$(1) \qquad M = f(x,y,z) \qquad \text{and}$$
$$D = g(\overline{x},\overline{y},\overline{z}).$$

Labor is measured in man-hours and the cost of one man-hour of labor is w, the wage rate. Labor inputs are assumed to be identical, and consequently producers in either sector would have no reason to prefer an hour of one man's labor over that of another's. The total endowment of labor, X_0, is fixed in a given period and represents the maximum number of man-hours available. The amount of labor used in sector M is denoted by x, that used in sector D by $\overline{x}$.

The capital stock consists of Y_0 units of identical capital inputs, which can be transferred between the two sectors in the given period of analysis. Sector M uses y units of capital and sector D uses $\overline{y}$ units. The cost of capital is denoted by r and can be thought of as the rental fee for using one unit of capital for a given period.

The transport sector is owned or otherwise directly controlled or regulated by the government, and t is the price of one ton-mile of service. Transport services are an intermediate good. This means that every ton-mile used as an input in producing M or D is itself an output of the transport sector. Capital and labor are used to produce these ton-miles. Unlike the capital and labor used in either the domestic or the modern (or monopoly) sectors, however, inputs employed in the production of transport are assumed to be fixed. With capital and labor inputs for transport fixed, it follows that for a given transport production function the total ton-miles of service available in a given period is fixed. This endowment is denoted by Z_0. Sector M uses z ton-miles, sector D uses $\overline{z}$ ton-miles.

---

3. This notation was suggested by the dualistic—modern and domestic—characteristic of the economies of today's underdeveloped countries or what Hirschman describes as the "coexistence and cohabitation of modern industry and of preindustrial and sometimes neolithic techniques." Albert O. Hirschman [F17], p. 125. Despite the fact that everyone seems to have much the same "dualistic" phenomenon in mind, no consensus exists as to how these economies should be divided. (For discussion of the dualism of underdeveloped countries, see Benjamin H. Higgins [F15], Chap. 14, and the essays by Higgins and Justus M. van der Kroef [F16], pp. 99–115; [F43], pp. 116–33.) For instance, rural-urban, industrial-agricultural, and foreign-local dichotomies have been suggested. It is not particularly important how these sectors are defined for the purposes of the present study, as long as there are two sectors with different market characteristics; that is, differences in their degree of monopoly, oligopoly, or competition.

The assumption that labor and capital are locked into the transport sector is obviously somewhat unrealistic. However, a characteristic feature of capital used to produce transport services is the extent to which it is sunk. It is difficult to use roads, locomotives, railroad tracks, or trucks outside the transport sector. Similarly, in many countries it is difficult either to lay off or to fire transport workers.[4]

In equilibrium, there will be no unutilized resources. That is, the total of all input used in M and D will always equal the total resources available to these sectors, which may or may not absorb all the resources in the economy because of "disguised" unemployment, and so on. Thus,

$$
\begin{aligned}
X_0 &= x + \bar{x}, \\
Y_0 &= y + \bar{y}, \quad \text{and} \\
Z_0 &= z + \bar{z}.
\end{aligned}
$$

(2)

To derive the conditions necessary for welfare maximization, an objective function that can provide a consistent ordinal ranking of various conditions in the economy must be stipulated.[5] To do this, the Bergson-Samuelson social welfare function will be employed. Assuming that income can be continuously redistributed in a utopian lump-sum fashion "so as to keep the 'marginal social significance of every dollar' equal," a social welfare function can be derived from regular individual indifference maps. Further, this social welfare function yields "'community or social indifference contours' with all the nice regularity properties of individual's indifference contours" where "nice" is primarily taken to mean convex to the origin. Again, following convention, these social welfare functions are assumed to depend "upon the totals of goods alone."[6]

Stipulating that the individual's indifference maps are convex and consistent and that there are no external economies or diseconomies, a social

4. In some underdeveloped countries the political pressures are such that not only are existing employees locked in, but unneeded additional workers must be periodically hired. In Chile, for example, despite a drop in ton-miles of services supplied and the introduction of more modern capital equipment into the railroads, the number of employees has increased.

5. Optimality implies that one person cannot be made better off with any reallocation of inputs without making at least one person worse off. Because this Pareto optimum does not require interpersonal utility comparisons, different distributions of utility among individuals cannot be ranked. For this reason, the criterion of Pareto optimality alone does not allow one to choose a single point at which utility is maximized. In order to choose that Pareto efficient point at which social welfare is maximized, one must make value judgments about income distribution. Vilfredo Pareto [F37], p. 44.

6. Paul A. Samuelson [F41], pp. 11 and 17.

welfare function that depends only on total outputs of the modern and domestic sectors can be defined. Thus,

$$(3) \qquad\qquad U = u(M,D).$$

The output of sector M can be maximized subject to the constraints of equation (2) and a predetermined level of production (D^*) in sector D by defining the function L, where λ is the unknown Lagrangian multiplier:[7]

$$L = f(x,y,z) - \lambda[g(X_0 - x, Y_0 - y, Z_0 - z) - D^*].$$

The conditions for production optimization are[8]

$$(4) \qquad\qquad \frac{\partial f/\partial x}{\partial f/\partial y} = \frac{\partial g/\partial \overline{x}}{\partial g/\partial \overline{y}} \qquad \text{and}$$

$$\frac{\partial f/\partial x}{\partial f/\partial z} = \frac{\partial g/\partial \overline{x}}{\partial g/\partial \overline{z}}.$$

These are the familiar marginal conditions: that for each product the marginal rate of substitution between any two inputs must be equal.

A product transformation curve can be defined as the locus of output combinations of M and D which can be produced by efficient production techniques with given endowments of the three inputs. The slope of this curve expresses how much D must be sacrificed to obtain an additional unit of M or the rate of product transformation, RPT. It can be easily proven that[9]

$$(5) \qquad RPT = -\frac{\partial D}{\partial M} = \frac{\partial g/\partial \overline{x}}{\partial f/\partial x} = \frac{\partial g/\partial \overline{y}}{\partial f/\partial y} = \frac{\partial g/\partial \overline{z}}{\partial f/\partial z}.$$

For social welfare to be maximized, the rate of product transformation between M and D must equal the marginal rate of social substitution. Since the marginal rate of social substitution is defined as $(\partial U/\partial M)/(\partial U/\partial D)$, welfare maximization implies that

$$(6) \qquad \frac{\partial U/\partial M}{\partial U/\partial D} = \frac{\partial g/\partial \overline{x}}{\partial f/\partial x} = \frac{\partial g/\partial \overline{y}}{\partial f/\partial y} = \frac{\partial g/\partial \overline{z}}{\partial f/\partial z}.$$

7. This proof is similar to that used by James M. Henderson and Richard E. Quandt [F11], p. 205.

8. Throughout the following analysis, it is assumed that the production and social welfare functions have the proper second-order conditions for maximization.

9. See Henderson and Quandt [F11], p. 68.

In other words, welfare is maximized and the economy is in equilibrium at the point where the product transformation curve is tangent to a social indifference curve.

For this optimum equilibrium to be reached through the market mechanism, the following price relationships must hold:

(4a)
$$\frac{\partial f/\partial x}{\partial f/\partial y} = \frac{\partial g/\partial \overline{x}}{\partial g/\partial \overline{y}} = \frac{r}{w}, \quad \frac{\partial f/\partial x}{\partial f/\partial z} = \frac{\partial g/\partial \overline{x}}{\partial g/\partial \overline{z}} = \frac{t}{w},$$

(5a)
$$\frac{\partial f/\partial x}{\partial g/\partial \overline{x}} = \frac{\partial f/\partial y}{\partial g/\partial \overline{y}} = \frac{\partial f/\partial z}{\partial g/\partial \overline{z}} = \frac{P_g}{P_f}, \quad \text{and}$$

(7)
$$\frac{\partial U/\partial M}{\partial U/\partial D} = \frac{P_f}{P_g}$$

where P_f and P_g denote the price of commodities M and D.

If there is perfect competition for both buyers and sellers in the factor market, then cost minimization on the part of every producer will ensure that the optimum conditions expressed in equation (4a) are reached.[10] That is, if the firms in each sector are perfect competitors, and input and output prices are given, profit maximization implies that the ratio of the marginal product of each input to its price equals the inverse of a firm's output price. If firms in both sectors pay the same price for inputs, rational behavior on the part of perfect competitors in the two sectors leads to an output–price ratio as expressed in equation (5a).[11] Finally, maximizing the social welfare function subject to a budget constraint yields equation (7)

In order to compare different equilibrium points under assumptions other than perfect competition, it is useful to derive a utility function, where utility is a function of the production functions, the social welfare function, and the factor endowments.[12] For the present model this would be

(8)
$$U^* = u^*(f,g,X_0,Y_0,Z_0,u).$$

In both equations (3) and (8) social welfare is the dependent variable. In (8), however, utility is expressed as a function of the model's parameters rather than of the commodity mix.

10. This can be proved easily by minimizing cost subject to an output constraint with fixed input prices. See Henderson and Quandt [F11], p. 51.
11. This can be established by defining a profit function for each producer and then maximizing this function with an output constraint.
12. Fishlow and David [B11], p. 533.

Market Imperfections: Distortion Parameters

The existence of product and factor market imperfections means that the conditions for a static welfare optimum will not, in general, be met. This poses questions about the effects that various transport pricing policies will have when these market imperfections exist.

To maximize profits, a firm expands production until marginal cost equals marginal revenue. In perfect competition, marginal revenue equals price, and profit maximization leads to the optimum output of M and D (as shown in the previous section). For a monopolist, however, marginal revenue does not equal price, for his demand curve is downward sloping. Consequently, when a monopolist maximizes profits by equating marginal revenue with marginal cost, the price he charges for his output at the optimum level of production will be higher than his marginal revenue or marginal cost. On the logic that a firm's monopoly power is reflected in its ability to establish an equilibrium price higher than its marginal revenue, the firm's ratio of marginal revenue to price can be used as an index of monopoly power.[13]

For each sector of the model, a parameter equal to the ratio of equilibrium marginal revenue to price can be set:

$$\mu_f = \frac{\text{marginal revenue } M}{P_f}$$

$$\mu_g = \frac{\text{marginal revenue } D}{P_g}.$$

If either μ_f or μ_g equals one, this implies that in equilibrium marginal revenue equals price, which is the case in perfect competition. As μ approaches zero, it represents a firm with an ever increasing monopoly power.

For production decisions, a monopolist uses marginal revenue, not price, to pick his optimum output level. By multiplying the price ratio on the right-hand side of equation (5) by the ratio μ_f/μ_g, marginal revenue can be substituted for price as the basis for production decisions. Thus, (5a) can be modified for the imperfect market case to read:

(5b) $$\frac{\partial f/\partial x}{\partial g/\partial \overline{x}} = \frac{\partial f/\partial y}{\partial g/\partial \overline{y}} = \frac{\partial f/\partial z}{\partial g/\partial \overline{z}} = \frac{\mu_g P_g}{\mu_f P_f}.$$

---

13. The measure of market power used here is a generalization of the Lerner measure of market power in the monopoly case. (It differs from Lerner's measure only by a constant of unity.) See Abba P. Lerner [B15], p. 169.

Varying the μ's will then cause the equilibrium mix of M and D to vary.[14] Imperfections in the product markets do not affect the efficient input mix, for this is determined solely by the relative prices of the inputs. Welfare maximization implicitly requires that different sectors be charged the same price for the same input. To allow for situations in which $w \neq \bar{w}, r \neq \bar{r}$, and $t \neq \bar{t}$, the following parameters can be introduced:

$$\delta_w = \bar{w}/w,$$
$$\delta_r = \bar{r}/r, \quad \text{and}$$
$$\delta_t = \bar{t}/t.$$

By assumption, factor price differentials do not represent any heterogeneity among inputs. If, however, the wages were higher in sector M because the workers were more skilled, this difference could be taken into account by redefining the production functions to allow for different types of labor. However, since all inputs are assumed identical, any differential in wages or capital costs in the model must be due to factor immobility, imperfect information, time lags, and other market imperfections.

Similarly, differential prices in the transport sector represent the government's pricing policy at any particular time. By assumption, the government controls the sale of transportation inputs and therefore has the power to set discriminatory prices. For example, if δ_t is less than one, this means the government is intentionally charging less per ton-mile in sector D than in sector M. Since all transport inputs are assumed identical, transport price differentials reflect true discrimination and not differences in cost to the government.[15]

If a firm maximizes profits, it uses each input until the ratio of the marginal product of that input to its price equals the inverse of the output price. For example, sector M is profit maximizing when

$$\frac{\partial f/\partial x}{w} = \frac{\partial f/\partial y}{r} = \frac{\partial f/\partial z}{t} = \frac{1}{P_f}.$$

For sector D profit maximization implies

$$\frac{\partial g/\partial \bar{x}}{\bar{w}} = \frac{\partial g/\partial \bar{y}}{\bar{r}} = \frac{\partial g/\partial \bar{z}}{\bar{t}} = \frac{1}{P_g}.$$

14. The variation of the μ's as parameters, although a neat procedure, is not wholly without cost. As Fishlow and David admit in a footnote, this technique of parameterization rests on the assumption that "the demand curves for the commodities are not related to the community utility surface." See [B11], p. 533.

15. For the semantics of this distinction, see Jack Hirshleifer [B13], pp. 451–62.

Dividing the first equation above by the second gives

$$\frac{\bar{w}\partial f/\partial x}{w\partial g/\partial \bar{x}} = \frac{\bar{r}\partial f/\partial y}{r\partial g/\partial \bar{y}} = \frac{\bar{t}\partial f/\partial z}{t\partial g/\partial \bar{z}} = \frac{P_g}{P_f}.$$

By definition of the δ's this reduces to

(5c) $$\delta_w \frac{\partial f/\partial x}{\partial g/\partial \bar{x}} = \delta_r \frac{\partial f/\partial y}{\partial g/\partial \bar{y}} = \delta_t \frac{\partial f/\partial z}{\partial g/\partial \bar{z}} = \frac{P_g}{P_f}.$$

Equation (5) is the special case of (5c) when the δ's are all equal to one or when $w = \bar{w}$, $r = \bar{r}$, and $t = \bar{t}$.

Imperfections in the factor markets change the allocation of resources in two ways. First, since the relative prices of inputs are different from those that would exist if there were no imperfections, firms will now use different input mixes to produce a given output. Consequently, the efficiency conditions expressed in equation (4a) will no longer be fulfilled and the economy's transformation curve will be lowered. This has been called the production effect.

Factor price differentials also affect the output mix of goods produced by the two sectors. For individual firms, profit maximization implies that marginal cost is equated to marginal revenue. Factor prices obviously affect marginal costs, and consequently they affect the level of output produced by each of the two sectors. Because changes in the output mix influence the relative prices of goods M and D, this has been labeled the price effect of factor market distortions. To use the three δ's as parameters, it is necessary to assume that, although commodity prices and resource demand might change, the price ratios to the sectors for a particular input remain constant.

By putting all the distortion parameters into the model, equation (5c) is modified as follows:

(5d) $$\delta_w \frac{\partial f/\partial x}{\partial g/\partial \bar{x}} = \delta_r \frac{\partial f/\partial y}{\partial g/\partial \bar{y}} = \delta_t \frac{\partial f/\partial z}{\partial g/\partial \bar{z}} = \frac{\mu_g}{\mu_f} \frac{P_g}{P_f}.$$

It is obvious that when $\delta_r = \delta_w = \delta_t = \mu_f/\mu_g = 1$, the model represents the special case of perfect competition. Also, whenever the monopoly indices are equal, the μ's drop out. This implies that, if there is equal monopoly power in the two sectors, there will be no change in the slope of the price line for the two commodities. If the ratio of the μ's is not equal to one, this ratio determines "the angle by which the relative price line deviates under monopoly from that under perfect competition."[16]

The expression for the utility surface can therefore be generalized as follows:

(8a) $$U^* = u^*(f,g,u,X_0,Y_0,Z_0,\mu_f,\mu_g,\delta_r,\delta_w,\delta_t).$$

To test the welfare implications of different transport pricing schemes, (8a) can be used to measure the effectiveness of manipulating transport prices as a second-best tool. By fixing all the parameters except δ_t, and measuring U^* with different values of δ_t, the effect on social welfare of various transport price ratios can be quantified.[17]

The Explicit Model

Up to this point, the model has been described in general terms. No specific functions have been stipulated, and no indication has been given as to the magnitude and direction of the parameters. More explicit specifications are required for quantification.

To begin, assume the following Cobb-Douglas production functions are valid:

(9) $$M = x^\alpha y^\beta z^\gamma \qquad \alpha + \beta + \gamma = 1$$
$$D = x^{\alpha'} y^{\beta'} z^{\gamma'} \qquad \alpha' + \beta' + \gamma' = 1.$$

The labor coefficients in sectors M and D are α and α', respectively, the capital coefficients are β and β', and the transport coefficients are γ and γ'. These functions are linear and homogeneous to the first degree. They show constant returns to scale. As the amount of an input is increased, its marginal product decreases if the other two inputs are held constant. Cobb-Douglas functions generate convex production isoquants which fulfill necessary second-order conditions for optimization. These functions also necessitate use of some of each input to produce any output.

A linear and homogeneous Cobb-Douglas function can also be chosen to represent the social welfare function. Thus,

$$U = M^c D^d \qquad \text{and} \qquad c + d = 1.$$

16. Fishlow and David [B11], p. 536.
17. Obviously these values for U^* depend on the distortion parameters, production functions, factor endowments, and the social welfare function. Consequently, the absolute value of any particular U^* is arbitrary. In a sense, all that is being done is to number each social indifference curve and use these numbers to compare levels of social welfare.

Convex community indifference curves characterized by diminishing marginal rates of substitution between the two outputs can be generated from this function. In other words, as one continues to remove one unit of M, one must add ever increasing amounts of D to leave social welfare at the same level. This function also implies that both sectors must produce something if there is to be any social welfare. If sector M produces nothing, no matter how much sector D produces there will be no social welfare. Considering the aggregated nature of each sector, this does not seem too unrealistic.

With the production and utility functions stipulated, it is possible to solve the model for the utility surface using equations (1, 2, 4, 5a, 6, and 7).[18] Equation (8) becomes

$$
(10) \qquad U^* = \left[\frac{X_0 \delta_w \alpha c \mu_f}{\alpha' d \mu_g + \delta_w \alpha c \mu_f} \right]^{\alpha c} \left[\frac{Y_0 \delta_r \beta c \mu_f}{\beta' d \mu_g + \delta_r \beta c \mu_f} \right]^{\beta c}
$$

$$
+ \left[\frac{Z_0 \delta_t \gamma c \mu_f}{\gamma' d \mu_g + \delta_w \gamma c \mu_f} \right]^{\gamma c} \left[\frac{X_0 \alpha' d \mu_g}{\alpha' d \mu_g + \delta_w \alpha c \mu_f} \right]^{\alpha' d}
$$

$$
+ \left[\frac{Y_0 \beta' d \mu_g}{\beta' d \mu_g + \delta_w \beta c \mu_f} \right]^{\beta' d} \left[\frac{Z_0 \gamma' d \mu_g}{\gamma' d \mu_g + \delta_t \gamma c \mu_f} \right]^{\gamma' d}
$$

In equation (10), utility is expressed in terms of sixteen parameters: six production coefficients, two utility coefficients, three factor endowments, and five distortion parameters. Again, it is assumed that the government can control only the transport differential (δ_t), while the production coefficients, utility coefficients, and distortion parameters for the capital, labor, and product markets (the exogenous parameters) are all outside of government control.

Two measures seem useful in calculating and comparing utility losses: (1) total percentage loss (*TPL*) defined as the difference between the maximum possible level of welfare, when all markets including the transport market are perfectly competitive, and any observed level of utility (with the same production and utility function) as a percentage of the maximum welfare; and (2) relative percentage loss (*RPL*) defined as the difference

---

18. One method of solution is as follows. Substitute the right-hand side of equation (1) for M and D in the left-hand side of (7). Now substitute this new expression of the output price ratio into the right-hand side of (5a). By substitution (from equation [2]), equation (4) reduces to three linear equations in three unknowns which can be used to solve for x, y, and z. By retracing our steps, with (2), $\bar{x}$, $\bar{y}$, and $\bar{z}$ can be found. These six expressions can then be solved and substituted into (6) to express utility in terms of the 16 parameters. This new function is equation (8).

between utility with optimum transportation pricing and utility with some other transportation pricing scheme, given imperfections in the product, capital, and labor markets, taken as a percentage of the welfare the identical economy would enjoy with the optimum transport price. Thus:

$$TPL = 100 \left[\frac{\text{utility under perfect competition} - \text{observed utility}}{\text{utility under perfect competition}} \right]$$

$$RPL = 100 \frac{(\text{utility with } \delta_t = \mu_g/\mu_f) - (\text{utility with } \delta_t \neq \mu_g/\mu_f)}{(\text{utility with } \delta_t = \mu_g/\mu_f)}.$$

How much of the maximum conceivable welfare has been lost because of various combinations of market imperfections is reflected by *TPL*. A transport administrator, however, must usually accept imperfections in capital, labor, and product markets as being beyond his control. Accordingly, he should be more interested in *RPL* or knowing what percentage improvement of utility could be achieved, given imperfections in other markets, if he pursued an optimum transport pricing policy.

To discover what transport pricing differential would maximize utility with any given set of exogenous parameters, the partial derivative of $U*$ with respect to δ_t is required:

$$(11) \qquad \frac{\partial U*}{\partial \delta_t} = \left[\frac{U* c d \gamma \gamma' \mu_f}{\delta_t (\gamma' \mu_g + \delta_t c)} \right] \left[\frac{\mu_g}{\mu_f} - \delta_t \right].$$

For $U*$ to be a relative maximum, this must equal zero. By inspection, the derivative always equals zero when $\delta_t = \mu_g/\mu_f$.

Because Cobb-Douglas production functions have unitary elasticities of substitution, the optimum price is determined only by the ratio of the market power coefficients in the model. In other words, no matter what imperfections exist in the capital and labor markets, the government's best pricing policy is to equate the transport differential with the ratio of these market power coefficients. Thus, pursuing a second-best pricing policy, the government would discriminate in favor of that sector with the greater market power (or lower market power coefficient).

The logic underlying this conclusion can be readily explained. Say that sector *M* has greater monopoly power than sector *D*. This implies that too much *D* and not enough *M* is produced. By discriminating in favor of sector *M*, the government is in effect lowering the marginal cost of that sector. In order to maximize profits, sector *M* will expand production until marginal revenue equals this new and lower marginal cost. At the new equilibrium, neither M nor D will be produced with an efficient mix of inputs, but the output mix will be on a higher social indifference curve. The welfare gains associated with the new mix of outputs more than compensates for the welfare loss occasioned by inefficient allocation of resources associated with discriminatory transport pricing.

An obvious alternative pricing policy would be that of neutrality or δ_t equal to unity. Indeed, given the assumption of homogeneous inputs, marginal cost pricing or any other cost-oriented pricing strategy would require that $\delta_t = 1$ in the model. A policy of $\delta_t = 1$ therefore will be called cost oriented.[19]

Pricing schemes might also be considered that are demand oriented in strategy. In the present model, demand-oriented schemes can be expressed by setting the ratio of transport prices charged to each sector equal to the proportion of the transport outputs used, that is, $\delta_t = \bar{z}/z$.

Note that neither the cost- nor the demand-oriented pricing schemes, as outlined, is identical to the concepts of any specific pricing theory, as discussed in Chapter 2. Instead, they are best construed as rough empirical or practical analogies to some of these concepts.

Perfect Competition

The relative percentage losses associated with different values of the transport differential when there are no imperfections in the capital, labor, or product markets is illustrated by the data in Table 5-1.[20] As one would expect, when no imperfections exist elsewhere, welfare is maximized when the transport differential is set equal to one. In this case, since $\mu_g/\mu_f = 1$, the optimum and the cost-oriented pricing schemes are the same. If demand-oriented pricing (DOP) is followed, the value of δ_t is set at 0.58 in the example of Table 5-1. In other words, the monopoly sector pays almost twice as much for transport services as the other sector. Despite this discrimination, the DOP leads to a utility loss which is less than one-third

19. No claims can be made, however, about testing the welfare implications of marginal cost pricing. The supply of transport services is assumed fixed at X_0 so the marginal cost of supplying a unit of transport up to this capacity is indeterminate. Instead, only the welfare effects of setting transport prices proportional to marginal or any other stipulated costs can be tested.

20. When all other markets are perfect, the relative percentage loss and total percentage losses are identical. When the optimum transport price is used, the economy is maximizing social welfare perfectly. In this case, $s_t = 1 = \mu_g/\mu_f$.

TABLE 5-1. *Relative Percentage Losses under Selected Transport Pricing Policies When All Other Markets Are Perfect*[a]

Transport differential δ_t	Relative percentage loss
1.00[b]	0
1.00[c]	0
0.58[d]	0.31
0.10	5.85
0.30	1.57
0.50	0.50
0.70	0.13
0.90	0.01
1.20	0.03
1.50	0.14
2.00	0.40
3.00	0.92
6.00	2.12
10.00	3.16

a. Definitions and values assumed for parameters of the model:

α = labor coefficient in sector M (= 0.55)
α' = labor coefficient in sector D (= 0.75)
β = capital coefficient in sector M (= 0.30)
β' = capital coefficient in sector D (= 0.20)
γ = transport production coefficient for sector M (= 0.15)
γ' = transport production coefficient for sector D (= 0.05)
c = coefficient of the social utility function for sector M (= 0.50)
d = coefficient of the social utility function for sector D (= 0.50)
δ_r = cost of the capital (= 1.00)
δ_w = wage rate (= 1.00)
μ_g/μ_f = ratios of marginal revenue for sectors D and M respectively (= 1.00)

b. Optimum pricing.
c. Cost-oriented pricing.
d. Demand-oriented pricing.

of 1 percent. Indeed, as shown in the lower part of Table 5-1, for any value of δ_t between 0.50 and 3.00, the relative losses are less than 1 percent; the loss rises to only 3.16 percent when δ_t is set at 10. Apparently, when there is competition elsewhere a transport pricing scheme must be sharply discriminatory before there is any significant loss in social welfare.

Factor Market Imperfections

Total and relative percentage losses under various transport pricing schemes when there are imperfections in the labor and capital markets are illustrated in Table 5-2. In the example, capital costs about 50 percent

TABLE 5-2. *Total and Relative Percentage Losses under Selected Transport Pricing Policies When There Are Labor and Capital Market Imperfections*[a]

Transport differential δ_t	Total percentage loss	Relative percentage loss
1.00[b]	4.01	0
1.00[c]	4.01	0
0.58[d]	4.30	0.31
0.10	9.62	5.85
0.30	5.52	1.57
0.50	4.48	0.50
0.70	4.13	0.13
0.90	4.02	0.01
1.20	4.04	0.03
1.50	4.15	0.14
2.00	4.39	0.40
3.00	4.89	0.92
6.00	6.04	2.12
10.00	7.04	3.16

a. The parameter $\delta_w = 0.50$; the parameter $\delta_r = 1.50$. For the values of other parameters and explanation of notation, see Table 5-1, note a.
b. Optimum pricing.
c. Cost-oriented pricing.
d. Demand-oriented pricing.

more in the competitive sector than in the monopoly sector, while wages in the monopoly sector are twice those in the domestic sector.[21] However, no product market imperfections are assumed. With imperfections thus restricted to the factor markets only, the optimum price still has the same

21. In the context of less developed countries this assumption might be justified on the conventional observation that labor and capital markets in most underdeveloped countries are something less than perfect. Hirschman ([F17], p. 126) writes that "probably one of the principal economic characteristics of any country where industrial development is incipient and spotty is the existence of two distinct wage levels, one applicable to the industrial sector and the other to the preindustrial sectors." As for the capital markets, Higgins ([F15], pp. 343–44) has said:

The industrial and rural sectors are not part of the same "economy." . . . Geographically, the plantations, mines, and oil fields are in the same country, but economically they may be more closely tied to the metropolitan country providing the capital, technical knowledge, and managerial skill than to the underdeveloped country in which the operation is located. The men who launch, organize, and manage these enterprises—even when they are the urbanites of the country itself—know little of peasant agriculture and village life. The rural capitalist relies for his success on his personal and firsthand knowledge of the villagers with whom he deals; he lends to them, sells to them, and buys from them. This is knowledge of a sort the foreign or urban capitalist does not have and does not wish to acquire.

value as in the example of Table 5-1 since the optimum price is determined for this particular model only by the ratio of the market power coefficients. Also, the relative percentage losses in Table 5-2 are identical with those in Table 5-1, since for this model, as long as μ_g/μ_f stays fixed, changing the imperfections in the capital and labor markets has no effect on the relative losses. A corollary of this is that in this model, or any model for which Cobb-Douglas production functions hold, transport prices cannot be used to compensate for imperfections in the other factor markets.

There are still social costs involved in having imperfections in the capital and labor markets. In the example, social welfare would be about 4 percent higher if there were perfect competition in the other factor markets.

Product Market Imperfections

As product market imperfections in an economy increase (see Table 5-3), more and more is to be gained by violating the usual normative conditions and discriminating in favor of the sector with monopoly power. However, as long as μ_g/μ_f is less than or equal to 2.00, the relative loss which results from using cost-oriented prices rather than the second-best prices is less than 0.5 percent. For the particular choice of exogenous parameters used in this example, cost-oriented prices yield a smaller relative loss than demand-oriented prices as long as μ_g/μ_f is less than 3.00. As μ_g/μ_f grows

TABLE 5-3. *Total and Relative Percentage Losses under Selected Transport Pricing Policies When There Are Product Market Imperfections*[a]

Ratio of marginal revenue to price	Total percentage loss with optimum price	Relative percentage losses with		Relative cost of discriminating the wrong way	
		Cost-oriented pricing	Demand-oriented pricing	$\delta_t = 0.50$[b]	$\delta_t = 0.10$[c]
1.00	0	0	0.31	0.50	5.85
1.33	0.89	0.08	0.50	1.03	7.31
2.00	4.97	0.50	0.85	2.11	9.52
3.22	13.69	1.57	1.43	4.00	12.45
5.00	22.27	2.87	2.01	5.85	14.84
10.00	37.68	5.85	3.21	9.52	18.92

a. For values of other parameters and explanation of notation, see Table 5-1, note a.
b. δ_t = transport differential; assumes the monopoly sector is charged twice as much for its transport inputs as the other sector.
c. δ_t = transport differential; assumes the monopoly sector is charged ten times as much for its transport inputs as the other sector.

larger, more D and less M is produced, and consequently the amount of transport used by each sector changes. This causes the demand-oriented prices to change in value as μ_g/μ_f varies. When μ_g/μ_f becomes great enough (about 3.00), the monopoly sector uses fewer transport inputs than the other sector, despite the fact that it is more transport intensive. For this high value of μ_g/μ_f, the demand-oriented prices will be less for transport inputs in the monopoly than in the more competitive sector. Thus, for this example, when μ_g/μ_f is greater than 3.00, the demand-oriented prices will discriminate in the right direction, and consequently will involve smaller relative losses than the cost-oriented prices. However, with smaller values for μ_g/μ_f, the monopoly sector will be consuming more transport inputs than the other sector; the demand-oriented prices will then discriminate in the wrong direction and yield higher relative losses than the cost-oriented prices.

Since, by assumption, μ_g/μ_f is never less than one, the optimum price never involves discriminating against the monopoly sector. In the last two columns of Table 5-3 the relative losses are shown if the monopoly sector were charged either twice as much ($\delta_t = 0.50$) or ten times as much ($\delta_t = 0.10$) for its transport inputs as the other sector. It is obviously costly to discriminate the wrong way, and the greater the value of μ_g/μ_f, the more expensive it becomes.

Production Parameters

The only production parameters in the model that affect the relative percentage losses associated with different values of δ_t are the transport production coefficients γ and γ'. The effect of changing the value of γ, the monopoly sector's transport production coefficient, on the relative losses with different pricing strategies is shown in Table 5-4. For these experiments, γ', the more competitive sector's transport production coefficient, was fixed at 0.05. In case 1, the two sectors are equally transport intensive. In case 2, the transport coefficient in the monopoly sector is three times that in the other sector. In case 3, the monopoly sector is five times as transport intensive as the relatively competitive sector.

When γ equals γ' (case 1) the demand-oriented price yields almost as much utility as the optimum price. By comparing the second column of Table 5-4 with the fifth, one can see that when both sectors use the same amount of transport to produce a unit of output (case 1) the demand-

TABLE 5-4. *Relative Percentage Losses under Selected Transport Pricing Strategies and Production Conditions When There Are Product Market Imperfections*[a]

	Relative percentage loss with cost-oriented pricing			Relative percentage loss with demand-oriented pricing		
Ratio of marginal revenue to price	Case 1 $\gamma = 0.05$	Case 2 $\gamma = 0.15$	Case 3 $\gamma = 0.25$	Case 1 $\gamma = 0.05$	Case 2 $\gamma = 0.15$	Case 3 $\gamma = 0.25$
1.00	0	0	0	0	0.31	0.79
1.33	0.05	0.08	0.09	0.01	0.50	1.13
2.00	0.29	0.50	0.58	0.07	0.85	1.72
3.33	0.85	1.57	1.90	0.22	1.43	2.67
5.00	1.46	2.87	3.57	0.39	2.01	3.57
10.00	2.73	5.85	7.68	0.78	3.21	5.44

a. For values of other parameters and explanation of notation, see Table 5-1, note a.

oriented price is superior to the cost-oriented price whenever there is any product market imperfection. The reason is quite simple: since both products are equally transport intensive, the demand-oriented price will always discriminate in favor of the monopoly sector whenever μ_g/μ_f is greater than unity. Of course, if one were to employ demand-oriented pricing that was inversely related to demand levels, as in most value-of-service schemes, this conclusion would be reversed. When cost-oriented prices and demand-oriented prices for case 3 are compared, it is apparent that if the monopoly sector is more transport intensive, the monopoly distortion must reach a certain level before the demand-oriented price is as good as the cost-oriented price. Specifically, the more transport intensive the monopoly sector, the higher the μ_g/μ_f ratio must be before the demand-oriented price is better than the cost-oriented price.

Different Utility Weights

In the preceding analyses, the two outputs, D and M, were weighted equally in the social welfare function. Changing these weights considerably has little effect on the relative losses incurred under different pricing schemes. This can be clearly seen in Table 5-5. Changing the weights has, however, a significant effect on the total losses. As one might suspect, if the output of the monopoly sector is favored, the society loses more as the degree of monopoly increases.

TABLE 5-5. *Total and Relative Percentage Losses under Selected Transport Pricing Strategies for Different Utility Functions*[a]

Ratio of marginal revenue to price	Total percentage loss with optimum pricing			Relative percentage loss with cost-oriented pricing			Relative percentage loss with discriminatory pricing		
	Case 1 $c = 0.75$ $d = 0.25$	Case 2 $c = 0.50$ $d = 0.50$	Case 3 $c = 0.25$ $d = 0.75$	Case 1 $c = 0.75$ $d = 0.25$	Case 2 $c = 0.50$ $d = 0.50$	Case 3 $c = 0.25$ $d = 0.75$	Case 1 $c = 0.75$ $d = 0.25$	Case 2 $c = 0.50$ $d = 0.50$	Case 3 $c = 0.25$ $d = 0.75$
1.00	0	0	0	0	0	0	0.20	0.31	0.28
1.33	0.73	0.89	0.63	0.05	0.08	0.08	0.32	0.50	0.44
2.00	4.35	4.97	3.33	0.32	0.50	0.44	0.57	0.85	0.73
3.33	13.05	13.69	8.84	1.11	1.57	1.28	1.00	1.43	1.17
5.00	22.48	22.27	14.15	2.17	2.87	2.18	1.45	2.01	1.50
10.00	40.71	37.68	23.88	5.01	5.85	4.07	2.47	3.21	2.41

a. For values of other parameters and explanation of notation, see Table 5-1, note a.

Conclusion

The specific findings reported in this chapter, given the limited generality of the model on which they are based, are not too important in and of themselves. In the main, they suggest that, as long as the economy is not dominated by a sector with very strong monopoly power and for which transport is a significant input, little appears to be gained by attempting to find the optimum second-best price. This tends to substantiate the suggestion made by several observers that in many instances the gains potentially realizable from increasing allocative efficiency are probably small relative to those which could be realized by greater attention to the managerial and organizational function of firms and to their internal efficiency.[22] Furthermore, the model illustrates the considerable information required to evaluate the effect of relatively uncomplicated pricing policies even in the context of a simple economic environment. No real world would be expected to be so simple. The complications of determining an optimum second-best price or the probable impact of other pricing policies would be correspondingly, and perhaps disproportionately, augmented in actual applications.

22. Harvey Leibenstein [B14], pp. 392–415.

CHAPTER SIX

Criteria for Evaluating Alternative Pricing Strategies

THE CHOICE OF ONE transport pricing strategy over another as a deliberate matter of public policy requires a formulation of what constitutes the public welfare and of how this welfare is increased or reduced by pricing decisions. Clearly, any concept of public welfare is likely to have many dimensions.

Transport prices have many dimensions as well. It has long been recognized, for example, that transport pricing policies can affect income distribution and location decisions. They may also influence inflation, technological change, and other aspects of macroeconomic policy.

Attitudes toward pricing alternatives will also be conditioned by assessments made of the surrounding environment. These assessments vary widely from one observer to another. The desirability of marginal cost pricing, for example, depends on the extent to which an individual believes that he observes such policies being followed elsewhere in the economy (because of second-best considerations).

Attitudes toward transport pricing policies can be conditioned by the political situation too. Thus, if one assumes that investment is needed for development, that government has a fairly high propensity to invest but limited ability to raise money through income or excise taxes, an argument might be made for employing substantial user charges or for setting rates on nationalized transport activities at levels that maximize profits.

Distributive Effects

Social welfare is also dependent on the distribution of benefits. Distributive effects arise with any pricing system, and transportation pricing is no exception. Indeed, neutrality is rarely, if ever, possible.[1] Transport pricing may be expressly designed to achieve income redistribution. Although other important and more direct means of achieving income transfers are often available, transport pricing may be a useful and expedient redistribution procedure in some contexts. For example, important favorable consequences for economic growth are sometimes thought to result from distributing the net benefits of a transport project to groups in society who have high propensities to save and invest.

As for the distributive consequences of any pricing policy, one obvious concern is the allocation of benefits between those who use a transport facility and those who do not. At one extreme, a bridge might be built and maintained from general tax revenues. If there is no charge for using the bridge (setting the price at zero is a pricing policy), the people who use the bridge get all the benefits, and the total cost is borne by society as a whole, users and nonusers alike. Consequently, redistribution of income from people who do not use the bridge to those who do should result.

By contrast, bridge tolls might be set at such a level that more funds would be generated than it cost to build the bridge and provide the service. The resulting income could be redistributed in different ways; it would depend on what the bridge authority did with this money. If the profits were used to lower the general tax burden, income would be redistributed in favor of taxpayers and probably of nonusers, since the taxpayers normally encompass some of the nonusers. On the other hand, if the bridge were very crowded and time costs were included in the marginal calculation, marginal costs might be greater than average costs and a surplus could result. Again, the effect on income distribution would depend on how this surplus was used.

Different pricing policies also can affect the distribution of benefits between various groups of users. Trucks might be charged enough to cover the full cost of the bridge, and automobiles permitted to use it free. The net benefits would then accrue to the automobile users. Similarly, peak-

1. J. de V. Graaff [F7], for example, argues that prices could and should be used to redistribute income. It will be argued here that a decision on this matter depends on a variety of circumstances and does not easily lend itself to generalization.

period pricing schemes can allocate costs (and hence net benefits) in a number of ways between those who use a facility during rush hours and those who use it during off-peak hours.

In addition, pricing policies can be used to distribute benefits in different ways among the users of a facility over the life span of the project. Price might be used in such a way that the total cost of a bridge is recovered in user charges as quickly as possible, perhaps over the first quarter of the life span of the facility. In this case, the people who use the facility during the last three-quarters of its life might be expected to reap relatively greater net benefits.

Transport planners cannot claim to know whether one distribution is better than another in any general welfare sense. At best they may be able to point out the economic implications of alternative distributions. It is almost impossible to make any a priori generalizations as to what distribution of benefits is optimum for a given economy. The important point is that virtually no pricing policy is likely to be neutral: implicit in any pricing policy is a distribution of net benefits. Which distribution is best depends on the values of society.[2] Which distribution is chosen will probably depend on the values of the policy maker, who must take into account the social priorities involved in using alternative pricing policies as policy instruments.

Location Consequences

Location consequences of transport pricing and investment decisions are often important in transport planning. Transportation is an intermediate good, used as a factor of production in manufacturing various products. Thus, if transport prices are set on a commodity by commodity basis, different transportation prices can be used to encourage or discourage the production of various types of manufactured goods or the growth of various sectors or regions of an economy.

---

2. Merely choosing certain types of transport pricing policies as policy instruments, even if neutral in their distributional aspects, may affect social welfare. Suppose the population of a particular country objects to price discrimination for some cultural reason. As a consequence, transport pricing schemes that entail price discrimination may be unacceptable even though they may contribute toward reaching other objectives. Similarly, toll roads may be unpopular—consequently, a project that does not have tolls might be preferred despite, say, a possible unfavorable income redistribution brought about by the necessity of subsidies.

This sort of pricing is often an important policy instrument in a context of economic development. For example, in the economic history of the United States there are several examples of transport pricing policies used to favor certain locations or regions. Traditionally, railroads in the United States charged more for shipping manufactured goods from west to east and south to north than vice versa.[3] Similarly, the port of Baltimore may have been given a boost in European trade by the North Atlantic Railroad Conference's equalization of ocean freight rates. Certain regions may also have benefited from differences in coal tariffs established by U.S. railroads.

Considerable distortion in capital allocation over time can occur when discriminatory transport tariffs are employed. The dangers of discrimination are multiplied when there are competing modes of transport, especially if the investment decisions for each mode are made independently. When the prices charged by each mode do not reflect the costs of supplying the services, there is always the danger that a high-cost sector with low prices will be expanded rather than a lower-cost sector with high prices.[4]

If all investment is closely regulated by some centralized authority which realizes that current transport prices do not reflect the costs of providing transportation services, the danger of unintentionally making inefficient investment decisions can be minimized with proper administration. The analytical knowledge and data flows required for such administration are, however, beyond the capabilities of most planning agencies. On the other hand, with decentralized control, it is possible that discriminatory prices will lead to inefficient investment decisions. Even a nationally owned industry operated on a decentralized basis can make inefficient investments as a result of inappropriate price signals. The commission managing a

3. There was some economic excuse for the railroads' behavior. Because agricultural and mining goods were shipped predominantly from west to east and south to north, railroads had excess capacity on the empty backhaul from east to west and north to south. See D. Philip Locklin [B17], and Isaiah L. Sharfman [B29], Pt. 3-B.

4. The Colombian experience is a case in point. Railroad rates once were well below costs, and as a consequence the demand for rail services was greater than supply. The government borrowed large sums from the World Bank to expand and modernize the rail system. Later, when the Bank realized that huge losses were accruing, it told the government it would make no future loans unless rail rates were raised. When the rates were raised, however, many shippers switched to the roads. As a consequence, the railroads then had excess capacity, and the roads, which were also subsidized, clamored for additional investment funds to expand capacity to accommodate the increased demand. Richard Weisskoff [F45]; see also Edwin T. Haefele, ed. [J2], pp. 122–76.

nationalized steel industry, for example, may not know the real costs of transport services and may, like the private producer, use the market price as a basis for investment decisions.

Inflation, Technological Change, and Macroeconomic Policy

An important source of pricing difficulty often arises from the long life of investments in transportation facilities. During their life new technological developments may mean that, per unit of capacity, the operating and even the replacement costs of a facility are much lower than the historical costs. It can be inferred from economic theory that prices related to the costs of a currently optimal operation will yield higher efficiency properties than prices related to historical costs. If lower prices justified by technological improvements are immediately adopted, however, refinancing problems may develop for transport enterprises. In such circumstances, even nationalized operators may encounter difficulty in obtaining the necessary financing.

Often inflation and technological change can counteract each other. At the same time that technological change is acting to lower the price of a unit of capacity, inflation can produce a tendency to raise it. Which force proves to be more important depends on the country and the circumstances. In the United States, technological change has perhaps been slightly more important than inflation in its impact on transport costs. In Europe, the race may be about equal. In some underdeveloped countries, inflation is more significant than technological change, and current costs are at least as high as historical costs.[5]

The problem need not arise if all technological changes are foreseen,

5. According to James R. Nelson [B22], p. 480:

No method of economic analysis can determine, scientifically, what to do about the gap between average and marginal cost. One E.D.F. [Electricité de France] answer to this, in the era of French inflation, was admittedly cynical: if most of the capital account takes the form of fixed-interest obligations, then the rate of inflation may exactly close the spread between average and marginal cost and permit marginal cost pricing to coexist with a balanced budget. This answer not only requires acceptance of the idea of an optimum rate of inflation, as Marcel Boiteux has pointed out; it also neglects the fact that different customers are likely to demand services which mingle cost dimensions in different proportions. Since decreasing costs are more significant in some cost dimensions than in others, no averaging-out process can produce a marginal cost rate structure.

so that all investments are properly amortized. In the economy as a whole, moreover, one could expect as many forecast errors to be made in one direction as in the other. If no financial stigma is attached to writing off overvalued assets, so that financing of the new equipment could proceed promptly, the problem would again be avoided. However, particular firms or industries sometimes miscalculate the economic lives of equipment, and bondholders tend to take a dim view of forfeitures. Thus, if prices are lowered immediately as new technology reduces costs, there is a very real possibility in a capitalistic or mixed market economy of harming the credit standing of the affected establishment and, therefore, its ability to finance future investments.

There is no pat answer to this problem. For individual cases, the correct price could depend on how a variety of equity questions are answered.[6] Moreover, while theoretically the problem should be easier to solve in a nationalized than in a private industry context (because of greater availability of general tax funds for transport subsidy and investment), experience suggests that the problems are not notably less complex in one than in the other. Parliaments often can be as insistent as investment houses on financial integrity, even though the reasons for such insistence may be very different; for example, a scarcity of tax revenues and a plethora of attractive welfare programs.

This problem lies close to a more general difficulty often faced by governments, particularly of the developing countries—the ethical question of whether a democratic government should continuously generate rates of inflation greater than those foreseen by private investors in order to make public investments financially viable. A practical issue—whether a government can long continue such policies—also exists. The nationalized Electricité de France, for example, discovered after World War II that private investors would purchase its bonds only if both the interest and the principal were tied to the price of electricity. Thus, bondholders were at least partially protected against unforeseen inflation. A government in an underdeveloped country may, of course, have an additional reason for not relying on inflation as a solution to its financial problems. Foreign governments or international organizations may demand a reduction in the rate of inflation in return for financial assistance.

Macroeconomic policy can also influence employment practices in the

6. For discussion of this problem, see Merton J. Peck and John R. Meyer [B24], pp. 199–241; Yale Brozen [B7], pp. 67–75 and 123–32; and James C. Bonbright [B6], pp. 16–23.

transport sector. For example, the perpetual underemployment and unemployment plaguing many less developed countries motivates their governments to employ as many workers as possible. A variant of Parkinson's law seems to be that, for most underdeveloped countries, the costs of providing nationalized transport services always seem to expand to absorb the revenues derived from such services. Hence, one often finds a rail system with excess capacity and an overly large labor force, neither of which can be reduced for political reasons. In such circumstances, it can be tempting to apply monopolistic price discrimination when establishing the railroad tariffs in order to maximize the revenues available to the railroad authorities. From a practical standpoint, however, such practices normally overlook the strong possibility of truck competition,[7] not to mention the potentially adverse effects on efficiency. In many underdeveloped countries, trucks are not effectively controlled, at least directly. Thus, once the roads are built, the government railroad runs the serious risk of being underpriced by its truck competitors if it continues to operate with highly discriminatory pricing. Therefore, the long-run feasibility of charging some users much more than costs is questionable.[8]

In the same context—excess rail capacity—highways are sometimes priced below full costs with an accompanying inducement to promote their use. This, in turn, increases the pressure on the government to expand the highways. An alternative to highway expansion would be the diversion of traffic from the highways to the railways, which could be accomplished either by lowering the price on rail traffic or by raising the price of highway traffic. Obviously, raising the price on the highways increases the average price of transportation, and lowering the price on the railways lowers the average price of transportation. Presumably, these two alternatives will have different effects on the overall demand for transportation and hence the performance of the entire economy.

7. Robert T. Brown ([F3], pp. 242–74) argues that unless an underdeveloped country is ruled by a strict totalitarian regime, political pressures will ensure that in a matter of time the country will have a network of roads and a competitive trucking industry.

8. Chile's experience is a case in point. When the truck entered the transportation picture ten years ago, the railroads were underbid by truckers, and consequently few high-value products are shipped by rail today in Chile. The trucks, in effect, stole the "cream" and left the railroads with only that traffic which they had always carried at a loss, a pattern not too atypical of many countries in all parts of the world after World War II. See Brown [F3], pp. 242 ff.

Miscellaneous Practical Considerations

A variety of practical considerations, involving political and administrative realities of particular circumstances, are also important in evaluating alternative pricing strategies. Customer realization that the government often has direct control over the rates for any given mode can create strong pressure to give special consideration to certain commodities, such as exempting them from a general rate increase. Once a government succumbs to a selective tariff policy, it must often cope with the problem of justifying any or all changes in rates.

Similarly, forces are almost always present to maintain transportation tariffs at their current level. Important pressures are awakened in any regulatory or political system whenever a change is proposed in transport charges. Consequently, transport prices are often inflexible. Rapid price changes are difficult to achieve and this has important implications. It means, for example, that pricing is often unavailable as a tool for balancing traffic flows and that there is little possibility of working off excess capacity at a sale price. It also means that mistakes may take much longer to correct in transport than in other industries.

Generally speaking, many observers, while accepting the basic notion that prices should vary with or roughly correspond to costs, either average or marginal, still feel that there are definite limitations on the number of price changes that can be tolerated within a given time period. Arguments for limiting the number of price variations relate to concepts of market stability or creating a workable competitive environment. Costs attach to varying prices in terms of creating instabilities and decision problems for both carriers and shippers, so that only a limited degree of price variation seems workable within many market environments.

Administrative feasibility may also impose limitations on price variations. This is particularly true when, as is often the case in transport, pricing policies are subject to regulatory review. Such reviews are normally public and require time (for example, to hear different points of view). Indeed, a rational management operating within an environment of public regulation is probably well advised to establish tariffs on the presumption that they cannot be modified on short notice. At a minimum, there will be little scope for sudden sharp upward or downward adjustment of rates or special sales in regulated industries. Among other problems, sharp variations in charges can create special advantages or disadvantages for shippers who are in competition. This consequence tends to conflict with a common regulatory constraint on transport pricing that different modes and shippers receive equal treatment. Of course, an exact definition of equality may not always come easily in this context.

Various practical considerations are also relevant in evaluating the more complex second-best or discriminatory pricing procedures. There is disagreement about technological capability to implement sophisticated and differentiated pricing schemes at a reasonable cost. In the past, most special pricing schemes such as highway or bridge tolls have required considerable input of labor to enforce. To reduce these labor requirements, the suggestion has been made that electronic or other sophisticated technological devices be used, but field experiments with such proposals are still limited.

Collection and implementation costs for tolls can be substantial. For example, highway toll collection costs, whether by automatic or manual collectors, range between 2 and 5 cents a vehicle trip in the United States. Thus for a typical urban trip, which in most urban areas averages less than five miles and uses a facility costing between 1 and 2 cents a vehicle mile, the institution of differential pricing systems would increase roadway costs between 20 and 100 percent.[9] There are also additional costs that may be imposed on the travelers if they must stop and wait for toll collection. In many circumstances, justifiable toll differentials may be so small relative to the extra collection costs required for differential pricing as to raise serious doubts about the advisability of establishing the tolls. In short, the costs of implementing a more complex pricing or other rationing scheme must be weighed against the value of the improvements thereby achieved. Marginal conditions for optimization clearly apply here as well as they do to other classes of economic decisions.

Evaluation

The choice of a pricing strategy, in sum, will normally depend to a considerable extent on policy objectives and subjective preferences. This is true even within a relatively limited and static view of technologies and demand structures. Broaden the range of issues to include relevant dynamic and administrative questions such as the government's ability to tax or the

9. See John R. Meyer, John F. Kain, and Martin Wohl [A5], pp. 244–325.

influence of the price structure on savings and investment rates, and generalization becomes quite difficult.

It appears that at least ten criteria for assessing pricing strategies might be identified. These are:[10] (1) resource allocation; (2) managerial efficiency; (3) income distribution; (4) administrative or regulatory requirements (such as information, data, and analysis); (5) price stability over time; (6) development of new or otherwise socially desirable transport modes; (7) inflationary adjustments; (8) technological change in both products and production technology; (9) investment choices; and (10) broad objectives of fiscal and monetary policy. The first three of these criteria are essentially static in character, the next five essentially dynamic, and the last two could be analyzed in either context.

Correspondingly, approximately six fundamental pricing strategies can be identified. These would be: (1) profit maximization; (2) average cost; (3) short-run marginal cost; (4) long-run marginal cost; (5) optimal second best; and (6) proportional markup (or markdown) of marginal costs with the budget constraint that total revenues equal total costs. For the most part, other pricing strategies mentioned previously can be described as derivatives or combinations of the above six. For example, the peak-period schemes adopted from public utility experience originated in marginal cost pricing concepts, though in practice they can sometimes include elements of value-of-service or discriminatory pricing as well. Similarly, the option or superpeak pricing schemes are almost invariably syntheses of two or more of the basic or pure strategies listed above. Indeed, in a strict sense, even the sixth strategy can be construed as a merger of marginal cost and average cost pricing principles, although it has sufficiently differentiable properties to be of interest in its own right.

Refinements or special forms of each of the pure strategies are also easily identified. In particular, average costs for pricing can be defined in several ways. At one extreme is the individual project or group approach in which average costs are determined for each identifiable project or group with particular needs or applications. At the other extreme is the continuing enterprise approach in which total cost is taken to be the aggregate amount expended for all purposes (maintenance, operation, and new construction) on an entire transport system. This includes both old and new linkages and

10. A similar and highly suggestive framework for evaluating efficiency problems in general can be found in Harvey Leibenstein [B14], pp. 392–415. Leibenstein particularly emphasizes the importance of managerial efficiency.

probably reflects both historical and current costs. Similarly, total volume would be measured as the total use made of the entire system. The profit-oriented pricing strategies also can be expressed in a wide variety of formulations.

One useful organizational scheme for systematic comparison of pricing strategies is to construct a matrix in which the different pricing strategies are rank ordered in terms of the different criteria. The rank ordering of different pricing procedures involves, of course, some highly subjective judgments, which will depend crucially on the specific economic and market environment in which they are made. For example, assuming that the transport sector is part of an economy where monopolistic pricing practices are pervasive, profit-oriented pricing practices may induce (on second-best arguments) a better static allocation of resources than the pursuit of marginal cost pricing within the transport sector alone.

Similar comments apply to the ranking of transport pricing schemes in terms of their impact on technological changes. Specifically, much depends on how one perceives the processes of technological change. One might adopt the Schumpeterian view that substantial profits, in excess of those normally needed to attract capital, are essential to financing research, development, and innovation.[11] In this case, the existence of monopoly and monopolistic profits will be considered an aid to technological advance. On the other hand, if one believes that competitive pressures and the restriction of funds to levels just adequate to cover costs and outlays provide the stimulus needed for research and development, then monopoly profits could be considered an impediment to technological change.[12]

Pronounced differences in the evaluations will also exist in different national environments—economic, political, and social. The value attached to achieving transport prices that serve, or at least do not conflict with, broader goals of national economic policy is likely to be greatest in the less developed countries. The explanation, in essence, is that the more advanced countries are likely to possess such a wide range of reasonably effective policy instruments for achieving their aggregate economic goals that they need not rely on transport pricing for these purposes. Furthermore, experience is likely to have demonstrated to the more economically

11. Joseph A. Schumpeter [F42]. For a concise statement and critique of this general position see Edward S. Mason [B18], pp. 371–81.

12. Such a view is strongly urged by Leibenstein [B14]. For an interesting case study, whose conclusions run strongly contrary to the Schumpeterian view, see Walter Adams and Joel B. Dirlam [B1], pp. 167–89.

advanced countries that transport prices are awkward, and often costly, instruments for achieving broad development or redistribution objectives. In addition, advanced economies usually possess highly developed infrastructures and a full range of modern technologies, so the options available to transport users are numerous. It is therefore difficult to channel transport activities via pricing incentives alone. In many less developed countries, by contrast, transport pricing may be one of the few effective policy tools available, for instance, for redistributing income or accelerating economic growth. The possibility of enforcing or sustaining discriminatory prices also may be greater, since underdevelopment implies a lesser number of economic and technological options.

By way of illustration, two hypothetical exercises in rank ordering of the six pricing strategies listed above are shown in Tables 6-1 and 6-2 in terms of different relevant evaluation criteria. Table 6-1 pertains to what might be described as reasonably typical conditions in a small, less developed country pursuing import substitution as a development policy within an essentially mixed public-private market economy. In Table 6-2, the same exercise is repeated, assuming conditions similar to those in the United States and accepting, quite arbitrarily, the Schumpeterian view that monopoly profits facilitate technological change. In both tables, simple rank orderings are presented for each pricing strategy according to how well each serves the particular evaluation criterion.

The rankings are in no way meant to be definitive. They are simply an illustration of one possible means of organizing the many diverse considerations that influence choices of pricing strategies. In short, the rankings are arbitrary, subjective, and possibly even erroneous. It should be obvious, moreover, that the only relevant rankings would be those made by the political authorities responsible for decisions.

An arithmetic average of these rank orderings or any other numerical operations on these rank scores to achieve a composite score for a particular pricing strategy in terms of all the evaluation criteria is not recommended. Such operations performed on ordinal scales generally imply particular assumptions as to the relative weight of the various criteria used in the measurement. Important differences in the weights attached to different criteria and, even more fundamentally, the extent to which a particular pricing strategy satisfies a specific evaluation criterion are obscured by any such aggregate weighting scheme. For example, optimal second-best pricing is, by definition, best able to serve most economic resource allocation and welfare maximization goals and thus would have one of the better average

TABLE 6-1. *Matrix of Rank Order Evaluations of Alternative Transport Pricing Strategies for a Small, Less Developed Country Pursuing Import Substitution as a Development Policy within an Essentially Market or Mixed Public-Private Economy*

Evaluation criteria	Profit maximizing		Average cost	Short-run marginal cost	Long-run marginal cost	Optimal second-best	Proportional markup	
	Price discrimination or value of service	Single price					Short run	Long run
Promotes efficient resource allocation	3	2	5	4[a]	8[a]	1[b]	7[a]	6[a]
Stimulates efficient investment choices	3	2	5	4[a]	7[a]	1[c]	8[a]	6[a]
Motivates managerial efficiency	8	7	3[a]	6[a]	1[a]	5	4[a]	2[a]
Motivates technological change	8[d]	7	1	6[a]	4[a]	5	3[a]	2[a]
Simplifies administrative or regulatory requirements	3	2	1	4	6	8	5	7
Minimizes price instability over time	5	4	3	8	1[c]	6	7	2
Provides a mechanism for re-distributing income	2	4	3	8	7	1[c]	6	5
Simplifies or aids promotion of a particular or new mode for non-economic purposes	1	2	8	4[a]	7[a]	3	6[a]	5[a]
Promotes broad aggregative or macroeconomic objectives	1	2	5	3[a]	8[a]	4	6	7[a]
Simplifies problems of adjusting to inflationary circumstances	1	2	5	3[a]	8[a]	4	6	7[a]

a. If economies of scale exist and marginal costs are likely to be above average costs because of overutilization of capacity in the short run.

b. If the optimal factor combination, technologies, product choices, and so on are known and observed by management.

c. If the detailed information needed to implement these policies over time is available.

d. If the existence or availability of monopoly profits does not encourage the search for cost economies or new technologies or products (that is, the Schumpeterian hypothesis does not hold).

TABLE 6-2. *Matrix of Rank Order Evaluations of Alternative Transport Pricing Strategies under United States Conditions*

Evaluation criteria	Profit maximizing		Average cost	Short-run marginal cost	Long-run marginal cost	Optimal second-best	Proportional markup	
	Price discrimination or value of service	Single price					Short run	Long run
Promotes efficient resource allocation	8	7	6	2	3	1[a]	4	5
Stimulates efficient investment choices	8	7	5	6[b]	2	1[c]	4	3
Motivates managerial efficiency	8	7	3[d]	6[d]	1[d]	5	4[d]	2[d]
Motivates technological change	1[e]	2	7[f]	3[g]	8[f]	5	4	6[f]
Simplifies administrative or regulatory requirements	3	2	1	4	6	8	5	7
Minimizes price instability over time	5	4	3	8	1[c]	6	7	2
Provides a mechanism for redistributing income	2	4	3	8	7	1[c]	6	5
Simplifies or aids promotion of a particular or new mode for non-economic purposes	1	2	8	4[d]	7[d]	3	6[d]	5[d]

a. If the optimal factor combination, technologies, product choices, and so on are known and observed by management.
b. This ranking would be considerably higher if the short-run marginal cost pricing were fully implemented to include its capital budgeting implications.
c. If the detailed information needed to implement second-best pricing policies over time is available.
d. If economies of scale exist and marginal costs are likely to be above average costs because of overutilization of capacity in the short run.
e. If it is assumed that the existence or availability of monopoly profits encourages the search for and financing of new technologies and products (that is, the Schumpeterian hypothesis holds). The assumption may be quite inaccurate in some cases.
f. If economies of scale are assumed.
g. An asymmetry is quite possible in this ranking. When too little capacity is available, short-run marginal cost pricing results in a sort of monopoly profit or rent that could finance invention and innovation (in the manner of Schumpeter); the contrary could well be true when too much capacity is available.

rank scores. As the information required to implement optimal second-best pricing is virtually impossible to accumulate at present, it is unrealistic to believe that any sort of reasonable approximation to optimal second-best pricing could be achieved. The low ranking given to optimal second-best pricing on the criterion of administrative simplicity reflects this difficulty, although the extent of the administrative inconvenience associated with this strategy may not be fully apparent.

To the extent that generalization is permissible, some kind of marginal cost pricing is likely to be among the more attractive alternatives in an advanced economy. This will be particularly true if one does not accept the Schumpeterian hypothesis. Indeed, such would almost seem to be official policy in Canada, the United States, the United Kingdom, and to a lesser extent Europe, today. In all of these economies, a tendency toward marginal cost pricing (occasionally short as well as long run) has character-ized public policy in recent years. Discriminatory value-of-service price structures for rail, which were established near the end of the last century and at the beginning of this one, are slowly being abandoned as policy and eroded by technological change.

By contrast, some sort of limited profit-maximizing strategy could be appealing, at least in the short run, in many less developed countries. Indeed, the very reasons such a strategy was adopted in Europe and North America in the nineteenth and early twentieth centuries, when those areas were also less developed, would in large measure explain the appeal they might have in Africa, Asia, and South America today. National goals ranging from promoting higher savings and investment rates to mitigating the effects of inflation to providing a mechanism for redistributing income and eco-nomic activity among different areas and groups are likely to receive a high priority in these areas. Not unlike North America and Europe late in the nineteenth century and early in this century, these countries may have few other tools of public policy available for achieving such goals. In addition, some heuristic evidence suggests that these countries possess less than fully competitive market structures, perhaps to such an extent that monopolistic pricing in the transport sector might not distort resource allocation unduly. Discriminatory pricing may also be relatively easy both to impose and to maintain in a less developed economy because the transport alternatives are limited.

Any short-term development or redistribution advantages derived from pursuing value-of-service or other discriminatory pricing schemes must be weighed, however, against the probability that such pricing will create other problems as an economy grows or develops (as in Europe and North America in recent decades). In fact, much will depend on the degree of administrative flexibility present in the transport sector of any given country. If reasonably well-developed institutions exist for making a transition from one pattern of transport pricing to another, the short-term gains from a more discriminatory pricing policy might be achieved with little future loss in transition costs. But the existence of such flexible and adaptive institutions seems to be more the exception than the rule. Any discriminatory pricing scheme will create vested interests, and those who benefit from such a scheme will oppose change and make this opposition known.

Indeed, virtually all less developed countries today tend to operate in a technologically more complex world, and specifically one with more transport choices, than characterized Europe and North America in the nineteenth century. In particular, the internal combustion engine is notably ubiquitous. Thus, the simplest solution to the transport pricing problem of many less developed countries may be the development of cost-oriented tariffs at a relatively early stage in their development. This is not to say that their transport tariffs need to be geared exactly to long-run or short-run marginal costs or any other specific cost concept. Indeed, a cogent argument can be made that it is well to retain at least some flexibility and demand orientation in transport charges in order to improve capacity utilization and adaptation to new situations. Furthermore, if there is private enterprise in transport, some markups over long-run marginal cost may be necessary in order to maintain financial viability and a reasonable rate of capital investment and development.

Summary

The attractiveness of any transport pricing solution will depend on the particular circumstances within which the transport system is operating: the objectives sought, the constraints to be honored, and the surrounding political and economic environment. And the worthiness of various theoretical solutions to transport pricing problems will depend on the extent to which the assumptions employed in deducing the theoretical solutions are approximated within the real world. Furthermore, pricing decisions are often executed within a developing, ever changing context. In such circumstances, simple static solutions or prescriptions are likely to be incomplete and potentially misleading. Throughout these chapters on pricing, therefore, the emphasis has been on relating different suggested or preferred transport pricing solutions to the broader developmental and welfare objectives of the society.

Clearly, the optimal policy for any single country is likely to vary with the specific circumstances. The choice must be made within the context of particular social, political, and economic institutions and in terms of the weights placed on the achievement of different objectives by policy makers. The transportation analyst can only point out certain interrelationships between different objectives and pricing strategies and indicate some of the less obvious hazards that may occur as one policy is adopted instead of another. The final choice must remain with the relevant political authorities. The analyst's greatest strength may be in pointing out that certain kinds of pricing strategies can conflict with efficient use of resources, particularly in a static sense. Perhaps even this advice should be tendered somewhat less than dogmatically since market imperfections exist in many economies, and their extent and influence is often not fully understood or documented.

A more satisfactory analytical approach to evaluating pricing policies may ultimately be achieved by using systems analytic techniques such as those described in Volume 2. Such an approach would provide more definite information on the macro or growth implications of alternative pricing strategies. This information should be useful since pricing strategies most conducive to static efficiency often are in conflict with growth or income redistribution objectives, thereby creating much of the uncertainty about the choice of one strategy over another.

PART TWO

Forecasting the Demand
for Transportation

CHAPTER SEVEN

Transport Demands: The Basic Framework

In a market economy, transportation demand presumably arises as a result of utility or profit maximization decisions by households and firms. Consumption of transportation services also tends to be highly complementary to the use of other commodities. The demand for transportation is therefore commonly labeled "a derived demand," in the sense that transport is not normally demanded for itself but as a derivative of buying or seeking some other service or commodity.

Early efforts to estimate transport demand relationships have been in large part what an economist would call neoclassical, Marshallian, and single equation in orientation: origins or flows of transportation demands are determined by relating output to price, income, and other variables. In practice, this approach has tended to conceal many of the important structural dimensions of trip makers' behavior. An alternative, multiple-equation format that attempts a more accurate representation of the underlying structure has therefore evolved slowly over time. This approach customarily begins with land-use or spatial-location characteristics and derives trip demands and trip destinations and then follows this with an assignment or allocation of these trips to a network. The procedure is portrayed schematically in the flow chart of Figure 7-1. Such multiequation systems are well suited to modeling the spatial location and macroeconomic determinants of travel. They are also especially useful for representing trip demands over complex networks with many substitute destinations, modes, and routings, as in urban areas.

99

FIGURE 7-1.   *Schematic Model for Forecasting Passenger and Freight Transportation Demand*

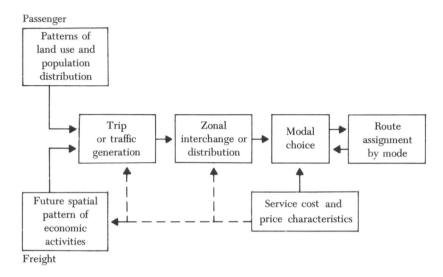

A basic determinant of transport demand is obviously location choice. However, location theory for households and firms is not well developed empirically. The location decision facing a firm is complex, involving evaluation of the cost of various inputs (in delivered prices) and the location of markets in which the firm sells. Classical location theory has concerned itself with the spatial location of input and product markets and cost minimization problems.[1] Generally, this abstraction provides little that is empirically useful in forecasting location choices.

The interrelationship between location choices and transport demands, especially the location or land-use feedbacks over time arising from transport system performance, might be modeled, for example, by using a large-scale behavioral simulation model—such as the model described in Volume 2. The simpler demand estimation procedures described in this volume are first approximations at best.

As will be seen in the review in succeeding chapters of specific attempts

---

1. For a discussion and bibliography of this literature, see Walter Isard [C8] and Edgar M. Hoover [C7]. The classic location problem formulated by Alfred Weber [C18] illustrates the nature of much of this literature. The problem is to locate a factory selling its product in one city, produced by two inputs bought in two other cities, so as to minimize transport costs. William Alonso [C1] has recently discussed this problem, indicating the difficulties of finding an analytic solution.

to model transport demands, many unsettled questions remain. In particular, too little empirical information exists about the influence on demand of price, scheduling, and service characteristics.[2]

In the remainder of this chapter, the general structure of transport forecasting procedures will be discussed. Succeeding chapters will consider particular forecasting methods as applied to urban and interurban passenger and freight demands, with substantial emphasis on the statistical methodology appropriate in view of the sample data normally available. Considerable attention is also given to developing those generalizations about transport choices that seem most justifiable in light of the limited evidence available.

Land-Use or Economic Location Patterns

All transport demand forecasts must begin with some knowledge of the geographic or spatial distribution of economic activities. This entails analyzing the present and the potential economy of the area affected by the proposed development, given the transportation system that serves it.

The basic spatial or location element in most passenger demand studies has been a land-use model of some sort. Essentially, land-use models are attempts to forecast the spatial distribution of people and their activities. The underlying behavioral assumption is that stable empirical relationships exist between patterns of land use and needs or demands for transportation services. In urban transportation studies, the primary emphasis has been on estimating residential and work-place locations and the relationship between them. In intercity studies, by contrast, the focus is shifted slightly to the estimation of what makes people interact with one another. Thus government and holiday centers are expected to interact with manufac-

2. The modeling of a transport system in Volume 2 of this study includes a demand model for shipment that shows a subjective weighting scheme which reflects these sorts of considerations. A measure of the transport service offered by a single transport link is represented as a linear combination of a set of performance factors, p_i and the corresponding valuation v_i, assigned to each factor by the shipper. Each element in the performance vector corresponds to the quantity of a particular attribute experienced as a result of traveling over the link under consideration—transport charge, travel time, probability of loss, waiting time. The weights in the valuation vector are those of the shipper. The product of the two vectors gives a measure of overall link rating. The transport services chosen by a shipper are then estimated by finding the route through the network from point of origin to point of destination which minimizes this overall rating, using standard minimum path algorithms.

turing cities or commercial centers in different ways than commercial centers are expected to interact with one another or with manufacturing cities.

To estimate the demand for freight transportation, the forecast of the future spatial pattern of economic activity is conventionally labeled an economic base study. These studies perform for freight transportation essentially the same function as land-use studies do in urban or intercity passenger forecasts: they provide a basis for predicting major needs for transport at specific geographic points. Ordinarily, an economic base study includes an appraisal of natural resources, the population and labor force, and the existing industry of the economy under consideration. It may also include some analysis of the social structure, attitudes, and incentives of the people involved. It attempts to identify those industries which are the primary users of transport facilities and to specify their present and potential future locations and level of output.

To be satisfactory for long-range transport demand forecasting, the economic base study should also incorporate regional growth characteristics—to explain migrations of labor and capital among regions, changes in the composition of output, and so on. Satisfactory regional models, however, are not readily available.[3] Circumstances will govern the choice of an appropriate model. It will differ, for example, for underdeveloped and developed economies, and for imperfect or highly regulated and relatively free or competitive market economies. For a context of perfect markets, Borts and Stein have conducted by far the most comprehensive analysis of regional growth. They suggest that differences in growth rates are best explained by modeling the market's response to regional differences in the rates of return on capital and labor, and the induced migrations in labor and capital that result.[4] There have been other empirical studies made of United States growth patterns, though the models implicit in the findings are not always obvious.[5] The task of modeling regional development is probably easier in simpler, less developed economies (though, again, little progress has been made to date). The crucial variables in these circumstances are probably the location of natural resources, entrepreneurship, and capital, and the accessibility of various areas.

Most location models or analyses focus on the decisions of producers,

3. For a survey of regional models in the literature, see John R. Meyer [C12], pp. 19–54.
4. George H. Borts and Jerome L. Stein [C3]; also George H. Borts [C2].
5. Daniel Creamer [C5]; Harvey S. Perloff and others [C15]; Victor R. Fuchs [C6].

apparently on the premise that capital is usually more mobile than labor. Considerable differences exist among industries in their responsiveness to the availability of particular inputs, the costs of their transport, and the location of product markets. An interview study by the University of Michigan revealed, for example, that, in addition to purely economic considerations, many qualitative and subjective dimensions affect industrial location choices—personal ties of the management with its markets and financial sources or personal tastes for a region as a result of being raised and started in business there.[6] In a project context, ad hoc heuristic procedures and sampling and survey techniques are probably sufficient to yield a reasonable estimate of basic industrial locations. However, in large-scale planning (for example, an intercity road network to be built during the next several decades) a systematic model of regional growth, incorporating the feedbacks of the transport system on that growth, can be imperative.[7]

Trip Generation

To be useful for transport planning, estimates of the future location of population and industry must be converted into physical estimates of the transportation requirements generated and terminated at different points in geographic space. The conventional nomenclature for this exercise is "trip generation." In the case of passenger trip generation, the usual unit of analysis will be the household. The forecasting exercise will seek to estimate how many trips the members of the household will make to work, school, place of recreation, retailing establishments, and so forth. Roughly similar models, with only slight modification, are used to estimate passenger trip demands for business firms or other basic behavioral units. When forecasting freight, this means estimating how many tons of freight must be transported into a plant or area in order to manufacture certain commodities, and how much transport away from the area is required to remove these final goods or commodities from their production sites to their markets.

No attempt is usually made when modeling trip generation to derive or estimate the directional flow of the actual travel demands (see Figure

6. Eva Mueller, Arnold Wilken, and Margaret Wood [C13].
7. The Northeast Corridor Project in the United States is one example. The second is the systems study in Volume 2. See Chapter 9, this volume.

7-1). Rather, the emphasis is on the estimated travel requirements for specific points of the system. In essence, trip generation provides a picture of the origins and destinations of different trip and travel demands but not of the flows or interchanges between different points within the system.

Zonal Interchange or Distribution

Given the number of trips originating in and destined to each area, zonal interchange models provide a description or forecast of travel between areas. The most familiar technique used for this purpose is the gravity, or inverse impedance, model.

The gravity model is based on the premise that the volume of transport between two areas, i and j, depends directly on the number of tons of freight or passenger trips originating in i, needed at or destined for j, and is inversely related to the distance, elapsed time, cost, or some other measure of separation between i and j. The customary statement of models of this sort assumes that flows between regions i and j can be statistically represented by one or more attraction parameters, such as population or income levels, and impedance parameters representing costs or other such effects.[8] Interzonal trips are normally stratified by commodity trips, trip purpose, land use, and other variables to obtain greater homogeneity and behavioral regularity.

Gravity models have a considerable history. In simplest form, they are used to represent pairs of zonal interchanges independently of each other.

8. For an excellent summary of gravity models, see Walter Isard [C9], Chap. 11. The gravity model is of the form:

$$x_{ij} = \frac{f(P_i P_j)}{d_{ij}}$$

where x_{ij} is travel between cities i and j, P is a measure of trip generation or activity level, for example, population, and d is distance or some representation of travel cost. The pioneers were John Q. Stewart [C16] and George K. Zipf [E32].

Usually functional forms that can be transformed to linear equations are chosen to make estimation easy, though there is only mixed evidence as to whether the distance variable or a suitable proxy can be represented linearly. Income has often been used as a measure of trip attraction. Thus this form

$$x_{ij} = k \frac{y_i^\alpha y_j^\beta}{d_{ij}^\gamma}$$

where y is income and k, α, β, and γ are parameters has become popular in practical applications, linear in logs. More sophisticated versions of the gravity model are described below in Chapters 8 and 10.

Urban transportation planners, however, have developed techniques for simultaneously determining interchanges: the model is calibrated (parameterized) so that travel from any one node is affected by service to, and the attractions of, all other nodes. Such simultaneous determination is especially important in urban demand forecasting since the network is more complex and the options to travelers more numerous. This allows more substitution between alternative destinations and routings. Basically, the objective in urban applications of interchange models has been to distribute a fixed set of trip requirements; internal consistency requires the inclusion of a variety of constraints in order that the demands and supplies of all nodes are met.

Another popular model for forecasting zonal interchanges is the intervening opportunity model. This model is based on the premise that total travel time from a point is minimized, subject to the condition that every destination point considered has a stated probability of being acceptable. The fundamental notion is that a trip is made to the closest acceptable location, regardless of time, distance, or cost. Acceptability is defined in a behavioral sense by varying the parameters of the model to achieve some sort of "best fit." The intervening opportunity model thus has considerable flexibility, much the same as the gravity model. Its use has generally been confined to urban transportation demand modeling, as will be described in Chapter 8.

A third approach to determining zonal interchanges is by linear programming. In this approach, thorough behavioral rationality is assumed, known, and sought. Specifically, the zonal interchanges are distributed so as to minimize costs, subject to the constraints on system capacity.[9] Lack

9. The mathematics of the linear programming can be stated quite simply. Flows between regions i and j are determined so that they minimize

$$\sum_{i=1}^{n} \sum_{j=1}^{m} C_{ij} F_{ij},$$

subject to the constraints:

$$\sum_{j=1}^{m} F_{ij} \leq S_i \qquad\qquad (i = 1, 2, \ldots, n)$$

$$\sum_{i=1}^{n} F_{ij} \geq D_j \qquad\qquad (j = 1, 2, \ldots, m)$$

$$\sum_{i=1}^{n} S_i = \sum_{j=1}^{m} D_j \qquad\qquad (F_{ij} \geq 0)$$

where S_i is the supply of that subcommodity produced at node i, D_j is the demand for the subcommodity at node j, and C_{ij} is the cost of transporting the subcommodity from i to j. Finally F_{ij} is the flow.

of data has often restricted the application of linear programming models. The model has important behavioral implications which may or may not be realistic. As one might suppose, it has proved to be most useful as an empirical description of behavior in fully competitive industries under conditions of spatial price equilibrium.[10]

Modal Choice

The choice of a particular mode and routing for meeting a transport demand between two points, as specified by the trip generation and zonal interchange forecast, requires an investigation of the basic economic and service characteristics of the available transportation modes and routes. Modal choice introduces major considerations on the supply side of the transport market; that is, an assessment of the capacity, cost, and performance of the existing or proposed transport system. Shippers and travelers can be presumed to select that particular mode or combination of modes which will minimize total cost or maximize utility. Nevertheless, these choices may be difficult to model.

In particular, a mode may have higher directly assignable costs for performing a transport service, but the savings on handling, packaging, inventory, and other distribution costs may more than compensate. Similar comments apply to choice of passenger modes: in any good analysis, time savings and comfort must be recognized as having value to the traveler choosing a particular mode.

The question of modal choice can be further complicated by the fact that services offered by each mode may in some instances be both complementary and competitive. This sort of complication is introduced by network topology. For example, a combination of modes may be needed in order to complete a trip between two given points. At the same time, modal interchange can introduce considerable costs. Consequently, the choice of mode by a shipper is not typically a simple choice of rail, truck, air, or water but is a complicated selection over a mix of possible modes, routes, and schedules. The choice is very much a function of the network and performance conditions that exist at any given time. Indeed, modal choice and routing are often considered problems to be solved simulta-

10. See Abraham Charnes [15], William W. Cooper and Alexander Henderson [19], James M. Henderson [122], and Frank L. Hitchcock [124], pp. 224–33.

neously by the shipper. This simultaneity may exist, moreover, even if the freight shipper does not really determine routing directly. Thus, in many circumstances, shippers may be picking a bundle of services that produces a certain transport result without knowing how this bundle of services is created in terms of modes. Though institutional and regulatory constraints often retard multimodal shipment, there are more and more such shipments, and more entry into the freight forwarding business, which uses all modes.

Route Assignment

Closely allied to the problem of determining modal choice is that of making route assignments by mode. Route assignment essentially maps zonal interchanges for a particular mode. Assignment provides specific estimates of demand placed on different links within a rail, highway, waterway, or air transport system and thereby details modal utilization.

Assignment is also closely related to network specification and coding.[11] Since route assignment involves specifying the particular patterns of flow on each transport system or mode, each modal network must be described in considerable detail, that is, in all of its relevant linkages. Once a description of interzonal travel and modal choices has been outlined, the assignment problem is that of allocating trips to the coded network.

Most assignment programs use some kind of minimum path algorithm. When a network is being modeled, there may be a large number of alternative paths that can be used for each interzonal trip, even within a specified mode. Minimum path algorithms select the shortest route (least time, distance, or cost) for each trip.

If link capacities were infinite, the assignment problem would be relatively simple and, in fact, largely irrelevant. However, as flows on a transportation network change, the cost-performance characteristics on the network also change. This is most evident on urban facilities during rush hours. But performance characteristics of freight and intercity passenger transport networks also react to changes in flow. Real world users adapt their behavior to local capacity shortages. If a shorter, faster route becomes congested (and thereby slower), users will shift to a less congested and formerly slower alternative. The result is a complex equilibrating process

11. Coding is the process of describing link characteristics in a quantitative scheme suitable for analysis and quantitative manipulation.

of travel demands, travel speeds, and link volumes. Analysts have found the description of this equilibrating behavior difficult but often essential.

The response of shippers to capacity–performance relationships on the system may be confined to shifts in routes within a single mode, but it may include changes among modes as well. This response, of course, suggests simultaneity between modal choice and route assignment decisions. In some cases, therefore, much can be said for performing the modal choice and route assignment simultaneously, for example, by using mathematical programming techniques. An adequate simultaneous formulation can, however, sometimes be difficult. Recognition must be made of the cost of transferring from one mode to another so as to avoid an unrealistically large number of intermodal transfers. Similarly, the underlying linearity (that is, constant cost) assumptions of conventional linear programming formats may also be questionable in a multimodal context since the cost–performance relationship of many facilities appears to be nonlinear. Proliferation of the network, and therefore of the number of possible linkages, can also greatly expand the computational burden of solving programming problems. These difficulties need not necessarily be insurmountable, however, so long as large electronic computers are available.

Summary

The demand forecasting procedure outlined in this chapter is essentially sequential. In particular, zonal interchanges are estimated before modal choices. After the modal choices have been identified, route assignments to specific modal networks or systems are made. Such organization adheres closely to conventional practice.

This procedure, however, clearly abstracts from much simultaneity or behavioral feedbacks observed in reality. For example, the performance of a transport system will affect modal choice and routing. It should also have some effect on how many trips are made and to what destination. Ultimately, too, transport system performance should affect location or land use, with firms' and households' choices responsive in some degree to the system performance.

Thus, while the flow chart portrayed in Figure 7-1 has some intuitive appeal, the rationale for this particular demand model, a recursive structure, is not compelling. Much of its popularity lies in the advantages it affords in conceptualizing and programming for the computer. As with any recursive model used as an approximation to a system with important simultaneous relationships, it will probably yield only rough approximations on initial application. Improvement can be expected in the quality of the forecasts if repeated loops, or iterations of the analysis, are used, both to improve the internal consistency and accuracy of the traffic forecasting and flows and to simulate better the reaction of the future economy to possible (hypothetical) changes in the transportation system.

To the extent that resources permit, a particular improvement in the quality of the demand forecast might be achieved if, after one iteration, the land-use or economic base studies were reassessed and the whole process repeated. Unfortunately, this feedback, though often discussed, is seldom incorporated into transportation demand analyses. Indeed, the greatest failure of individual project evaluation techniques is typically that these macroeconomic or location feedbacks or loops are rarely analyzed in depth. Even in many purported systems analyses, the transportation land-use feedback is not one of the system effects well treated.

One fascinating aspect of the development of transport demand models is the extent to which similar methods are increasingly being employed for estimating different types of transportation requirements. The underlying logical flow of the procedures used for estimating intercity freight and passenger transportation needs is becoming more and more akin to that employed (and usually pioneered) in urban passenger demand studies. The only major differences tend to be in the underlying economic analyses: passenger models are concerned, quite naturally, with land-use and population migration patterns while freight models are almost invariably founded on some kind of economic base study. These differences, of course, merely reflect the fact that passenger and freight systems serve different needs. A question still to be answered is whether this emerging consensus on technique provides a sufficient basis for adequate project evaluations.

CHAPTER EIGHT

Forecasting Urban Passenger Travel

THE CONVENTIONAL METHODOLOGY for estimating demand for urban transportation closely follows the scheme outlined in the previous chapter. The analysis typically begins with land-use projections and proceeds sequentially to develop travelers' choices as to number of trips, destination, and routing.[1]

Land-Use Models

Attempts at systematic land-use forecasting have involved a wide variety of procedures. One early suggestion is a simple deviant of the intervening opportunity model. In applying this model to land-use forecasting, new activity is located in increments about the center of an opportunity surface (the central business district, CBD), with the extent of dispersion in new locations controlled by changing a single parameter that affects how tightly packed the distribution will be. The opportunity surface is often defined in terms of airline distance to the CBD, in which case the land-use pattern will be a smooth function with respect to distance, and with declining density as distance to the CBD increases. Alternatively, the effect of transport accessibility or costs from any point on the surface

1. For an excellent survey of urban transportation planning, see Richard M. Zettel and Richard R. Carll [D59].

to the center can be represented by using minimum time or cost paths in defining the opportunity surface. Particular zoning or open space reservations also can be included as constraints on the allocations.[2]

In order to better represent the interaction of transportation with location decisions, Hansen, in a study of Washington, D.C., for the period 1948 to 1955, elaborated the basic intervening opportunity model by postulating that residential growth in an area was a function of its relative accessibility to employment centers and its supply of vacant land.[3] Similar accessibility and availability measures have been used in a number of subsequent land-use forecasting exercises.

In recent land-use models, efforts have been made to estimate and represent simultaneously the effects of many variables, with the use of multivariate regression techniques. Variables such as vacant industrial land, sewage availability, zoning protection, and accessibility to work areas and schools have been included.[4] The empiric model developed for the Boston area is perhaps the most elaborate example; it uses linear multiple regression equations to explain changes in nine land-use variables (four population and five employment categories) for each of 626 traffic zones.[5] The dependent variable is in difference form, the change from 1950 to 1963. Explanatory variables include transport accessibility, a dummy variable representing the availability of utilities, and measures of land availability for various purposes.[6]

These regression models, though often including a parameter reflecting the accessibility of the transport system, only crudely represent the feedbacks between transportation and land use. They largely rely on the stability of prevailing trends in metropolitan growth patterns and decentralization for their accuracy in forecasting. Actually, only two efforts to model the transportation to land-use feedback explicitly have been made to date:

2. George T. Lathrop and John R. Hamburg [D35], pp. 95–103.

3. Walter G. Hansen [D18], pp. 145–51.

4. Charles F. Barnes, Jr. [D1], pp. 1–12, and Alan M. Voorhees, Charles F. Barnes, Jr., and Frances E. Coleman [D56], pp. 1–9.

5. Donald M. Hill [D24], pp. 111–20; Neal A. Irwin and Daniel Brand [D28], pp. 520–40; Daniel Brand, Brian Barber, and Michael Jacobs [D4], pp. 53–67.

6. The authors use a gravity model variant to represent accessibility of a zone in their study of Boston. Accessibility of zone j to activity k, A_{jk}, is defined as

$$A_{jk} = \sum_{i=1}^{n} Z_{ik} e^{-\beta T_{ij}}$$

where Z_{ik} = activity measure k in zone i; T_{ij} = travel time from i to j; β = a parameter measuring the propensity of zones i and j to interact in activity k. Brand and others [D4].

the first as a part of a study of the Penn-Jersey (that is, Philadelphia) metropolitan area and the second in a Pittsburgh area study.

The basic behavioral premise of the Penn-Jersey land-use model involved the trade-off between transport costs and land value. Total population was stratified by time period and socioeconomic class, with each class postulated to have a certain preference in housing (in terms of the model, a price it would pay for housing of a given type in each particular zone). Each household type was given a location budget, defined as the portion of its income to be spent on transportation and housing combined. Transportation costs associated with each zone were based on that zone's accessibility, defined by likely trip destinations and their costs. Subtraction of these transport costs from the location budget yielded the amount available for housing. All households were postulated to choose a location so that this residual available for housing was maximized. This was framed as a linear programming problem.[7] The model was staged in five-year increments, with new locations calculated for a certain portion of the total population each five years. Input data included land available, industry location, population and income levels, and accessibility of each area to employment. Many of these data inputs were calculated endogenously in separate submodels (for example, employment locations, housing market costs, transportation or accessibility costs, tastes of different population groups for housing and their propensity to relocate).

The Pittsburgh model, while somewhat less ambitious, is a landmark study in terms of its suggestions of where the greatest payoffs are likely to be in future modeling efforts. The model was conceived in connection with a planning study for the Pittsburgh region. It was then developed extensively by its originator, Ira Lowry, as an individual effort at RAND, and subsequently extended under the auspices of the city of Pittsburgh into a simulation model aimed largely at urban renewal planning.[8]

As originally formulated, the Lowry model was a static, cross-sectional location model. A distinction was made between basic, or site-oriented, employment sectors, which were treated as exogenous, and market, or service-oriented, employments, which were located (endogenously) near

---

7. The basic linear programming formulation of the behavioral premise representing the transportation location trade-off was by John D. Herbert and Benjamin H. Stevens [D23]. A series of papers by Britton Harris extended this model: [D20], pp. 305–19, and [D21].

8. John F. Kain and John R. Meyer [D31]; Ira S. Lowry [D37]; William A. Steger [D50], pp. 144–50.

household residences.[9] The model consisted of a set of simultaneous equations that endogenously determined employment and land use in retail and service trades, the quantity of residential land developed, and the number of households in residence in each zone.

Two basic behavioral premises were employed. First, residential locations were related to employment locations by a gravity model, with employment locations inversely weighted by their travel distance to the zone in question. Second, retailing and service employment locations were dependent on the number of residences in all surrounding zones, again in a gravity format, with the number of residences weighted inversely by the distance to the zone in question. Thus, a limited simultaneity is involved since residential choices are related to employment locations, some of which are jobs in the retailing sectors, which in turn locate so as to be near household residences. Since the model itself consisted of nonlinear simultaneous equations, iterative procedures were used to obtain a solution. The model was fitted with the use of 1958 cross-section data, and a zone was defined as one square mile.

As a static, market equilibrium model, the Lowry formulation is not directly suited to land-use forecasting. While recognizing this limitation, the author attempted some forecasts based on his best estimate of the future location pattern of basic industry. The city of Pittsburgh has subsequently converted this into a simulation format, modeling changes over one- or two-year time periods in a recursive manner. In these simulations, a certain share of households are deemed mobile—they adjust their location patterns over the city. Basic industrial sectors are located, as are commercial sectors, as a function of a variety of attributes of each potential zone; for example, accessibility as influenced by the transport system. The transportation component of the Lowry model and its behavioral feedback to land use were not refined in these subsequent adaptations.

Trip Generation

The standard approach to estimating the number of trips originating in or destined for each area or zone is to assume that trip generation rates

9. The exogenously determined, or basic, industries were manufacturing, wholesaling, public utilities, research facilities, central administrative offices, government, hospitals, recreation, and agriculture and extractive. This amounts to just over half of all employment in the Pittsburgh area.

depend on the type and intensity of land use. Focus on this relationship is one of the major contributions of the Detroit study of 1953 and has served as the basis for forecasting transport demand in virtually every urban transportation study since.[10] Various kinds of residential, commercial, and industrial land usually generate a different number of trips per unit. The basic assumption in forecasting is that the level of trip generation in each zone can be estimated by applying appropriate parameters for each specific class of land use.

In particular applications, land area, employment, population density, and number of dwelling units have been used to estimate trip generation. The early studies tended to emphasize land use and area measures, while recent studies have stressed economic activity measures such as employment, retail sales, and school enrollment.[11] Measures such as acres of land use or floor area are basically proxies, of course, for levels of employment, production, households, and other kinds of trip-generating activity located within a particular zone.

Particular attention has been focused on the development of behavioral trip generation models for home-based trips. Person or vehicle trips per household, per capita, or per dwelling unit have been hypothesized to vary with car ownership, net residential density, distance from the central business district, family income, and size of families. Numerous simple and multiple regression models have related trips per household or per capita to one or more of these explanatory variables. However, high intercorrelation of many of the explanatory variables in most samples has hindered attempts at equation specification for econometric estimation, and hence the nature of the underlying structure tends to be unclear.

For example, traffic analysts have discovered that car ownership alone explains as much or more of the total variance of zonal trip generation data as all the other variables combined. Despite the impressive evidence that car ownership is a good predictor of trips, it seems plausible that residential density and income might affect trip making above and beyond their effects on car ownership. An elaborate analysis conducted by William Mertz and Lamelle Hamner of trip generation rates per dwelling unit for 95 Washington, D.C., census tracts illustrates the point. They found that

10. Michigan State Highway Department [D41].
11. For a survey of practices to date, see Paul W. Shuldiner [D45], pp. 73–88; B. C. S. Harper and H. M. Edwards [D19], pp. 44–61; Alan Black [D2], pp. 1–7; Paul H. Wright [D58], pp. 152–68; Donald E. Cleveland and Edward A. Mueller [D9], Fig. 47.

the simple correlations between trips per dwelling unit and each of the explanatory variables of car ownership, residential density, income, and distance from the CBD were all high and had the expected signs. However, the explanatory variables were all highly intercorrelated so that good fits of trip generation were obtained when subsets of the variables were employed in the regression equation for trip generation.[12]

Thus, specifying the appropriate model and obtaining reliable parameter estimates from the available sample data remain a challenging task. Moreover, only limited attention has been directed to the problems raised in extrapolating these relationships into the future, or in developing generalizations across cities. Trip generation rates tend to be inversely related to city size, being especially low in the oldest of the large standard metropolitan statistical areas.[13] To the extent that regularities can be ascertained in trip generation behavior across cities, extensive sampling of travelers in every city being studied for transport requirements may not be necessary. Substantial time and money could thus be saved when developing urban transport plans.

Peak-Hour Characteristics of Trip Generation

Proper representation of the peaking characteristics of urban travel demand is crucial. Peak-hour traffic exceeds off-peak travel by a considerable margin—to such an extent that peak-hour congestion has become synonymous with "the urban transportation problem." Peaking arises

---

12. William L. Mertz and Lamelle B. Hamner [D40], pp. 170–74; Gordon B. Sharpe, Walter G. Hansen, and Lamelle B. Hamner [D44], pp. 88–99.

The following two equations taken from the Mertz and Hamner study illustrate the effect of excluding or including residential density in an equation with car ownership:

$$T = 2.88 + 4.60A \qquad R = 0.827$$
$$T = 3.80 + 3.79A - 0.0033D \qquad R = 0.835$$

where

T = mean number of resident vehicular trips per dwelling unit
A = mean car ownership per dwelling unit
D = population per net residential acre
R = correlation coefficient

The size of the regression coefficient for automobile ownership is sensitive to the equation specification, a typical result when there is little independent variation in the exogenous variables in the sample data.

13. Herbert S. Levinson and F. Houston Wynn [D36], pp. 1–31.

largely from the work trip, which is highly concentrated twice a day (except in Latin countries where because of the siesta it can occur four times daily). The afternoon peak tends to be spread over a longer time span and is usually the time of day when the capacity of the transportation system is most overtaxed. This is because of shopping and other trips in the afternoon peak not present to the same extent in the morning. Transit service, through its predominant orientation to commuting trips, experiences far sharper peaks in the day than automobiles and usually experiences a dramatic reduction in demand on weekends.

Peaking is basically a demand phenomenon and an important dimension of trip generation. It is therefore somewhat surprising that most urban transportation studies handle the peaking problem by an adjustment on the supply side. Typically, street and highway volumes are determined, analyzed, and forecast on a 24-hour basis. Peaking is then accounted for by assuming that peak-period volumes are a constant proportion of all 24-hour volumes at every location and for every kind of facility.[14]

This practice is usually justified by the contention that the sampling errors for 24-hour interzonal volumes are much smaller than those for peak-hour volumes or those for any particular trip purpose (because of larger sample sizes). There is little systematic evidence to support this widely used argument, and indeed the converse may be the case. Origin and destination studies are subject to significant underreporting of trips, but little of this underreporting appears to be attributable to work trips. The latter may therefore comprise the better sample and provide more useful trip forecasts.[15] Furthermore, substantial savings in data processing could be

14. Thus if F_{ij}^{24} is the number of trips between i and j in a 24-hour period, peak-hour trips, F_{ij}^{p}, are represented by a constant proportion, λ:

$$F_{ij}^{p} = \lambda F_{ij}^{24}.$$

λ often varies with the facility type. For example, in the Southeastern Wisconsin study, peak-hour flows on the expressway and arterial highway were assumed to be 10 percent of total average weekday flows, 8 percent on freeways. Southeastern Wisconsin Regional Planning Commission [D49], p. 75.

15. For example, the following equation may describe current and future peak-hour travel demands more accurately than the equation in the previous footnote:

$$T_{ij}^{p} = \phi T_{ij}^{w}$$

where

T_{ij}^{p} = the number of peak-hour trips between i and j
T_{ij}^{w} = the number of work trips between i and j
ϕ = a constant relating peak-hour trips to work trips between i and j

achieved if intensive data analysis were limited to work trips, since only about one-fourth as much data would be involved. In general, it is probably easier to forecast the size of the labor force and its spatial distribution, and hence work-trip generation, than the heterogeneous group of activities that generate all trips over a 24-hour period.

There are, however, even more fundamental reasons than these for being dissatisfied with a proportionality hypothesis for estimating peak-period demands. Peaking relationships include behavioral parameters that depend on the extent of existing congestion. The duration of the peak period varies greatly among and within communities. By definition, the peaking phenomenon is inadequate capacity at those hours or minutes when many travelers would like to depart. As a result, a "queuing" problem exists in most urban transport systems. Many trip makers are forced to or voluntarily shift their trips forward or backward in time to alleviate the queues, forgo trips altogether, or make trips to alternative locations.[16]

A forecast based on a simple proportionality assumption therefore does not permit evaluation of the performance of existing or new capacity in meeting peak-hour trip demands. If congestion is severe, additional capacity may not appear to alter peak-period performance of the system significantly in terms of vehicle speed or trip-time measures; only the time duration of the peak may be reduced. Additional capacity, in essence, permits some travelers to schedule their trips more conveniently, at preferred departure or arrival times. These effects are hard to measure and even more difficult to evaluate. The recognition that increments to capacity may not reduce congestion as much as they affect the consumption of other commodities (such as service at the desired departure hour and alternative location choices) requires that these more subtle dimensions of demand be investigated.[17]

Interzonal Flow Models

Attempts to model zonal interchanges for urban areas almost always start with a mapping of the actual flows over the existing transport network, as based on the existing patterns of origins and destinations. This requires

---

16. This queuing dimension of peak-hour demands is discussed by Gerald Kraft and Martin Wohl [D32], pp. 205–30.

17. To better understand these time-of-day effects, see Tillo E. Kuhn [D33], pp. 297–325.

some kind of traffic survey. In most studies, these travel data are obtained from household interviews and are augmented by traffic counts at so-called cordon lines. In the earliest studies, future interzonal travel was projected by applying a constant growth rate to these observed interzonal travel volumes. When the results of this crude procedure proved unsatisfactory, more sophisticated procedures were developed. The most widely used of these improved methods fall into three categories: (1) the Fratar method; (2) the gravity model; and (3) the intervening opportunities model.

The Fratar expansion method represents a logical extension of the simple growth factor method.[18] It corrects the most obvious inadequacies of the growth factor model by recognizing that the growth of different parts of the region or metropolitan area often will differ significantly and that as a result the increase in interzonal travel in various parts of the region will also differ. In essence, the Fratar expansion method assigns a different growth factor to each zone. Future interzonal travel forecasts are derived from the present level of interzonal trips and the different zonal growth factors. The zonal growth factor, G_i, is simply the ratio of future to present trip generation ($G_i = T_i^*/T_i$, where the asterisk denotes trip generation in the future). Total expected future zonal interchange from i to j, T_{ij}^*, is given by:

$$T_{ij}^* = T_{ij} \cdot G_j \left[\frac{\sum_{j=1}^{n} T_{ij} \cdot G_i}{\sum_{j=1}^{n} T_{ij} \cdot G_j} \right].$$

This expansion thus forecasts zonal interchange by a weighted sum of zonal growth factors, the weights given by present interchanges. Application of this formula to any two zones will give two different results, depending on which zone's growth factor is employed (that is, whether G_i or G_j is used as the term just preceding the brackets in the above expression). In practice, an average of the two is generally taken.

When forecasts of zonal interchanges done in this way are aggregated over all zones, the resulting estimate of trip generation by zones generally will not agree with the trip generation estimates obtained from the trip models. In order that the trip-end estimates be consistent, an iterative process is required, in which trip ends resulting from the first iteration are used to update the growth factors, and so on. Trip-end estimates obtained in this manner have converged fairly quickly in applications.

18. Thomas J. Fratar [D14], pp. 376–84.

The gravity model, the second commonly used method of projecting interzonal travel, determines a set of flows from every point to every other point in such a way that the trips supplied to each point equal the total number of trip attractions at that point. Trips originating at each point are thus influenced by the choice of all possible destinations. The simplest formulation relates trips originating at zone i to an attraction factor at all other zones and inversely to an impedance factor, transport costs or time raised to a power. Defining T_i as the total trips originating in zone i, T_{ij} as trips from zone i to j, A_j as the number of trips attracted to any zone j, and D_{ij} as the distance from i to j,[19] a typical gravity model can be described as

$$T_{ij} = kT_i \frac{A_j/D_{ij}^b}{\sum_{j=1}^{n} A_j/D_{ij}^b}.$$

The exponent b is the only parameter affecting the distribution.[20] It will be a function of both trip type and the definition of zonal size. When the value of the exponents is large, flows tend to be satisfied as close to the demand point as possible; a small value gives greater weight to the distant points. In the extreme, a zero exponent would allow demands to be satisfied at each point in direct proportion to the percentage of the total supply available from that point. The exponent of friction varies with trip purpose[21] and with urban areas. As a broad generalization, when the impedance factor is expressed in travel time, the exponent tends to be about 1.0 for work trips, 2.0 for shopping trips, and 3.0 for social trips. For shopping trips, low values of the exponent tend to be applicable for very specialized and high value items, while large exponents are appropriate for low value

19. This was developed in the context of urban modeling by Alan M. Voorhees [D54], p. 37. See also Voorhees [D55], pp. 46–56.

20. In situations where there is only one demand point or one supply point, the exponent can assume any positive value less than infinity with no effect on the resultant distribution. As the number of supply or demand points increases, the exponent begins to have an effect on the distribution. Since the attraction (D_j/T_{ij}) is standardized by the sum of the attractions as a denominator, the constant k will be unity when b is zero. When b assumes a nonzero value, this equation does not generate flows in such a way that the sum of terminating flows at every point is equal to the demand at that point. Hence, to maintain the equality of the sum of inflows to the demand at every demand point, k must assume a value different from unity.

21. For a discussion of these differences, see J. Douglas Carroll, Jr., and Howard W. Bevis [D5], pp. 183–97.

items.[22] Limited experimentation has been conducted with nonlinear forms of the gravity model, usually to account for the fact that very short distance trips seem to show no correlation with distance.[23]

In more complicated forms of the gravity model, a common procedure is to use several empirically determined travel time friction parameters in place of the standard inverse exponential function, which has a single exponent for travel time. The following general format illustrates these extensions:[24]

$$T_{ij} = \frac{T_i A_j F_{ij} K_{ij}}{\displaystyle\sum_{j=1}^{n} A_j F_{ij} K_{ij}}$$

where

T_{ij} = trips produced in zone i and attracted to zone j

T_i = trips produced in zone i

A_j = trips attracted to zone j

F_{ij} = empirically derived travel time factors that are a function of the spatial separation between the zones; these express the average areawide effect of spatial separation on trip interchange

K_{ij} = specific zone to zone adjustment factor to allow for the incorporation of the effect on travel patterns of social or economic linkages not otherwise accounted for in the gravity model formulation

This more sophisticated formulation of the gravity model has enough free parameters to fit the data to almost any degree of accuracy desired. Typically, the friction parameters, F_{ij}, are estimated empirically with the special adjustment factors, K_{ij}, used to account for unusual flows. This representation of the impedance factor is determined in an iterative way. Sometimes it is fitted empirically; sometimes an initial set of values based on other urban area studies is assumed. Interzonal flows predicted from this set of friction parameters are then plotted to determine a trip length frequency distribution. In subsequent iterations, the travel time factors for

22. For such differences in shopping trip distribution, see David L. Huff [D26], pp. 81–90. Another good example of a gravity model estimated for shopping trips was that for the Baltimore region. T. R. Lakshmanan and Walter G. Hansen [D34], pp. 134–43.

23. For a bibliographic sketch of these attempts, see Gunnar Olsson [C14], pp. 16–17.

24. Walter G. Hansen [D16], pp. 67–76; Richard J. Bouchard and Clyde E. Pyers [D3], pp. 1–43; U.S. Bureau of Public Roads [D51]; and U.S. Bureau of Public Roads [D52].

trips of each length are adjusted to improve the fit of the predicted distributions to the actual. A few iterations are usually sufficient to obtain a close fit. Gravity model calibration of this sort is now a fairly routine procedure in urban transportation studies.

Intervening opportunities, the third model in wide use to forecast zonal interchanges, involves a stated probability of every destination being accepted. Total travel time is minimized for every origin, subject to the constraint that every potential destination is considered. A trip originating in zone i thus has less probability of being served by zone j as the number of intervening opportunities increases. Specifically, if

$P(V_j)$ = total probability that a trip will terminate before the jth possible destination is considered,

V_j = "subtended volume," or the possible destinations already considered, that is, reached before reaching zone j, and

L = constant probability of a possible destination being accepted if it is considered,

the expected interchange from zone i to zone j (T_{ij}) is the number of trip origins at zone i (O_i) multiplied by the probability of a trip terminating in j:[25]

$$T_{ij} = O_i \left[P(V_{j+1}) - P(V_j) \right]$$

or

$$T_{ij} = O_i \left[e^{-LV_j} + 1 - e^{-LV_j} \right].$$

The parameter L shapes the distribution of interchanges, with a larger value of L leading to a more concentrated set of trips, given any surface of opportunities. Basically, the model allocates trips on an incremental basis over an opportunity surface that has been delineated or rank ordered by travel time to the origin zone, i.

This model is not dissimilar to the gravity model. A relationship to

25. The mathematical formulation as the basis of this derivation is as follows:

$$dP = L[1 - P(V)]dV$$

where dP = probability that a trip will terminate when considering dV possible destinations. The other notations are as above.

The solution of the differential equation (L) is:

$$P(V) = 1 - e^{-LV}.$$

See Earl R. Ruiter [D43], pp. 1–21.

distance (in travel time or cost) arises since the number of intervening opportunities is a cumulative function as distance increases. The results are identical when the number of intervening opportunities are a linear function of distance.[26]

Practical applications of the intervening opportunity model are becoming increasingly complex and sophisticated. Data for subtended volumes are not usually available and hence use of the model has turned to trip distance as the basis for estimation of L. Trip-end density data are the usual basis for calibration, the objective being to replicate as well as possible the existing distribution of trip lengths. Iterative procedures have been employed in which an initial value for L is calculated, and so on, until a good fit is achieved. The significance of differences in the definition of the size of a zone has also been noted.[27] Since a different value of L can apply to each origin zone i, zones in various directions with separately calculated values of L have been classified. Density of trip originations and average trip lengths are the usual basis for classification.

All three of these zonal interchange models are based on empirical generalizations about travel behavior, and their behavioral implications are not always obvious or well articulated. Still, as empirical generalizations, how well they fit and how accurately they predict can be tested, and some tests have been made. There remains considerable disagreement, however, about the interpretation of the empirical results. The disagreement is to some extent irrelevant since all do quite well empirically. Large planning budgets and the availability of computers have permitted elaborate specification and the use of many free parameters in all of the basic models. As a result, there is little difference among them in terms of how well they fit or forecast. The empirical differences that do exist result either from their application to particular situations or from the choice of evaluation procedures.

Nevertheless, some generalizations can be made about the relative merits of the three models. The Fratar growth method does least well where structural changes tend to be large. It typically underestimates future trips from the suburban fringe, where structural changes are likely to be rapid, but seems to perform slightly better than the other models in predicting trips to and from the core city, where stability is such that the growth factors are more reliable.

26. For a discussion of the comparisons, see Walter Isard [C9], pp. 540–44, or Olsson [C14], pp. 13–45.
27. W. Stearns Caswell [D6], pp. 22–35.

There is little basis on which to choose between the gravity and inter-vening opportunity models in terms of closeness of fit. For example, in one systematic comparison, both models fitted current data equally well and did as well as the Fratar model. Moreover, both models proved superior to the Fratar model in predicting travel in rapidly growing areas. When only friction parameters were used in the gravity model, it did less well than the intervening opportunity model, but when the zonal adjustment factors were added the opposite result was obtained.[28]

The emphasis in these three models on forecasting accuracy rather than the development of behavioral concepts introduces some risk of substantial error when predicting traffic into a distant future. In a few urban areas (for the United States only), comprehensive land-use transportation plans have been conducted for two or more points in time, thus permitting comparisons of trip patterns over time. In these comparisons, a notable decline has occurred in transport demanded from and to CBDs, arising mainly from decentralization of workplaces and their exit from CBDs.[29] This reduction in trip demands to the CBD has been accompanied by changing interchange patterns, most significantly an increase in crosshaul trips from one portion of less central urban areas to another, but perhaps passing through or near the CBD.[30] This crosshaul pattern contrasts sharply with the predominantly radial pattern of trips in the large cities a decade or so ago and still observed in smaller cities today. Changes in the surface of zonal interchanges if and as decentralization continues may be such that their representation by adjusting parameters in a gravity or any other largely empirical model may prove difficult.

Modal Choice

Urban modal choice models represent attempts to develop relationships that determine what share of total traffic will use each mode, with most attention usually devoted to the split between transit and private auto-mobile. While all urban transportation studies include modal split models, there are important differences in their level of sophistication, and in the

28. Kevin E. Heanue and Clyde E. Pyers [D22], pp. 20–50.

29. John R. Meyer, John F. Kain, and Martin Wohl [A5], pp. 84–88; Jacob Silver [D46], pp. 153–76; John R. Walker and Gary R. Cowan [D57]; David A. Gorman and Stedman Hitchcock [D15], pp. 213–20.

30. Edward H. Holmes [D25], pp. 3–86; Walter G. Hansen [D17], pp. 73–76.

variables included. Modal split models developed in recent years can be classified as either trip-end or trip-interchange models.

Trip-end models were originally developed for, and still have their most widespread use in, highway-oriented origin and destination studies. In the United States, the principal objective of most urban transport studies has been, and normally still is, the design of freeway systems for the metropolitan area. Thus, the emphasis has been on forecasting future automobile travel, with transit travel regarded as a residual to be subtracted from total trip generation before the resulting trips are assigned to the highway network. These highway planning studies have been little concerned with the relative performance of alternative modes. Rather, they tend to focus on long-term increases in income and car ownership and accompanying suburbanization of the population, which, as will be seen below, are powerful forces resolving the modal choice question toward the automobile.

By contrast, trip-interchange models initially were developed for, and still have their most widespread use in, transit feasibility studies.[31] The important difference between trip-interchange and trip-end models is that the trip-interchange models usually emphasize comparative travel time, costs, and service by competing modes. The interest in travel time, costs, and service differentials for transit feasibility studies is hardly surprising since proponents of these systems contend that better transit performance will attract automobile commuters to transit. Implicit is an emphasis on forecasting a marked "one-shot" improvement in the relative performance of transit and its impact on the level of transit use. The differences in philosophy behind the two approaches are reflected in the choice of variables used, as shown in Table 8-1, where the variables used in nine urban transportation studies—four trip-interchange models and five trip-end models—are listed.

In the earliest and simplest trip-end modal split models, some proportion of trips originating in each zone was subtracted from total trip generation before assigning the trips to the highway network. This transit-use proportion was often specified as a function of car ownership, net residential density, income, or a combination of these variables. A typical modal split

---

31. The distinction between highway type, origin, and destination studies and transit feasibility studies has begun to blur in recent years as the comprehensive origin and destination studies have been extended to large metropolitan areas where transit modes are very important, and as transit planning becomes more adequately represented in the transport planning process.

TABLE 8-1. *Variables Used in Modal Split Transportation Models, Nine Urban Area Studies, 1955–61*[a]

	Trip-end models					Trip-interchange models			
Variables	Chicago	Pittsburgh	Erie	Puget Sound	Southeastern Wisconsin	Washington, D.C.	Twin Cities	San Juan	Buffalo
Trip characteristics									
Number of trip purposes used	2	5	1	4	7	2	3	2	2
Length of trip	—	—	—	—	—	—	—	—	x
Time of day	—	—	—	—	—	x	—	—	x
Orientation to central business district	x	x	—	—	—	—	—	—	—
Trip-maker characteristics									
Automobile ownership	x	x	—	x	x	—	—	x	x
Residential density	—	x	—	x	—	—	x	—	—
Income	—	—	—	x	—	x	x	—	x
Workers per household	—	—	—	—	—	—	—	—	—
Distance to central business district	—	x	—	—	—	—	—	—	—
Employment density	—	—	—	—	—	—	x	—	—
Transportation system characteristics									
Travel time	—	—	—	—	—	x	x	x	x
Travel cost	—	—	—	—	—	x	—	x	—
Parking cost	—	—	—	—	—	x	x	—	x
Excess travel time[b]	—	—	x	—	—	x	—	—	—
Accessibility[c]	—	—	—	x	x	—	—	—	—

Source: Martin J. Fertal and others [D12], p. 3, Table 1.

a. An x indicates that a particular variable, as described in the Variables column, was used to explain modal split in the particular model described in that column. A dash indicates omission of the variable in that model

b. Time spent outside the vehicle during a trip: walk, wait, and transfer times for transit trips, and parking delay time for automobile trips.

c. A measure of the level of travel service provided by the transit or highway system to trip ends in the study area.

model of this kind may be expressed by the following pair of equations:

$$T_i^B = \alpha_0 + \alpha_1 A_i + \alpha_2 D_i$$

$$T_{ij}^B = T_i^B(T_{ij})$$

where

$T_i^B =$ the proportion of trips originating in i by mode B
$A\ \ =$ automobile ownership
$D\ \ =$ net residential density

Obviously, such formulations are adequate for small places and for urban areas without major transit systems, but for large, dense metropolitan areas having extensive transit systems, more elaborate models are needed.

The most common extensions of these trip-end models have been trip stratification by purpose and estimation of separate relationships for trips made to and from the central business district and those made to and from the remaining zones. Examples of trip purposes accorded special attention in modal split models are school trips and work trips. Transit is generally competitive with other travel modes for regular trips to and from work, and most school children are captives of transit because they are unable to drive. Estimating separate relationships for transit travel to and from the CBD and for transit travel to and from all other parts of the region represents recognition of the large qualitative differences in the levels of transit service to the CBD and to other parts of the region. Furthermore, high-density central business districts are frequently served by rapid transit and commuter railroads, which provide a higher speed and qualitatively different form of transit than is available in most other parts of a city.

The most thorough effort to date to model modal choices was in a zonal interchange model developed for Washington, D.C. In this study, conducted for the National Capital Transit Authority, zonal interchange data for 1955 were stratified by trip purpose (work and nonwork), and by the ratio of highway trip costs to transit trip costs, the ratio of transit service to automobile service, and the median income in residence zones. This stratification defined 160 subclasses. Diversion curves relating the percentage of transit usage to the ratio of highway travel time to transit travel time were then obtained for each subclass.[32] This produced a reasonably close

---

32. Thomas B. Deen, William L. Mertz, and Neal A. Irwin [D10], pp. 97–123; and Arthur B. Sosslau, Kevin E. Heanue, and Arthur J. Balek [D48], pp. 44–68.

fit of actual modal choice for the sample data, especially for work trips to the CBD. Transit trips not oriented to the CBD were not as accurately forecast. Travel time ratios for nonwork trips were taken from off-peak periods and had to be applied to both peak and off-peak periods, which probably contributed to the less satisfactory results in modeling nonwork trips.

A major result of this study is its suggestion of a much greater sensitivity of modal split to the performance of the highway system—parking delays and costs and walking time—than to the performance of the transit system. The model implies that a fifteen-cent across-the-board fare increase (about a 50 percent increase) would result in only a 5 percent decline in total transit trips. This relatively small fare elasticity is consistent with other empirical studies. However, transit operating time was also judged to be of about the same significance, for example, a 50 percent rise in waiting and transfer times would reduce transit use by about 15 percent.[33]

The conventional procedures for determining modal split just described are somewhat at odds with the conventional economic theory of demand. Modal split is calculated independent of the level and destination of trips, which in turn are determined independent of such supply characteristics as the price of trips. This presumes that alternative modes are largely competitive and that their availability or performance does not greatly alter overall trip demand. That is, travelers first decide whether to make a particular trip and then choose a mode on the basis of service and cost characteristics of the available choices.

In a substantial departure from this conventional planning format, Domencich, Kraft, and Valette developed a model that treats trip generation, interchange, and modal choice simultaneously.[34] Rather than let price or other service characteristics affect only the modal choice of a predetermined level of directed trips (that is, with origins and destinations determined), they allow such influences to act on the level of trip making as well. After stratifying demand by trip purpose, their model fits an equation to zonal interchanges by each mode, and uses as explanatory variables both transport system supply characteristics, such as travel cost or time, and basic economic variables, such as the type of land use, income levels, and family size. The model therefore closely resembles conventional econometric demand models.

33. Sosslau, Heanue, and Balek [D48], pp. 5–19.
34. Thomas A. Domencich, Gerald Kraft, and Jean-Paul Valette [D11], pp. 64–78.

This model by Domencich and associates has a sounder conceptual basis as a behavioral representation than most modal choice models. It gains this, however, at the expense of some estimation difficulties. High intercorrelation of the many independent variables included in the model makes parameter estimation difficult and necessitates the introduction of additional information into the estimation in the form of constraints on the regression parameter estimates. As a result, the fit of the data is not as close as is typical of conventional interchange or gravity models.

The Domencich-Kraft-Valette model was applied to a cross-section sample of Boston trips, classified by two modes (car and transit) and four purposes (work, social and recreational, personal business, and shopping). The results generally agree with much of the other evidence (often of a more heuristic nature) that is available regarding modal choice. For example, transit demand was generally far more sensitive to travel times than fares, with elasticities for the former on the order of -0.50, and for the latter of -0.10 and -0.30 for work and shopping trips, respectively. This agrees with the common observation that service rather than price is the major factor in determining transit system ridership.[35]

All of these modeling procedures for modal choice abstract from certain interdependencies or, at best, attempt to approximate them by iterative procedures. For example, the characteristics of alternative transport systems can be only very broadly defined before the actual flows over them are known. Relative travel times and costs of highway and transit modes are functions of existing capacity and congestion levels which can be determined only after trips have been assigned to the network. Similarly, schedule and other service characteristics of transit systems tend to depend on the density and total demand for transit services. Recalculating modal split after traffic assignments have been made and system performance determined is the obvious solution, and one which is becoming more commonplace.

Other behavioral feedbacks may occur when considering a longer time horizon. As noted, automobile ownership plays a predominant role in predicting modal split; urban transport demand models typically use simple extrapolations of trends in car ownership per capita in their forecasting. When forecasting far into the future, the obvious question to raise is: Can car ownership be properly regarded as an exogenous or fixed variable, or

35. A more systematic statement of the model and the empirical results is in Charles River Associates [D8], Chaps. 2–5.

will changes in residential form, travel demand, or the available transport system and its performance affect car ownership? In particular, transit service characteristics may affect people's decisions to own a car, particularly a second one. Conceivably, if many people chose to forgo a car and used transit instead, transit service would improve; the greater density of ridership would reduce transit headways, for example. This suggests that three sorts of variables—transport demand for the two modes, service characteristics, and car ownership—are all interrelated and should be treated endogenously in a model of modal choice. In defense of the customary procedures, it must be noted, however, that transit system availability has not proved to be significant in studies to date in explaining car ownership.

If the behavioral feedback of the transport system on location choices is included within the model, the procedures become more complicated. Residential density will change as demands on the transport system and its performance evolve, and hence the relationships between income, location choice, and car ownership, all as endogenous variables, will have to be represented.[36]

Despite the variety of models and applications, the results obtained from modal split studies are similar in important aspects. For example, in Figure 8 1 aggregate modal diversion curves (forecasting transit's share of total trips as a function of the ratio of travel time by transit to that by automobile) obtained by zonal interchange modal split models in a number of cities are presented. Their similarity is noteworthy. All of these curves indicate that public transit usage drops quickly when, and if, any disadvantage appears in time required for transit trips. The major difference in the results appears to be the level of the captive transit market in each city represented by the existence or nonexistence of a right-hand tail on the diversion curves. This minimal level of transit use will vary depending on demographic, social, income, and density characteristics of the city.

Combining these empirical findings of observed modal choices with an examination of the basic structure of cost and service characteristics associated with the different modes in different circumstances can provide a reasonably accurate forecast of the modal split which can be expected to prevail in the long run.

Directly assignable operating costs, which do not include capital costs,

36. Kain has fitted a simultaneous equation model of this type for the Detroit area, in which causation runs from residential density to auto ownership, and then to modal choice. John F. Kain [D29], pp. 55–64.

FIGURE 8-1. *Percentage of Total Personal Trips Diverted to Rapid Transit or Highway Facilities, by Travel Time, Eight Urban Area Studies, 1953–59*

Percent

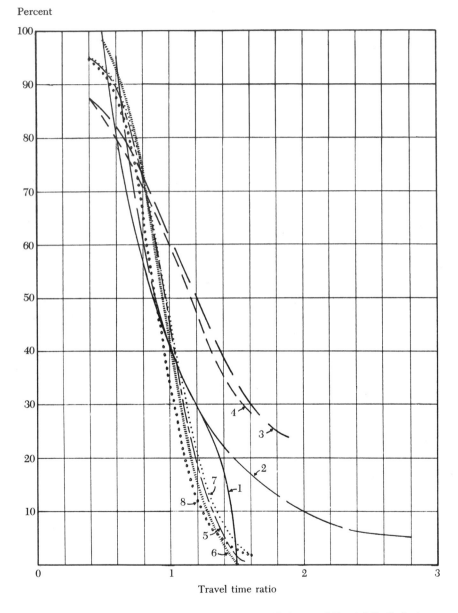

Travel time ratio

Source: Henry D. Quinby, "Traffic Distribution Forecasts—Highway and Transit," *Traffic Engineering*, Vol. 31 (February 1961), p. 24.

Explanation of Curve Numbers

Curve number	Line symbol	Curve developed by	Year	To be used with[a]
		Rapid transit curves		
1	————————	Washington, D.C., Mass Transportation Survey	1953	Nonoriented trips of all types potentially divertible to R.T.
2	——— —	Chicago Transportation Usage Study	1957	Nonoriented work trips to and from CBD and outlying areas
3	——— ————	Chicago Transportation Usage Study	1957	Nonoriented work trips to and from CBD only
4	— — — —	San Francisco Transportation Technical Committee	1959	All trips of interest to local San Francisco R. T. to CBD (all orientations, all times of day, all purposes)
5	—— - —— - ——	Southern New Jersey Rapid Transit Study	1959	All trips of interest to Southern New Jersey R.T.
		Highway curves		
6	ꜛꜛꜛꜛꜛꜛꜛꜛꜛ	U.S. Bureau of Public Roads	1956	All vehicular trips of interest to Interstate Freeway System
7	....	American Association of State Highway Officials	1957	All vehicular trips of interest to urban freeways
8	●●●●●●●●●●●	American Association of State Highway Officials	1957	All vehicular trips of interest to urban major streets

a. R.T. = rapid transit; CBD = central business district.

tend to be remarkably similar for the different urban modes in a variety of operating circumstances. For example, they were in the general range of 1.5 to 2.0 cents per *available* seat mile in the United States in the early 1960s.[37] Differences in costs per *revenue* seat mile will therefore be mainly a function of differences in the rates of utilization that can be achieved by the different modes and differences in their capital costs.

Specifically, the crucial factor normally will be the volume of traffic along a particular traffic corridor during the rush hours. Forecasting such volumes with any accuracy in particular applications requires a detailed analysis of different overall systems applied to each specific situation. In general, residential and work-place densities are crucial in determining modal costs and service characteristics, since these densities largely determine the important factor of peak-hour corridor volume. Thus, only broad conclusions can be reached about urban transportation costs in general, as each city is likely to have its own peculiar geographic and other characteristics influencing both volume densities and costs.

37. The following discussion of urban transportation costs is abstracted from Meyer, Kain, and Wohl [A5], Chaps. 8–11.

With these limitations in mind, the usual cost relationships, counting all costs including capital, under United States conditions seem to be as follows: (1) if less than 8,000 to 10,000 trips per rush hour are available to a mode in a particular traffic corridor, automobile or some combination of bus and automobile on public highways will be most economical; (2) if 10,000 to 20,000 trips per rush hour will travel on one mode in a corridor, buses traveling on reserved or otherwise uncongested highways will be most economical; (3) if over 20,000 trips per rush hour are available to one mode in one corridor, buses on reserved right-of-way highways and rail transit will both be quite economical. Of course, if rail lines are already in place and there is no intention of replacing them, a good case can be made for ignoring many of the capital costs of a rail system. In this case, rail becomes relatively economical even at volumes beneath 20,000 per hour. Similarly, rail will generally be more attractive, everything else being equal, if tunnels must be used for any considerable distance on the route, or if the existing city streets are narrow and have low capacity.

As for time in transit, a consideration so important in commuter choices, rail mass transit provides a faster mode of travel for downtown destinations than highway modes in large and densely populated cities. However, the speed advantage of rail transit over buses operated like a rail system on exclusive right-of-way highways may not be pronounced. Indeed, both the automobile and the bus may be no more time consuming in terms of total elapsed travel time than the train, because usually more time must be spent going from the point of origination or termination to the line-haul vehicle when traveling by train than by other modes of urban transport. This is mainly a reflection of the facts that trains have less divisibility and a more limited geographic coverage than highway vehicles.

As a consequence of these cost and demand factors, shopping and recreational travel in North American cities is increasingly the province of the passenger automobile. Commuting, on the other hand, presents a much more complex and diverse picture. If the costs of private automobile operation are not too prohibitive in terms of either money or traffic congestion, a preference seems to exist for commuting by automobile. However, in the large United States cities, where the cost of automobile commuting can be high in both money and time, public transportation facilities remain competitive for many trips.

Essentially the same pattern of preferences in urban transit modes seems to prevail in other countries. Differences, if they do appear, seem mainly attributable to high United States income levels, which permit more people to adopt private automobile options—though the differences between Europe and North America in this regard seem to be rapidly disappearing. Government tax policies also tend to make the use of automobiles less feasible in many parts of the world. Specifically, fuel taxes are a major source of general tax funds in many countries, whereas in the United States they are usually earmarked for highway development and are relatively low. The pattern varies widely, however, because fuel taxes in parts of Latin America, Africa, and Asia are nonexistent or even negative. There may be other sources of differences. Low labor and high capital costs in the developing countries often have had the effect of making buses relatively more attractive than automobile and rail modes. Indeed, if it is assumed that private automobile ownership is not too extensive, buses should have particularly attractive cost characteristics in countries that have low labor costs, at least if urban streets are reasonably wide and not too congested.

Network Assignment

After projections of interzonal travel by each mode are obtained, these trips must be assigned to the available or projected highway and transit networks. Techniques for performing highway assignments have evolved from the use of ad hoc manual methods to the use of complex iterative computer programs. Assignment to transit networks is identical in principle, but the network alternatives are usually so few that the assignment problem is trivial.

The earliest assignments were restricted to limited freeway networks, were made manually, and usually were subjective. Typically, they involved allocating traffic to, or dividing it between, two alternatives (usually an existing arterial road and a proposed freeway) linking a pair of origin and destination zones. These assignments generally were based on diversion curves similar to those developed for trip-interchange modal split models.

In 1957, a computer algorithm was developed for finding the minimum path through a network, and a new era of network assignment modeling was born.[38] The Chicago Area Transportation Study was the first to apply these minimum path techniques. Subsequently, other studies have developed more sophisticated programming models for use in assignment. These models assign traffic to a network on the assumption that the traveler minimizes travel time or cost.

38. George B. Dantzig [I11], pp. 270–73; and Edward F. Moore [I30].

In the attempt to represent the effects of capacity constraints on route selection, an interesting problem has arisen. An assumption of infinite capacity for each link produces peculiar and unrealistic results. A minimum cost algorithm for mapping flows over a network without capacity constraints will map all traffic onto high performance expressways. Such minimization algorithms produce an all or none sort of mapping which either overloads links or assigns no traffic to them. The omission of a feedback of capacity on link performance is an obvious problem.

All efforts to incorporate capacity constraints use some form of iterative procedure, in which continually updated travel times are used in the minimum path algorithms. For example, in the Chicago and Pittsburgh studies the network assignments were made node by node, adjusting time costs as a function of the loading after each node's addition. Travel times for all interchanges from a single node were calculated, traffic from that node was loaded onto the network, a capacity cost function was used to recalculate times, and other nodes were successively introduced and treated in an analogous fashion. The nodes were introduced randomly.[39] This random solution procedure appears to work well for major links, but the results for smaller capacity links are more sensitive to alternative loading sequences. Alternative procedures include loading the entire network before capacity adjustments are made or loading partial networks before incorporating capacity feedbacks.[40] The capacity constraints on travel speeds is variously represented mathematically as a continuous or discrete function of traffic volume.

Land-Use Feedbacks and the Need for Simulation Models

There has been an undercurrent of dissatisfaction with conventional land-use and urban transportation planning models, largely arising from the failure to incorporate feedbacks between transportation and urban development adequately. Critics argue that the land-use transportation models may prove correct because they are self-fulfilling prophecies. Future

39. Illinois Department of Public Works and Buildings [D27], pp. 104–10; U.S. Bureau of Public Roads [D53]; Theodore J. Soltman [D47], pp. 122–40.
40. For a survey of assignment techniques, see William L. Mertz [D39], pp. 94–105; Brian V. Martin and Marvin L. Manheim [D38], pp. 69–84.

urban travel may result from the transportation investment specified by the transportation plan rather than from future urban development as postulated in the model. That is, the causal sequence implied in the conventional models is: (1) increases in population and employment; (2) changes in urban development, largely increasing decentralization; (3) increases and more dispersal in future urban travel; and (4) additional needs for highway investment. However, some critics suggest that the actual sequence of events might be: (1) forecasts of future urban development and travel; (2) increased urban highway investment; (3) urban expansion; and (4) increased urban travel. Indeed, many urban planners seem disposed to label highway investments as the major causal factor producing urban sprawl and a variety of other external consequences they regard as noxious. On the other hand, highway planners and engineers claim that they are merely facilitating what is an inexorable trend, increasing automobile use and decentralization.

The truth probably lies in between. While the empirical evidence is by no means definitive, there is considerable literature on the factors that are influencing land-use and location decisions in urban areas. Admittedly, most of the work is of a partial nature, focusing on only a few variables at a time. Nevertheless, it is clear that passenger transportation systems are one, though not the only, determinant of location patterns. Technological changes in manufacturing and retailing are another fundamental consideration. Similarly, rising incomes appear to be important in allowing people to live in single family dwellings, a preference that also seems to be conditioned by demographic and work-force participating factors.

Obviously, too, simultaneity between investment and its use—for example, increased highway facilities built concomitantly with urban expansion—may simply reflect good planning. Clearly, what is at issue is the cause of location changes. New highways cannot claim greater travel as a reflection of their benefits if their existence alone caused the change. Satisfactory transportation planning, therefore, requires that the effect of transportation investment on urban development, as well as the demand implications of alternative forms of urban development, be taken into account. Unquestionably, urban transportation investments have some effects on urban development, and it is desirable to introduce a feedback loop into demand forecasting models and system planning. The important issues are what both the nature and the strength of these feedbacks are and how they can be incorporated into planning procedures.

As noted earlier, none of the attempts in land-use modeling have been addressed to all aspects of urban development. Generally speaking, they represent only a meager beginning. The Lowry model developed for Pittsburgh and subsequently extended to a time-series simulation comes the closest to the ideal through its representation of basic industries' location effect on other employment and residences. However, the model is essentially a static, general equilibrium model; its strongest claim, that of presenting a reasonable solution to the land-use allocation problem at a point in time, does not qualify it as a satisfactory behavioral simulation of the many interrelations between transport investments and location choices occurring over time.

What is clearly needed is a recursive or feedback model that incorporates the many behavioral dimensions behind location decisions, basically a time-series model or simulation of urban development. No such model exists at present in spite of continual agitation for its development.[41] Developing such a model, moreover, may by no means be compatible with the objectives of ongoing urban transportation planning efforts. Extending the state of the art with respect to modeling land-use feedbacks clearly involves more risk than most city planning efforts, or cities' consultants, can afford. Also, a time-series data bank on location choices must be available. This requires a continual and substantial investment in the planning effort. The absence of consistent time-series data on land use is indicative both of the present state of the art and of the incentive structure that has led practical planning to focus on the one shot or static representation of metropolitan land use and transportation development.

41. A discussion of a simulation model of this sort appears in John F. Kain and John R. Meyer [D30], pp. 171–78.

CHAPTER NINE

Modeling Intercity Passenger Demand

INTERCITY PASSENGER DEMAND STUDIES, though numerous, have usually been much less comprehensive than urban transportation studies.[1] The prevalent form of intercity passenger demand research has been the estimation of a single linear forecasting equation for a particular mode. These efforts have usually been built on a simple gravity model formulation. Only lately have the models been expanded to incorporate price, income, and similar effects that economists normally consider paramount when estimating demand relationships. In essence, most recent intercity passenger demand models have represented a merger of simple gravity models with relatively conventional economic demand models.

There has been considerable experimentation, however, with the methods used for estimating these models. Some of the most advanced and complex econometric estimation techniques have been applied. These techniques include constrained regression, Bayesian estimation, and iterative techniques for fitting nonlinear functions. A similar air of innovation has characterized the development of data sources. Everything from case studies

---

1. The one exception is the Northeast Corridor Transportation Project, which has attempted to develop multiequation feedback models. *Studies in Travel Demand* [E26]. For a sketch of the planned representation of these feedbacks, see Stephen H. Putman [E19]. This model arose in large part out of a research effort by the CONSAD Research Corporation to survey and evaluate a variety of possible means of modeling these system feedbacks. See CONSAD Research Corporation [E7]. For a survey of the problems in data collection, especially in the Northeast Corridor, see Mark L. Rose [E25], pp. 134–56.

of particular experiences to elaborate time-series to large cross-section samples have been used.

This experimentation with estimation techniques and inventive exploitation of data sources is easily explained. There is little historical information available on intercity passenger travel that is appropriate for estimating the kinds of intercity passenger demand equations needed for planning and public policy purposes. The information in the few data that are available is limited. In the statistical vernacular, all the available series on intercity travel tend to be highly correlated. If the data are from time series, trends are so dominant that almost nothing else can be observed. If the data come from cross-section observations, such as travel between individual city pairs, it is usually difficult to observe much variation in prices or even in income characteristics. The result is that individual investigations have rarely been conclusive.

Nevertheless, a consensus about the characteristics of demand for different intercity passenger travel modes seems to be emerging. Clearly, both air and automobile travel are income elastic; as incomes rise the demand for both these modes increases markedly. Air travel also seems to be sensitive to the prices charged for airline services: a 1 percent reduction in air travel cost usually results in a 1 percent or more increase in the use of airline services. By contrast, the two other major public modes of intercity passenger transport, rail and bus, are relatively insensitive to income considerations. Both rail and bus, though, tend to be sensitive to the prices charged not only for their own services but for competitive services rendered by the other: that is, there is a positive cross elasticity of demand between bus and rail fares. Service characteristics can also condition the relative attractiveness of the different intercity modes. In particular, any improvement in the performance time of one of the public modes over that of another tends to be advantageous to that mode.

In this chapter, much of the documentation for these tentative generalizations is summarized. Considerable attention is also devoted to the methodologies and statistical techniques used to arrive at these conclusions.

The Gravity Formulation and Its Basic Extensions

The gravity model has typically been the starting point for intercity passenger demand studies, having both a long history and a continuing usefulness in forecasting trip generation and zonal interchange.[2] The variables commonly used to represent attractions at the origin and destination are population and income, with the impedance term variously represented as a function of performance or supply characteristics, such as distance, price, or travel time. Such models have been used in several ways; for example, to estimate total travel,[3] travel by a particular mode,[4] and the aggregation of travel over all modes.[5]

Probably the most elaborate gravity model yet used for an analysis of intercity passenger demand was one developed for application to the Northeast Corridor of the United States.[6] In this effort, the demand model was essentially conceived as a combination of a gravity model, representing the interactions between points and hence determining trips generated and their destinations, and a modal choice formulation based on price, time, and service characteristics of alternative modes. The model consisted of eight equations: the four major intercity travel modes serving corridor cities, each stratified by business and personal travel. Logarithmic demand equations were used.

As the gravity component in the personal travel equations, the explanatory variables were the logarithms of the product of the population at origin and destination, incomes, and a measure of attractiveness at the destination city.[7] Employment was substituted for population in the business travel equations. Price and travel time variables for the given mode and for competing modes were included. Travel time was measured from portal to portal, in an effort to include schedule or waiting time and the time spent in the collection or distribution phases (time spent traveling from the line-haul vehicle to the origin or destination) as well as line-haul time. It can be argued that different individual elements of travel time would

---

2. Gerald A. P. Carrothers ([E6], pp. 94–102) surveys the historical development of gravity models. See also George K. Zipf [E32]; Fred C. Ikle [E9], pp. 123–36.

3. A recent example is by Solita Monsod, who used a single gravity model to fit intercity demand for common carrier travel with a sample of 50 city pairs in the Northeast Corridor in 1961. See [E13], p. 167.

4. Several air studies have been made: Daniel M. Belmont [E2], pp. 361–68; Samuel B. Richmond [E24], pp. 65–73; Carl Hammer and Fred C. Ikle [E8], pp. 306–16; and John B. Lansing, Jung-Chao Liu, and Daniel B. Suits [E12], pp. 87–95.

5. Roger E. Alcaly [E1], pp. 61–73.

6. For a complete description of the model, see Systems Analysis and Research Corporation [E27].

7. A discussion of the rationale of equation specification in the model is contained in Systems Analysis and Research Corporation [E27], Chap. 5, pp. 3 and 12. The arguments are reviewed by Gerald Kraft and Martin Wohl [D32], pp. 10–15.

have different weights or parameters in a demand function. Unfortunately, the data problems were such that this level of disaggregation was deemed infeasible. Indeed, no really definitive study of the effects of different elements of travel time has been made to date.

In notation the complete model can be described as:

$$\text{Log } D_{ij}^{mp} = \log K_{mp} + e_m \log (E_i E_j) + \sum_{q=1}^{4} P_{mp}^q \cdot \log P_{ij}^{qp}$$

$$+ \sum_{q=1}^{4} t_{mp}^q \log T_{ij}^{qp} + Y_{mp} \log Y_i + a_{mp} \cdot \log A_j$$

where

D_{ij}^{mp} = the number of round trips originating at city i going to city j via mode m for purpose p

K_{mp} = a constant for the demand model for mode m for purpose p

e_m = the elasticity of demand for trips via mode m for business with respect to the weighted employment product

E_i, E_j = the employment in city i and city j respectively, weighted by trips per employee

P_{mp}^q = the elasticity of demand for trips via mode m for purpose p with respect to the price of trips via mode q for purpose p

P_{ij}^{qp} = the one-way cost of travel between cities i and j via mode q for purpose p

t_{mp}^q = the elasticity of demand for trips via mode m for purpose p with respect to the travel time for trips via mode q for purpose p

T_{ij}^{qp} = the one-way travel time between cities i and j via mode q for purpose p

Y_{mp} = the elasticity of demand for trips via mode m for purpose p with respect to per capita personal income

Y_i = per capita personal income in city i

a_{mp} = the elasticity of demand for trips via mode m for purpose p with respect to destination city attractiveness

A_j = the attractiveness of city j

The large number of variables in the model presented some considerable estimation problems. Cross-section data on traffic flows between cities were used to estimate the functions. However, many of the variables were highly correlated, which reduced the extent to which the available historic sample information could be used to estimate the relationships among variables.[8] A conventional solution to this multicollinearity problem is that of changing the specification of the model, usually by simply omitting variables. Such variable omission or alteration of the model, however, can introduce potentially serious errors of misspecification.[9] To avoid such misspecification, the major alternative is to incorporate additional or outside information (that is, in addition to the sample) into the estimation.

In the case of the Northeast Corridor study, additional information was employed in the form of linear constraints on the range of values which the estimates of the regression coefficients could assume, these constraints being based on prior information. This procedure has been labeled the constrained regression model.[10] In the corridor study, each demand elasticity was constrained to have the correct sign; thus, a mode's own price elasticity was constrained to be negative and cross elasticities were constrained to be positive. In addition, a maximum value was specified for each elasticity. For example, all own elasticities were constrained to lie in the range between minus five and zero. In the actual estimation, the zero constraint proved to be effective in several cases, thus limiting the parameter estimate from a reversal of sign which was inconsistent with the prior economic theory. In no case was the constraint on the maximum absolute value of a parameter binding.

The elasticities estimated in the Northeast Corridor study appear highly plausible. The results appear in Tables 9-1 and 9-2. For example, the business travel equation for rail yielded an employment product elasticity of 0.9, a rail cost elasticity of −0.35, a bus cost cross elasticity of 2.3 (indicating rail and bus travel are highly competitive in terms of price), a rail time elasticity of −4.4 (suggesting the demand for rail travel in the corridor would be strongly affected by improvements in travel time), and a cross elasticity for air travel time of 0.36. Other findings suggest that the demand for business trips for all modes is inelastic (less than unity) with respect to own price, with air travel exhibiting the highest price elasticity of demand. Personal travel demand appears to be more elastic with respect to own price than business travel for all modes except bus transportation.

8. For an introduction to the problem of multicollinearity, see John Johnston [H6], pp. 200–07, or Donald E. Farrar and Robert R. Glauber [H3], pp. 92–107.
9. Ta-Chung Liu [H8], pp. 855–65.
10. The original development and application of the constrained regression model was in John R. Meyer and Robert R. Glauber [H11], Chap. 8.

TABLE 9-1. *Constrained Regression Estimates of Elasticities of Intercity Passenger Transport Demand, Business Trip Demand Model, United States Northeast Corridor*[a]

Mode	Elasticities with respect to: Employment product	Rail cost	Bus cost	Air cost	Automobile cost	Rail time	Bus time	Air time	Automobile time	Income	Attractiveness	R^2
Rail	0.893	-0.354	2.283	0	0	-4.376	0	0.361	0	b	b	0.91
Bus	0.802	0	-0.740	b	0	0	-1.700	b	0	b	b	0.73
Air	0.929	0	b	-0.891	0	0.973	b	-2.103	1.078	1.418	0.836	0.92
Automobile	1.067	1.127	0	0	-0.358	0.844	0	0	-3.410	b	0.333	0.71

Source: Systems Analysis and Research Corporation [E27], p. v-47.
a. The Northeast Corridor is the area along the Atlantic Coast between Boston and Washington.
b. This variable was not in the model.

TABLE 9-2. *Constrained Regression Estimates of Elasticities of Intercity Passenger Transport Demand, Personal Trip Demand Model, United States Northeast Corridor*[a]

Mode	Elasticities with respect to: Population product	Rail cost	Bus cost	Air cost	Automobile cost	Rail time	Bus time	Air time	Automobile time	Income	Attractiveness	R^2
Rail	0.854	-3.003	3.150	0	0	-2.636	0	0.052	0.056	0.465	1.601	0.89
Bus	0.673	0	-0.689	b	0	0	-1.589	b	0	2.542	1.869	0.78
Air	0.911	0	b	-0.914	0.095	0.857	b	-2.213	1.120	1.905	1.020	0.91
Automobile	0.794	0.185	0	0.489	-0.929	0.458	0.074	0	-1.364	1.523	1.574	0.90

a. For source and notes, see Table 9-1.

The authors minimize the importance of travel costs for short trips like ∽ those found in this megapolitan corridor, and suggest that other factors, particularly travel time, are more important in determining intercity passenger travel. For both business and personal trips, and for all modes, demand is elastic with respect to own travel time. Personal rail travel does not appear to be as elastic with respect to time as it does with respect to cost. However, estimates of the time elasticities for both personal and business travel are very high, the demand for business trips usually being more time sensitive than the demand for personal trips.

The corridor model, as just described, lays great stress on obtaining sophisticated estimates of the impedance terms. A. J. Blackburn has initiated an extension of the basic gravity model in another direction, that of better estimating the attraction term. Blackburn explicitly introduces the substitution by the traveler of one destination for another as a function of the attractiveness of different sites. As noted earlier, this sort of consideration is implicit in many urban interchange models.

Blackburn assumes that the total number of trips originating from zone i is positively related to the total gravitational influences of all zones. These he proxies in the conventional way: they are to be positively related to population and inversely to distance.[11] Thus, the attractiveness of zone i for the traveler at zone k, denoted by G_i, is:

(1) $$G_i = P_i \cdot \psi(d_{ik}) \qquad \psi' < 0$$

where $\psi(d_{ik})$ denotes the inverse functional relationship of distance to demand and P_i is population of i. Total expected journeys (t_k) are then postulated to be positively related to total gravitational influences on the origin zone k, these influences being represented in the form:

(2) $$t_k = \alpha(\sum_i G_i)^n.$$

The interchange between any pair of zones i and k is assumed proportional to the total gravitational influence times the total number of trips:

(3) $$t_{ik} = \frac{G_i}{\sum_j G_j} t_k = \alpha G_i \left(\sum_j G_j\right)^{n-1},$$

which is the conventional gravity model in the special case where n is one, but results in a substitution of one potential destination for another if n

---

11. Anthony J. Blackburn [E4], pp. 111–24.

is less than one. Assuming a simple exponential representation of the impedance term, this generalization of the gravity model and its contrast to the simple gravity model can be expressed in log form as follows:

Generalized gravity model:

(4)
$$\ln t_{kj} = \ln \left\{ \alpha_1 P_k P_j e^{-\alpha_2 d_{kj}} \left[\left(\sum_{i \neq k} P_i e^{-\alpha_2 d_{ki}} \right)^{\alpha_3} \right. \right.$$
$$\left. \left. + \left(\sum_{i \neq j} P_i e^{-\alpha_2 d_{ij}} \right)^{\alpha_3} \right] \right\} .$$

Conventional gravity model:

(5)
$$\ln t_{kj} = \ln \left[\alpha_1 (P_k P_j)^{\alpha_5} e^{-\alpha_2} d_{kj} \right] .$$

In estimating the generalized gravity formulation, a system of equations which are nonlinear in the estimates of the unknown parameters must be solved. Blackburn used an algorithm by Marquardt to find a solution.[12] He has applied the model to cross-section data for seventeen city pairs in California, data which are not completely satisfactory in all respects. In general, his empirical comparisons of the generalized and conventional models were inconclusive, and neither model yielded a significantly better fit to the data. Whether a full-scale passenger demand model should include substitutions arising from the availability of alternative destinations, especially given the considerable complications introduced because of nonlinearities in the functions and the attendant difficulties in their estimation and statistical inference, remains an open issue.

Abstract Mode Models

In the above demand analyses, each mode is defined according to the administrative entity that controls its operations or the sort of physical equipment it employs, and a single demand equation is estimated for each mode. In the abstract mode approach, by contrast, the demand for transportation is represented by a single equation which reflects passengers' choices for all modes.

12. Donald W. Marquardt [H10]. Blackburn [E4] tried three forms of the distance impedance term:

$$\psi(d_{ij}) = d_{ij}^{-\beta}$$
$$\psi(d_{ij}) = e^{-\beta d_{ij}}$$
$$\psi(d_{ij}) = (d_{ij} + c)^{-\beta}.$$

A major motive for the abstract mode formulation is that of data saving. The number of observations available for estimating one abstract mode equation will be equal to the number of modes times the number of city pairs; whereas in a formulation employing an equation for each mode, the sample size available for estimating each equation equals the number of city pairs.

These data economies can be important. The absence of intercity demand data has been noted. In addition, the collinearity problem existing in available data is such that samples often contain less effective information for purposes of statistical estimation than is typically desired. As will be seen below in the discussion of time-series estimation of airline demand, this problem can be especially relevant when estimation must rely on time-series data. Sometimes, and even with cross-section samples, these collinearity problems can only be met by introducing prior information and employing more subjective estimation procedures such as constrained regression. Unfortunately, subjective procedures complicate the reporting and interpretation of results.

The original formulation of the abstract mode model was by Quandt and Baumol,[13] again designed to model passenger travel in the Northeast Corridor. Quandt and Baumol used a single-equation representation of passengers' modal choices, for all modes, linear in the parameters. Each mode is characterized by several independent variables describing its supply characteristics. These variables are defined relative to the level of that variable attained by the best mode between the city pair in question. These relative performance dimensions then determine modal choice. Their first formulation of the model was as follows:

$$T_{ijk} = \alpha_0(P_i)^{\alpha_1}(P_j)^{\alpha_2}(C_{ij}^b)^{\alpha_3}(C_{ijk}^r)^{\alpha_4}(H_{ij}^b)^{\alpha_5}(H_{ijk}^r)^{\alpha_6}(D_{ijk}^r)^{\alpha_7}(Y_{ij})^{\alpha_8}$$

where

T_{ijk} = the number of trips between the two nodes i and j

P_i, P_j = the populations of i and j

Y_{ij} = the weighted average income at i and j

H_{ij}^b = the shortest travel time between i and j

H_{ijk}^r = the travel time for the kth mode divided by the least travel time

C_{ij}^b = the least travel cost between i and j

13. Richard E. Quandt and William J. Baumol [E21], pp. 4–31; and Quandt [E20], pp. 33–34. The model also appears in Quandt and Baumol [E22], pp. 13–26.

C^r_{ijk} = the cost for the kth mode divided by the least cost

D^r_{ijk} = the departure frequency for the kth mode divided by the highest departure frequency

This is basically a linear demand model, with both attraction and impedance terms entering.

Noteworthy in the abstract mode conception is its premise that a traveler when choosing a mode compares its performance in a particular service quality to the mode that is best in that regard. That is, a bus traveler considers bus time relative to air time, the mode with the fastest time, but neglects the times of other modes. Thus, one mode can be compared to another in terms of time, but a third or a fourth is compared in terms of other service characteristics. This implies a certain discontinuity in preferences with regard to modal choice. Changes in service characteristics, if they do not qualify that mode as the best in that respect, have no effect on demand. For example, automobile travel will be unresponsive to changes in bus or rail times, since it is only the best time, that of air, which enters into people's decision to make an automobile trip. Introduction of a mode that does not exceed any service dimension's best level in time or cost has no effect on demand. Conversely, the introduction of a mode that reduces the prevailing minimum travel time regardless of the new mode's price produces effects on demand.

The empirical application of the abstract mode model has not been notably successful. The model was initially fitted using sixteen city pairs in California for air, bus, and automobile travel. The major premise to be tested was whether the travel demand for all modes could be parameterized as a single equation and hence be estimated by pooling data across modes. In a comparison of the abstract mode formulation to single mode demand equations, using analysis of covariance tests, the abstract mode models came out second best.[14] Also, the automobile mode data proved difficult to pool with data for the other modes. The income elasticity estimated from the abstract mode formulation appears to conceal considerable differences in the income elasticity among users of different modes, especially of automobile users. In addition, the abstract mode formulation yielded parameter estimates with higher variances than models individually specified for each mode.

Attempts have been made to modify the original abstract mode model

14. Kan Hua Young [E31], pp. 3–38.

in view of these findings.[15] The major step taken has been to provide for different income elasticities for the different modes and routes by introducing dummy variables into the equation. This sort of accounting for differences across modes, of course, makes the abstract mode model less abstract. Equations were fitted with both the California data and a sample that had been compiled for intercity flows in the Northeast Corridor. Significant differences in the income elasticity among city pairs were revealed, with the values ranging from about one to over three. This is an outcome not easy to interpret.

In general, an abstract mode demand function representing travelers' choices among modes as a single equation, with each mode's performance represented relative to the time or costs of the best mode serving a city pair, does not appear superior to a conventional multiequation gravity formulation. The more conventional approach presumes that disaggregation in demand estimation is necessary because of the complexity of the underlying utility functions and demand curves, and the very practical difficulties in empirically representing the relevant dimensions of each mode and the choices among modes. The empirical tests appear to substantiate this presumption.

Neither approach, the individual modal models or the abstract mode models, is well grounded in the theory of consumer behavior. The specific formulations have been largely determined by how well they fit existing data. Blackburn[16] has suggested an alternative that is more appealing on theoretical grounds. He postulates differences among individual travelers in their underlying utility functions and income levels, and hence their responses to the service characteristics of different modes. Some will choose

---

15. Richard E. Quandt and Kan Hua Young [E23], pp. 39–74. Provision for different income elasticities among routes but the same income elasticities for all modes on any given route was expressed as follows:

$$T_{ijk} = \alpha_0 (P_i P_j)^{\alpha_1} (C_{ijk}{}^r)^{\alpha_3} (H_{ijk}{}^r)^{\alpha_5} (D_{ijk}{}^r)^{\alpha_6} \cdot \exp\left\{ \alpha_{11}\left(\frac{C_{ij}{}^b}{Y_{ij}}\right) + \alpha_{12}\left(\frac{H_{ij}{}^b}{Y_{ij}}\right) \right\}.$$

The other alternative that proved useful was to relate relative service characteristics of the mode to income:

$$T_{ijk} = \alpha_0 (P_i P_j)^{\alpha_1} (C_{ij}{}^b)^{\alpha_2} (H_{ij}{}^b)^{\alpha_3} \cdot \exp\left\{ \alpha_{13}\left(\frac{\ln C_{ijk}{}^r}{\ln Y_{ij}}\right) + \alpha_{14}\left(\frac{\ln H_{ijk}{}^r}{\ln Y_{ij}}\right) + \alpha_{15}\left(\frac{\ln D_{ik}{}^r}{\ln Y_{ij}}\right) \right\}.$$

16. Anthony J. Blackburn [E3], pp. 47–89.

rail, others air, as a function of their valuation of such characteristics as time and costs.

These differences among potential travelers are the basis for differences in choice of mode. It is also assumed that there are differences in the amount of travel individuals with the same choices of mode will desire. Several parameters are used to represent these underlying behavioral differences among potential travelers with respect to performance characteristics of the available modes. A multivariate probability distribution is assumed over the parameter space. This probability distribution is then employed to determine the expected number of travelers taking each mode, that is, market demand, for each possible set of price and service characteristics across modes.

Only the basic rudiments of this procedure will be outlined here, since both the parameterization and the estimation of the model is complex. The total costs of making a trip from i to j on mode m for a randomly selected individual is given by the following linear equation:

$$(1) \qquad C_m = p_m + \sum_{k=1}^{r} u_k s_{km} + u_m$$

where C_m is the total cost, p_m the price, s_{km} the service or time variables, u_k their monetary valuation, and u_m a random variable. The individual will choose to make the trip by mode m only if C_m is lower than similar evaluations of traveling by other available modes. Both u_m and u_k are assumed to be random variables that vary over all individuals according to some probability distribution. The total number of people choosing mode m, and hence the expected number of trips, is thus a random variable determined by taking the expectation over all individuals.

Blackburn's explicit formulation of the u's, representing the nature of the utility function and the multivariate distribution of the parameters, was largely conditioned by analytic and computational ease. Time was the only service variable included; the mean valuation of time was expressed as a random variable, related to the average level of incomes (in the two cities of origin and destination) by the following:

$$(2) \qquad E(u) = ce^{\alpha + \beta y}$$

where c, α, and β are parameters and y represents income. Time and price were thus the two determinants of trip costs and hence modal preferences, but only the valuation of time varied with income levels across travelers.

The level of demand for a traveler choosing mode m was related inversely to changes in trip costs, positively to population of the two cities, and positively to per capita income. These are, respectively, the three terms in brackets in the following expression:

$$(3) \qquad \phi_m = \left[e^{-\lambda c_m}\right] \cdot \left[\left(\frac{P_i}{P_i + P_j}\right) \cdot P_j^\alpha + \left(\frac{P_j}{P_i + P_j}\right) P_i^\alpha\right] \cdot \left[\alpha v Y^\beta\right]$$

where ϕ_m is per capita travel on mode m; P_i and P_j are population in cities i and j respectively; and α, λ, v, and β are parameters. Per capita demand on mode m as represented is thus a random variable.

The total expected travel on mode m requires calculating the probability that any person will choose mode m, multiplying by the populations at origin and destination, and taking expected values of demand over all travelers with respect to the random variables in the demand function. Total expected travel on mode m is thus:

$$(4) \qquad T_m = [\alpha_0 P_i P_j (P_k^{\alpha_1} + P_j^{\alpha_1})(P_i + P_j)^{-1} \\ \cdot [E(v e^{\alpha_3}\{p_m + u z_m + u_m\})] \cdot [\bar{P}] + e_m$$

where z_m is service time on mode m, u is the monetary valuation of service time, and u_m is a random variable associated with service on mode m. The second term in brackets represents the expected value of the price of mode m, as denoted in equation (1), given that mode m is chosen; $\bar{P}$ is the probability that mode m is chosen over all other modes; and e_m is a random error term. All but the first term in equation (4) are a function of the underlying probability distributions of the random variables—the random terms in the valuation of different modes' services, u_m; the valuation of time across the population of potential travelers, denoted by u; and the effect of income on their trip demands, denoted by the random variable v.

In order to make the problem tractable, multivariate normal distributions were used to specify the probability space of these underlying parameters.[17] The probability that the typical traveler will choose mode m entails evaluating a definite integral over a specific range of values for u, the

17. The multivariate normal is the only tractable continuous multivariate probability distribution. The u_m's were assumed normal, while u and v were assumed log-normal. These latter variables representing the value of time and the level of demand were assumed to have a log-normal distribution, since the latter is everywhere nonnegative and thus avoids the problems of negative levels of demand and of negative values of u which would imply that people preferred higher trip times. Blackburn [E3], pp. 59–60.

valuation on time, and taking the expectation of total demand with respect to the random components v and u_m.[18]

The parameters of this model can be estimated, given cross-section data on modal characteristics, income and population, and modal choice. Estimation by minimizing the sum of squared errors, however, entails solving a nonlinear function, which poses considerable computational difficulty. A numerical procedure of the iterative type is needed to minimize the error sum of squares. In Blackburn's application, evaluating the function requires a numeral approximation of six integrals. This function must be evaluated at each data point for each specified parameter set being tried. The computations thus become quite expensive.[19]

Blackburn obtained numerical results based on the California sample; these are not of notable interest and the fit was not good by usual standards. However, the elasticities for price, income, and travel time all assumed the appropriate sign. The elasticities varied across city pairs because of differences in income levels; the income elasticity seemed low, usually between 0.5 and 1.0; the price elasticities varied considerably by mode, with air generally exhibiting the highest; time elasticities were usually higher than price elasticities, with air again exhibiting the highest value.[20]

The real contribution of Blackburn's model, however, is its imaginative introduction of differences in tastes and income at the micro level and the setting of travel demand in terms of a demand function consistent with the theory of consumers' choice. That the effects of new modes can be estimated illustrates the model's potential usefulness. A new mode with different price and service characteristics will be valued differently by trip makers and will induce some of them to make a different choice of mode. It will also induce more travel by improving service. Aggregation of these varied responses is necessary to estimate new market demand functions. The ultimate use or contribution of the model depends in part on the extent to which more efficient numerical means can be devised for solving nonlinear functions defined over many definite integrals. Imple-

18. Equation (4) can be expressed as a function of a vector of random variables, U, where U has a joint normal distribution. The elements in U are the random variables discussed in the text. Determining the expected level of travel on mode m entails taking the expectation that the elements of this vector of random variables assume certain values, which determine the expected value of that portion of the total traveling population which will choose mode m and the number of trips they will make. There are six elements in the vector U; hence taking this expectation involves valuing the function over six definite integrals.

19. Blackburn [E3], pp. 68–73.

20. Blackburn [E3], pp. 74–83.

mentation also requires far better intercity passenger travel data than have been available to date.

Cross-Section Studies of Air Travel

Cross-section studies have long played an important role in econometric forecasting of demand functions. Because larger samples are typically available and the data in cross-section samples can be richer in information than time series, cross-section studies have been considered an attractive alternative means of estimating parameters for which time-series data are ill suited.[21]

Cross-section travel data are especially well suited to calibrating models of trip generation or zonal interchange of the gravity type; for example, estimating attraction coefficients such as population and the effect of impedance terms such as distance and time. On the other hand, reliable estimation of price elasticities is not so easy to achieve with cross sections. Most observed cross-section variation of fares is due to differences in the class of service offered or in trip length, arising from the fact that fares per mile tend to reflect differences in costs. The fact that different classes of service are the source of the price variation means, of course, that it is easy to misspecify the equation, mixing up service and price effects. However, the existence of substantial differences in service, particularly schedule frequency or the availability of nonstop or multistop service, suggests that service elasticities are a reasonable target in cross-section estimation.

Probably the most successful cross-section air study thus far was that done by the Civil Aeronautics Board (CAB) of the 300 most heavily traveled city pairs in the United States.[22] Number of passengers was the dependent variable. The set of explanatory variables was comprised of price, income, travel time, quality of service, and, as a measure of the community of interest factor, the average number of business daytime telephone calls between each city pair. Price was represented by average fares per mile for each class of service weighted by the number of passengers, and travel time was taken to be the average travel speed (time on the ground was

---

21. Pooling data cannot be done indiscriminately. For a review of the problems that must be considered, see Edwin Kuh and John R. Meyer [H7], pp. 380–93; James Tobin [H20], pp. 113–41; and Richard Stone [H19].

22. U.S. Civil Aeronautics Board [E28].

included) of the four most direct flights in each direction. Quality of service was proxied by dummy variables for the frequency of nonstop flights among the four best flights serving each city pair. Linear regressions for both 1960 and 1964 were estimated. The results are shown in Table 9-3.

All coefficients were significant statistically; the regressions explained

TABLE 9-3. *Regression Coefficients from Cross-Section Analysis of Air Travel in 300 United States Domestic City-Pair Markets, 1960 and 1964*[a]

Independent variable	Intermediate stop dummies			
	1960		1964	
	Included	Excluded	Included	Excluded
Constant	7.20	9.21	6.87	8.43
Fare per mile	−1.76	−1.81	−1.94	−1.96
	(0.32)	(0.33)	(0.40)	(0.41)
Time per mile	−0.68	−1.27	−0.56	−1.06
	(0.21)	(0.18)	(0.20)	(0.17)
Distance	−0.92	−1.34	−0.88	−1.27
	(0.14)	(0.11)	(0.15)	(0.12)
Telephone calls[b]	0.28	0.30	0.32	0.31
	(0.04)	(0.04)	(0.04)	(0.04)
International passengers	0.14	0.15	0.12	0.13
	(0.02)	(0.02)	(0.02)	(0.02)
Income products[c]	0.18	0.18	0.20	0.24
	(0.03)	(0.03)	(0.04)	(0.04)
One stop	−0.14		−0.13	
	(0.03)		(0.03)	
Two or more stops	−0.26		−0.33	
	(0.07)		(0.11)	
Second carrier (60%–99%)[d]	0.07	0.07	0.10	0.12
	(0.02)	(0.03)	(0.03)	(0.03)
Second carrier (20%–59%)[d]	0.05	0.05	0.06	0.08
	(0.02)	(0.02)	(0.02)	(0.02)
R^2	0.89	0.88	0.87	0.86
Sy	0.157	0.163	0.171	0.177
N	300	300	300	300

Source: U.S. Civil Aeronautics Board [E28], p. 9.

a. The city pairs are the 300 most heavily traveled in the United States. All variables are expressed as logarithms. The dependent variable is the number of passengers. The numbers in parentheses are the standard errors.

b. Average number of business daytime telephone calls between each city pair.

c. The product of the aggregate incomes in the Standard Metropolitan Statistical Areas of each city pair.

d. The traffic carried by the second largest carrier in the market as a percentage of the largest carrier's traffic.

nearly nine-tenths of the variation in air travel among city pairs in both years. Fare elasticities were about -1.8 in 1960 and -1.9 in 1964. Travel time elasticities were very sensitive to the inclusion of dummy variables for the number of intermediate stops. In 1960, the travel time elasticity was less than unity (-0.68) when the intermediate stop dummies were included and greater than unity (-1.27) when they were omitted. Both were somewhat lower in 1964. The authors concluded that the true time elasticity probably lies somewhere between the two estimates, since intermediate stops are likely to have a deterrent effect on travel.

The CAB study also disaggregated its results to perform an implicit analysis of covariance test. For example, trip length may be a source of potential heterogeneity in time or fare elasticities since substitute modes of travel such as rail, automobile, and bus are readily available for shorter trips, whereas in long-haul markets good substitutes for air travel do not exist. This suggests that the effect of different fares on the demand for air travel should be greater in the short-haul markets. Accordingly, the two annual samples of 300 cities each were combined, then the city pairs were stratified into several length-of-trip groups. The same equation was fitted. The effects of stratification on the fare and travel time elasticities appears in Table 9-4. The investigators found that fare elasticities for the shortest and longest flight stage lengths were low or insignificant. The time elasticities increased as trip distance increased.[23]

Another disaggregation was performed by class of service. The CAB staff estimated separate first-class and coach travel characteristics by fitting an equation to each. This procedure yielded a meaningful estimate of the cross elasticity of demand for the first-class fare in the coach model and vice versa. The fare elasticity for coach service in the coach equation was -2.9, the cross elasticity for the first-class fare was 1.6, and travel time elasticity was -0.9.[24] Attempts to estimate fare and time elasticities for the submarkets defined according to the relative extent of business and personal travel were inconclusive.

Time-Series Models of Air Travel and More Sophisticated Pooling Techniques

As noted, cross-section data are not completely satisfactory in all respects. Lack of sufficient independent variation in some variables such as fares

23. Samuel L. Brown and Wayne S. Watkins [E5], pp. 24–25.
24. U.S. Civil Aeronautics Board [E28], pp. 16–17.

TABLE 9-4. *Cross-Section Regression Analysis of Air Travel in 600 United States Domestic City-Pair Markets, 300 Each from 1960 and 1964, Stratified by Distance*[a]

Independent variable	Coefficients and standard errors by distance (miles)		
	0–799	800–1,799	1,800 and over
Constant	8.00	6.11	8.28
Fare per mile	−2.10	−1.94	−0.64
	(0.35)	(0.38)	(0.77)
Time per mile	−0.69	−0.57	−1.23
	(0.20)	(0.23)	(0.43)
Distance	−1.12	−0.44	−1.48
	(0.16)	(0.18)	(0.31)
Telephone calls	0.28	0.51	0.22
	(0.05)	(0.06)	(0.04)
International passengers	0.13	0.10	0.15
	(0.02)	(0.02)	(0.03)
Income products	0.19	0.05	0.29
	(0.03)	(0.05)	(0.07)
One stop	[b]	−0.13	−0.19
		(0.03)	(0.05)
Two or more stops	[b]	−0.14	−0.30
		(0.08)	(0.09)
Second carrier (60%–99%)	0.10	0.03	0.12
	(0.03)	(0.03)	(0.04)
Second carrier (20%–59%)	0.05	0.04	0.07
	(0.03)	(0.03)	(0.04)
Clock time[c]	0.11	0.13	0.004
	(0.03)	(0.03)	(0.04)
R^2	0.82	0.86	0.89
Sy	0.173	0.149	0.154
N	226	249	125

Source: U.S. Civil Aeronautics Board [E28], p. 9.
a. See Table 9-3, note a.
b. "Stop" variables omitted because of lack of observation.
c. Expressed as 0 for 1960, 1 for 1964.

is one problem; the necessity to aggregate different sorts of underlying behavioral demand structures can be another. These problems are such that time-series analysis is often used as an alternative means of obtaining reliable estimates of price and income elasticities. Unfortunately, the data problems in time-series analysis appear to be at least as formidable as in cross-section.

Perhaps the simplest time-series estimation procedure is to compare case studies over a short time horizon by examining the short-run effect of a specific change in price within a particular market. Typically, a correction is made for the change in traffic from one period to the next for normal secular increases. Then the ratio of the percentage change in normalized traffic, corrected for secular trend, to the percentage change in fares or other variables is calculated. In such comparisons over a short time period, and in circumstances where the change in fares or service frequency is dramatic, accuracy in the adjustments for trend and other factors is not necessarily crucial.

One of the most interesting of these case studies was carried out for the Los Angeles-San Francisco air travel market by the CAB. Analysis of the Los Angeles-San Francisco air travel corridor is of special interest for several reasons. First, travel between Los Angeles and San Francisco is heavier than that of any other city-pair market in the world and has experienced a remarkable growth in recent years; from 1957 to 1964 the number of yearly passengers flying between Los Angeles and San Francisco increased by 250 percent as compared to a 70 percent increase in passenger miles for all United States trunk airlines.[25] To a significant degree this rapid growth in air travel has been caused by the unusually rapid growth of the West Coast communities. It can also be attributed, however, to intensive price competition among competing carriers generated by Pacific Southwest Airlines (PSA), a small intrastate carrier. This price competition affords an interesting opportunity to estimate price effects on demand.

Average fares in the Los Angeles-San Francisco market declined from a 1961 level of about $18 to about $15 in 1964. Based on past trends, increases in income, population, and other factors could account for about one-third of the almost 200 percent increase in traffic during this four-year period, whereas the other two-thirds seems attributable to the fare changes. An estimate of the price elasticity of air travel in the Los Angeles-San Francisco market can be determined by relating the increase in demand above the normal trend over the three-year period 1962–64 to the reduction in fares; this procedure yields an estimate of the price elasticity of -1.3.[26]

Obviously, such a case study approach tends to be ad hoc in nature and depends on the extent to which cases can be selected so that the normal trends in demand can be isolated from the special factors. In conventional time-series analysis, a multivariate regression equation is used for this

25. U.S. Civil Aeronautics Board [E30], p. 5.
26. U.S. Civil Aeronautics Board [E30], pp. 20–21, 321.

purpose. Time-series equations of airline demand have been estimated for single city-pair markets, in city-pair markets aggregated into a corridor or region, and for an entire country. When applied to market aggregations (of several different city pairs), neither the dependent nor the independent variables are normally homogeneous. Indeed, they may be so aggregative as to provide information only on rather long trends. Since long-run trends dominate the time path of many of the variables normally of interest, statistical estimation of the effects of particular independent variables is difficult. Somewhat greater homogeneity in the variables is obtained in single-market time-series studies, though at the expense of introducing the problem of empirically representing the special economic characteristics of the travel market in question. This may not be easy. For example, short-run time-series data on local income levels are generally not available.

Despite the problems involved, the CAB staff has attempted to estimate an overall air passenger demand model for the United States using time-series data. They first estimated a simple equation relating output to price, income, and a time trend, an equation linear in logs, using quarterly data for 1953–64. The intercorrelation of income and the time trend was so high that a reliable estimate of the income elasticity could not be obtained—the estimate changed markedly when a time trend was included. Specifically, the CAB researchers found that

$$\log RPM = -1.637 - 0.967 \log FARE + 2.497 \log DPI$$
$$(0.180) \qquad\qquad (0.069)$$
$$\bar{R}^2 = 0.98$$

and

$$\log RPM = 2.910 - 1.180 \log FARE + 0.658 \log DPI + 0.007\, TIME$$
$$(0.171) \qquad\qquad (0.509) \qquad\qquad (0.002)$$
$$\bar{R}^2 = 0.98$$

where RPM is total revenue passenger miles per capita; $FARE$ is real fares (revenue per passenger mile plus the transportation tax, deflated by the consumer price index); DPI is disposable personal income in 1954 dollars per capita; and $TIME$ is a time trend. In order to reduce the collinearity in the sample, first differences in the logs were fitted. A stratification was also made in the sample over time as a means of testing whether changes in the elasticities were occurring. The following results were obtained:

1953–64:
$$\Delta\log RPM = 0.0346 - 0.972\, \Delta\log FARE + 1.59\, \Delta\log DPI - 0.0007\, TIME.$$
$$(0.143) \qquad\qquad (0.279) \qquad\qquad (0.0002)$$

1953–57:

$$\Delta \log RPM = 0.0375 - 1.208 \, \Delta \log FARE + 1.087 \, \Delta \log DPI - 0.0009 \, TIME.$$
$$\quad\quad\quad\quad\quad\quad (0.576) \quad\quad\quad\quad\quad (0.362) \quad\quad\quad\quad (0.0005)$$

1958–64:

$$\Delta \log RPM = 0.0722 - 1.207 \, \Delta \log FARE + 3.103 \, \Delta \log DPI - 0.0021 \, TIME.$$
$$\quad\quad\quad\quad\quad\quad (0.228) \quad\quad\quad\quad\quad (0.568) \quad\quad\quad\quad (0.0007)$$

The CAB staff concluded that air travel is price elastic with a short-period fare elasticity of demand for air travel in the neighborhood of -1.2, and that this elasticity is probably rising slightly over time. Their results also suggest that air travel is income elastic.[27] These estimates are, of course, average elasticities and should not be uncritically applied to any individual market.

Straszheim has estimated a similar model to explain yearly passenger travel between the United States and Europe.[28] The North Atlantic is a useful market for study because reliable data are available and considerable variation in price and class of service has occurred. Demand equations were estimated for total demand for the period 1948–64 and for adjusted tourist demand for 1954–64. In the latter, data were adjusted to exclude the effect of first-class travelers who in the period 1961–64 were diverted to tourist-class service by the unusually high differences in fares of the two classes.

A linear logarithmic demand equation was used, similar to those used in the CAB study for the United States; the dependent variable was the number of trips, and the explanatory variables were the air fare from New York to London deflated by the United States consumer price index, real United States per capita income, and a time trend. As in the CAB efforts, multicollinearity among the explanatory variables presented a serious estimation problem, as both price reductions and income increases proved to be highly correlated with time. This high intercorrelation is typical in markets in which demand has grown at roughly 15 percent annually, as has the North Atlantic air market since World War II. A time trend alone can explain most of the variation in demand. The remaining variation in the historical data was insufficient to obtain reliable parameter estimates for the other variables by the use of ordinary least squares regressions.

As suggested previously, the only solution to this problem is the incorporation of additional outside information. To this effect, both constrained and Bayesian regression estimation methods were used by Straszheim. The former proved to be unsatisfactory, largely because the interrelationships

27. U.S. Civil Aeronautics Board [E29], pp. 28–33.
28. Mahlon R. Straszheim [A11], Chap. 6 and App. C.

of the independent variables were such that a large variation in parameter estimates would provide an essentially comparable and excellent fit of the data. There was thus little to choose among the various constraint sets and their resultant parameter estimates.[29]

The Bayesian regression model[30] provides a more flexible format for the incorporation of additional information. In Bayesian regression, outside information is included in the form of a prior distribution on the parameters in question, after which sample data are incorporated simultaneously to produce revised estimates of the distribution. A normal distribution was assumed for the prior. The prior was based on Straszheim's examination of the North Atlantic over this period as well as other markets in which price or service changes had occurred. Fairly tight priors produced seemingly reasonable estimates. For example, using a prior distribution on the price elasticity with mean at −2.0 and standard deviation of 1.0 (implying that the decision maker believes that the price elasticity is twice as likely to lie between −1.0 and −3.0 as outside that interval) and a prior mean on the income elasticity of 1.75 led to an estimate of the price elasticity of total demand of −1.5 and an income elasticity of 2.0 (Table 9-5). The unexplained shift in demand attributable to all other factors as represented in the coefficient on the time trend was about 5 percent. This can be construed as the annual increase in demand due to higher speeds, better schedule frequency, changes in tastes, and so forth.

The estimates are, of course, sensitive to the priors employed, and hence a sensitivity check was run on the prior distribution. These results are also shown in Table 9-5. The high collinearity in the sample is such that the prior to a considerable extent affects the assignment of the weights to the three explanatory variables.

Bayesian estimation procedures were also applied to selected individual city-pair routes to and from the United States. Individual markets are more amenable to a precise determination of the price or service changes which occurred, though netting out the effects of special circumstances affecting particular markets may be a problem. Two one-month periods (March and September) each year from the earliest date of service after World War II to 1965 were used as the sample data. (In most cases, service began in

29. A comparison of constrained and Bayesian estimation procedures is made in Straszheim [A11], App. C, pp. 275–86.

30. The definitive work on Bayesian statistical analysis is Howard Raiffa and Robert O. Schlaifer [H16]. For the normal regression model, see their Chapter 12.

TABLE 9-5. *Bayesian Estimates of Demand Function for North Atlantic Air Market and Sensitivity Check on Prior Distribution, 1948–65*

| | Elasticities of variables and time trends | | | |
| | Prior distribution assumed for elasticities | | Posterior distribution | |
Types of demand and elasticity, and time trend	Mean	Standard deviation	Mean	Standard deviation
Total demand, 1948–65				
Income elasticity	1.75	0.585	2.0440	0.517
Price elasticity	−2.00	1.000	−1.5041	0.894
Time trend	0.10	0.050	0.0557	0.043
Adjusted tourist demand, 1954–65				
Income elasticity	1.75	0.585	1.8192	0.522
Price elasticity	−2.00	1.000	−1.4223	0.818
Time trend	0.10	0.050	0.0620	0.046
Sensitivity checks on prior distribution, total demand, 1948–65				
Price elasticity	−2.00	1.000	−1.6170	0.894
Income elasticity	1.17	0.585	1.7150	0.517
Time trend	0.10	0.100	0.0630	0.043
Price elasticity	−1.00	1.000	−0.6280	0.894
Income elasticity	1.17	0.585	1.3870	0.517
Time trend	0.10	0.100	0.0980	0.043
Price elasticity	−3.00	1.000	−2.3030	0.894
Income elasticity	1.17	0.585	1.5780	0.517
Time trend	0.10	0.100	0.0490	0.043
Price elasticity	−2.00	2.250	−1.0840	1.234
Income elasticity	1.17	1.170	1.5860	1.046
Time trend	0.10	0.100	0.0810	0.058

Source: Mahlon R. Straszheim [A11], p. 283.

the late 1940s.) A prior distribution with a mean price elasticity of −2.0 and a mean income elasticity of 1.17 was specified.

The resulting estimates and their comparison to ordinary least squares regression estimates appear in Table 9-6. The Caribbean markets, largely tourist oriented, exhibit a significant price elasticity, as one would expect. In the Canadian and Pacific markets, the Bayesian priors yield reasonable estimates for the income elasticities and residual time trends but no significant price effects. Price effects thus appear to be relatively unimportant in the long routes in the Pacific over the sample period, though one would expect price effects to show up in the West Coast–Honolulu route which is a more tourist-oriented market.

TABLE 9-6. *Ordinary Least Squares and Bayesian Estimates of Demand Function, Selected Air Market City-Pair Routes, Late 1940s to 1965*

City-pair routes	Type of elasticity and time trend	Ordinary least squares regression estimates		Bayesian regression estimates, posterior distribution[a]	
		Mean	Variance	Mean	Variance
New York–San Juan	Price elasticity	0.2081	0.3661	−1.7504	0.6211
	Income elasticity	3.6099	1.6773	2.3177	0.9803
	Time trend	0.1223	0.0097	0.0862	0.0021
Miami–San Juan	Price elasticity	0.1665	0.3551	−1.7355	0.6682
	Income elasticity	3.5218	0.4996	1.6507	0.2717
	Time trend	0.1204	0.0212	0.1610	0.0032
Miami–Port au Prince	Price elasticity	0.3370	0.6110	−1.4629	0.8223
	Income elasticity	−0.0301	0.7042	0.8920	0.3120
	Time trend	0.1862	0.0123	0.1139	0.0021
Anchorage–Tokyo	Price elasticity	−0.0635	0.8646	−0.4339	0.3263
	Income elasticity	1.6882	2.0481	2.0841	0.1067
	Time trend	0.1486	0.0809	0.1258	0.0019
Sydney–San Francisco[b]	Price elasticity	3.1285	1.3306	−0.8367	0.3123
	Income elasticity	−0.1500	0.2295	1.8621	0.1030
	Time trend	0.1426	0.0128	0.0808	0.0021
Tokyo–Wake–Honolulu[c]	Price elasticity	−1.7868	1.3421	−0.3965	0.3440
	Income elasticity	5.2646	2.6659	2.1052	0.1127
	Time trend	0.0102	0.1075	0.1444	0.0019
Los Angeles–Honolulu	Price elasticity	−0.3119	0.6211	−0.4144	0.4234
	Income elasticity	3.5034	1.7032	2.0950	0.1409
	Time trend	0.0802	0.0127	0.1302	0.0021
New York–Montreal	Price elasticity	−0.8613	0.0962	−0.8370	0.5322
	Income elasticity	0.3915	2.6923	1.8483	0.1774
	Time trend	0.1153	0.0036	0.0783	0.0030
Chicago–Toronto	Price elasticity	−0.7601	1.0026	−0.7119	0.5510
	Income elasticity	5.3873	6.2530	1.9210	0.1839
	Time trend	−0.0175	0.0081	0.1126	0.0024
New York–Toronto	Price elasticity	0.0554	0.4991	−1.2230	0.6883
	Income elasticity	0.1620	0.1223	0.8395	0.3777
	Time trend	0.1101	0.0092	0.0822	0.0062

Source: Straszheim [A11], p. 285.

a. Prior distribution assumed:

	Mean	Variance
Price elasticity	−2.00	1.00
Income elasticity	1.17	0.3364
Time trend	0.10	0.01

b. Passenger travel via Qantas Empire Airlines only.

c. Includes both traffic stopping at Wake and nonstop Tokyo–Honolulu traffic.

These city-pair market comparisons are generally more amenable to interpretation than the North Atlantic case, since the multicollinearity is not so severe, and thus sample data bear a greater weight in the estimation. Bayesian estimation applied to many such city pairs in this fashion is a useful means of sorting out broad differences among markets. A single prior applied to many samples amounts to an implicit analysis-of-variance test on some broad market differences.

Generalizations about Modal Choice

This chapter has thus far been focused on the methodology for obtaining structural estimates of the important parameters in intercity passenger demand functions. While the statistical results are less than complete, a number of important generalizations about modal choice can be made, many of which may be important in forecasting demand for intercity passenger travel. The crucial problems in passenger transport forecasting tend to center around determining the valuation placed on different service characteristics by individuals making trips for different purposes and delineating the extent to which the different modes of transportation meet these more important service characteristics at a reasonable cost.

The major modes of domestic intercity passenger transport are bus, automobile, train, and airplane. For the more utilitarian forms of intercity passenger transportation—rail coach, bus, and private passenger automobile—the costs incurred in the United States in 1965 were in the neighborhood of 1.5 to 2.0 cents an available passenger mile of service performed; on a passenger mile basis, these costs were between 2.5 and 3.0 cents for bus and automobile and substantially more for rail. For higher quality service, such as rail day-night coaches, rail parlor cars, and long-haul tourist-class air service, the costs tended to be somewhat higher, at between 2.0 and 2.5 cents an available seat mile, although occasionally rising to 3.0 cents or more for the shorter airline hauls and some of the more deluxe rail parlor car services; on a passenger mile basis the range was between 3.0 and 7.0 cents depending crucially on load factors achieved. Furthermore, even a good quality of first-class air travel did not cost much above this level as long as the haul was about five hundred miles or more. Then the cost of an available seat mile was approximately 2.5 to 3.5 cents and 4.5 to 7.0 cents a passenger mile. Finally, at the top of the quality scale were first-class rail and first-class short-haul air travel. These tended to cost between 5 and 10 cents a revenue passenger mile, the exact level depending on a number of service considerations.

To these direct fare costs must be added expenses, such as tipping and extra logistic expenses, and a valuation for service differentials. A careful accounting of these tends to reduce the effect of the above fare differentials among modes. For example, while intercity touring by private passenger automobile tends to be a remarkably low-cost form of travel when a family unit of four or more persons is making a trip, some of the differences in the cost per mile between the automobile and public modes will be absorbed in extra costs for lodging while en route. Private automobile passenger travel is generally slower (only the bus is as slow in most cases) and inherently not a 24-hour-a-day mode. Furthermore, when compared with tourist-class air service, passenger travel by private automobile usually has higher associated food costs, since an allowance for meals is normally incorporated into the air fare structure. On the other hand, the automobile provides a complete door-to-door service, not requiring taxis, porters, and supplementary bus rides, which, while usually trivial by themselves, can be fairly costly in the aggregate.

There are also logistic and supplemental cost differences between the different modes of public passenger travel. Rail coach seems to cost the most in addition to the basic transportation fare, the bus second most, and air service the least. The net effect of this is that the higher costs of air travel are at least partially mitigated. On the other hand, since basic rail coach fares tend, if anything, to be slightly higher than bus fares, the supplemental charges accentuate the cost differences between these two modes.

There are some substantial differences in the schedule flexibility the various modes can provide. One of the most serious yet least understood economic and service disadvantages of passenger train travel is that the unit of efficient operation is relatively large. It often does not pay to schedule a passenger train with less than 200 to 300 seats, or sometimes even 1,000 seats, of passenger capacity. An immediate consequence is that the train cannot be efficiently scheduled for many departures except in the highest volume markets. The bus and airplane, with an efficient operating unit of about 50 and 100 respectively, can conveniently schedule many more departures for a given size of market than can the train. In addition, the greater schedule flexibility of both the bus and private automobile substantially reduces the probability that the traveler will lose time waiting for connections. Lack of schedule flexibility is one of the important explanations of the decline in intercity rail passenger service in the United States. The individual private passenger automobile, of course, has more schedule flexibility than any public mode.

With regard to operating speeds, the bus, rail, and automobile modes are nearly the same. While both bus and automobile tend to have somewhat higher line-haul times than the train, this disadvantage can easily be exaggerated since neither highway mode usually requires as much time going from the line-haul vehicle to points of origin and termination as the train. Obviously, air travel is in a class by itself when it comes to performance speed, particularly on trips of more than 200 miles. Indeed, even on relatively short intercity trips, air travel will retain a speed advantage if airports are not too inconveniently located. Moreover, much of the early inconvenience of remote airport locations has been eliminated in recent years with the improvement of transportation facilities to airports and, perhaps even more importantly, the increasing relocation of many formerly central city activities to the vicinity of airports. Today, an airport located at the outskirts of a city may be more convenient for travelers who originate or terminate their trips at residential points than a railroad terminal placed in an older part of the central business district. In short, despite much comment about the relative amount of time consumed by land travel as a percentage of the total time spent on an air trip, it is usually difficult to improve on the overall performance speed of air travel as a mode of intercity transportation for trips of roughly 250 miles or more.

One factor, not thus far mentioned, that conditions passenger modal choices to an indeterminate extent is safety. The conventional view is that safety considerations favor rail most and air least. Such a ranking, moreover, has some basis in the comparative safety statistics for the different modes. This is particularly true if safety is measured exclusively in terms of passenger fatalities per million miles of travel since a significant proportion of the fatalities on all the surface modes, including rail, does not involve passengers, while air fatalities are mainly confined to passengers. The actuality seems to be that people react to the passenger fatality figures and that these diminish the relative attractiveness of air and automobile travel, and perhaps of buses as well. It also appears that older travelers are more fearful about the safety of air travel than younger travelers, so the importance of air safety as a demand consideration may diminish over time even if air travel does not become relatively safer as time passes (though there is every reason to expect that it will). The overall importance of safety considerations, therefore, as a future determinant of passenger transport choices is difficult to forecast.

Finally, the present technological trends do not seem to indicate any pronounced likelihood that the basic patterns of modal choice will be changed in the near future. For example, considerable publicity is periodically given to the possibility of greatly improving the speed and other performance characteristics of rail passenger transport by using new technologies. Most of these do not stand up as real commercial possibilities, however, under close economic or engineering scrutiny, except when applied in travel corridors characterized by exceptionally high volumes. In addition, when extrapolating any large changes in basic traffic patterns because of technological improvements, it must be remembered that there is a strong tendency for improvements to occur in all fields. The common practice of making optimistic projections for one particular mode on the basis of improvements that might be made in that mode involves considerable risk that the effects of these developments will be offset by equally advantageous improvements in competitive modes.

Clearly, given the many dimensions involved, any generalizations about modal choice and preferences are subject to some degree of hazard. Nevertheless, intercity passenger transport should fall into reasonably well-defined patterns in the future unless dramatic changes occur in the technologies. For trips much in excess of 500 miles, air travel would seem to be not only the cheapest but usually the service preferred by most travelers. Only private automobiles should prove competitive and then only for family-group tourism and similar purposes. The automobile should also be dominant for trips of less than 500 miles, at least where income levels are sufficient to permit a high level of automobile ownership. The relative attraction of the different public modes for the shorter trips will depend mainly on travel volumes. The train should prove competitive or important only in very large volume markets with the bus dominant elsewhere. Air service will also be important for certain kinds of short-haul service. Sharply improved travel times for train services might affect these relationships, at least marginally. Both bus and rail intercity passenger transport face, however, a significant obstacle over the longer term, since with rising incomes people can be expected to shift increasingly to either air or automobile travel.

CHAPTER TEN

Forecasting Demands for Intercity Freight Transport

Techniques for estimating freight transport demands are, in general, not well advanced. Freight demand models have been relatively crude, single-equation fits to empirical data. Only recently has attention been devoted to study of land uses and the industrial structure as the basis for estimating freight demands, in a fashion analogous to that used in urban transportation studies.

Estimating Traffic Generation

Forecasting the demand for freight transport should begin, like any other transport demand forecasting exercise, by defining the main sources of traffic. One way of doing this is to employ a so-called economic base survey. These surveys typically include open-ended examinations or appraisals of the natural resource base, the population and labor force, the existing industries of the area under consideration, and possibly the social structure, attitudes, and incentives of the people. In identifying those industries that will be the main users of the transport facilities and in specifying their present and potential future location and level of output, any base study essentially must encompass three broad elements: (1) a determination of productive potential, including both physical and human resources; (2) an investigation of market potential; and (3) an assessment of entrepreneurial potential, or the response of the local or regional economy to profit-making opportunities, including government and private investment plans.[1] For forecasting freight transportation demand, the industrial, mining, and agricultural structure is usually the most important component of the economic base analysis, since these industries are major sources of freight traffic.

The patterns of growth and interdependencies of industry are also important in determining freight traffic demands. One means of representing the interrelationship among industrial sectors that can be particularly useful is the input-output model. This model represents all intersectoral transactions by a set of equations. These equations assume constant linear relationships between the amount of input from all other sectors needed to produce a unit of output in any one industrial sector. Such an input-output model can be used to determine the level of productive activity in all sectors of the economy required to satisfy any given bill of final demands.[2] These activity levels provide both a good base for estimating traffic generation and important clues on traffic flows.[3]

The underlying input-output coefficients can be estimated in several ways. The purposes of a study will have a bearing on the choice of input-output estimation procedures. For example, if an input-output model is to be used for making practical pricing or investment decisions, considerable disaggregation may be required. On the other hand, for determining broad economic impacts of a change in final demand (for example, a cut in defense expenditures or a change in investment), the usefulness of disaggregation may not be so obvious.[4] For freight transport forecasting, two dozen sectors is often sufficient disaggregation of an economy if the sectors are appropriately defined, minimizing within class heterogeneity with regard to transport demand or supply characteristics.

The type of country or economy being examined can also be relevant to choice of the level of input-output aggregation. For example, the economies of some of the less developed countries are far less complex than the United States economy, and fewer sectors will suffice for their descrip-

---

1. A procedure for conducting such an economic base study and the sources of information for studying transport in a less developed country are described by Clell G. Harral [F8].

2. Wassily W. Leontief [C10].

3. About 49 percent of transport gross sales was for shipping intermediate goods in the United States in 1958. Karen R. Polenske [E18], p. 8.

4. Wassily W. Leontief and others [C11], pp. 217–41.

tion, all other things being equal. Generally, aggregated estimates, as derived from manufacturing studies or censuses employed to obtain an approximate picture of the relationships among sectors, tend to be adequate for transport planning.

By contrast, estimating the regional or spatial dimension of input-output relationships, something that is usually essential to transport planning, is almost always a serious practical problem. Regional data are often unavailable.[5] The determination of regional activity must usually be based on individual regional surveys, with frequent reliance on proxy measures for regional output derived from employment or tax records and application of common (national) input-output relationships to the estimates of output for each region. The objective is to provide necessary disaggregation in intersectoral flows, indexed by their origin and destination.

Projections of future regional activity are perhaps even more difficult, especially the location of industrial demand inasmuch as this entails forecasting resource and market potentials and future industrial investment. Also, location projections involve knowledge of the future transport system since changes in transportation performance can significantly feed back on resource and industrial development.[6]

Interzonal Flow Models

For estimating freight traffic patterns, "who sells to whom" must be determined. By far the simplest approach to this interzonal flow estimation problem is to use a "trade model," which can be described as an assumption that the zonal distribution of a good is some fixed proportion of the total amount of the commodity consumed or produced in a region. Thus, the distribution of internal flows, x_{ij}, can be related by a trade coefficient matrix to levels of regional consumption or output.[7] The trade coefficient matrix is then used for forecasting. In notation,

$$x_{ij} = c_{ij}x_{0j} \text{ for } i, j = 1, \ldots, n$$

5. In the United States, a few states have developed such tables: Utah, California, Washington, Oregon, and Mississippi. See Polenske [E18], p. 39.

6. This sort of system effect is a major motive of the model developed in Volume 2.

7. Chenery and Moses are the leading developers of this kind of forecasting model. Hollis B. Chenery [C4] and Leon N. Moses [E15], pp. 803–32.

where

$$\sum_{i=1}^{n} x_{ij} = x_{0j}$$

$$\sum_{j=1}^{n} x_{ij} = x_{i0}$$

$$\sum_{i=1}^{n} x_{i0} = x_{00} = \sum_{j=1}^{n} x_{0j}$$

and

n = the number of regions
c_{ij} = shipment from i to j divided by total consumption in region j
x_{ij} = shipment from i to j
x_{i0} = production in region i
x_{0j} = consumption in region j
x_{00} = total production and total consumption in all regions

The above is called a fixed column coefficient model. The matrix of trade coefficients, c_{ij}, is determined by dividing flows in the base year by consumption in each region, each column of x_{ij} being divided by the base-year level, x_{0j}. In a fixed row coefficient trade model, the division is by total production over rows in the c_{ij} matrix (that is, $c_{ij} = x_{ij}/x_{i0}$). Either version can be employed for forecasting; the consumption model presumes that the trade relationships among zones are invariant to changes in final demand, while the production model assumes that they are invariant to changes in supply.

Another model commonly used to estimate interzonal commodity flows is the gravity model. In it, interzonal flows are related proportionally to the total production and consumption in two regions and assumed inversely proportional to the total. In a sense, the gravity model combines the two versions of the trade model. In notation,

$$x_{ij} = \frac{x_{i0} x_{0j}}{x_{00}} G_{ij} \text{ for } i,j = 1, \ldots, n$$

where G_{ij} equals the gravity friction parameter and the same equalities hold as before for the trade model. The crucial gravity coefficients, G_{ij}, can be derived from an interzonal trade matrix or represented by some function of transport time or costs. Obviously, the gravity model has more parameters than the simple trade models.

Polenske has compared the performance of the trade and gravity models in predicting interzonal flows of fruit and vegetables in the United States. Using data for both rail and truck for the years 1960–64, she found that the gravity model calibrated on the 1960 flows was a significantly better predictor of the 1964 distribution than either version of the trade model. This result is not too surprising in view of the much larger data input needed for the gravity models.[8]

Another type of interzonal flow model is the linear programming model which allocates shipments between regions to meet a given regional distribution of demand. Linear programming models have the appeal of embodying the premise of economic rationality. This premise, of course, can be a mixed blessing; shippers' rationality may be of a more complex order than simple transport or other cost minimization. For example, marketing considerations, such as an effort to achieve long-run market penetration, may mean that transport costs play a relatively minor role in a firm's current decision making.

The solution of programming models produces two special characteristics that are relevant to their applicability. First, only a small portion of potential routings normally can or will be used in a programming approach. For a system of n regions and one interconnection between each, only $2n - 1$ of the potential routings (of which there are n^2) will be employed. Second, no crosshauls or backhauls will occur. If one bushel of wheat or ton of coal is like all others, transport costs are not minimized by hauling some of the commodity both from point A to point B and from point B to point A.

Many linear programming models of freight flows have been developed. Karl Fox fitted such a model to feed grain movements among ten regions in the United States. Morrill and Garrison found that wheat movements in the northwestern United States, at least within a single season, could be predicted quite accurately by using linear programming. Henderson, in a study of the United States coal industry, came to the same general conclusion for coal shipments.[9]

The success of linear programming models in predicting freight transport patterns largely depends on a commodity classification's homogeneity. Specifically, homogeneity reduces the need for any crosshauls. Observed

8. Karen R. Polenske [E17], pp. 73–103.

9. Karl A. Fox [I18], pp. 547–66; R. L. Morrill and W. L. Garrison [E14], pp. 116–26; James M. Henderson [I22].

crosshauling of commodity classifications is largely attributable to the fact that conventional and practical definitions of commodity groups encompass diverse goods, some of which are produced at particular points but consumed widely. Patterns of seasonality lost through aggregation of data also can be an important source of commodity heterogeneity, especially in agricultural products. For example, area A may be the source of a food crop in the fall while area B is the supplier in the spring. A linear programming model will not predict such crosshauling unless fall and spring flows are separately treated.

Thus, the nature of the available data, especially the level of aggregation, is relevant in the selection of models to predict zonal interchanges. Studies of the empirical applicability of linear programming and gravity models under varying circumstances confirm this hypothesis. For example, Polenske found that a programming model was inapplicable for modeling fruit and vegetable shipments in the United States because of the considerable crosshauling observed. Mera studied the usefulness of both a gravity model and a linear programming formulation to explain Pakistan railway data on shipments of domestic wheat, rice, and "all other agricultural products." Using a number of different measures for comparing the fit of observed to calculated data, he found, in general, that a gravity model was most useful for predicting the interregional flows of the more aggregated commodity types, such as "all other agricultural products" or textiles, and programming models were better for very homogeneous commodities, such as domestic wheat and rice. In all cases, the disaggregation of commodities into more specific commodity types provided better fits when using programming techniques.[10]

Modal Choice

Modal choice will depend initially on the type of commodity being shipped, since shippers of different commodities will value cost, travel time, or other performance variables differently. Traditionally, there have been three properties of freight considered particularly important or relevant in determining modal choices: density or weight of the freight per cubic measure, volume of shipment (that is, the demand for transportation services

10. Polenske [E17], pp. 38–44. Mera's study is summarized in Appendix A.

per unit of time), and the dollar value of the product per unit measure. In addition to these basic properties, there are a number of other product characteristics which can be important, such as perishability, fragility, volatility, and seasonality or daily peaking. The adaptability of a product to reduction to or suspension in common liquids may also be important in some cases since it raises the possibility of using specialized pipeline transportation.

While convenience and other relatively subjective conditions play an important role in the allocation of freight traffic, the freight market is essentially an industrial market. Freight traffic is therefore particularly sensitive to changes in the prices charged for different transport services. Broadly speaking, the price that a shipper will be willing to pay for a transportation service will be related to the basic product characteristics listed above. Willingness to pay is usually a negative function of density, volume of traffic per time period, seasonal steadiness, and schedule flexibility, and a positive function of value per unit of weight, perishability, and most of the other characteristics enumerated. The relationship between the willingness to pay for a transportation service and the characteristics of the product to be transported obviously reflect the underlying cost realities of moving products through a distribution system. The costs of holding inventory, the probability and extent of product damage, and the costs of loading and transshipping are all examples of costs which are considered in assessing the proper mode of transport.

The relative ability of different modes of transport to supply transport services can be fully assessed only in terms of the underlying cost structure of different modes. In the long run, transport charges should and to a considerable extent do reflect differences in cost. Approximate estimates of long-run marginal costs for the United States under 1960 conditions are shown in Table 10-1 for the principal modes of freight transport. The cost estimates shown are for the most part minimal, that is, they pertain to the most economic or advantageous rather than to typical operations. The only important reductions that might be made in these costs would involve the use of new and highly specialized equipment. The cost effects associated with the introduction of such equipment are often speculative because the economic life of such installations is uncertain. There has been considerable stability in transport costs in the United States since 1960 (productivity gains roughly balancing increased costs of factor inputs), so these figures would be only slightly modified by updating.

Cost comparisons by modes for developing countries would not be very

TABLE 10-1. *Minimum Long-Run Marginal Costs of Freight Transport in the United States, by Mode, 1960*

(In 1960 mills per revenue ton-mile)

Mode of transport	Minimum marginal cost
Intercoastal tanker and lake bulk carrier	0.5
Pipeline	1.0
Barge (bulk commodities only)	3.0
Rail carload (bulk commodities)[a]	7.0
Piggyback	9.0
Rail carload (manufactured commodities)	9.0
Truck	25.0
Airline	100.0

Source: Adapted from John R. Meyer and others [A7], Chaps. 3, 4, 5, and 6, and other sources, mainly information provided by the carriers.

a. Costs as low as 4 or 5 mills per revenue ton-mile can be achieved in certain special cases by the railroads but only if *no* empty return haul or specialized equipment and extremely heavy loadings per car are assumed. Also, unit trains for movement of bulk commodities can reduce these costs to 5 or 6 mills in some cases.

different, at least in a *relative* sense, from those reported in Table 10-1.[11] Although there are substantial differences in capital and labor costs between developed and underdeveloped countries, the lower labor costs in South America, Africa, and Asia are counterbalanced by greater use of labor and higher capital, equipment, and maintenance costs; higher fuel costs may be experienced in many instances as well. Indeed, using free market foreign exchange rates, it appears that the absolute level of costs for the different modes are roughly identical with those reported in Table 10-1 in those developing countries for which reliable data are available, for example, Chile, Colombia, Ghana, Nigeria, Pakistan, Sudan, Uganda, and Venezuela.

The only major qualifications to this generalization, according to the limited evidence available, are that the minimum achievable truck costs are a penny or so lower in countries that have both low fuel and low labor costs, as in Colombia and Nigeria. However, full realization of cost economies in trucking is impeded in many countries, particularly of Asia, because of residual barriers to highway commerce. Highways, too, are often unpaved or of low quality in Africa, Asia, and South America with serious consequences for fuel consumption, tire wear, and operating speeds.[12]

11. Detailed cost and performance data for a variety of transport systems in Colombia are assembled in Volume 2.

12. Armando M. Lago [E11]; Richard M. Soberman [A9], pp. 55–70.

There is also evidence that rail costs can be higher in some developing countries than in the United States or Europe.[13] Relatively higher rail costs may simply be because railroading is a capital-intensive and often an import-dependent mode of transport; hence costs reflect the high cost of capital and scarcity of foreign exchange that typifies many underdeveloped countries. But other factors also influence costs. Railroads are often vastly overstaffed in these countries, a reflection either of the fact that the railroads are viewed as a politically expedient form of work relief or of the relative strength of the railroad bureaucracy. Many railroads in Africa and South America operate with very low volume densities; this is characteristically an impediment to the achievement of low-cost rail transport. Operations of a railroad can involve complex problems of management and coordination, especially when general merchandise cargo is to be handled. Finally, railroad equipment utilization is often low in some of the developing countries because import restrictions or delays in shipment of needed spare parts hinder quick and efficient maintenance.

It should be noted that the figures in Table 10-1 may make insufficient allowance for many important components of overhead or, perhaps, the need for private enterprises to achieve a certain amount of profitability to attract capital. Specifically, threshold and common costs that cannot be readily allocated to specific traffic are not included. That is, the reported costs are not fully distributed costs. The figures in Table 10-1 are also based on the assumption of large volumes, long hauls, low fragility, and virtually all other conditions needed to bring costs down to minimum achievable levels.

The ability of different modes to adjust costs and services to meet varying transport needs should also be noted. For example, piggybacking is a hybrid of rail and truck operations in which origination and delivery of shipments is made by truck tractor and trailer on highways while the line haul (the long-distance movement between cities or major terminal points) is performed by placing the truck trailer on a flatcar for conventional movement by rail. Piggybacking is, of course, only one example of containerization, a technique using freight containers which are transferable from one mode of transport locomotion to another. The objective of containerization is to effectuate economies by using each form of locomotion wherever it is most advantageous in reducing costs or meeting service objectives.

Similarly, the small unit size of the truck trailer as compared with the

13. Richard M. Soberman [A8].

rail boxcar and the low cost of moving the truck trailer from one location to another give it an advantage in consolidating many small shipments into larger loads. Such consolidation often can eliminate extra handling and freight sheds. The truck trailer is also generally a better vehicle from the standpoint of controlling loading and inventory costs. Similarly, the truck tractor involves a much lower capital outlay than the rail switch engine, the ratio of their purchase prices being 10 to 1 or higher. Additionally, the truck tractor, when used as a local service vehicle, requires a crew of only one as compared with two or more for the rail switch engine under commonly accepted railroad operating rules. Indeed, because of these characteristics, a properly organized, high-volume piggyback operation will have most shipment classification performed at the time of loading the trailers on the freight cars of the piggyback train, thus reducing the need for involvement in rail classification yards. Bypassing classification yards can be a major means of shortening the amount of time required for a rail shipment to be completed as well as a cost-reducing device.

The major advantage of rail operation, low intercity line-haul costs, is also largely retained with a containerized system.[14] In the United States, it is usually difficult to reduce truck line-haul costs for general merchandise shipments much below 2 cents per revenue ton-mile, while line-haul costs of 0.7 to 0.8 cent per revenue ton-mile are achievable by rail boxcar. Containerized operations by rail usually have somewhat higher line-haul costs than with boxcars because of a lower revenue to gross weight ratio and higher capital investment per available ton of carrying capacity. However, these disadvantages can be at least partially offset in a well-organized container operation by achieving a much higher utilization rate on rolling stock or by designing the container more efficiently (for example, elimination of wheels or undercarriages).

Costs are incurred when a transfer is made from one mode of locomotion to another, even when such a relatively simple technology as piggybacking is used. Therefore, since the origination and termination costs of piggybacking are essentially the same as those for all-truck transport, the real key to deciding whether or not piggybacking pays is whether the length of the line haul is sufficient to yield enough line-haul cost savings to offset the extra costs of transferring from one mode of locomotion to another. Generally speaking, under North American conditions, line hauls of less than 200 miles are not sufficient to provide the needed offset, line hauls

14. John R. Meyer and others [A7], pp. 151–55.

of over 400 miles are, and line hauls between 200 and 400 miles tend to be in a zone of indifference, where the correct choice depends on specific characteristics like terrain, commodity density, and other special factors.

Experiments also have been conducted with containerization in other modes of transport. For example, considerable testing has been made of fishy-backing, which is essentially the same as piggybacking except that a ship is used for the line haul instead of a train. One difficulty, particularly when in competition with direct land transport, has been the high cost of putting a ship into port, which means that it rarely pays to bring a ship in unless a considerable number of trailers are waiting for loading or unloading at a particular spot. Thus, fishy-backing will either increase inventory costs because of longer required shipping times or increase the length of the line haul, and therefore line-haul costs, because of circuitous routings needed to push the shipments through major ports. Another major disadvantage of fishy-backing is that ship costs, unlike rail costs, are mainly a function of cubic space rather than weight; trailers with their wheels attached represent a considerable waste of cubic space when placed in a ship's hold, so the most practical application of the container concept in shipping has been with containers that are separable from their wheels. Among the major economies in containerized shipping are the elimination of longshoring, pilferage, and similar costs at dockside. Transfer times between ship and shore vehicles are also reduced by containerization. This decreases the ship's time in port and attendant costs, and inventory holding charges as well.

When related to the demand characteristics of different products, the minimal long-run marginal costs reported in Table 10-1 permit a rough approximation to what constitutes a rational allocation of freight traffic between various modes of transport (and a likely one with an approximation to marginal cost pricing). It is reasonably clear that if it is possible to move a low-value commodity in a coastal tanker or lake bulk carrier without incurring intermodal transfers or an overly circuitous routing, these modes have a clear-cut advantage even over such a low-cost competitor as the pipeline. However, wherever circuity or intermodal transfers exist or the commodity is not amenable to water transportation but is, like natural gas, a liquefiable product moving in large, steady volumes, it is transportable with minimum cost by pipeline. If the liquefiability characteristic is not present, or if the bulk product moves at low or unsteady volumes, then barge transportation, where it is available, is usually the next lowest cost alternative. Finally, if the bulk commodity is not conveniently located to water transportation or cannot be pushed through a pipe, rail hopper or boxcars are usually the lowest cost system.

For manufactured commodities, rail boxcars and piggyback or other containerized operations are the most economical modes of transport (at least in North America and Europe) that simultaneously provide a service up to the minimal standards required by higher valued goods. The truck, however, usually renders a superior transportation service, which is often accompanied by significantly lower warehousing, inventory, and other distribution costs for the shipper. For some commodities, these may more than offset any transport cost disadvantage. Some of these economies are due to inherent truck advantages over rail transportation, and some are attributable to the greater flexibility and service orientation of truckers. For example, one reason for some of the competitive successes of the trucking industry may be a decentralized marketing structure. Local truckers and truck representatives, motivated by some form of direct profit sharing or profit incentive, have proved very flexible, even creative, in meeting special shipper needs.

These generalizations about the cost structure as it conditions modal choices are substantiated if one examines the modal split of twenty-nine commodity groups in the United States for 1960, as assembled by Kent and shown in Table 10-2. These largely conform to what would be forecast on the basis of cost and service characteristics, particularly if allowance is made for the substantial portion of truck tonnage attributed to relatively local carriage on short hauls. The tendency for rail and water carriage to be more involved than truck transport with high density (usually bulk) commodities is directly illustrated by the data in Table 10-3 pertaining to tonnages hauled by the different modes classified by shipping density.

Further substantiation of these modal split generalizations is provided by one of the few extensive single-equation investigations of surface freight demand using United States data. This was by Perle, who estimated a demand equation for five commodity groups (products of agriculture, animals and products, mines, forests, and manufacturing and miscellaneous) in each of nine regions, as a function of relative prices of various modes.[15] His dependent variable, tons of freight traffic originated within a region by mode, abstracts from the origin and destination of shipments. The study was largely oriented toward modal choice, and his estimation efforts were

15. Eugene D. Perle [E16], pp. 119–26. His procedure is analogous to the urban demand modeling format that begins with a representation of trip demand and then estimates modal choice before going on to zonal interchange and assignment.

mainly directed at determining price elasticities. Perle found that motor carrier demand was somewhat price elastic for forest and mine products, slightly inelastic for manufactured goods and products of agriculture, and highly inelastic for animal products. Hence, the low-valued, bulk goods were most responsive to price, and high-valued goods the least responsive.

The limited extent of the market for air cargo as compared with the more conventional forms of transportation is readily explained by the high costs of air freight. (The 100-mill air cargo cost reported in Table 10-1 is probably too low for all but a high density, all-cargo jet operation.) Normally, only very high perishability or extremely high value per pound, factors that make inventory costs important, will justify air cargo. Small shipments, particularly of an emergency nature, also are well adapted to air transport.

In general, most of the air cargo in Europe and North America is a result of the creation of new transport markets rather than of a diversion from existing markets. Air cargo may have a more significant role to play in developing countries, particularly where the terrain is mountainous, and, to a lesser extent, where jungle or other wet terrain exists and there is no good river or other water access. In such cases, air cargo has the advantage of bypassing heavy expenditures required for development of ways, either of road or rail, an advantage often accentuated by the relative factor prices. Specifically, lower pilot and other labor costs make air cargo marginally more attractive in less developed countries than in the United States and Western Europe even under relatively conventional geographic conditions. Continued development of jet technology promises to extend the role of air cargo in the near future. Indeed, very large jet freighters may well make air cargo competitive with the truck for longer hauls of high-value cargo.

Concluding Observations

Improvements in modeling procedures and statistical methodology promise to extend our knowledge about intercity transport demand. As noted in Chapter 7, evolution toward systems representations in demand estimation is almost certain, though the character of the emphasis in passenger and freight modeling is likely to differ somewhat. In the case of passenger demand, forecasting location and income changes appears to be far less important than characterizing tastes with regard to price and service dimensions. Trends in the basic macroeconomic determinants of

TABLE 10-2. *Tons and Ton-Miles of Freight Hauled in the United States, by Commodity Group and Mode of Transport, 1960*

(Tons in thousands, ton-miles in millions)

Commodity group number[a]	Commodity group[a]	Railways Tons	Railways Ton-miles	Inland waterways Tons	Inland waterways Ton-miles	Domestic coastlines Ton-miles	Highways Tons	Pipelines Tons	Airlines Tons
01	Farm products	127,936	57,067	15,220	12,059	1,688	367,715	—	—
08	Forest products	6,040	2,503	4	0	78	10,301	—	—
09	Fresh fish and other marine products	48	38	23,136	1,194	84	86	—	—
10	Metallic ores	117,760	24,958	72,579	53,918	421	3,446	—	—
11	Coal	314,400	91,741	125,241	26,193	3,201	131,497	—	—
13	Crude petroleum, natural gas, and natural gasoline	1,888	855	35,251	8,630	60,167	27,996	334,105	—
14	Nonmetallic minerals, except fuels	188,413	32,943	85,562	16,984	6,164	1,043,834	—	—
19	Ordnance and accessories	0	0	0	0	0	0	—	—
20	Food and kindred products	84,104	54,591	5,834	2,130	13,452	122,049	—	—
21	Tobacco products	491	608	1	0	119	448	—	—
22	Basic textiles	772	764	40	23	109	5,984	—	—
23	Apparel and other finished textile products, including knit apparel	395	327	4	0	78	768	—	—
24	Lumber and wood products, except furniture	81,720	49,038	24,637	957	10,332	181,551	—	—
25	Furniture and fixtures	1,174	1,149	0	0	0	4,541	—	—
26	Pulp, paper, and allied products	41,360	27,614	2,434	446	1,405	57,849	—	—
27	Printed matter	540	689	0	0	0	1,491	—	—

28	Chemicals and allied products	55,963	29,890	11,109	6,664	10,812	92,301	—	—
29	Petroleum and coal products	48,197	18,112	114,867	26,094	193,395	303,552	118,027	—
30	Rubber and miscellaneous plastics products	1,484	1,087	20	1	45	1,483	—	—
31	Leather and leather products	102	108	2	0	29	765	—	—
32	Stone, clay, and glass products	44,291	11,795	6,393	1,511	1,543	90,206	—	—
33	Primary metal products	37,603	16,237	9,993	6,551	7,108	59,618	—	—
34	Fabricated metal products, except ordnance, machinery, and transportation equipment	31,233	13,353	12	3	96	70,872	—	—
35	Machinery, except electrical	3,535	2,988	331	43	245	10,316	—	—
36	Electrical machinery equipment and supplies	2,730	2,503	65	8	386	8,686	—	—
37	Transportation equipment	14,860	9,992	907	133	374	30,193	—	—
38	Instruments, photographic and optical goods, watches, and clocks	0	0	0	0	0	0	—	—
39	Miscellaneous products of manufacturing	10,253	6,552	6,349	248	2,400	49,628	—	794
40	Waste and scrap materials	31,063	6,019	11,390	1,012	85	67,270	—	—
	Total	1,247,565	463,521	551,381	164,802	313,816	2,744,446	452,132	794

Source: Malcolm F. Kent [E10], p. 3, Table 1.
a. Official U.S. Bureau of the Budget classification system.

TABLE 10-3. *Tons of Freight Hauled in the United States, by Shipment Density and Mode of Transport, 1960*

(In thousands of tons)

Shipping density (pcf)[a]	Railways	Inland waterways	Highways	Pipelines	Airways
5–9.9	5,640	60	35,693	—	—
10–14.9	11,219	1,428	86,314	—	—
15–19.9	4,883	609	15,974	—	—
20–24.9	15,177	694	46,991	—	—
25–29.9	36,643	9,102	119,006	—	794
30–34.9	63,905	2,719	103,973	—	—
35–39.9	122,302	9,497	145,251	—	—
40–44.9	97,837	96,319	253,821	92,462	—
45–49.9	112,498	33,333	286,448	—	—
50–54.9	328,190	126,246	146,578	—	—
55–59.9	34,718	101,300	237,409	359,670	—
60–64.9	2,521	1	2,952	—	—
65–69.9	9,541	1,196	30,686	—	—
70–74.9	4,588	527	13,247	—	—
80–84.9	7,225	—	4,520	—	—
85–89.9	141	—	671	—	—
90–94.9	69,226	5,310	81,807	—	—
100–104.9	102,656	78,137	919,948	—	—
105–109.9	10,606	—	7,455	—	—
110–114.9	2,114	—	7,134	—	—
115–119.9	658	—	13,791	—	—
120–124.9	—	1,798	—	—	—
130–134.9	10,351	2,193	39,853	—	—
135–139.9	—	171	—	—	—
145–149.9	27,118	3,368	53,813	—	—
155–159.9	1,866	—	427	—	—
160–164.9	76	283	2,181	—	—
165–169.9	1,029	—	997	—	—
170–174.9	7,590	198	—	—	—
180–184.9	4,615	343	2,865	—	—
185–189.9	36,300	—	60,476	—	—
190–194.9	—	34	—	—	—
195–199.9	1,529	1	352	—	—
215–219.9	1,201	—	1,183	—	—
220–224.9	9,795	4,743	6,631	—	—
225–229.9	4,902	1,213	15,167	—	—
250–254.9	941	7	—	—	—
290–294.9	96,847	70,551	—	—	—
310–314.9	1,417	—	832	—	—
Total	1,247,865	551,381	2,744,446	452,132	794

Source: Malcolm F. Kent [E10], p. 4, Table 2.
a. Pounds per cubic foot.

demand tend to be fairly stable. In contrast, attitudes toward scheduling considerations that affect travel time appear to be quite critical. This is reinforced by the need to evaluate and predict the effects of future technologies that promise to be oriented more toward service improvements than toward cost reductions.

In the case of forecasting intercity freight transport, representation of firms' location choices and the nature of their distribution process tend to be fundamental. Once a firm's location and distribution decisions are made, its transport alternatives are constrained. The feedback of the transport systems' performance on these decisions tends to be considerable, but only with a time lag. Modeling these feedbacks will be a task far more difficult than that of representing shippers' preferences for alternative modes, given fixed locations. Even this relatively static demand estimation problem has, however, proved formidable. As a consequence, forecasting and quantification of freight demands are among the least understood aspects of transportation planning.

PART THREE

Project Evaluation

CHAPTER ELEVEN

Benefit Measurement
for Transport Projects

Transport project evaluation, like all public investment evaluation, is directed at an assessment and choice among project
proposals. In economic analyses of these problems, the usual goal is to
maximize net social gains subject to prevailing economic and political
constraints.[1] The systematic evaluation of benefits and costs and the development of investment criteria for individual public projects have been
labeled benefit-cost or cost effectiveness analysis, which is essentially the
development of criteria for planning, designing, and evaluating specific
public projects.[2] The foundations of benefit-cost analysis lie in welfare

1. The significance of any benefit measure will depend on the type of capital budgeting
procedure used. The individual project analysis discussed in this and the next few chapters
involves an accept or reject decision for each project. The choice of a benefit measure tends
to be most important or sensitive when adopting a project-by-project approach of this kind.
This is in contrast to the mathematical programming approach discussed in Part 4, where
projects are evaluated collectively. In the context of a programming approach, the measure
of benefits for each proposed project essentially provides a rank ordering of all proposed
projects. Errors in benefit measurement may to some extent be offsetting in such circumstances. The constraints incorporated in the programming—in particular, the budget constraints—determine the cut-off point for project acceptability rather than the benefit measure
itself. In this latter approach to project evaluation, therefore, the benefit measure tends to
be somewhat less critical.

2. A recent survey of the literature and an excellent bibliography is contained in A. R.
Prest and R. Turvey [F39], pp. 683–731. Marglin has also presented an excellent summary
of both the method and the theoretical foundation of benefit-cost analysis. Stephen A. Marglin
[F26], especially Chap. 1.

economics and microeconomic theory. The objective is to develop means for making decisions on the allocation of resources that will reflect the most desirable use of those resources in terms of allocative efficiency or some other goal defined by society.

The Dimensions of Social Benefits

The net social gains or net benefits of public projects are not easily defined. Transport projects are no exception. The objectives of public projects and hence the relevant benefit measures generally include more than profits, the predominant motive of the private sector. The social benefits of a project can include a variety of market and nonmarket consequences—consumers' valuations of the product purchased, income redistribution, induced increases in employment, income, or productivity, and often a variety of other consequences society deems worthwhile. Transport projects can be subject to an especially large number of these indirect external benefits.

The most common economic criterion for measuring project benefits, and the usual starting point for consideration, is that of maximizing the value of goods consumed, as reflected in consumers' willingness to pay. Consumption benefits are often labeled market-oriented benefits since they are usually traded in some approximate fashion in the marketplace. As noted earlier, however, the nature of transport pricing is such that quantitative assessment of these benefits is often difficult in practice. With market imperfections, prevailing prices sometimes provide an approximate measure only of marginal benefits or opportunity costs.

A variety of external and indirect benefits and costs of a proposed project can be incorporated into the measure of project benefits. Income distribution effects are typical of these. Economists have tended to treat the distribution problem independently of decisions about resource allocation, which are usually directed at achieving the highest aggregate consumption benefits for any given income distribution. The presumption is that redistribution of these aggregate benefits can then be considered in formulating tax or other transfer schemes, to the extent that redistribution is deemed necessary.[3] The presumption that appropriate income redistribution can

3. Mera has developed measures of the trade-off between economic efficiency and equity when there are constraints on redistribution by lump sum transfers. Koichi Mera [F29], pp. 658–74.

be effectuated has, however, not always proved to be realistic. Distribution consequences are therefore typically deemed relevant in public project evaluation, and hence an addition or subtraction from benefits to account for them is sometimes made.

Adjustments for other social or external effects can be similarly achieved. However, political judgments generally are necessary in defining the nature of these social benefits. The planner's or economist's role is usually best limited to describing the nature of a project's effects so these can be evaluated.

The extent to which social and indirect effects should be included as benefits is difficult to determine. Counting external and social benefits in evaluating some projects but not others can distort the allocation of resources, and hence an argument can be made for maintaining consistency in treating externalities. The discipline of the marketplace is so easily forgotten in these situations that some empirical market evidence about benefit projections may be important as an antidote to the excesses of particular lobbies or bureaucracies.[4] One widely advocated antidote is the imposition of user charges. Recovering benefits with user charges suggests a profit-oriented benefit measure based on market prices.

Perhaps the most difficult issue in measuring an individual project's benefits is that of interpreting the system effects through the rest of the economy; for example, changes in demand and cost curves, employment, or productivity. These system effects can be substantial when the project being contemplated is large. Particularly important secondary effects which need to be examined are whether sectors affected by a proposed project will enjoy economies or diseconomies of scale and whether any induced changes in factor productivity occur. In an individual project evaluation, these adjustments are often made on an ad hoc basis as well as possible. Many can only be treated satisfactorily, however, in a full systems approach.

Benefit Measurement in a Conventional Welfare Context

The conventional theory of welfare economics is based on maximization of utility subject to constraint and is typically translated to the maximization

4. Roland N. McKean [F25].

of the value of consumer benefits. In perfectly competitive market economies, consumers' valuation of the consumption benefits of any commodity will be reflected in the demand curve, which indicates willingness to pay. Maximizing the total value of consumption benefits in the economy is equivalent to maximizing the area under the demand curve for all commodities, the price indicating the value of each incremental change in output. In Figure 11-1, this would be the area *ABCE* for a typical commodity, where *AB* measures the quantity consumed and *AD* the price.

An allocation of resources such that their marginal benefit in each sector equals their marginal cost ensures that the value of total consumption benefits, or net benefits, is maximized. If all commodities are perfectly divisible, the satisfaction of this condition can be expressed in terms of the marginal conditions of welfare economics.

The marginal analysis of standard welfare economics is inapplicable, however, when discrete changes in output are being contemplated and, in particular, for discerning whether any one good should be forgone completely or a new product produced. For projects that constitute discrete changes in output, observed market prices no longer serve as adequate measures of benefits and costs for nonmarginal changes. These prices typically understate the value to consumers of a discrete change in output. This is best illustrated by reference to the total area under the demand curve for a typical commodity. Consumers will pay an amount, generally

FIGURE 11-1. *Marshallian Demand Curve*

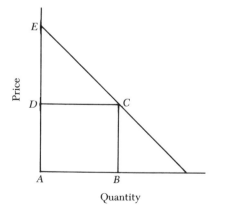

labeled consumers surplus, in excess of the single price charged.[5] When a finite increase in output occurs, there will usually result a positive consumers surplus which will need to be evaluated. Similarly, there will be nonzero consumers and producers surpluses[6] forgone everywhere in the economy as a consequence. Strictly speaking, it is the net effect of all these changes that is required for a decision.[7]

Use of the market demand curve to estimate consumers surplus as a measure of benefits presumes that monetary amounts under the demand curve adequately represent satisfaction or utility. This relationship between the demand price and utility or social welfare, implicit in the aggregation of individual's demand curves to a market demand curve, will depend on the distribution of income.[8]

Some subtle difficulties arise concerning the adjustment for income effects as different prices are employed. Since the marginal utility of money will usually differ as a good's price changes, every unit of expenditure indicated by a demand curve need not be of equal value. For example, if demand for the commodity is elastic, an increase in price reduces total expenditure on the commodity, and hence the greater expenditure on other commodities implies that the marginal utility of a dollar is falling. If demand is inelastic, the reverse occurs. Hence the area under a typical demand curve can be a poor estimate of benefits measured in dollars of constant marginal utility. It has sometimes been suggested that this inaccuracy be mitigated by

5. This would usually be defined as the area CDE in Figure 11-1. Much effort has been expended in the literature in a discussion of what is the best or appropriate definition of consumers surplus. Marshall's original definition was the amount of money people would be willing to pay in excess of the current price for that amount which they now consume. (Alfred Marshall [F27].) Subsequently, it was pointed out that a distinction should be made between the compensation a person must be paid to forgo the commodity versus the amount he would pay for the opportunity to buy it. There will be no difference when there is no income effect, that is, the marginal utility of income remains constant. This discussion, extensive in the postwar literature, is not very important from a planning viewpoint, since income effects are generally assumed negligible in practical applications.

For a discussion of meaning and measurement of consumers surplus, see Alexander Henderson [F10], pp. 117–21; J. R. Hicks [F12], pp. 68–74; E. J. Mishan [F30], pp. 27–33; J. R. Hicks [F13].

6. Producers surplus is defined analogously to consumers surplus as that amount by which the competitive supply price exceeds the minimum paid to factors to keep them from switching to an alternative use.

7. This form of the compensation test is suggested by Nicholas Kaldor [F19], p. 549.

8. Hla Myint [F34]; Hicks [F13]. For a summary of consumers surplus and its role in conventional welfare theory, see Mishan [F30], pp. 197–250.

defining a demand curve that has been adjusted downward for the positive income effect created by lowering the money price of a good, an adjustment such that the marginal utility of income remains constant for all price levels. Unfortunately, making these adjustments typically requires more knowledge about underlying utility functions than is generally available.

Because of the difficulty of making such adjustments, an alternative procedure has been suggested: estimating the maximum number of dollars, regardless of utility value, that people would pay rather than do without a particular good or service; that is, the revenue a discriminating monopolist might extract for his product. If this figure is larger than the total cost of providing the good or service, production is usually considered to be economically justified. This is an attempt at a direct measure of the so-called compensation test: For any project, would the gainers be able to compensate the losers, who are the previous claimants on the resources?[9] This measure, however, is also not easy to derive. Perfect price discrimination would reduce the amount of money income a consumer would have available at each level of price and output for the commodity. The income effect of perfect price discrimination would shift downward the conventional demand curve relating how much the consumer would pay.[10] The larger the share of the budget the commodity represented, the larger the shift would be.

In general, important conceptual problems with consumers surplus measures arise from the fact that the demand curve and associated consumers surplus for any one commodity is a static, partial equilibrium concept. As such, all the problems of using partial equilibrium measures in a welfare context must be faced.[11] Consumers surplus in any single market is uniquely defined only for a particular income level and its distribution and resource allocation decisions in all other markets. Increased demand for any commodity normally will result in reductions in output in other sectors, unless there is less than full employment or induced productivity changes. Significant effects on relative prices and changes in the pattern of output may result. Such changes result in changes in con-

9. There is also no guarantee from a single conventional measure of consumers surplus that a proposed project would meet the "Samuelson criterion" that the consumers surplus should be positive for all conceivable welfare distributions. Paul A. Samuelson [F40], pp. 1–29.

10. This would occur as long as the good were not inferior, meaning that less would be consumed as incomes fall.

11. Ian M. D. Little [F23], pp. 174–77. E. J. Mishan [F31] presents a good summary of this problem.

sumers surpluses throughout the economy. It is therefore necessary to weigh the positive consumers and producers surpluses in the project in question against the surpluses forgone in alternative uses of the resources, in either the public or the private sector as the case may be.

Neglect of these forgone surpluses can be correct only under certain restrictive assumptions. For example, if the economy is perfectly competitive and constant costs exist everywhere, there will be no producers surpluses and they can be ignored. In addition, if the change in the pattern of output induced by the investment in a particular project results in only marginal changes throughout the economy, no effects on consumers surpluses occur, since under these assumptions there is no consumers or producers surplus lost on the marginal unit of output forgone in any sector. To be correct, these marginal changes must consist of infinitesimal changes. There are no a priori grounds to justify this particular assumption (except in the limit, which, of course, defines away the problem). In most practical planning circumstances, and certainly for large projects, the possibility of nonincremental changes should at least be explored.

Simple pragmatic (but nevertheless important) difficulties can arise, moreover, when attempting to measure empirically the full area under a portion of a demand curve. The investigator trying to estimate a demand function normally can observe only a limited number of closely clustered price and quantity data, to which he can give only a first approximation to a best-fitting demand function. This will be particularly true for new products or services. Conventional empirical procedures will only yield information about the impact of price, scheduling, service, or other variables in the neighborhood of the immediate observations. Little of substance is known about the shape of the demand function beyond the limited range of the available data. Coupled with the information about demand, pricing, and cost in alternative sectors necessary to value the possibility of forgone surpluses elsewhere, the data requirements are obviously extensive.

In sum, for large projects involving discrete changes in output, the conventional marginal analysis is usually difficult to apply. Somewhat paradoxically, it is in these cases that straightforward marginal analysis typically gives way to consumers surplus measures.[12] The problems, conceptually and empirically, of employing consumers surplus measures are

12. For a good defense of the usefulness of consumers surplus measures, see Myint [F34], and Hicks [F12], p. 68. Mishan ([F31], p. 245) probably summarizes the views of many when he concludes his discussion of consumers surplus with the plaintive query: "After all, what other practical procedures are open to us in a comparison of true situations?"

also most acute in such circumstances. Generally speaking, there are no really satisfactory simple, partial equilibrium measures of benefits when market imperfections or indivisibilities render the usual market information an incomplete reflection of benefits and costs.

In assessing the effects of a large project throughout the economy, a number of approximations must be made of systemwide consequences.[13] The estimation of benefits is perhaps the area where this problem is most acute, with pricing consequences a close second. This also explains much of the ambiguity and the lack of a consensus on what is an appropriate measure of project benefits. Large projects are also, of course, the cases for which evaluation might be most aided by a systems analysis aimed at tracing broad developmental implications over time. Indeed, the distinguishing feature and major advantage of a systems analysis is that many effects of a particular capital investment, which are considered to be external in the individual project planning methodology, are incorporated into the planning process via the systems approach.

Transport Benefit Measures in Practice

Conflicting views on project benefit measurement generally reduce to recommendations that different areas under the demand curve be used to measure benefits. Many of these views are the result of different assumptions as to how the facility is to be priced. Varying user prices will affect the rate at which the facility is used and therefore the benefits to be realized. There are also conflicting opinions about the evaluation of any increase in demand that results from a new facility.

Among the more commonly employed or proposed benefit measures for transport project analyses are the following:

Single price measures
1. The current price charged for the facility multiplied by the expected increase in the quantity of transportation consumed. This measure seems most appropriate when the new facility reduces travelers' costs or time,

---

13. Nor is the problem of evaluating system effects in a project planning context confined to public transport planning. The considerable literature in benefit-cost analysis which has arisen from water resource planning struggles with this difficulty. McKean [F25]; Maynard M. Hufschmidt, John V. Krutilla, and Julius Margolis, with the assistance of Stephen A. Marglin [F18]; or Arthur Maass and others [F24].

hence inducing more trips, but where the facility charge remains unchanged.

2. The existing quantity of output multiplied by the increase in price made possible by the increase in the quality of service. This measure presumes the price increase is such that no change in output occurs. With emphasis on the change in price rather than the change in quantity, a project is suggested that improves the performance of a facility qualitatively; for instance, an airport landing system that increases the safety of air travel.

3. A determination of the maximum revenue that can be obtained from the facility by a single price.

4. A determination of the maximum profit that could be obtained from the facility, subject to the constraint that only one price be charged. This measure amounts to pursuing single-price profit maximization, as described in Chapter 2.

Multiple price measures

5. A determination of the maximum profit (or revenue) that could be extracted by a perfectly discriminating monopolist. Such a full area measure would correspond, at least roughly, to the consumers-surplus-oriented benefit measures discussed above.

6. An important special case of a multiple pricing measure is that of simulating any discriminatory pricing practices employed by alternative or competitive facilities. This measure may be especially relevant in a mixed market environment where considerations of second best suggest that pricing of public facilities should follow or adapt to private practice where such behavior deviates from pure competitive behavior.

A simple example from the highway area can be used to illustrate some of these benefit measures. Assume that Figure 11-2 illustrates transportation users' cost curves (operating and time costs) before and after a new facility becomes available, for example, a new road. The cost curves AC_0 and AC_1 denote average operating costs on the existing and new facilities exclusive of user charges. $AC_0(P_0)$ is average cost including a facility user charge of P_0. The average fixed cost curve representing facility costs is shown as AFC_0. An average cost pricing scheme is portrayed by the price P_0, which results in demand Q_0 and receipts that just cover the existing facility's capital and maintenance costs. The area OP_0XQ_0 is the user charge revenue realized for the existing facility. As noted in Chapter 2, this sort of average cost pricing scheme aimed at financial recoupment of capital costs is fairly

FIGURE 11-2. *Illustrative Highway Demand and User Cost Curves*

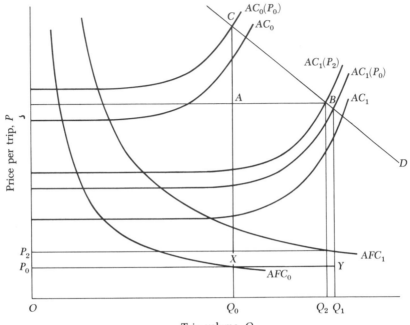

typical in transportation systems. While different benefit measurement schemes tend to be related, at least implicitly, to different pricing schemes, it does not necessarily follow that adoption of any benefit measure implies use of the corresponding pricing policy.

Figure 11-3 portrays the demand curves for the existing and new facilities (D_0 and D_1) as functions of the facility charge employed. These are constructed by subtracting vertically the costs incurred by the user from the user demand curve, D, shown in Figure 11-2. For example, at quantity Q_0 the facility demand curve, D_1, for the new facility would be defined by the distance (on Figure 11-2) from C to the intersection of the Q_0 line with the cost curve AC_1; for the old facility—that is, the D_0 curve—the relevant distance at Q_0 would be from C to the cost curve AC_0. This construction nets out of the demand curve the cost of resources directly borne by the user. (Presumably travelers value all costs at their marginal worth, including their own time cost.) Consequently, the facility demand curves define the excess of the demand price over average costs or the maximum which can be recovered to defray the costs of the facility.

As noted, the demand for a new project or facility and often the benefits are typically derived from changes or improvements in operating or other travel costs. This conforms to the standard cost-benefit analysis that appears in the transportation literature, in which cost and time savings, safety improvements, and so forth are the basis for estimating benefits. Average operating and fixed costs for the new facility are denoted in Figure 11-2 by AC_1 and AFC_1 respectively. Inclusive of the previous charge of P_0, the perceived costs to the traveler are $AC_1(P_0)$ in Figure 11-2. The quantity Q_1 will be consumed if price P_0 is charged. Total facility receipts are $P_0 \cdot Q_1$ and the increase in facility receipts would be XQ_0Q_1Y. This measure has a considerable history as a proxy for project benefits, with the increase in user receipts from the old to the new project used to value the new project. It corresponds to the first measure in the above listing of alternatives.

FIGURE 11-3. *Derived Facility Demand Curves*

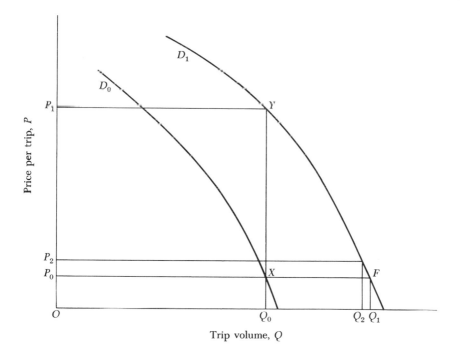

Alternative pricing schemes, of course, may be relevant, and they will have an impact on the measure of benefits. Referring to Figure 11-3, a common benefit measure, and one suggested fairly early for highways, is to multiply the travelers' cost saving resulting from the new facility by the previous quantity of trips made (shown as area P_0XYP_1 in Figure 11-3). This is equivalent to the second measure—benefits measured by multiplying current use by the toll which would reduce demand to its former level—in this case P_1.

The third measure—revenue maximization at a single user price—would have the user price set at the unitary elastic point on the demand curve D_1. The fourth—a profit maximizing pricing policy—would require selecting that facility price where the marginal revenue curve corresponding to demand curve D_1 intersects the marginal cost curve derived from the costs arising from facility use. A profit maximizing pricing policy will result in a somewhat higher price than the revenue maximizing alternative, except in the special case where additional users entail no added operating costs (for example, road maintenance may be relatively insensitive to use in some circumstances), in which case the two criteria are identical.

Each alternative pricing scheme will result in a different use of the facility and different amounts of benefits realized and user receipts collected. For example, marginal long-run capacity costs might be used as the basis for pricing; or some other pricing scheme intermediate between average and marginal costs might be employed. One alternative, P_2, just sufficient to cover the new average capacity costs, is shown in Figures 11-2 and 11-3. Although in Figure 11-2 unit costs of capacity are portrayed as increasing, the discussion is independent of this particular portrayal of scale effects.

Similarly, the short-run congestion toll solution outlined in Chapter 4 would entail varying the facility toll as the facility size is changed. These tolls serve as a means of optimally allocating the fixed facility in the short run but are also properly viewed as an economic rent or price for capacity, which should be compared to the marginal cost of added capacity, as in the conventional theory of the firm. Regarding these short-run congestion toll receipts as the benefit measure, facility size is adjusted until the marginal increase in benefits equals the marginal cost of added capacity. For facilities of divisible size, these correspond to typical marginal benefit and cost curves.

Finally, of course, there are a variety of multiple-price policies which might be pursued in order to raise revenue, effect certain income transfers, or induce a better pattern of resource use. The fifth and sixth measures are two typical examples of such policies, though they hardly exhaust the possibilities. As noted, introduction of multiple-pricing schemes raises the problem of how to treat intramarginal gains to induced travelers. Quite common in the economic literature is the suggestion that some form of consumers surplus be used to measure gains to new users, although induced travelers have in some cases been omitted from the calculations.[14]

A typical recommendation is that the benefits to new travelers be valued as the area under the demand curve (area *ABC* in Figure 11-2), plus payments in the form of user charges. As suggested earlier, and usually recognized by the advocates, such consumers surplus measures are subject to the important qualification that the change in travel demand represents a small portion of travelers' incomes, which allows the presumption that the marginal utility of income is essentially constant. In addition, for such measures, it is helpful if facility users are participants in reasonably competitive markets (to avoid measuring how much market prices diverge from marginal social costs and other associated second-best difficulties).[15] Abstracting from externalities, consumers surplus measures are, of course, the upper limit on any sensible benefit measure based on the demand curve. Only in one notable case, the American Association of State Highway Officials "Red Book" recommendation in the highway area, was an even larger benefit measure employed for induced travelers—the change in operating cost times the increase in volume.[16] This, in effect, is an area twice that of *ABC* in Figure 11-2.

No one of these alternative measures of benefits is necessarily correct in all circumstances. As the earlier discussion of pricing policies indicated, the choice of an appropriate pricing procedure can be very complex. The same is true for the closely related question of benefit measures. Nevertheless, observations on the relative utility of the different measures can be made.

To begin, the full-area benefit measures, based implicitly on multiple-pricing schemes, aside from whether or not they are recovered, are clearly difficult to apply rigorously. Their appropriate use entails quite complex accounting of system or general equilibrium effects. In many transport

14. Clarkson H. Oglesby and Laurence I. Hewes [F36], pp. 84–90.
15. David M. Winch [F47], pp. 46–48; Herbert Mohring and Mitchell Harwitz [F33], pp. 50–52.
16. American Association of State Highway Officials [F1], pp. 14–15.

applications, the net gains to intramarginal travelers may be relatively small if fairly and exhaustively calculated, netting out all the systemwide effects. In economies characterized by relatively well-developed and competitive markets and near or at full employment, transport demand increases will tend to be at the expense of demand reductions elsewhere. For example, the high price elasticity noted for intercity air passenger travel is, in the case of pleasure trips, largely a diversion from private automobiles, and in the case of business air travel may reflect reductions in other marketing or management expenses such as telephone services. Similarly, in the case of air freight, increased demand may be more and more often at the expense of intercity trucking.

It is difficult to make a case that the net results of these substitutions or changes in demand as a result of changes in relative prices yield a large net gain in consumers surplus. In less developed countries, consumers surpluses may be more significant. There, however, the induced effects on income levels and other macroeconomic changes are likely to be of more concern than the static welfare changes implied by consumers surpluses.

As compared with the usual market criterion based on a single price, full-area measures may also establish a different standard for determining whether the production of a good is economically justified in the public rather than the private sector. In a private market economy, the entrepreneur will be expected to follow profit maximization in determining his pricing strategy and in making his investment allocations. Normally, he will have only limited scope for price discrimination. His test for determining whether a good should be produced is that, at some level of output, the price that consumers are willing to pay for it is greater than its cost at that output. By contrast, the entire area under any demand curve, or price-discriminating monopolistic practices, will normally result in higher estimates of benefits and therefore could suggest the production of goods that would be excluded if reasonably conventional private market criteria are used.

In short, for discrete projects for which intramarginal surpluses exist, market prices, even when markets are perfect, usually do not provide all the information necessary for good benefit measures. Caution and prudence in interpreting and assessing these intramarginal benefits is probably the best advice. Indeed, a reasonably strong case can be made for counting as gross benefits only the area under the demand curve which can be recouped by a single price. Similarly, using the same pricing procedure for the project in question as employed by competing facilities (implying a benefit measure like the fifth listed above) has much to recommend it.

Social and External Effects

Market prices may not accurately reflect social values for a number of reasons. As an important consequence, the incentive structure created by reference to market information may not lead to a socially optimal resource allocation. Hirshleifer classifies these potential divergences as being of two types: extra economic values; and incorrect market values.[17]

The most familiar example of an extra economic value relates to the distribution of income. As noted, measures of willingness to pay are dependent on the distribution of income, with alternative distributions of income leading to different demand functions and different market information. The prevailing distribution of income will thus influence market pricing and resource allocation decisions. Moreover, direct means for redistributing income may not be readily available in some environments, for example, many less developed countries. The distribution of income, among income classes and especially among regions, can thus be an important consideration in some project evaluations. Furthermore, transport projects often have a considerable impact on regional location decisions, again potentially implying income redistribution effects of considerable importance.[18] It is therefore hardly surprising that motives of income redistribution have a way of appearing implicitly or explicitly in the rationale for many public transport investments.[19]

Other nonmarket values have been deemed important in transport project evaluation. Military preparedness has long been a basis for many investments in intercity highways and airport and airways facilities, for subsidizing construction and operation of a merchant fleet, and for support of airline operations. Similarly, in the international airline market, externalities such as international prestige or balance-of-payments considerations have become a major force in shaping the industry.[20] The contributions of trans-

17. Jack Hirshleifer, James C. de Haven, and Jerome W. Milliman [G11], pp. 74–75.
18. In the context of economic development where capital markets and tax systems are not well developed, regional income effects can be of substantial importance.
19. In the urban transportation framework, for example, the income distribution effects which tend to be of concern often take on a strong locational bent. Much of the agitation for public transit support in the United States appears to have as one of its major motives that of providing support to central business districts. Mass transit systems are generally construed as conducive to more centralized location patterns and of positive benefit to downtown business locations and residences. Federal subsidy support is thus one means of transferring income to the core city and providing relief of part of the tax burden facing downtown mayors.
20. Mahlon R. Straszheim [A11], especially Chaps. 2 and 11.

portation to economic development also have been much advertised. In many instances, these externalities can be difficult to assess in any objective quantitative way.

As for divergences between market prices and social values, most attention is usually given to cases where market prices omit any reflection of certain social costs. Thus, much publicity has been given to the fact that urban highways create noise, smog, and poor aesthetics. These clearly are consequences that are external to the decision making of private automobile, truck, and bus owners and, generally speaking, to decisions to invest in public road building. Another prominent example is airport noise. Still another case, which may merit particular attention in the coming decade, is the sonic boom likely to be associated with the operation of large supersonic aircraft.

Divergence between market prices and social values may also arise from market imperfections. For example, monopolistic practices in product markets, sometimes even in regulated ones, may maintain prices in excess of marginal costs. As noted earlier, if this circumstance is widespread in an economy, the costs of producing a project's service or product may understate the value of the output forgone in other sectors since the price, or the value of marginal social benefits, elsewhere may be above marginal factor costs. Monopsony or distortions in factor supplies can have similar effects. In this case, factor payments include a monopoly rent which should be excluded when calculating social costs. The difficulty of making adjustments in pricing to compensate for such second-best considerations was considered in Chapter 5. Unfortunately, adjustment in any one sector's benefit measure for these effects is a difficult, if not practically impossible, task.

Scale economies and diseconomies can constitute another important class of externalities. The conventional model of welfare economics assumes that factor and product prices are independent of the output of the project in question; hence prices reflect social valuations exactly. This assumption is violated if significant productivity changes are induced by a project. Evaluation of these productivity changes entails an examination of scale economies or diseconomies in all affected sectors.

Again, the empirical relevance of such effects is most important when the project is large. However, this is also true when many other systemwide effects occur in the economy; for example, price and cost changes resulting from changes in the pattern of output. Identification of the productivity increases induced by and solely attributable to the project in question will be hazardous. Nevertheless, such calculations will probably be needed when reviewing large projects, especially in less developed economies. If such induced productivity measures are attempted and prove substantial, they are often accompanied by considerable changes in investment patterns, employment rates, and location effects.

Location effects are often suggested as an externality particularly worthy of evaluation with transport projects. Care must be exercised, however, that what is labeled a benefit is not merely a transfer of wealth or change in value of present assets. For example, examining changes in land rents as a reflection of the change in valuation that occurs because of a new transport facility too often considers only the increases in land values around the new facility but not the corresponding reductions that may occur elsewhere.

Induced longer-term effects on employment and investment will be relevant mainly when there is less than full employment and when there are capital market imperfections. If unemployment exists, market prices for factors presumably overstate real costs. However, adjustment in benefit evaluation in these circumstances is by no means straightforward. A distinction between sources of unemployment is relevant. Often unemployment will be attributable to market imperfections in matching available labor skills with demands. To the extent that transport projects can employ otherwise unemployed labor whose location is such that other means of relief are not readily available, transport projects may have special benefits. Nevertheless, means of relief other than undertaking transport projects usually exist. Consistency in investment allocations requires that the positive employment effect which can arise from other expenditures possibly displaced by the transport investment be taken into account.

Because of social and external benefits, more sophisticated scoring systems for benefit evaluations than a monetary scale are sometimes suggested for public investment programs. Specifically, a unit of measurement is sought for benefits which allows almost any desired weighting of economic, social, and political consequences.[21] One obvious difficulty with any such scoring system is that it increases the possibility that investment decisions will be made on purely subjective grounds. Also, relating these more general benefit

21. Some experiments with these broader scoring systems have been undertaken as part of the program to apply program budgeting techniques to the evaluation of the civilian welfare programs of the United States government. For an account of some of the problems involved in making such application, see David Novick, ed. [F35], and Robert Dorfman, ed. [F4].

measures to monetary estimates of project costs is by no means straight-forward. One suggestion for placing costs and benefits on an equivalent basis in such cases might be to calibrate the number of benefit units realized per dollar expended on previous projects. After both benefits and costs are expressed in the same units, project evaluation can, of course, proceed with the same techniques as when monetary measures are directly employed.

Finally, in any assembly of external benefits, it must be borne in mind that externalities normally do not enter into rankings of alternatives within the private sector of a mixed or market economy. This is not an argument for excluding these broader considerations in the public sectors, but, as in the case of forgone producers or consumers surpluses, suggests an evaluation of the net external benefits and costs that might be forgone because a public project displaces private activity.

Summary

There is seemingly no simple practical (as contrasted with theoretical) measure of benefits that can be used for individual project evalutions which will always yield unique and unambiguous results, particularly when considering public investments. Essentially, the difficulty is that the supply and demand curves of conventional, static economic analysis, which are necessarily the basic analytical and empirical tools of individual project evaluations, do not convey all the information that a government agency desires or needs to make rational investment choices. All the dynamic implications of investment choices, including a compendium of all the adjustments induced in the rest of the economy, would be desirable, but that much information is seldom, if ever, available.

Disregarding external effects, the benefit measure which would normally produce a rough parity between the public and private sectors in a mixed economy would be one based on a pricing policy for the public sector which best simulates private enterprise in the same society. This usually should be simple profit maximization or some close variant. By the same token, if there is extensive monopolistic price discrimination in the private sector, a reasonable policy for determining the level of public investments might be the application of discriminatory pricing principles in the public sector as well.

The existence of significant external effects, however, interferes with any attempt to establish identical accounting schemes in the public and private sectors. External effects often cannot be recouped by user charges. In cases where recouping indirect benefits is infeasible, the inclusion of indirect effects in the benefit measure can affect the relative size of the capital budgets of the public and private sectors. Decisions regarding the weighting of indirect benefits can also involve the determination of an alternative to monetary valuations and the general question of the advisability of transport subsidies.

In general, the benefit measure to be preferred depends on decisions about capital budgeting and pricing and on other broad considerations such as the government's ability to sustain subsidy costs, the fiscal position of the government, and the extent to which resources in the economy are being effectively used. The pricing and investment procedures followed throughout the rest of the economy are also relevant. The advantages and disadvantages of using a variety of pricing schemes implied by the various market measures of benefits, within the context of individual project evaluation, will be considered in greater detail in Chapter 14.

CHAPTER TWELVE

Discounting Benefits
and Costs

CAPITAL BUDGETING CRITERIA were developed by economists in the context of private investment decisions and are an integral
part of the economic theory of the firm.[1] Their application in the public

1. The best procedure for evaluating benefits and costs which occur over time almost
invariably is to determine the discounted present value of a project, sometimes called
discounted present worth of net benefits. This criterion is usually simple to apply and has
fewer disadvantages than any other standard criterion conventionally employed for project
evaluation. The advantages are discussed in Appendix B.

In notation, the discounted present value (DPV) is

$$DPV = \sum_{i=0}^{n} w_i(GB_i - C_i)$$

where

GB_i = gross benefits of the project in year i
C_i = the cost of the project in year i, excluding depreciation but including any amortization payments on foreign debt associated with the project
w_i = the weight assigned to the net benefits in year i
n = the number of years in the life of the project

The usual weight, w_t, for the net benefits occurring in year t is found by letting w_t equal
$1/(1+d_t)^t$ where d is the interest or discount rate. When the discount rate is the same for
each succeeding pair of periods the formula reduces to one quite commonly given in the
literature:

$$DPV = (GB_0 - C_0) + \frac{(GB_1 - C_1)}{(1+i)} + \frac{(GB_2 - C_2)}{(1+i)^2} + \text{etc.}$$

This is a convenient simplification though it is not always empirically justified.

sector, which is almost invariably the major concern of transport planners, involves several unsettled issues.[2]

The potential welfare implications or advantages of using the market rate of interest for discounting are quite well defined in the case of a perfect capital market. The market rate of interest then reflects the terms on which consumers are willing to trade present for future consumption. Insofar as the government regards itself as an individual competing with other members of society for scarce economic resources, it should behave as conventional economic theory indicates private individuals should behave, undertaking all investments that have a positive present value when discounted at the market rate of interest. With competition, use of the market rate should assure that the marginal utility of the last dollar spent in the public sector equals that of the last dollar spent in the private sector.

The argument that the government should use the market rate of interest is by no means compelling, however, in all circumstances. The public sector may have broader objectives than income maximization. The existence of externalities, the need for income redistribution, or the pursuit of full employment, price stability, or foreign exchange conservation may suggest public action at odds with that suggested by market rates. For example, job creation may be construed as the most important current objective of public policy; the discount rate for comparing alternative patterns of employment opportunities over the next decade need not be the discount rate that would be used to compare different time patterns of consumption benefits. Moreover, capital markets may not be perfect. In short, the public sector cannot usually act in the capital market without cognizance of its effects on the price of capital, or on other important variables in the economy.

Several alternatives to the market rate of interest for discounting have been suggested for public projects. The advantages and disadvantages of using market rates or some alternative discount rate will be reviewed below, with particular attention to the circumstances in which the market rate is an appropriate or inappropriate choice.

2. Analysts of investment projects often act as if the date at which either benefits or costs occur is irrelevant. In a survey of twenty preinvestment studies financed primarily by the Agency for International Development and the International Bank for Reconstruction and Development, it was revealed that in only one of the studies were weights assigned to gross benefits and costs according to when they occurred. In all other studies, estimated benefits were added together. Clell G. Harral and Tillo E. Kuhn [F9], p. 169.

The Market Rate of Interest in the Context of Perfect Capital Markets

The welfare significance of the market rate of interest rests fundamentally on the assumption of perfect competition. Each individual is assumed (1) to have a known and certain stream of future income; (2) to face a market rate of interest that indicates the terms on which he can borrow or lend money; (3) to desire to maximize his welfare over time; and (4) to depend for his welfare only on his own levels of consumption in different time periods. Each individual maximizes welfare over time by borrowing or lending at the prevailing interest rate, subject to the budget constraints implied by his income stream. Each borrows or lends until his marginal valuation of an additional dollar of future income, his marginal time preference, equals the market rate of interest, the terms on which he can exchange present for future income. The market rate of interest will therefore reflect individuals' marginal time preferences, or the preferences for extra future consumption relative to extra present consumption.

Firms are assumed to behave similarly. Each firm is assumed to be confronted by a set of productive investment opportunities, each opportunity yielding a known future income. In addition, each firm (1) has a given present income and assets; (2) faces a market rate of interest which indicates the terms on which it can lend or borrow money; (3) wishes to maximize its welfare over time; and (4) depends for its welfare only on the amount of its net income in each time period. A firm maximizes its present net worth if it chooses that kind of productive investment with the highest present value, financing this investment by borrowing or lending as the situation dictates. The discount rate used is the market rate of interest.[3]

The actions of all individuals and firms, who behave as if their conduct had no effect on the market rate of interest, collectively determine that rate. If the capital market is perfect, the resultant market rate of interest indicates how all households and firms value a marginal trade-off of present versus future income. This valuation will be based on the prevailing distribution of income, and hence the normative significance of the market rate of interest will depend on that distribution.

3. Irving Fisher [G6]. For a mathematical presentation, see any standard work on mathematical economics, such as James M. Henderson and Richard E. Quandt [F11], Chap. 9; or Jack Hirshleifer [G10], p. 226.

Determining the market rate of interest as a measure of time preference is a difficult empirical exercise in practice. For example, Krutilla and Eckstein sought to estimate the national preferences for future consumption relative to extra present consumption for the United States based on actual borrowing and lending decisions.[4] They began with the observations that different individuals borrow at different interest rates and that an individual usually cannot lend at the same interest rate at which he can borrow. (This discrepancy, of course, is a deviation from the perfect capital market model.) Three categories of households were considered: lenders, borrowers in the mortgage market, and borrowers obtaining short-term consumer credit. Households were also separated into ten levels of annual income. When a household had both consumer debt and mortgage debt, the higher interest rate (that is, on consumer debt) was assumed to be the marginal rate. When a household had an annual income above $15,000, only the lending rate of interest was considered, and an average lending rate was calculated for each income group as the weighted average of the after-tax average rate of return for all types of financial assets owned by the income group. The Krutilla and Eckstein calculations for the United States suggest an average annual rate of preference for extra present consumption relative to extra future consumption ranging from 4.6 percent for households with annual income in excess of $15,000 to 7 percent for households with annual incomes below $3,000.

This represents an important attempt, the most ambitious effort to date, at measurement of time preference in a context of relatively perfect capital markets. Nevertheless, as the authors realize, this study is unsatisfactory in certain respects and yields only approximate results.[5] Krutilla and Eckstein were forced to use the average interest rate rather than the interest rate on the marginal amount borrowed or lent. They were also unable to isolate risk premiums on various financial assets or the effects of liquidity, default, and changes in the general price level on the structure of interest rates. Their calculation of the preference for extra future consumption relative to extra present consumption for each income group was based on an assignment of equal weights to each household within each income group. In short, even in a circumstance in which the assumptions of a perfect capital market are not strained beyond credulity, empirical deter-

4. John V. Krutilla and Otto Eckstein [F21], Chap. 4.
5. For a detailed criticism of the study by Krutilla and Eckstein, see Martin S. Feldstein [G5], pp. 117–34.

mination of the marginal rate of time preference or *the* interest rate that reflects private decisions in the capital markets is a difficult task.

As a practical matter, of course, the assumption of a perfectly functioning and riskless capital market is only a first approximation, and one which may not be realistic in many circumstances. Even relatively sophisticated North American firms do not always follow the prescription derived from the conventional economic model, which compares the present value of various investment projects when discounted at the market rate of interest. If private entrepreneurs are not, in fact, using the market rate of interest in their discounting as a basis for their borrowing and lending decisions, the welfare implications of prevailing market rates are not obvious. Similarly, price may not play a fundamental role in capital rationing. Particularly in the developing countries, capital may be allocated at least partially on the basis of family, religion, or caste, and usury laws or other public regulation may affect interest rates. Even where more highly developed capital markets exist, the predominance of internal financing through retained earnings, reinforced by market power due to advertising and entry barriers, may imply that capital rationing will not always be closely attuned to market rates. Defining the optimal rate of time preference in these circumstances is a difficult second-best problem.

The Case for a Social Rate of Discount below Market Rates

An additional criticism of the conventional or competitive capital market model is that there may be important external or social effects that the market rate of interest does not reflect. That is, the assumption that an individual's present welfare depends only on the level of his own consumption at each point in time is challenged. Marglin has been the principal spokesman for this point of view, arguing that an individual's welfare depends not only on his own level of consumption, but also on the consumption of other members of society. Because of this particular external effect, Marglin suggests that citizens may rationally instruct the government to undertake certain investments because each one wants the government to force everyone else to reduce his present consumption in order to increase the consumption of future generations. The existence of such external effects, and the state's ability to force all members of society to participate, may imply a social rate of discount below the market rate of interest. Hence, the amount of public investment chosen by the present generation acting collectively will not, in Marglin's model, usually be the same as would be chosen by people acting unilaterally.[6]

The essence of this argument is that because the social rate of discount may be below the market rate (the private rate of time preference and the yield on private investments) private saving at a full employment market equilibrium is too low. In these circumstances, government could use fiscal and monetary tools to raise private savings, or it might undertake the necessary projects itself, financing the investment through bond issue or taxation. As Marglin has pointed out, many governments may not have monetary and fiscal means at their disposal to raise private savings, especially in the developing countries, and, short of resorting to direct controls, they are likely to remain unable to do so.[7] They will, therefore, be faced with undertaking public investments, financed by bonds or taxes, whose internal rate of return is less than that which is realized on marginal private investments.

The suggestion that there is a social preference for more savings has not been universally accepted.[8] Opponents of the greater savings view have argued, for example, that society has a choice between helping the poor of this generation and helping that of the next and that society is more likely to prefer the former.[9] This, of course, may imply a higher rather than a lower social rate of discount. The fact that future generations should be wealthier than present generations because of general economic growth tends to reinforce this supposition.[10]

There is virtually no empirical evidence that can be brought to bear on this controversy. Determination of the social rate of discount requires examination of public budgeting processes. The assessment of benefits of public projects has hardly begun, and hence inferences as to the social

6. Stephen A. Marglin [G16], pp. 95–111. Baumol initiated this sort of reasoning when he suggested that an individual may indicate a preference for a different interest rate for public projects to which all are forced to contribute. William J. Baumol [F2], pp. 91–93.

7. Stephen A. Marglin [G15], pp. 274–75.

8. A closely related argument as to why the social rate of interest may lie below the risk-adjusted market rate of interest stems from the observation that society, unlike an individual, will not die. That is, the present generation may give insufficient attention to the interests of future generations; to the extent that the government represents society in perpetuity rather than the current population, the government might therefore appropriately choose a lower discount rate. Robert C. Lind [G12], pp. 336 ff.

9. Gordon Tullock [G24], pp. 331 ff.

10. E. J. Mishan [G17], p. 140.

discount rate implicit in these decisions are difficult to make with any confidence or accuracy.

The Public Sector's Role in Capital Markets and Its Opportunity Cost

While market imperfections and externalities may to some extent obviate the welfare implications of the perfect capital market model and the market rate of interest, the particular role of the public sector in capital markets appears to be an even greater complication. It is quite obvious that the public sector in most circumstances is not just another participant in a perfect capital market. Most national governments play too large a role in their domestic capital markets to act as if their borrowing and lending activities do not influence the domestic market rate of interest. The pursuit of monetary and fiscal policies aimed at achieving growth, price stability, or employment objectives typically is given much greater priority than public borrowing or lending so as to achieve a particular time stream of benefits from public expenditures. Periods of budget imbalances which result from discretionary fiscal policy testify to the fact that the public sector is usually not free to alter at will its time stream of benefits and costs in the capital markets, at least not without considerable cost.

Because of the government's pervasive role in the capital markets of most nations, the opportunity cost of public funds is a function of the private consumption and investment displaced by public financing and of the reinvestment possibilities associated with affected private and public projects. Determining the opportunity cost of public funds involves examining the incidence of taxes and the nature of the government bond market, as well as the private capital markets in which borrowing and lending occur.[11]

Again, Krutilla and Eckstein have made one of the few serious efforts to measure such a cost (specifically the opportunity cost of public tax

11. Reported rates of return depend heavily on the measurement of capital and hence on the tax laws, especially the treatment of depreciation. Adjusting the reported figures to produce an accurate measure of the return on equity can be difficult, and certainly an imprecise process. Also in some of the less developed countries, private rates of return may be inflated because government enterprises such as transportation and electric power follow pricing practices which subsidize private firms. On the other hand, private firms are subjected to many indirect taxes, which may or may not place an incidence on capital. In some cases, observed private rates of return reflect monopoly profits, while in others the observed rates of return may be artificially low because of government regulation.

receipts in the United States) by examining the marginal returns forgone in the private sector. They defined the effect of a general increase in income taxes on real resources diverted from the private sector as a weighted average of the marginal return in each private sector taxed, where the weights were based on the structure of the taxes. They found that in 1955 the average rate of return before taxes on private investments in the United States ranged from 5.5 percent for residential real estate to 21 percent for large corporations.[12]

In much the same fashion, Reuber and Wonnacott examined the impact on private investment in Canada of the sale of government bonds. They concluded that the marginal rate of return ranged from 5.55 percent on inventories of large businesses and private utilities to 6.25 percent on investments by small businesses.[13] These levels are somewhat higher than the corresponding yields on public bonds at the time, and as one would expect, closely resemble the interest costs on private debt.

Government bond rates will generally differ from market rates on private debt of comparable maturity since government debt is generally presumed relatively liquid and risk free. Since the government has the legal authority both to print money and to tax, it need never default on its bonds, at least to domestic holders. This raises the question whether the public sector should discount projects at its borrowing cost rather than the marginal return on displaced private investment. It can be argued that use of the lower public borrowing rate arising because of the state's unique role is inadvisable since different time discounting procedures may distort the allocation of capital between public and private projects. The state's fiducial powers exemplify this unique role. However, the considerable pooling of risks in investment in the public sector would seem to constitute a potentially legitimate basis for using a slightly lower discount rate for the government than in the private sector. Whether this advantage is separable from the state's other powers as a source of lower rates is debatable.

Another issue raised by the existence of imperfect capital markets is whether a distinction between consumption and investment forgone must be made in the discounting. Marglin suggests that such a distinction is necessary, based on the assumption that the social rate of discount is below the market rate and hence that the overall level of investment in the economy is not optimal. His recommendation for evaluating public projects is to discount benefits at the social rate of time preference and to evaluate

12. Krutilla and Eckstein [F21], pp. 106–16.
13. G. L. Reuber and R. J. Wonnacott [G20], p. 52.

the opportunity cost of initial capital outlays at a shadow price that reflects the private consumption and investment opportunities forgone. Changes in consumption resulting from the project are treated at their face value and discounted at the social rate, whereas investment forgone is inflated by a factor that represents the discounted value of the rate of return on the marginal private project.[14] This procedure results in the acceptance of all projects whose discounted present value of benefits exceeds initial capital outlays so inflated; in short, projects whose ratio of benefits discounted at the social rate to capital outlays exceeds some specified level.

The applicability of this procedure rests on particular assumptions about imperfections in the capital markets, assumptions that would seem separable from the question whether the social rate of discount is below the market rate. The critical question is whether the capital markets are judged relatively perfect (that is, all firms and households are able to borrow or lend unlimited amounts at the prevailing rate of interest) with respect to private investment opportunities and consumption, or whether external effects or imperfections lead to a divergence between the private and the social discount rate. If the capital market is perfect, no distinction need be made between consumption and investment forgone in the discounting. As Mishan points out, a perfect capital market implies that there is always an opportunity to invest funds in the private sector yielding some return, ρ, in perpetuity, which just equals consumers' marginal time preference. This is, therefore, the appropriate measure of the marginal worth of private investment *or* consumption forgone, and hence the opportunity cost of that part of a dollar of tax receipts which was previously consumed as well as that part which represents displaced investment if properly valued at

---

14. Stephen A. Marglin [F26], pp. 52–55.

If $B(x,t)$ is the benefits accruing in time t of a project of scale x, with cost $k(x)$, the net present value criteria is

$$\int_0^\infty B(x,t)e^{-rt}\,dt - ak(x), \quad \text{and} \quad a = \theta_1\,(\rho/r) + (1 - \theta_1)$$

where a is the shadow price of a dollar of income to the private sector which is taxed to finance this public project; θ_1 is the percentage of a dollar saved and invested by the private sector; r is the social rate of discount; ρ is the private opportunity cost of capital.

Marglin proposes inflating only the costs of the initial time period, for he assumes that costs incurred in later time periods are paid out of the additional gross national product generated by the project. However, if project costs in every time period reduce private investment in that time period, then all project costs should be inflated. See Marglin [G15], pp. 274–89; also Martin S. Feldstein [F6], pp. 114–31.

the rate, ρ.[15] Thus, if private capital markets are perfect, or can be assumed to be not too imperfect, Mishan suggests using the market rate of interest when discounting both benefits and costs of public projects.

In short, only when participation in the capital market by the particular citizens who are being taxed is constrained by market imperfections or institutional reasons is it necessary to look beyond the market rate of interest in determining the real opportunity cost of funds; and only then is it necessary to make a distinction as Marglin does between private consumption or investment forgone. In these circumstances, it is necessary to look at all the margins affected by a public project, that is, the effects on consumption and investment of both public borrowing and taxing. Reinvestment opportunities associated with public versus private projects are also relevant. Clearly, such an examination can quickly become a very substantial task.

Concluding Observations

The selection of a discount rate for government investments is usually based on the presumption that government seeks to maximize the discounted present value of consumption or, equivalently, the discounted present value of the nation's assets. For a variety of reasons the market rate of interest may or may not be judged relevant for making the normative inferences related to this objective. Those countries with well-developed capital markets and distributions of income which have had the blessing of the political process are those where the market rate is likely to be most relevant. Obviously, identifying whether a particular country empirically fits such a description can be a difficult and subjective exercise.

Since the public sector is not likely to be a perfect competitor in the capital markets, determination of the opportunity cost will require examination of the incidence of public taxing or borrowing on private investment. In countries where the capital markets are reasonably well developed, or to a first approximation, perfect, the rate of interest on long-term private borrowing should closely approximate the opportunity cost of capital to the public sector. If capital markets are judged reasonably perfect in their

15. Mishan [G17], pp. 139–46.

balancing of opportunity and impatience, no distinction will be necessary in discounting consumption and investment forgone, and between benefits of the project, recouped or not. The market rate of interest is a useful simplification and a reasonably good approximation to the correct rate in such circumstances.

Conversely, where capital markets are not well developed, the appropriate discount rate is not obvious, and some difficult second-best problems must be faced. In the underdeveloped countries, for example, the marginal return or worth of private expenditure displaced by public borrowing or taxing may be well above the nominal public borrowing rate and many private interest rates as well. In such circumstances, the opportunity cost of public financing may be difficult to ascertain.

As the preceding discussion suggests, there is not yet a consensus among economists regarding the theoretically correct discount rate for public investments in all circumstances. Hirshleifer, for example, would argue that in selecting projects the government should use "the market yield rates comparably placed in the rate structure—taking account of risk, term, illiquidity, etc."[16] By contrast, Samuelson concludes that "one can derive by appropriate assumption, conclusions that disagree or agree with Professor Hirshleifer's tentative dictum that government should use the same high interest rates that industry does."[17] Specification of the appropriate discount rate (or rates) for many public objectives is necessarily a political judgment. When capital market imperfections or externalities render market rates of less usefulness, this conclusion is reinforced.

However, the precise discount rate or rates employed in project evaluation may not be the issue most worthy of attention. For much public project evaluation, and transport projects are no exception, the necessity to include social or external effects as benefits for which there is little evidence, especially from the marketplace, suggests that the analyst might better direct his scrutiny and attention to the nature of the benefit measure. In this regard, it may be useful to relate the choice of a discount rate to the kind of benefits at issue and the uncertainty involved in their realization. For many sorts of public projects, project justification will hinge on the inclusion of external and social effects not readily quantifiable and, more importantly, typically subject to political pressures and oftentimes considerable exaggeration. Conservative discounting procedures using interest

16. Jack Hirshleifer [G9], p. 84.
17. Paul A. Samuelson [G22], p. 95.

rates comparable to returns on private projects may be a useful antidote in such circumstances.

The accept or reject decision for any project depends as well on the pricing procedures followed. As suggested in the next two chapters, the complications created by the interdependency of pricing, capital budgeting, and subsidy decisions may substantially lessen the practical significance of economists' inability to agree on *the* relevant discount rate.

CHAPTER THIRTEEN

Uncertainty and Facility Design

THE PLANNING AND DESIGN of transportation projects normally entail considerable uncertainty in the estimates of future conditions. Decisions must often be made as to capacity needed in a relatively distant time period. As noted in preceding chapters, transport demand can fluctuate even in the short run in response to economic and social variables external to the project itself. Variation may arise because of changes in economic conditions. It may also arise as a result of differences in the performance of the rest of the transport system, for example, when weather problems at one airport result in a shift in landings to other sites. Because of the lumpiness that often characterizes transport investment, capacity cannot always be adjusted immediately and continuously (at least not cheaply) to this variation in demand. As a consequence of these uncertainties and discontinuities, periods in which fixed transport capacity is either overbuilt or underbuilt may result.

Similarly, instantaneous adjustment of facility prices to variations in demand is usually difficult, if not impossible, in practice. Changes in demand over the short run may be such that the prices based on demand expectations and a particular pricing strategy are too high or too low in relation to specified objectives in certain time periods. The consequences of unforeseen changes in demand are obviously most significant when administrative costs or institutional circumstances inhibit the adjustment of prices, and when congestion costs are important, creating nonlinearities in facility

216

supply or performance curves. As noted in Chapter 4, an important characteristic of most fixed transport facilities is an ability to serve a range of outputs at varying costs or performance levels. The performance of a facility can only be properly represented by a complex and often nonlinear set of outcomes as demand fluctuates. If peaking characteristics are also pronounced, so that demand fluctuations produce a wide variety of results over the operating cycle, this result is magnified.

All too often conventional planning neglects the consequences which may arise from erroneous forecasts or the stochastic nature of demand. "Point estimates" of project benefits based on an assumed demand level and a fixed facility pricing policy, and hence estimates of savings in operating and time costs, are the usual procedure. At best, ad hoc and usually arbitrary adjustments for uncertainty will be employed, as described in the next section.

The Conventional Treatment of Uncertainty

The traditional adjustment for uncertainty, when it is recognized, "is simply to be conservative."[1] This principle applied at the stage of overall project evaluation implies more stringent criteria of acceptability. In practice, this is often achieved by one or more of the following schemes:

1. Assuming the useful life of the project or system under design to be less than its most likely physical or economic life.

2. Adding a risk premium to the interest rate used for discounting future cost and benefit streams to the present.

3. Reducing final net benefits in some rule-of-thumb proportion, generally by hedging estimates of engineering costs and benefits in specific, arbitrary proportions.

The list is indicative, not exhaustive. The adjustments may be applied singly or in some combination, but in no case are they satisfying devices for handling uncertainty. The values used for each of the several hedges may have no tangible relation to the important planning variables for the problem at hand. Furthermore, the consequences of the crude adjustments may not be explicitly traceable through the planning and subsequent construction processes.

The appropriateness of these adjustments for uncertainty will vary with

1. Otto Eckstein [F5], p. 469.

circumstances. Those that limit the assumed economic life of the project or shorten the length of the planning period may be useful in some cases, most commonly as an allowance for the rate of technological change, which is almost invariably difficult to forecast. Addition of a risk premium to the interest rate used for discounting accomplishes the same thing, perhaps more sensitively, since more distant future returns are progressively discounted more heavily. Use of a high discount rate is a popular means used by the private sector as a hedge against uncertainty associated with future market or technological developments. As noted in Chapter 12, however, determination of an appropriate rate (or rates) of discount is a difficult problem which is only compounded in complexity by attempting to incorporate a premium for uncertainty. Moreover, there is at present no unassailable empirical method for specifying the appropriate premium.

The principle of conservatism also applies at the design stage, with planners sometimes attempting to hedge an entire project by building adaptability or flexibility into it. These two terms generally refer to the ability to adjust the system efficiently to discrepancies between the capabilities built into the system and the amount and nature of the realized demand for the system's outputs. Outputs of most productive plants or projects can be varied over a limited range by changing combinations of variable inputs. In the case of a transport system, for example, output or capacity can be altered in response to input changes such as signal timing, speed limits, lane markings, and the like, depending to a large extent on the initial design of the system. The susceptibility of a system to changes of this type might be described as adaptability, with the term "flexibility" reserved to indicate the ability to change relatively fixed inputs, including, in the transportation case, the physical size of the system, the right-of-way requirements, and so forth.[2] Recognizing the existence of uncertainty in all planning activities, one observer has suggested that the planners and the decision makers should consider the trait of flexibility as "a virtue in itself, a virtue worth paying for at the seeming sacrifice of other standards of performance."[3]

2. The terms "adaptability" and "flexibility" are taken from George Stigler [A10], pp. 314–16. Stigler draws a similar distinction between flexibility and adaptability with reference to productive plants. With his line of reasoning, flexibility and adaptability may differ, but the greater the range of adaptability, the less need exists for flexibility. He shows, though, that even with complete adaptability flexibility may be desirable. "The real need for flexibility, however, clearly arises when there is only partial adaptability. . . . The amount of flexibility built into the plant depends on the costs and gains of the flexibility."
3. Raymond Vernon [C17], p. 196.

One standard means of incorporating flexibility into a system is to provide excess capacity. Excess capacity is not, of course, a free good; hence the pertinent question is how much extra capacity to purchase, given the objectives to be maximized, the controlling economic constraints, and the uncertainty of forecasts of future conditions. The optimum facility design will change with each planning problem and its controlling parameters.

At a slightly more sophisticated level, recognition that capacity may be underbuilt or overbuilt during certain periods may be represented by the implicit assumption that the costs of too much or too little capacity at any given moment vary symmetrically about a single-valued estimate of demand. In general, of course, there is no particular reason to assume, a priori, that the cost of using additional resources in constructing too much capacity would be equal to the costs (losses) of congestion resulting from the construction of too little capacity. The proper relationships are almost invariably asymmetric and nonlinear, especially when congestion prevails. Congestion costs, or costs due to inadequate capacity, will be based on shippers' and passengers' valuation of time delays, increases in the variance in trip time and operating costs as a result of exceptionally heavy demands on the system, and so forth. These costs need not respond in the same way as those of excess facility capacity, which presumably will be affected primarily by the opportunity cost or discount rate for committing more rather than less capital earlier rather than later.

In short, while certain ad hoc methods for handling uncertainty have the advantage of simplicity, in most circumstances there is little guarantee that these procedures will lead to optimal results. The normative implications of the implicit weighting of costs and benefits in these ad hoc procedures are generally not obvious. The obviously sensible alternative is to apply the principles of modern decision theory in one form or another.

An Introduction to Decision Theory

The basic procedures of modern decision theory can be relatively easily summarized.[4] First, it is assumed that the planner can employ whatever sample data, knowledge, or experience is available to estimate subjective probability distributions over the range of future outcomes, given the

4. For a more complete exposition of decision theory, see R. Duncan Luce and Howard Raiffa [H9], Chap. 2, and Howard Raiffa [H14].

options open to him. Then, every possible specific outcome resulting from a particular act or decision is assigned a numerical value or preference when related to some objective function. The appropriate decision is that which maximizes the expected value or utility of outcomes over the set of possible decisions. The expected value, or mathematical expectation, of a decision is the weighted average of the numerical value of all the possible outcomes resulting from the decision, each outcome's value being weighted by its assigned probability.

The explicit basis for this formulation of the problem of decision making under uncertainty lies in several assumptions. Essentially these require the decision maker to quantify his preferences among certain simple problems and to accept certain axioms of consistency or rationality as an aid in handling more complex choices involving conditional outcomes. The axioms basically premise the following: first, that the decision maker can order elements of a set of certain outcomes by indicating the probability in a standard gamble between an unattractive and an attractive outcome which he regards as bracketing the outcome in question; second, that his ordering of preferences among lotteries or uncertain situations is complete and transitive; and third, that his preferences among lotteries are not altered by substituting for any outcome an alternative outcome (which might be a lottery) that he regards as indifferent. These axioms allow complex decision problems to be analyzed in a simple manner. They imply that there must be a utility function which reflects preferences among sure outcomes and, moreover, for which consistent choices among sure or risky alternatives can be represented by ordering all situations according to their expected utility.

The key to the existence of a utility function that leads to consistent choices when maximizing expected utility is the postulate that choices among complex lotteries can be represented by summing the utility of component outcomes using probability calculus. This sort of axiom rules out certain kinds of behavior. In particular, the love or fear of gambling is eliminated. A person must be impartial about two situations with the same expected utility and cannot choose or reject one situation because of the suspense or excitement of the long series of gambles it entails. The other axioms can be and have been questioned as well,[5] and there is some empirical evidence that in certain circumstances people will make choices that violate the assumptions of transitivity and substitutability.[6] A distinc-

5. For a defense of the criticisms, see Leonard J. Savage [H17], pp. 100–04.
6. Daniel Ellsberg [H2], pp. 643–69; and William Fellner [H4], pp. 670–89.

tion must be made, however, between an analytic and a descriptive decision model. Of interest here is an appropriate analytic model. Many decision makers, when informed of their irrationality in some particular experiment or circumstance, will choose to change their decision, arguing that they really want to act consistently with the axioms and only acted inconsistently because of a spur-of-the-moment judgment.[7]

It must be stressed that the procedure applies to situations in which the probability distribution for the occurrence of possible outcomes may or may not be known.[8] When the probability distributions cannot be obtained through observation or repeated trials, the question is raised whether the decision maker or planner with no objective probabilities at hand must assume total ignorance of the probabilities of the future outcomes or whether the judicious selection of a subjective distribution of probability weights is appropriate. The tenets of modern statistical decision theory assume that the planner, given the options open to him, can employ whatever knowledge and experience are available to estimate a priori or subjective probability distributions over the range of future outcomes.[9]

Several methods for determining probability distributions on outcomes exist. These range from informal methods of information gathering and assessment to more intricate statistical analyses of trends or sampling results.[10] In the situations of concern here, sample data are often very limited or unavailable and hence the planner or designer must quantify a priori probability distributions on the range of possible outcomes. If the number of required probability assessments is small, a consistent distribution can often be obtained by considering each outcome individually, assigning it a tentative value, and then finally adjusting the tentative values so that they sum to one. When the number of possible outcomes becomes large, such a procedure becomes infeasible and probability density functions will prove more useful as a means of consistently reflecting judgmental proba-

7. Howard Raiffa [H15], pp. 690–94.

8. The distinction is usually made between risk and uncertainty, the former meaning a situation where the outcomes are stochastic but obey a known probability distribution, the latter a situation where the distribution itself is unknown. Luce and Raiffa [H9], pp. 13–14.

9. Savage [H17] has synthesized personalistic probability and modern utility to establish the basic framework of the subjective school of modern probability theory. His book also contains a complete bibliography of the history of the development of decision theory.

10. In the Bayesian approach to statistical decision theory, the probability distribution used for calculating the expected values is the conditional a posteriori distribution, obtained through use of Bayes' theorem together with evidence obtained from sampling and the a priori subjective probability distribution. Howard Raiffa and Robert O. Schlaifer [H16].

bility. Often the general shape of the density function is first decided, and then the assessment of outcomes is sharpened by reference to the cumulative distribution. For example, a useful procedure may be to ask the decision maker to divide the admissible range of possible outcomes into two equally likely subintervals, then to divide the two subintervals in turn into two equally likely halves, and so forth, and thus obtain fractile assessments in each case. This can be continued to whatever level of accuracy the decision maker feels his judgment warrants. The resultant fractile points may be plotted and a curve fitted to them, giving the cumulative distribution function over the admissible range. Density functions that approximate these numerical distributions may then be derived.

Application to Facility Design

The first step in applying decision theory to project design under uncertainty is to translate expected variation in demand into a probability distribution on performance for a given facility. Then, expected cost and output levels can be calculated for each facility; once this is done for all facilities under consideration, the optimal facility design for any expected output is the facility with the lowest expected total costs for that output.

The assumption of constant marginal utility of income is implicit in the objective of minimizing expected costs in facility design. Accordingly, the variance and the higher moments of the probability distributions of cost and output outcomes are disregarded. One obvious alternative response to uncertainty is to make design concessions that reduce the variance (presumably at the expense of a reduction in the expected value of project benefits). In the typical transportation planning context the critical issue is usually not the differences in the performance of a given facility, but rather the distribution of outcomes for some subset of the entire transportation system, probably the projects making up the current budget. Thus, centralized decision makers' attitudes toward risk and the probability distributions of outcomes for this large subset of projects must be consulted. Translation of risk considerations at this level of aggregation into decision rules, to be employed at the project or facility design stage, that will reflect the mean and the variance of outcomes involves very substantial conceptual and administrative problems. Since the variation in the sum of uncertain consequences of many projects will be less proportionately than that of any individual project, the aggregation of uncertain outcomes in the entire transportation investment program will generally go a long way toward reducing problems associated with the high variance of an individual project. Accordingly, design concessions to reduce the variation in a particular project that is part of a larger program may be judged unnecessary.[11]

The performance of a facility facing a stochastic demand curve will depend on the extent of variation in output as determined by the probability distribution on demand, the manner in which the facility is priced, and the shape of the facility cost curve. Determining facility performance is complicated when demand fluctuations result in the intersection of demand and perceived facility costs in the output range where facility costs are nonlinear. For example, in Figure 13-1, demand is assumed to be a linear function of price, with the intercept of the demand curve on the price axis assumed to obey a symmetric probability distribution (denoted by $F(a)$ in Figure 13-1). The subjective techniques discussed in the previous section can often prove helpful in the specification of this probability distribution. The demand functions associated with the lower and upper limits of demand variation are denoted by D_l and D_u. In this example, facility price is, by assumption, a fixed charge to be added to average variable cost and is represented by the distance between AVC and AC; thus AC represents total perceived costs to the user for the particular facility diagrammed. The family of demand curves defined by the probability function, $F(a)$, intersects perceived facility costs in some instances where costs are increasing and nonlinear. The result is a distribution (under normal assumptions, skewed) of output actually purchased, $F(Q)$, lying in the range of Q_1 to Q_2. The mean of this distribution represents expected output for the facility in question under the assumed demand conditions. Expected costs for this facility will be the sum of points along the average total cost curve (ATC) in the range Q_1 to Q_2 weighted by the probabilities defined by $F(Q)$.

The particular assumptions about the demand distribution and facility pricing strategy employed in this example are not immutable. The assumption of symmetry in demand could be replaced by any probability distribution on demand. (In practice most demand forecasts will probably assume

11. To the extent that project dependencies are such that the variance of outcomes must be considered, centralized capital budget decisions can mitigate the problem by their simultaneous selection of projects to be accepted. Uncertainty in a central budgeting context will be considered in Chapter 16, where higher moments of the probability distribution (than simply the mean) will also be considered.

FIGURE 13-1. *Expected Facility Use Given Stochastic Demand*

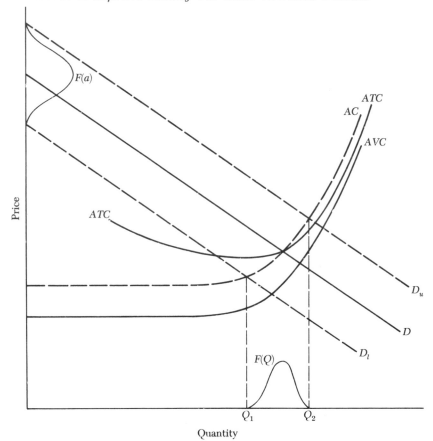

symmetry, with a normal distribution being by far the most popular.) Also, any pricing strategy, such as marginal or full cost pricing, might be employed which would lead to different distributions of actual outputs purchased and hence different expected outputs and costs for a specified facility.

The choice of an optimal facility design requires that expected costs and outputs of each candidate facility be derived for a specified distribution of demand functions and a pricing policy. This must be done for all time periods and the results discounted at the appropriate rate of interest. The locus of minimum expected cost levels for all expected output levels defines a long-run average expected total cost curve. In essence, this curve is equivalent, under conditions of stochastic demand, to the conventional envelope curve of the theory of the firm. The critical point of this exercise is that it permits trade-offs in facility design to be made in view of uncertainty so as to minimize expected total costs. Facility design is typically a decision option in many transportation planning exercises.

The procedure is flexible and permits any sort of demand and cost functions and probability distributions. In practice computational considerations will condition the choice of distributions employed. The search procedure is simplified if the cost relationships among basic types of facilities are invariant to scale. This assumption, together with a constant facility pricing policy, linear demand functions, and one frequency distribution for the demand function's price intercepts, as assumed above, implies that the probability distributions of realized costs and outputs are invariant to scale. The choice among the basic types yielding lowest expected average cost can be determined by deriving their expected costs at any one level of output, which, under the assumptions, indicates which of the basic facility types is optimal at all levels of output. The envelope curve is defined by the costs of that particular type of facility at all levels of output. Without such simplifications, an electronic computer will be needed in order to handle the many possible assumptions or estimates about future demand and performance of different types of facilities. Developing practical means of representing the interaction of probability distributions on demand with nonlinear facility cost curves is a challenging computational and programming problem.[12]

Time Staging Considerations

The design procedures described above can also be used to address a number of dynamic staging problems. In any practical planning circumstance, discontinuities in supplying capacity must be recognized. Capacity cannot be varied continuously. Nor will its costs in general be independent

---

12. A fairly simple example of this facility design problem has been programmed. A small number of discrete designs was envisioned; similarly, the level of realized demand was limited to several discrete levels. Constant long-run cost functions were assumed. The performance of each facility as a function of demand was represented by two functions; a family of rectangular hyperbolas represented the fixed costs of excess capacity when demand was below the output level where variable costs are increasing; hyperbolic sine functions were used to reflect costs caused by congestion when demand exceeded the range of constant variable costs. Leon M. Cole, "Planning Capital Investment under Uncertainty with Application to Highway Transportation Systems" (Ph.D. dissertation, Harvard University, 1965).

of its incremental staging; in transportation, it is often much cheaper to construct a large facility all at once than successively by small pieces. Provision must therefore be made in the planning process for questions of capacity staging over time. In addition, it will often be wise to design now in anticipation of the need for adding more capacity later (for example, selecting local service and regional airport sites which can eventually be upgraded in terms of runway length and approaches to handle larger planes).

To analyze staging problems of this sort, the most important requirement is a careful definition of construction and congestion costs as a function of the staging of capacity increments. The presumed effect of combining stages in construction is to reduce total construction costs in the future as demand increases but at the cost of carrying a larger capitalized valuation. The decision to construct ahead of demand can also reduce such costs as those caused by congestion and disruption during construction phases. These costs may be sufficiently large, for example, in certain urban or port facilities to favor a relatively early staging of capacity introduction. Clearly, the balance of any savings on construction and congestion costs versus the costs of carrying an inappropriately large capacity level for an interim period is a complex empirical matter, and one that must take into consideration how a facility performs at varying levels of demand.

One obvious way of handling these staging decisions would be to perform an exhaustive search of alternative staging paths for the project being proposed. In many cases the relevant options will be few. The usual questions are, When should an expansion be made? Should a two-stage (occasionally, more than two-stage) expansion be consolidated into a single step? (For example, at what point should a road or airport runway be paved? Should a runway extension be made suitable for jets now, in anticipation of jet use in a few years, rather than making improvements piecemeal?) In short, only a few obvious cases will normally require testing in order to determine the effects on construction costs at the margin of building the facility in pieces or all at once. If the probability distributions and cost functions lend themselves to easy iteration on the computer, this search procedure may be feasible.

Conclusion

The treatment of uncertainty as recommended in this chapter is at the project design stage. Specifically, a procedure is suggested for analyzing the trade-offs between facility costs, performance, and design, given expectations regarding the stochastic nature of demand. This is essentially a systematic procedure for choosing among a variety of possible designs, each of which has associated with it a set of consequences that obeys some probability distribution. Such a format permits, first of all, uncertainty in the demand side to be explicitly introduced into facility planning. It also enables one to systematically incorporate complex and often nonlinear measures of performance of alternative facilities into the analysis of facility design, in particular, asymmetry in results arising from demand variations in the face of underprovision or overprovision of capacity.

The effects of uncertainty in project analysis can be included at two distinct levels: in decisions concerning the pricing strategy for a given facility and in the facility design stage itself. The determination of appropriate prices, given expectations about the distribution of demand, involves a variety of institutional and administrative considerations and, in particular, the minimum practical and worthwhile length of time between price adjustments. How these considerations condition pricing policy for cyclic or multiple time-period demand variation was introduced in Chapter 2 and is illustrated at some length in the discussion of project evaluation in the next chapter.

CHAPTER FOURTEEN

Individual Project Evaluation: An Outline of a Decision Procedure

THE ASSESSMENT of individual projects involves an evaluation of project consequences, which in turn are the result of policies for benefit estimation, pricing, subsidies, and capital budgeting. For example, the exclusion or inclusion of social or external benefits may be instrumental in the acceptance or rejection of projects. Similarly, the pricing policies pursued, which might be based either on a government's ability to sustain deficits or on the requirement that projects be self-financing, are important. Indeed, the pricing decision is the crucial interface between benefit measurement and the capital budgeting decision.

While innovations in pricing policies may result in significant improvements in transport project evaluation, construction, and operation, most theoretical pricing rules, however intrinsically sound or interesting, are seldom attempted in real situations. In this chapter a decision procedure for project pricing which attempts to close the gap between salient aspects of theory and its application is outlined. The procedure, while geared toward seeking the simplest solutions for defined objectives, nevertheless provides a systematic, integrated, and flexible approach to decision making, and one, it is to be hoped, that is sufficiently pragmatic to give promise of real usefulness and application.

Specifically, in the procedure presented here, pricing policies are recognized as planning or administrative instruments to be used in achieving certain specified objectives which are established for a particular project or facility. Further, since pricing and capital budgeting are considered to be closely interrelated aspects of the same planning problem, project evaluation and capital budgeting are executed in close connection with considerations of pricing.

Attention is not restricted, moreover, to narrow economic issues or measurements affecting the project or facility under consideration. Pertinent broader issues can and do influence capital budgeting and pricing decisions, especially in the public sector. The difficulty lies in considering these broader, more qualitative issues in some systematic way commensurate with the traditional economic variables. The proposed procedure grapples with these problems directly, accommodating qualitative variables and judgments explicitly in the decision procedure; this contrasts with the more informal procedures of much current practice.

In essence, an iterative decision procedure for pricing and evaluation of public transport projects is advocated and described. This iterative approach permits a sequential examination of the advisability of alternative pricing and subsidy policies. By varying policy instruments or data inputs, a sensitivity test of the consequences of various policies for project evaluation and investment decisions can be performed.

Pricing Procedures: Objectives, Feasibility, and Acceptability

Several objectives or criteria may be involved in pricing transport projects, particularly for public facilities. In choosing among these, the question whether or not to impose similar investment criteria on both the public and the private sectors of the economy can be especially relevant. For example, a case is sometimes made for constraining the public sector to a single price or, in general, to that pricing practice which best simulates the sector of the private economy most like the public sector under consideration. In some cases, this leads to the simple pricing rule that the government should charge that single price which maximizes net revenue. An investment criterion analogue would be to undertake all public projects that could be financed from their own revenues, possibly subject to stipulated constraints on pricing practices.

The administration of prices and the capital budgeting problem would be relatively simple in these simulated private enterprise circumstances. Under such rules, it would be necessary only to determine whether the expected net profits of an additional transport project would be sufficient to pay the capital costs of the undertaking after meeting operating and all other costs. The transport agencies, public or private, would then proceed like private enterprises.

In most cases, however, public pricing policies are not likely to be so simple as profit maximization subject to the constraint that a single price be charged. The feasible set of transport project objectives with its implications for actual pricing policies can be extremely large, depending on the detail of the specifications. Normally, though, there are at least two broad objectives which are considered: (1) maximize the net present revenue (profit) generated from the use of the facility (at a specified discount rate); or (2) maximize the consumer use of the facility, subject only to the constraints that net present value is at least nonnegative and that every user pays a price no lower than the short-run marginal cost of what he consumes. The maximum use objective (subject to self-recovery of facility costs or any alternative stipulated budget constraint or subsidy limit) is usually closely aligned to the economist's objective of maximizing net benefits, has strong intuitive appeal, and in most cases is probably a close approximation to accepted public policy.

These and other public policy objectives may, moreover, lead to the use of discriminatory or differentiated pricing policies. For example, multiple or differentiated pricing may sometimes be recommended to increase facility use, raise additional income, or both. At least three common forms of price differentiation can be discerned: (1) cyclical price differentiation, normally geared to regular variations in the rate at which a service is consumed; (2) interconsumer, or interpersonal, price differentiation, where different prices are charged to different consumers within a single time interval; and (3) intertemporal differentiation, where the price charged to consumers increases or declines over time on a secular rather than cyclical basis.

Cyclical, or peak and off-peak, price discrimination in situations where it can be cheaply and effectively administered is the most likely of the various multiple pricing schemes to yield social benefits and the least likely to produce undesirable external consequences. It is often recommended in conjunction with demand peaking and is generally associated with the objective of increasing either facility use or the service amenities available to present users. Peak and off-peak prices can be set so as to maximize either the use of the facility or net present revenue (or any other revenue level). This sort of cyclical price discrimination can be easy to establish, especially if it accompanies obvious variation in the costs or demands associated with producing the system's services. The fact that cyclical price discrimination has too often been misapplied in transportation should not conceal its usefulness.

Interconsumer price differentiation involves more difficult questions, both as to the net social consequences and as to its political, administrative, and economic feasibility. Such discrimination may have considerable potential for distorting resource allocation and inducing less than optimal investment patterns over time. The income redistribution can also be substantial Therefore, a public policy decision to use such pricing involves some broad social and economic issues.

Interconsumer price differentials may also be difficult to implement, particularly for any length of time. Experience suggests that interconsumer price differentiation is easiest to apply and administer if it is related to some sort of actual cost differential; for example, if it can be established that there are distinctly different operating or other costs or that there are different levels of capacity or performance specifications associated with different classes of consumers.

It may also be possible to implement interconsumer price differentiation on the basis of differences in demand characteristics. Those consumers whose demands are relatively inflexible are generally assumed to object less to higher prices than consumers whose desires are more price elastic. Unfortunately, value-of-service pricing of this sort may be difficult to implement or maintain over time. Those who have to pay higher markups over costs (those discriminated against) are unlikely to accept their fate willingly. They will seek—and are likely to find in a world of modern and rapidly proliferating technologies—alternatives to accepting the higher markups. For example, they may move plants closer to markets or raw materials, or substitute truck transportation for rail transportation, even though truck transportation may not be cheaper in terms of total social costs or resource requirements. Transport planners historically have tended to underestimate the extent to which shippers can avoid discriminatory value-of-service pricing. Caution, therefore, is advisable when a project's justification and budget rely heavily on monopolistic price discrimination for needed revenues.

Intertemporal price discrimination of the secular type has a considerable history in transport pricing. A steady secular decline in real prices is almost invariably associated with the introduction of new products or services, as, for example, with the development of commercial jet airline services. Intuition and the limited evidence available suggest that declining prices for new transport services will be readily accepted in most cases. By contrast, secularly increasing prices on transport services can be troublesome to implement, as indicated by the difficulties railroads and other common carriers often have in raising rates to reflect increasing costs. In general, administrative simplicity and political acceptability tend to work against any random or idiosyncratic price changes from year to year.

The possible variations and combinations of these basic pricing schemes are numerous. The particular pricing scheme chosen will depend not only on stated objectives but also on the economic and political context affecting or surrounding a specific facility. Broadly speaking, a pricing policy should be politically feasible, conceptually and administratively simple, and should provide an efficient solution to the problem posed, such as the maximization of revenue or facility use subject to relevant constraints. In this regard, the smaller the number of separate prices charged for the use of a particular facility, the easier it normally will be to satisfy the consumer and execute the pricing policy. Thus, in the project pricing and evaluation procedures outlined in this chapter, complex pricing schemes are considered only after simpler pricing strategies have been rejected. The relative feasibility or acceptability of the different price discrimination schemes will vary from one set of economic, social, and political circumstances to another. As a first approximation, however, the following ranking seems reasonable: cyclical price differentials between peak and off-peak users will be relatively most acceptable; secularly declining prices will be second in acceptability; secularly increasing prices will be next; and interconsumer price discrimination will be least acceptable.

A Transport Project Pricing and Evaluation Procedure

As noted, no individual transport project evaluation procedure will yield unambiguous results under all conceivable assumptions or circumstances, and hence it is important to organize the search for feasible or desirable projects in a systematic and logical fashion. A useful search strategy is to begin with narrow, well-defined, relatively objective, and widely accepted lines of inquiry and then to extend the inquiry only as required, making explicit the implications of all the assumptions and qualitative judgments as they are introduced. Such a procedure must be flexible enough to include any combination of objectives with regard to differential facility use, amount of monetary deficit or surplus, and so on. At the same time, signals should be provided that indicate how well particular pricing or other regulatory decisions meet these objectives.

A flow diagram illustrating one decision process is shown in Figure 14-1. This schematic is focused on three basic decisions: the accept or reject decision, the choice of a capacity level, and the pricing scheme to be employed. As noted, all are highly interrelated. Input data (top box in Figure 14-1) include all the relevant demand, supply, and cost data associated with the facility under consideration. The interest rate for discounting must be specified. This will depend on the circumstances; for example, the market rate will be appropriate when capital markets are reasonably perfect. In addition, there are several broad social and economic considerations relating to overall means and ends which arise in the evaluation procedure. Consideration of these transcends the decision with regard to any particular project; as such their resolution is essentially an input when viewed at the project decision level. One factor is the viewpoint toward subsidy, both the amount and how it is to be financed, including whether price discrimination schemes might be employed to minimize subsidy costs.

The desirability of more or less capacity is another issue. Thus the discounted value of facility costs for all facility sizes must be determined (second box). Higher capacity levels may be possible only at the sacrifice of other objectives, for example, higher facility profits (see boxes G, H, I).

The first step in the evaluation procedure is to determine the net present value of the project when only cyclical price discrimination is permitted (box B). If net present value is negative (box C) a decision with regard to subsidy must be made. Built into Figure 14-1 is an assumption of skepticism toward public transportation investments for which the expected monetary costs exceed the expected revenues. Governments are called upon to supply many services which are difficult to sell, such as national defense, or which affect so many people that it is considered unwise to sell them, such as primary education and public health. Transportation, by contrast, is a government service that in many applications can be financed by direct user charges without any extensive social disadvantages or difficulties.

Nevertheless, for a variety of reasons, strict self-financing may be considered undesirable for certain transport developments. In such cases, policy

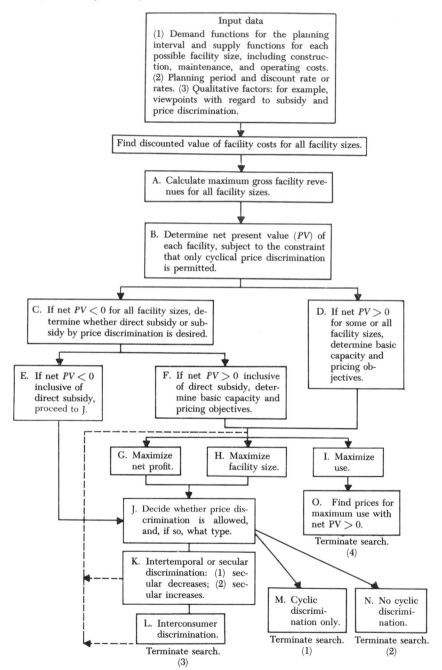

makers should be asked to specify exactly what level of subsidy they would be willing to pay for the expected unrecoverable or indirect benefits. Whatever level of subsidy is deemed appropriate can be added to the net present value of the project, and the evaluation can proceed.

Whether it is preferable to use a direct subsidy, rather than introduce subsidies indirectly by, say, lowering the discount rate, is difficult to specify a priori. A low public rate of discount indicates that the private sector underestimates the value of future consumption. Even when the social rate of discount is deemed below the market rate, it is not obvious whether the lower social rate of discount should be used to justify an extended public budget or whether direct subsidy principles are preferred.

Special pricing procedures may be employed as an alternative to direct subsidy. A proposed project with negative present value inclusive of direct subsidies might be reviewed systematically under increasingly complex pricing plans in an attempt to achieve the level of facility receipts needed for project acceptance. For example, the initial rule might be to accept only projects that are self-financing under administratively simple pricing rules (intertemporal) and to proceed on to more complex pricing regimes (interconsumer discrimination) subsequently. In terms of the procedures diagrammed in Figure 14-1, this means going from box C and branching to boxes E and J.

The underlying presumption of this procedure is that secular decreases or increases in prices are likely to be more acceptable than interconsumer price discrimination. Since it should be easier to capture monopoly rents on a new service, intertemporal price discrimination might be initially restricted to experiments with prices that declined over time. In addition, only simple and minimal changes might be permitted in the first tests. If, however, interconsumer price discrimination seemed sensible and administratively feasible, the procedure could be easily modified to test such prices early in the evaluation.

If a discriminatory pricing scheme does prove to justify the project, choices must then be made as to facility size and use, and also whether minimization of direct subsidy should be pursued at the expense of greater facility size or use. The trade-offs among facility size, use, and net revenues as they relate to facility pricing are shown in boxes G through L. The dotted lines denote the interrelationships between capacity and prices. (These are best explained by example, as done below.)

If positive net revenues are expected from a project (box D), the same trade-offs among facility size, use, and price must be considered. Perhaps the most obvious objective would be to maximize the profit derived from the facility. (Some aspects of the design of an algorithm for finding a profit-maximizing price are discussed below.) If the maximum profit objective is selected, the extent to which price discrimination will be used must be specified (box J). Obviously, any one or a combination of the three basic types of discrimination could be employed. Cyclical price discrimination of the peak and off-peak variety is probably the most moderate. If the decision is to follow the simple peak and off-peak strategy but not to permit either interconsumer or secular price differentiation, then the prices arrived at previously (when evaluating the financial feasibility of the project under the initial conservative assumptions) would be the relevant prices to implement. (It should be stressed that these cyclical price differentials are aimed at profit maximization and not at use maximization.) Of course, if all types of price discrimination are to be considered, the same sequence of procedures used to test various forms of price discrimination to reduce or eliminate subsidy could be reviewed.

Alternatively, one might choose to increase either facility size or facility use, at the expense of profit maximization. Again, all sorts of price discrimination might be employed in pursuing these objectives. If profit maximization is forgone in the choice of capacity and prices, the number of alternatives when facility size, use, and profitability are traded off quickly becomes large. As seen in Figure 14-1, at least four different terminal pricing solutions, corresponding to different specific criteria for project acceptance and different pricing objectives, can be identified or determined from this sequential procedure. These four are: (box M) no price discrimination other than simple cyclical discrimination (but projects possibly needing subsidy are included); (box N) the single price solution that yields the maximum net revenue on a project, excluding all forms of price discrimination; (boxes K and L) a set of intertemporal or interconsumer as well as cyclically discriminatory prices within certain administrative and feasibility constraints that yields a net present revenue equal to a given level (ranging from zero for projects that would otherwise require subsidy to maximum positive profits from the project); and (box O) the cyclically differentiated prices that maximize the use of the facility.

The evaluation procedures outlined here are quite flexible. A number of options are available at almost all the major decision points. With slight reorganization, the procedures could be made to adjust to different value judgments about administrative simplicity, the acceptability of different types of benefit measures, and so forth.

An Example of Project Evaluation in a Context of Price Differentiation, Cyclic and Temporal

The procedure just described for reviewing the interrelationships of pricing strategies and project evaluation can be illustrated in greater detail by relating it to a specific example. The analysis will address three questions: whether any facility of a given type should be built, what capacity level is appropriate, and the pricing policies to be pursued. For this purpose, an example involving distinctly different peak and off-peak service needs would seem particularly appropriate. The example illustrates certain analytical problems encountered when administrative or other constraints are operative, though solutions are not provided to all these analytical problems and no guarantees are given for the optimality, efficiency, or convergence properties of the paradigms presented.

To begin, all relevant demand and supply functions (for example, for peak and off-peak periods) for each time or discounting interval of the total planning period should be estimated. For convenience, define the supply functions so that they pertain only to all factors other than the fixed facility—the offering of all labor, administrative, and other skills needed to complete the project's productivity when joined with the fixed capital for the type of project under investigation. Assume, moreover, that the capacity is at choice and continuously variable over the whole range of outputs. Then, by the usual conventions of the theory of the firm, this supply function would be defined by the long-run average variable cost curve or the envelope of the short-run average variable cost curves for the plants of optimal design for each output level. (If stochastic demand is assumed, the supply curves are defined by the facilities deemed optimal at each output level, as described in Chapter 13.)

Separate demand functions are assumed for peak and slack periods, though any number of different time dimensions could be employed. Moreover, the procedure can also be applied in circumstances where only one demand curve is relevant to each basic time discount period. Following the usual conventions for the definition of supply, cost, and demand curves for transport services, quantity is measured by the rate of flow of output.

The effective demand for a facility can be obtained for the peak and off-peak periods by subtracting the supply from the demand functions for each (see Figure 14-2). Net curves represent the derived demand for the facility itself after all costs other than charges for facility use have been

FIGURE 14-2. *Derivation of Transport Facility Demand Curve from Linear Demand and Supply Curves*

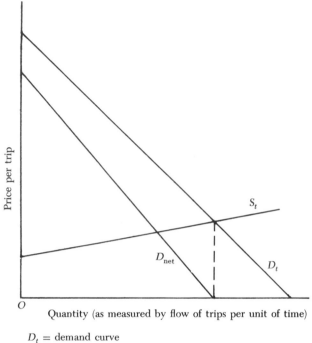

D_t = demand curve
D_{net} = derived demand curve ($D_t - S_t$)
S_t = supply curve

subtracted. Facility demand curves provide a basis for evaluating different pricing policies and thereby the potential benefits of a proposed capital investment; in this particular example, they can also be used to determine the amount of capacity to be installed for the type of facility under investigation.

For computational ease, linear facility demand curves are assumed. Whether this will be a good approximation depends on the circumstances, that is, the shape of the underlying demand and supply functions.

Composite peak and slack period discounted facility demand curves that represent the average situation over the planning period can greatly simplify the analysis. Without such an artifice, each time period would need to be analyzed separately and its calculated revenues available for facility amortization appropriately discounted. With a separate analysis for each period, a good deal of trial and error calculation would be needed to determine which combination of pricing policy and related capacity level would best serve the stipulated policy objectives. Even with a computer these calculations could be somewhat burdensome. However, composite curves accurate enough for most purposes can be found by taking discounted price observations at selected quantity intervals on all the individual facility demand curves of a given type (for example, peak and off-peak) and then fitting a line to these observations by, say, least squares.

How much accuracy is sacrificed by using such approximations? The approximation should significantly affect the price and capacity levels subsequently determined only if the individual facility demand curves vary over a wide range, or if there are very few time intervals being considered. Nevertheless, it is probably good procedure to check any tentative decisions on capacity and pricing by doing the detailed period-by-period calculations for the trial values before making any final choices.

By experimenting with different pricing schemes using the linear composite discounted facility demand curve (or the individual curves for each period if the composite curve is considered too gross an approximation), pertinent qualitative decision points can be identified. For example, a project evaluation might proceed, at least initially, by determining the maximum gross facility revenue of a project subject to the constraint that only two prices be charged throughout the life of the project, one for the peak of the operating cycle and one for the off-peak. The prices that determine this will be those associated with the unit elastic points, such as B and H in Figure 14-3, on the composite discounted effective demand curves for peak and off-peak periods respectively. The capacity level to be provided in this case would be OG. The conventional net present value test to see if the project is justified with such a pricing policy would be to sum the facility revenues over all periods for both peak and off-peak (the rectangles $OGHI$ and $OABC$ respectively in Figure 14-3) and compare this with the cost for a facility with a capacity OG; if the revenues exceeded costs the project could be at least tentatively accepted; if vice versa, rejected. When the composite approximation curves are used, the relevant total of revenues will be simply $n(OGHI + OABC)$ where n is the number of discounting periods embodied in the composite curve. No discounting is necessary before making the comparison of revenues with costs because discounted values were used to define the composite demand curves.

Maximization of gross revenue is not, of course, an appealing objective on almost any conceivable economic grounds, even though it does seem to have had appeal to some involved in transport management or policy.

FIGURE 14-3. *Determination of Peak and Off-Peak Prices of a Transport Facility to Yield Maximum Gross Revenue*

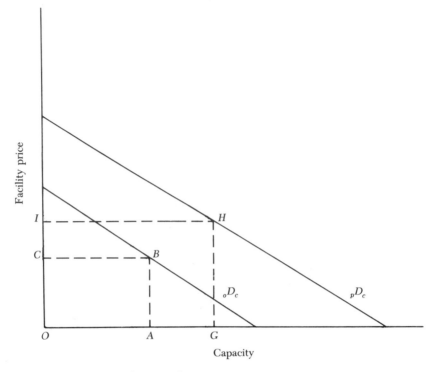

B, H = points of unitary elasticity
OA = capacity used in off-peak period
OC, OI = maximum revenue prices for the peak and off-peak periods respectively
OG = capacity level
$_pD_c$, $_oD_c$ = composite discounted peak and off-peak period facility demand curves

(Maximization of gross revenue, for example, seems to have been an objective widely held by many railroad traffic managers in the United States prior to the early 1950s.) If revenue maximization is to be sought, net rather than gross revenue would seem a more legitimate objective. In the present context maximization of net revenue would require that the relation between facility costs and output also be defined, and then subtracted from total revenue possibilities as defined by the relevant demand curves. Though there is logically a strong case for computing maximum net revenue before testing other objectives and pricing schemes, it is convenient to delay its exposition until after considering the maximum use case.

Thus, assume that maximizing the use of the facility is the objective, subject to the constraints that facility costs be recouped and that prices charged to any class of users not be less than the marginal costs of their service. For such an objective a pricing scheme more akin to those illustrated in Figure 14-4 would be appropriate. In Figure 14-4, the peak and off-peak net outlay curves have been combined vertically; the point, K, where off-peak demand is at its maximum, defines the kink in this combined curve.

The first step in the analysis, using composite facility demand curves, would be to determine the constant facility revenue per period needed

FIGURE 14-4. *Optimal Peak and Off-Peak Prices for Maximum Use of a Transport Facility to Yield a Net Present Value of Zero*

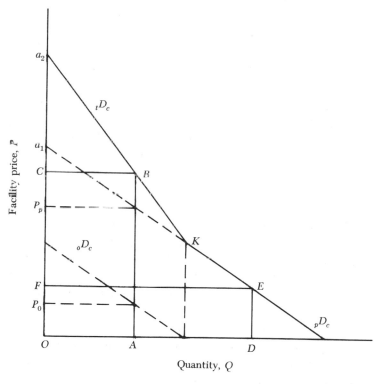

C = revenue sufficient to amortize cost of facility
$_pD_c, \ _oD_c, \ _tD_c$ = composite discounted peak, off-peak, and total period demand curves
F = single peak-period price
$P_p, \ P_o$ = peak and off-peak prices for maximum use

to yield a net present value of zero for a specified level of capacity; this would simply be the cost of the facility divided by n, the number of discounting periods. Since the objective is to maximize use, and therefore the level of justified capacity, the first trial should be made with the peak-period demand curve. Let that demand curve be represented by the function $P = a_1 - b_1Q$ where Q is quantity, P price, a_1 the intercept of the peak-period demand function with the price axis, and b_1 the slope of this demand function. Let $C = f(Q)$ define the facility revenue per period needed to amortize capacity Q. Then the first relevant question is whether a nonnegative solution for Q exists in the following function equating facility costs and receipts:

(1) $$f(Q) = a_1Q - b_1Q^2.$$

If a nonnegative solution greater than or equal to the quantity associated with K exists, the largest such Q is the capacity sought. The "revenue rectangle" (equal to C and therefore sufficient to amortize the facility's cost) would fit below the kink, for example, like $ODEF$ in Figure 14-4. The relevant facility charge, P, would be a single peak-period price, like OF in Figure 14-4. If OF were charged to all peak-period consumers and a zero, or no facility charge, levied for the off-peak, the use of the capacity would be maximized.

If no such solution exists, the upper portion of the combined demand curve should be tested. If a_2 is the intercept of the upper demand curve with the price axis and b_2 the slope, then the equation to be solved is

(2) $$f(Q) = a_2Q - b_2Q^2.$$

Again, the largest nonnegative solution defines the relevant capacity. In Figure 14-4, OA might represent such a capacity, $OABC$ the sufficient revenues, and OC the price dimension. In such a solution, the actual peak and off-peak prices, however, as shown in Figure 14-4, would be P_p and P_o for maximum use; that is, at these prices capacity OA would be fully used in both the peak and off-peak.

This solution represents a generalization of the Boiteux price and capacity solution with constant returns to scale for a shifting peak. As noted in Chapter 4, with constant returns, short- and long-run marginal and average costs are all equal to price, in conformity with the usual prescriptions of marginal cost pricing. However, if increasing returns prevail, the pricing solution outlined here will result in less capacity being justified than with a marginal cost-pricing scheme; conversely, with decreasing returns more capacity would be justified than with marginal cost pricing.

If no positive solution exists for either the upper or the lower portion of the demand curve, then no solution exists within the context of the problem. Abandonment of the project would be one alternative. Relaxation of the constraints would be another. For example, subsidies might be entertained as a possibility (which amounts to relaxing the self-financing constraint or lowering the value of C); alternatively, more elaborate and differentiated pricing schemes might be employed.

If the subsidy route is chosen, the minimum subsidy requirement would be the loss defined by a solution to the net revenue maximizing problem. Let net revenue, π, be defined by

$$\pi = PQ - f(Q).$$

Maximization of this function is a straightforward exercise in the calculus. The only special complication, differentiating this problem from its conventional form in the economic theory of the firm, is that all relevant demand functions must be explored. In the peak and off-peak case just described, this would mean that both $P = a_1 - b_1 Q$ and $P = a_2 - b_2 Q$ should be tried.

The objective of pricing policy in a situation characterized by sharply different peak and off-peak demands might not always be oriented to either profit maximization or use maximization. The reasons for adopting other objectives might not appeal to economists, but they may convince those who make policy. For example, the objective could be a single price for all users yet one which is fully compensatory in a financial sense. The grounds might be administrative expedience or some simple (perhaps even simple-minded in an economist's view) equity concept that everyone should pay about the same price. Alternatively, price elasticities of demand could be so low that price discrimination simply might not seem worth the effort or extra administrative cost.

For example, the situation might be as illustrated in Figure 14-5. Again, let the demand curves represent the effective composite demands for capacity: $_oD_c$ for the off-peak and $_pD_c$ for the peak. Let P_c be the single price that will yield sufficient revenue to pay for the capacity, OC, if levied against both peak and off-peak users. Let P_p be the price that would yield the requisite amount for the capacity, OB, which, say, is the justifiable capacity if the facility costs are charged to peak-hour users only. As drawn

FIGURE 14-5. *Effects of a Single and Fully Compensatory Price Charged to All Transport Facility Users, in a Peak and Off-Peak Period Demand Situation*

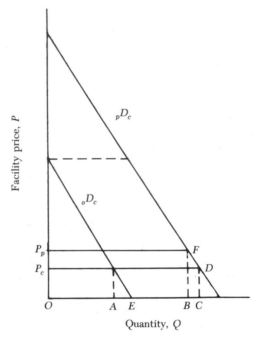

$_pD_c, _oD_c$ = composite peak and off-peak demand curves
P_c = single price charged to both peak and off-peak users
P_p = peak period only price (all facility costs are charged to peak)
OA = usage in off-peak with P_c
OB = usage in peak if all facility costs are charged to peak
OC = usage in peak with P_c
OE = usage in off-peak if no facility charge is made for off-peak

in this example, off-peak users would be charged nothing under the usual marginal cost-pricing rules for capacity OB since no shift in the peak would occur at this charge. Therefore, the effect of levying a single price in both periods is to increase the capacity needed, and to reduce (quite uneconomically) usage in the off-peak period from OE to OA and to increase it from OB to OC in the peak period, while redistributing the burden of the capacity costs away from peak and onto slack period users. In this particular illustrative case, total use is apparently decreased by a common price. The reverse, however, could be true in real applications, depending on the relative price elasticities of demand in the peak and off-peak periods. Again, it is possible that under some circumstances any reduction in usage or efficiency occasioned by a single price might be viewed by policy makers as a small cost to pay for the administrative simplicity or distributional effects of a single price system.

If a project does not yield a positive net present revenue under any relatively simple pricing scheme, including differentiation between peak and slack period users, interconsumer and intertemporal price discrimination strategies might be tested. To illustrate the latter, suppose an intertemporal price differentiation scheme is to be tested, subject to the constraint of a maximum of two price levels over the total planning period. As noted, this sort of constraint on the number of price levels may arise from political or social judgments about disadvantages (for example, of distribution or relocation effects) of having prices change more frequently.

A solution requires ascertaining the lengths of the two subperiods of the total planning period, and the price levels that are to prevail within each subperiod, such as peak and off-peak. An additional assumption, which seems realistic in many cases, particularly for government-regulated or -owned facilities, and which also helps keep the number of possible permutations within reasonable bounds, is that prices must systematically decline (or, if one prefers, rise) over time. In this simple two-level intertemporal pricing scheme, the second price base might be constrained to some fraction of the initial price. As noted, such a constraint seems realistic, particularly when considering the introduction of new products or services. The opposite assumption of positive price increments is also permissible within the procedure, but it may often seem less plausible. (Still, it might arise: for example, where the initial price constitutes some kind of special introductory offer to acquaint customers with a new service.)

The required analysis is basically combinatorial and lends itself to computer solution. For any subperiod made up of more than one time interval, the analysis is just as before. The difficulty is that prices and associated capacities must be determined for each possible combination of subperiods within the total planning period; furthermore, these different capacities and their related revenues must still be tested to see which choice best serves the specified objective function over all time periods. It seems possible, moreover, that the best capacity might be some compromise between the designated subperiod choices. When only two price levels are permitted, the possibilities are quite small. But as the number of permissible intertemporal price levels is increased beyond two, a substantial increase in computational effort will be needed (as a result of the increase in trials implicit in making a finer classification of the planning period). If inter-consumer price discrimination is also permitted, the same general procedures will apply, though care must be taken in ascertaining the appropriate discounted composite peak and off-peak net outlay curves, and the calculations become a good deal more burdensome.

It should be stressed that in large part these procedures and computations arise because of the need to plan in an environment of imperfect knowledge, where administration and procedural changes are not costless. Otherwise, one could simply vary the price, instantaneously if necessary, in order to maximize profits or use or net benefits as one's objectives dictated. In short, administrative simplifications complicate the analytical life much as analytical simplifications complicate the administrative life.

Summary

The project pricing and evaluation procedures presented in this chapter differ in several significant respects from more conventional project planning techniques. Benefit measurement, pricing, and capital budgeting are here considered integrally. There is no unique, unambiguous benefit concept deemed applicable to all circumstances, nor, for example, any hard and fast rules as to the virtues of subsidy or price discrimination. Assorted social and economic consequences are included in any pricing policy or project evaluation criterion. These interdependencies are here brought into the project planning process explicitly—particularly into benefit measurement, pricing, and capital budgeting decisions. Traditionally, these decisions have been treated in a narrower framework.

Clearly, a variety of assumptions and constraints, with varying subjective content, is involved. In the planning procedure outlined in this chapter, a mechanism is developed for specific incorporation of assumptions, constraints, and objectives as they are introduced into the planning analysis. Policy makers must decide such questions as the extent to which consistency is sought in the decision processes employed in the public and private sectors, whether profit or use maximization or some other objective is considered the socially most suitable goal, the possibility and justifiability of subsidization, the value attached to simplicity in the administrative mechanism, and so forth. The basic objective of the suggested planning procedure is to employ as few subjective assumptions or constraints as possible and to make explicit these assumptions as they appear.

One aspect of this framework deserves particular emphasis: the integration of the effects of alternative pricing schemes into the overall project selection and evaluation process. Pricing policies here are recognized as instruments which can be used directly to help achieve the objectives of the project and can be instrumental in determining the significance of subsidy or budget limits. Thus, the review of the many possible objectives, viewpoints, and consequences of pricing decisions as made in Part 1 is an indispensable element in the planning scheme outlined in this chapter.

PART FOUR

Project Interdependencies and Programming Techniques—An Introduction to System Planning

CHAPTER FIFTEEN

Selecting and Staging Additions to a Transport Network

Even in simple transport systems, additions to the network introduce dependencies among projects. Adding new links can significantly change interconnections and the resulting patterns of network usage and performance. Often a new link in a transport system will substantially affect the use made of another link or facility, not only parallel or complementary to the new link but sometimes considerably removed from and not obviously related to it. Proposed additions should therefore properly consider how the new pattern of linkages will affect the use of the overall transport system.

Important interdependencies may also arise from the nature of capital markets and the public budgeting processes for transportation investment. As noted earlier, when capital markets are imperfect, the opportunity cost of funds cannot be represented simply by the market rate of interest. In many public budgeting situations, the political process determines the size of investment budgets and hence the availability of funds for new projects in general program areas. Such budget constraints imply an opportunity cost of funds which, in general, will not be directly related to the market rate of interest or to the overall cost of funds to the public sector. In this sort of budgeting environment, individual project evaluation techniques cannot readily be applied since there is no exogenously determined opportunity cost of public funds. The relevant opportunity cost is known only after all project proposals have been reviewed and the best subset of projects has been selected, within the prescribed budget constraints.

Project dependencies of these two types are discussed in this chapter and Chapter 16. As an incorporation of limited system dependencies, they are a logical extension of the project evaluation procedures discussed earlier. As such, they represent a first or preliminary step to the systems viewpoint developed in Volume 2.

The unifying theme of the discussion is the application of basic mathematical programming procedures, in which a set of proposed projects is reviewed and that subset chosen to maximize some (typically linear) objective function subject to constraints. In the applications discussed in this chapter, the constraints represent the topology of the network and the limit on the investment budget. The planning problem in this case is to represent dependencies among projects that arise as a result of a new link's substantially altering routings of shipments throughout the system. A programming approach is employed to choose that set of link additions to a system which minimizes total transport costs subject to a constraint on the total transportation investment budget. A normative procedure is also developed to indicate a preferred time staging of these investments. In Chapter 16, a programming model is formulated to choose the subset of proposed projects that maximizes net benefits subject to annual budget constraints; this procedure is oriented toward financial dependencies rather than dependencies arising from network topology.

Network Planning as an Integer Programming Problem

Predicting the system effects of new links in a transport network is difficult, and past efforts have tended to be more subjective than quantitative. In large measure, this merely reflects the fact that so many possibilities must be evaluated, even in relatively simple systems with only a few nodes. Of course, the more potential additions under consideration, the greater the number of possibilities. The number of situations needing evaluation to determine the optimal set of link additions in a system can therefore become large very rapidly. For example, in a network with n potential link additions there are approximately 2^n possible combinations.

Fortunately, with the use of electronic computers and modern analytical techniques, such evaluations are not impossibly expensive today.

In this chapter, a simple model that will perform these evaluations with reasonable efficiency is described. The model involves the combined use of mathematical and dynamic programming. Mathematical programming is used to select the best possible solution for a particular stage of network development. To guide the search from one stage to another, dynamic programming techniques are used. Such techniques will indicate the most promising timing of investment configurations, as these are selected at each stage of the mathematical programming formulation.

The basic problem of planning link additions to an existing system for a single time period can be formulated as follows.[1] Let the network be defined as nodes, which correspond to production and consumption centers, and links, which are equivalent to individual transport routes. Commodities to be transported are expected to enter the network at the nodes and travel from link to link to their respective destination nodes. Associated with each link is a cost incurred by a unit traveling over it. Also identified are the set of possible new links (or projects) from which link additions will be selected. The problem is one of selecting from the set of all feasible projects that subset that minimizes both the cost of building new links and the cost of using the overall network.[2]

Each link in the system can be thought of as a project site at which one or more alternative projects may be constructed. Consideration of a network containing several potential link additions can be viewed as a grouped-projects analysis rather than as a full-scale systems analysis, since some essential aspects of the real world system, such as demand responses to changes in costs, are missing. Thus the programming techniques provide a fairly adequate analysis of the physical effects of system additions but do little or nothing to capture the interactions between the physical system and the economic system.

The problem, in summary, is to minimize the sum of future discounted

1. Monroe L. Funk and Paul O. Roberts [120], and Abraham Charnes and William W. Cooper [17], pp. 628–56.

2. The selection of such a simple objective function is defended only on the basis of ease of formulation. A higher level objective, such as value added or growth in gross national product, might be more consistent with development goals. However, most real world transportation planning problems are subject to a variety of subtle constraints which are difficult to quantify. Furthermore, if commodity and passenger flows could be accurately forecast at each stage, the difference between this simplified objective and the two higher level objectives mentioned above should be insubstantial.

costs for both constructing link additions and operating vehicles over the entire system, subject to the following constraints: (1) all supplies and demands of each commodity type must be met by flow over the network, in which the sum of flows into each node must equal the flows out; (2) if a link is not built, then there can be no flow over it; (3) the amount of funds committed to building new links must not exceed the available budget; and (4) the projects must either be constructed or not, that is, partial construction of a project is not permitted. Thus, the objective function to be minimized is

(1)
$$OBJ = \sum_{k=1}^{A} \sum_{j=1}^{m} c_j^k x_j^k + \sum_{J \in j} K_J P_J$$

subject to constraints on:
  Node flow equilibrium

(2)
$$\sum_{j=1}^{m} a_{ij}^k x_j^k = E_i^k$$

  Flow blocking constraints

(3)
$$\sum_{k=1}^{A} x_j^k - U_J K_J \leq 0$$

  Budget limitations

(4)
$$\sum_{J \in j} K_J P_J \leq B$$

  Integer requirements

(5)
$$K_J = \begin{cases} 0 \text{ if link is not built} \\ 1 \text{ if link is built} \end{cases}$$

  Nonnegativity

(6)
$$x_j^k \geq 0$$

in which

> OBJ = the value of the objective function
> c_j^k = the discounted unit cost of travel on the jth link for the kth commodity
> x_j^k = the volume of commodity k flowing on the jth link
> P_J = the discounted future cost for building project J
> K_J = the decision to build or not build project J

J = a project designation, consisting of one or more links in the set j

a_{ij}^k = the incidence relation of the jth link to the ith node (so that when j is inflowing, $a_{ij} = +1$, outflowing, $a_{ij} = -1$, and not connected, $a_{ij} = 0$); the a_{ij} are normally the same for all k, although this is not always true

E_i^k = the quantity of the kth commodity originating at or destined to node i

U_J = an upper bound on the flow on project J

B = total construction budget available during the period under analysis

The distribution portion of this formulation is equivalent to that of a transportation or Hitchcock problem with transshipment.[3] This type of distribution is a good approximation to the market process for homogeneous products.

An example to demonstrate the model is illustrated in Figure 15-1 in which two commodities are distributed over the network shown. Proposed link additions are shown as broken lines, existing links as solid lines. The budget is 600. To the right of the network is a set of node flow equilibrium equations. The detached coefficients of these equations become the link-node incidence matrices, in the block-diagonal portion of the initial simplex tableau shown in part (c) of Figure 15-1. By manipulating the slack variables, denoted as K's, and the corresponding right-hand-side element, the slack variables may be set to either zero or one. Artificial columns to get an initial solution or start are required but not shown.

---

3. The formulation and solution of the transportation problem has been known for some time. The transportation problem is to choose $x_{ij} \leq 0$ so as to minimize

$$T = \sum_{i,j} x_{ij} C_{ij}$$

subject to

$$\sum_{i=1}^{m} x_{ij} = b_j$$

$$\sum_{j=1}^{n} x_{ij} = a_i$$

$$\sum_{i=1}^{m} a_i = \sum_{j=1}^{n} b_j = N.$$

For example, see George B. Dantzig [110], pp. 359–73; or L. R. Ford, Jr., and D. R. Fulkerson [117], pp. 24–32.

FIGURE 15-1. *Example of Network Link Addition*

(a) Network

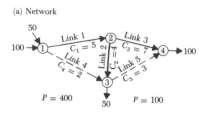

(b) Node flow equilibrium equations

$$
\begin{aligned}
① \quad -X_1 && -X_4 && +100 &= 0 \\
② \quad X_1 - X_2 - X_3 && && &= 0 \\
③ \quad X_2 && X_4 - X_5 && &= 0 \\
④ \quad X_3 && + X_5 - 100 && &= 0
\end{aligned}
$$

(c) Initial simplex tableau

	Commodity 1					Commodity 2					Integer variables				Slacks			Flow requirements
	5	4	7	2	3	5	4	7	2	3	400	0	100	0	0	0	0	
	X_1^1	X_2^1	X_3^1	X_4^1	X_5^1	X_1^2	X_2^2	X_3^2	X_4^2	X_5^2	K_4	K_4'	K_5	K_5'	S_1	S_2	S_3	
Flow requirements at node ①	-1	0	0	-1	0													= -100
②	1	-1	-1	0	0													= 0
③	0	1	0	1	-1													= 0
①						-1	0	0	-1	0								= -50
②						1	-1	-1	0	0								= 0
③						0	1	0	1	-1								= 50
Flow blocking constraints			1					1			-150	0	0	0	1			= 0
				1					1		0	0	-150	0		1		= 0
Integer constraints											1	1	0	0				= 1
											0	0	1	1				= 1
Budget											400	0	100	0			1	= 600

(d) Final optimal tableau

	Commodity 1					Commodity 2					Integer variables				Slacks			Flows	Basis	Elementary costs
	5	4	7	2	3	5	4	7	2	3	400	0	100	0	0	0	0			
	X_1^1	X_2^1	X_3^1	X_4^1	X_5^1	X_1^2	X_2^2	X_3^2	X_4^2	X_5^2	K_4	K_4'	K_5	K_5'	S_1	S_2	S_3			
	1	-1	-1	0	0													= 0	X_1^1	5
	0	1	1	1	0													= 100	X_4^1	2
	0	0	1	0	1													= 100	X_5^1	3
						0	0	1	0	1								= 0	X_5^2	3
						1	-1	-1	0	0								= 0	X_1^2	5
						0	1	1	1	0								= 50	X_4^2	2
	-1	-1				-1	-1				0	0	0	0	1			= 0	S_1	0
		-1					-1				0	0	0	0		1		= 50	S_2	0
											1	0						= 1	K_4	400
													1	0				= 1	K_5	100
																	1	= 100	S_3	0
	0	7	0	0	0	0	7	0	0	0	0	0	0	0	0	0	0	1,100	Objective	

The tableau of the optimal solution which, in this case, corresponds to building both links, is shown beneath the initial tableau of Figure 15-1(c). Note that in this problem neither link 4 nor link 5 is economically feasible when constructed individually. Both links must be built simultaneously or not at all.

The integer requirements may be met by any one of several techniques. One method which has been employed in practical problems is that proposed by Land and Doig.[4] It involves the solution of a series of linear programming problems in which the integer variables are set first to zero, then to one. Variables are successively constrained until an integer optimum is found. Land and Doig have shown that a solution obtained in this way is, in fact, optimal.

A Multitime Period Staging Formulation

The previous analysis describes how to define the optimal (as defined by the objective function) set of link additions which should be made to a network given a single period budget constraint. In most planning situations, the further problem must be resolved of how best to order these projects over time as budgeted funds become available. The steady state, single time period formulation developed in the previous section can be extended so that multiple time periods may be handled[5] and, in particular, so that the appropriate time staging of investments can be undertaken.

To do so, it is again assumed that supplies and demands are constant over all network configurations and are not a function of the network itself. It is also assumed that the network in any given stage n is a subset of the network which will exist at the next stage $n+1$ (since work proceeds from the last stage backward through time to the first stage in typical dynamic programming fashion). Cost reductions achieved by selecting a particular network configuration therefore apply only to traffic in the future and not to that of the past. The implications of these assumptions will be examined more carefully after the process has been explained.

The multistage analysis starts by looking at the final period of the planning life. This stage is designated stage N in Figure 15-2(a). The network, which will exist after construction of the links added during stage

4. A. H. Land and A. G. Doig [I26], pp. 497–520. See also Norman Agin [I1] and E. L. Lawler and D. E. Wood [I27].
5. P. N. Taborga and Paul O. Roberts [I36].

FIGURE 15-2. *Multistage Planning for Network Link Additions*

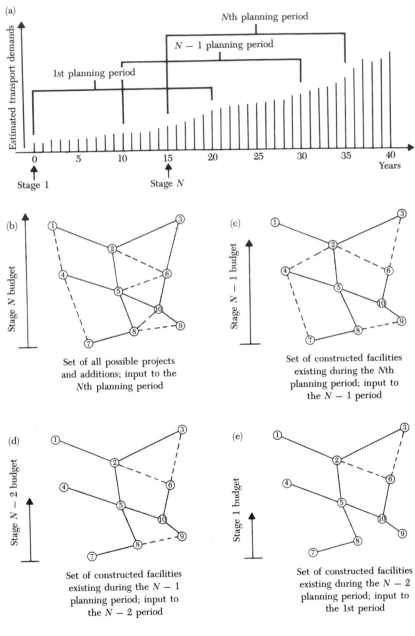

N, is based on the traffic that will use the system between years N and $N+20$ (assuming a twenty-year project life). The present discounted value of the total budget for stages 1 through N is assumed available for constructing this final, or Nth-stage, network. A selection is made from the set of all possible links (Figure 15-2[b]) to find that set which optimizes the objective function subject to the N-year budget constraint. This set of links selected by mathematical programming corresponds to the optimal transport system for the Nth planning period (Figure 15-2[c]). Links of the original set of all possible projects which are not built by stage N are deemed not economically feasible and need not be considered in other analysis periods, that is, those periods preceding N. Thus, the network for year $N-1$ must be a subset of the network for year N.

The $N-1$ stage is considered next. The budget available in year $N-1$ must be the sum of the discounted budgets from stage 1 through stage $N-1$. The set of links from which a plan must now be chosen are those which should be built by the end of the Nth planning period as determined previously. The optimal configuration for year $N-1$ is selected from this Nth-year set of links, subject to the reduced budget available in year $N-1$; the calculations are also based on the traffic forecast for the system during the $N-1$ planning period. The resulting network, which because of the stricter budget constraint is necessarily smaller than the network for period N, is shown in Figure 15-2(c). Stage $N-1$ represents the set of links out of which a plan must next be chosen for stage $N-2$ (Figure 15-2[d]) and so forth back to period 1.

By noting the differences between the networks at the $N-1$ and Nth stages, the $N-2$ and $N-1$ stages, and so forth, those links which are to be constructed during a particular stage can be determined. The entire time-staged plan is thus eventually obtained, by continuing to solve each stage in this fashion by working backwards from period N to period 1 (Figure 15-2[e]). The procedure is a simple application of dynamic programming techniques,[6] with the minimal cost solution at each stage determined by integer programming as described in the preceding section. The whole process is shown schematically in Figure 15-3.

The time-staging problem can be stated mathematically by adding to the original formulation of the problem a subscript, N, for stage, to both the choice variables and the flow requirements, and by adding another

6. Richard Bellman [14], pp. 191–95.

FIGURE 15-3. *Use of Dynamic Programming to Determine Optimal Staging Plan*[a]

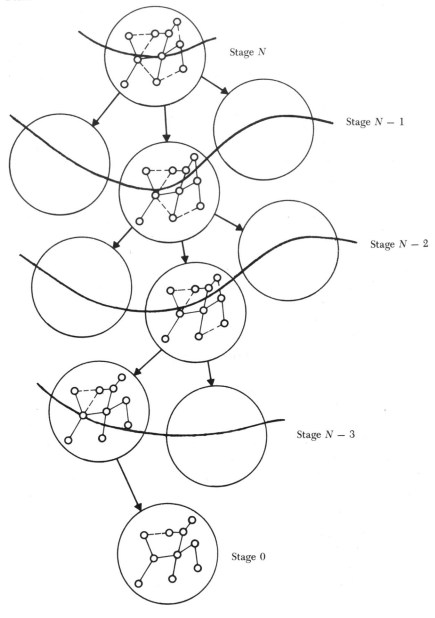

Stage N

Stage $N - 1$

Stage $N - 2$

Stage $N - 3$

Stage 0

a. Search for optimum at each stage performed by linear programming.

constraint for each of the integer variables. This new constraint is

$$K_{J,N-1} \leq K_N$$

which states that the decision variable K_J must not be greater than it was during computations for the preceding stage. In other words, if a link was not built during stage N, then it must not be considered during stage $N-1$.

The staging plan obtained is not rigorously optimal in the usual sense. Traffic patterns in the last planning period are the only ones that affect the selection of the highly important final, or Nth-stage, plan. Today's volumes merely determine which links of this final plan to build early. There is, therefore, an element of commitment to the Nth-stage plan, once it is determined.

An Illustrative Application

An application of the model provides an opportunity to demonstrate its capabilities as well as its shortcomings.[7] To this end, the model has been used to analyze possible additions to the road network of Colombia.

Colombia is characterized by extremely difficult topographic conditions. Three major ranges of the Andes Mountains divide the country and complicate the transport system. Prior to 1950, the country had little modern transport equipment and few facilities. There were three major modes of freight transport rail, highway, and river steamer. The rail system was unconnected, and there were no rail connections between the major seaports and the major industrial and governmental center, Bogotá. Similarly, goods from the important industrial city of Bucaramanga could reach the sea only by a combination of rail (or truck) and river transport. The highway system was incomplete, poorly maintained, and, because of the mountains, indirect. River operations were limited by floods, dry seasons, aged equipment, and lack of any direct or trunk connection to important cities in the highlands.

In the 1950s, Colombia entered into an extensive transport development program during which an important new railroad was constructed which connected Bogotá, Medellín (an important commercial and industrial center), and Bucaramanga with the north coast. In addition, a major effort

7. This example was first presented in Paul O. Roberts, P. N. Taborga, and Robert E. Burns [135].

was made to upgrade and modernize the road system. The result was a large commitment of funds to transportation in general and to a new Magdalena River valley (the so-called Atlántico) railroad in particular. Speculation arose that with this program Colombia had perhaps over-invested in transportation.

To apply the model, the basic data requirements are supplies and demands by commodity over time and a description of network topology and costs. Supply and demand data for Colombia were obtained from a variety of material, published and unpublished. The commodities treated were imports, exports, domestic agriculture, domestic livestock, and domestic manufactured articles. Imports and exports were taken primarily from an engineering study done for the Ministry of Public Works. For domestic agriculture and livestock, supply figures were available, but demand had to be estimated on the basis of population. A similar approach was required for the consumption of domestic manufactured articles for which supply but not demand distribution was available. A more detailed description of the assumptions underlying this distribution is given elsewhere.[8]

No attempt was made to use the model for the full multiple time period analysis as outlined in the preceding section. It was decided instead that runs should be made for a single stage at some point midway through the planning period in order that feasibility of the approach, computer running times, and so forth, might be evaluated. Since the integer programming routine had been run on only small test problems, it appeared desirable to test the algorithms with reasonable real world figures prior to full-scale analysis.

A reasonable approximation to the full intercity trunk transport network for Colombia is shown schematically in Figure 15-4. This network has 53 nodes, 230 links, and includes highway, rail, river, and transfer links with 32 possible projects.[9] The resulting matrix for the integer programming has 373 rows, 1,245 columns, and 4,041 matrix entries. Running times for this network with the set of flows previously described were on the order of 8 minutes per solution with a second-generation computer. It was immediately apparent that a problem of this size and with this number of lattice points would exceed available computer time allotments. It was therefore decided that the overall scale of the problem should be cut, both in number of links and in number of potential projects (which reduces the number of lattice points).

8. Parsons and others [J3], pp. 148, 149. See also Robert E. Burns [J1].
9. Figure 15-4 shows 36 principal nodes. Transfers from road to rail or vice versa were represented by an artificial link and hence an additional node.

FIGURE 15-4. *Schematic Sketch of Full Colombian Transport Network, 1950*

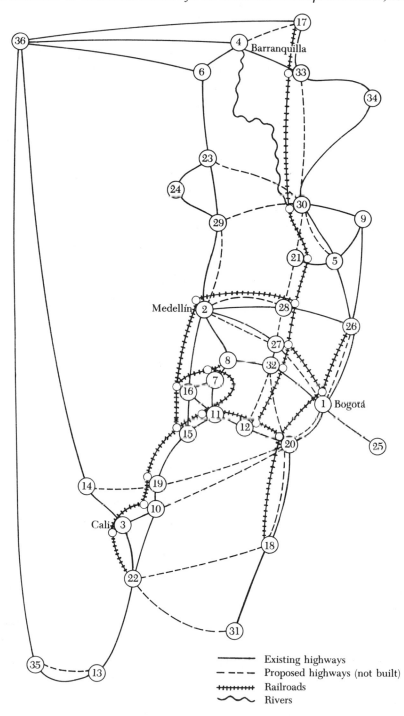

Existing highways
Proposed highways (not built)
Railroads
Rivers

The resulting reduced network is shown in Figure 15-5. It corresponds roughly to the Colombian highway network with potential link additions in the place of the Magdalena River railroad. It is made up of 36 nodes and 152 links; the matrix has 236 rows, 837 possible columns, and 2,779 entries with 27 possible projects. Running times for this network averaged 2 minutes 20 seconds for each solution. A Land and Doig tree of successively constrained solutions is shown in Figure 15-6.

The run was terminated three times prior to completion and the tree was pruned to reduce the total number of lattice points in the problem. The consequence of pruning is that any optimal integer solution obtained is no longer guaranteed to be globally optimum. Five integer solutions were found. The best solution is shown in Figure 15-7.

Although only three solutions were perfect integers, the others came so close that for practical purposes they were considered to be integers as well. The difference in the value of the objective function between the best and next best solution was less than 0.05 percent. All integer solutions were within 0.5 of 1 percent of one another. Examination of the links specified for building in the integer solutions reveal that the plans are nearly identical (see Figure 15-8).

It is interesting to compare the integer solutions obtained by use of the model with other possibilities. One obvious possibility is the NULL solution—that obtained by not building any new facilities, as shown at the upper left in Figure 15-9. The value of the resulting objective function was about 10 percent less than the best integer solution.

Three other plans were also tried; all are shown in Figure 15-9. These represented three diverse possibilities. The plan at the upper right represents approximately the network that has been built. At the lower left is a scheme incorporating the links referred to as the Andes bypass (or Marginal de Selva), and the lower right panel shows the best scheme that could be conceived with a number of transverse connections across the country.

The Andes bypass was by far the most expensive and thus least desirable of the plans investigated. It had an objective function valuation which was 17 percent higher (and therefore worse) than the best obtained. The network actually built appeared to be slightly less attractive than the NULL alternative, while the alternative emphasizing the transversals was about 5 percent better.

The results suggest that manipulating the topology of the network may produce significant cost savings. The results are quite dependent, however, on the relative accuracies of the costs of new construction and those for

FIGURE 15-5. *Schematic Sketch of Reduced Colombian Transport Network, 1950*

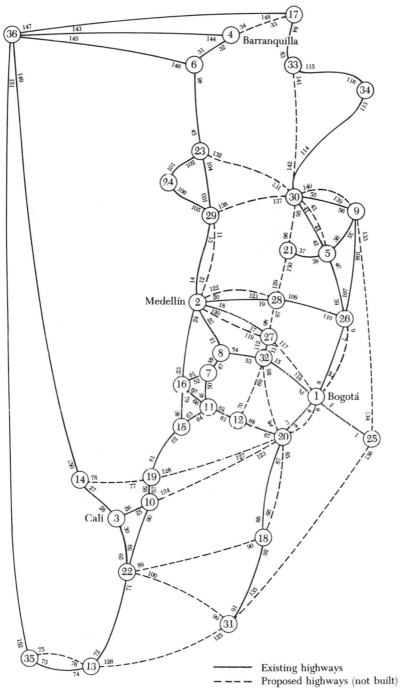

Existing highways
Proposed highways (not built)

FIGURE 15-6. *Solution Tree for Integer Programming, Colombian Transport Network, 1950*

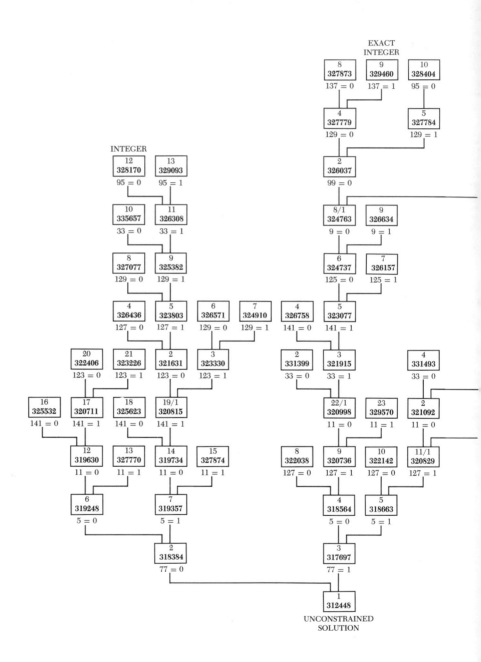

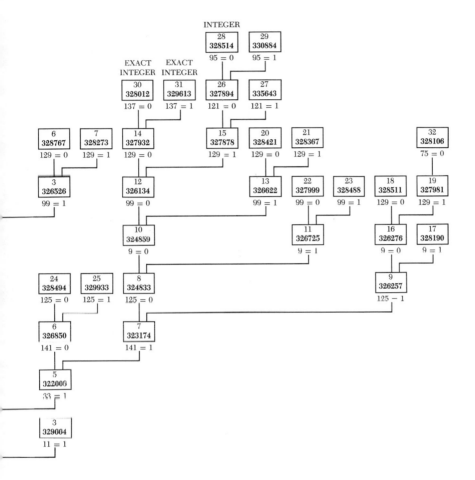

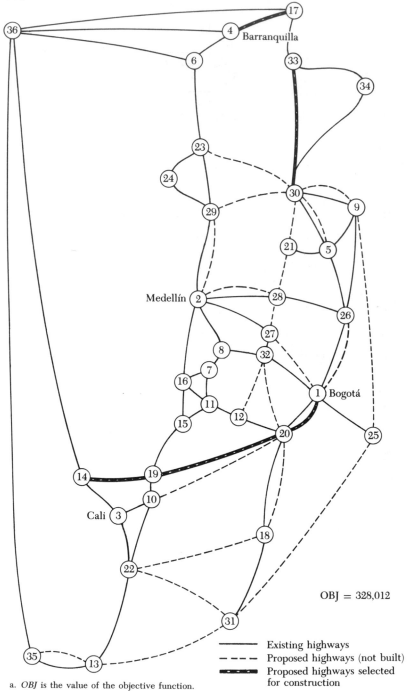

OBJ = 328,012

Existing highways
Proposed highways (not built)
Proposed highways selected for construction

a. *OBJ* is the value of the objective function.

operation over the links. Although considerable care was taken to estimate construction costs accurately, there is, of course, no substitute for cost estimates based on engineering location studies.

As for the constraint on computer time, there are several solutions. One, as in the present example, is to decrease the scope of the solutions. Another is to attempt to decrease the necessary computing times by improving the efficiency of the computer programs or the algorithms.[10] Another possibility, obviously, is to use more computer time as needed. The increase in costs may be quite trivial when compared to the magnitudes of the construction money involved.

An obvious simplification is to subdivide the problem into more manageable segments, for example, regional sublevels. Slightly smaller systems, on the order of 20 nodes, 5 commodities, and less than 10 link additions, can be solved readily with the existing routines. Decomposition into a series of smaller problems would also allow more commodities to be handled.[11]

The modal choice and routing aspects of the model might be greatly improved if the unit shipping costs for each link in each network reflected the shippers' preferences with respect to all the time and cost trade-offs that ordinarily exist in transportation and distribution activities. As these figures are specified for each column separately in linear programming, this adaptation can be relatively easy.

Summary and Critique

A major hurdle to applying the link-addition model as outlined in this chapter is its extensive computational requirements. The extent of this problem depends on the size and efficiency of available linear programming codes and of the computers on which these codes are used. The model employs an integer programming subroutine which can handle problems with approximately 400 constraint rows or, in terms of the problem, approximately 50 nodes. Running times depend primarily on the extent of the flows.

However, large-scale industrial applications of linear programming are

10. An obvious method for doing this is by means of storing the current basis and restarting from it.

11. Another approach is to determine commodity flows by means of other procedures (such as the gravity model), then to let each copy in the mathematical programming formulation represent the flows between a single origin and multiple destinations. This procedure will provide a solution to the problem posed by the distribution of commodities which do not behave in the fashion predicted by linear programming.

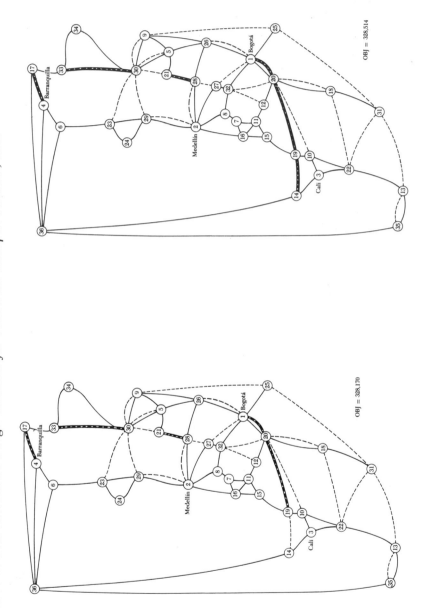

FIGURE 15-8. Four Alternative Integer Solutions for Colombian Transport Network, 1950[a]

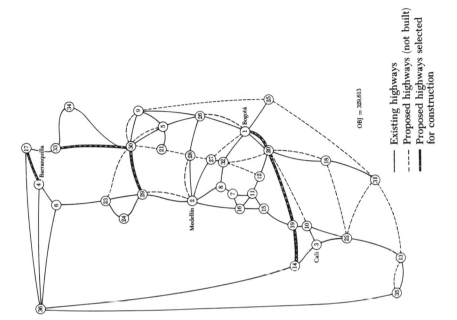

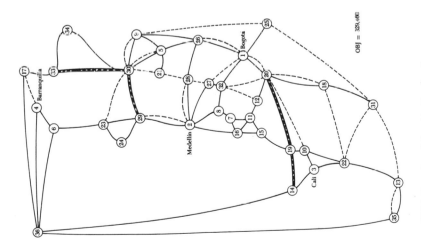

a. *OBJ* is the value of the objective function.

FIGURE 15-9. *Integer Solutions for NULL, Current, Andes Bypass, and Transverse Connections Plans for Colombian Transport Network, 1950*[a]

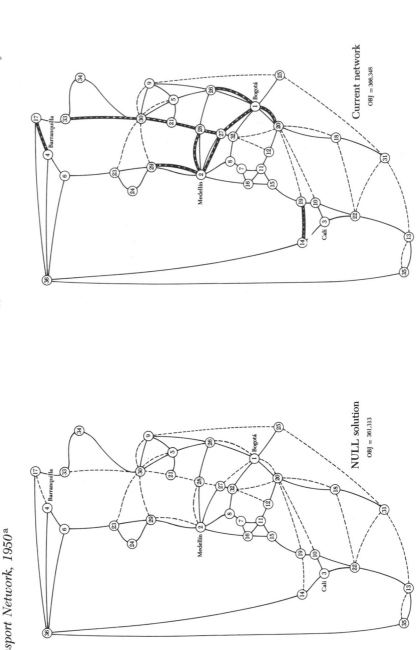

NULL solution

OBJ = 361,313

Current network

OBJ = 366,348

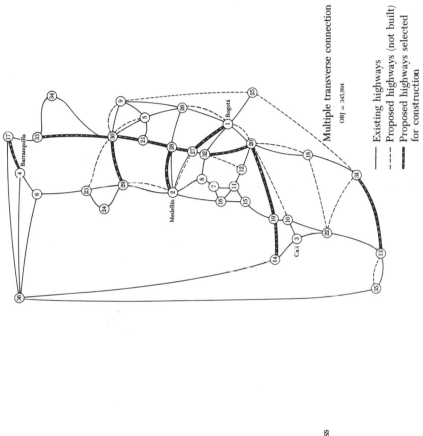

Multiple transverse connection

OBJ = 345,894

—— Existing highways
----- Proposed highways (not built)
━━━ Proposed highways selected
        for construction

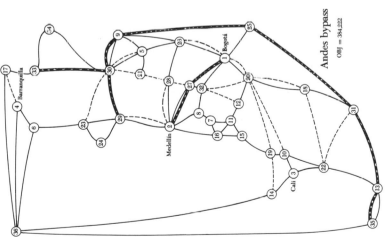

Andes bypass

OBJ = 384,222

a. *OBJ* is the value of the objective function.

273

both extensive and impressive. Progress in both equipment and software is continually being made. Computers increasingly will have dynamic memory allocation, which should help relax constraints on memory size. In terms of the link addition problem, this will increase the size of the network that can feasibly be analyzed. There are also ways in which the computation problem may be reduced by decomposing the matrix. Thus, in the long run, problem size should not offer a serious constraint to practical use of the procedure

In a different vein, the assumption of steady state flows in the model tends to ignore the effect of congestion on the network. However, capacity constraints to reflect congestion can easily be introduced if needed. A more serious problem from a practical planning viewpoint is the lack of seasonal or similar peaking in the model. Peaking may be quite important in the design of some aspects of physical systems. Specifying shorter time periods than a year may thus be necessary in certain applications. Similarly, the assumed flows represent the backhaul of empty vehicles only in a simplified way. By the introduction of more variables, this problem can also be handled, though not without adding considerable complexity.

As noted, the model requires that the supply and demand requirements over time for each of the various nodes be predicted at the outset. It would be highly desirable if the prediction of these regional supplies and demands of the various commodities were founded on basic macroeconomic relationships and trends in regional productivity and investments. In addition, transport demand in the real world depends both on the network configuration that exists at each stage and to some extent on its evolution through each of the previous stages. The obvious question is how significant this interaction might be. A simple iterative technique could be used to represent this simultaneity between transport demand and transport investment decisions. Once the staging plan is obtained, the supply and demand requirements could be recalculated and the entire procedure repeated, though the computation requirements might become quite burdensome. Moreover, the model is not well suited to develop a full macroeconomic feedback of the transport system on economic activity. The representation of full system feedbacks is, in fact, the major motive for the simulation modeling described in Volume 2.

In general, mathematical and dynamic programming formulations hold promise for transport planning in those cases where a number of combinatorial possibilities must be evaluated and where a single, simplified, linearized objective can be accepted. This should be possible during that phase of transport planning in which a preliminary search for good alternatives is being undertaken. After that phase has been completed and the choice is between a few well-defined but basically different development strategies, and where there are multiple and conflicting goals or where linearity cannot be presumed to hold, the use of simulation models is more appropriate. Nevertheless, even where a larger-scale behavioral model is available and applicable, programming techniques can be extremely useful in identifying and sorting the more important transport needs from those of lesser priority.

CHAPTER SIXTEEN

Investment Planning with Capital Budget Constraints

A PERFECT CAPITAL MARKET MODEL is often not the most realistic representation of the capital budgeting environment in which transport project decisions are made. The public sector does not typically participate in a perfect capital market. If the supply of savings is inelastic at the prevailing rates of interest, as it is in many countries, the market rate of interest may be a poor approximation to the opportunity cost of additional public investment. Similarly, taxing powers are seldom such that tax revenues can be rapidly increased if larger numbers of projects appear to have a positive value. Realistically, the feasible range in the size of the public budget will be bounded by the prevailing income distribution, tax systems, capital markets, and the level of private investment demand. It is thus unlikely that public budgets will be determined by assembling all projects which planners suggest have a positive net present value.

The usual administrative or organizational representation of constraints on public investment within the public sector is to specify limits on budgets for particular program areas. Planning within each program will involve selecting sets of projects that achieve particular goals within such bounds and these may reflect other considerations than a comparison of marginal rates of return based on net present value discounting. A budgeting environment such as this creates obvious financial interdependencies among projects. Individual project evaluation procedures or the use of simple decentralized rules based on the maximization of net present value are inappropriate in such circumstances.

When the complications of multiple period budgets or project indivisibilities are few, the choice of an optimal set of projects can be handled simply by a trial and error, iterative search. However, as the number of projects, indivisibilities, and interdependencies increases, the scanning, selection, and verification of a set of projects for which net present value is maximized (or any alternative objective) quickly become a formidable task. All possible combinations of projects must be examined in order to determine the optimal set that will exhaust the budgets prescribed. Such optimal program seeking under budget constraints obviously can become a large-scale problem in combinatorial analysis with all of its attendant difficulties. In such circumstances, a systematic search procedure using recent concepts in computer-based mathematical programming can be useful.

Both the programming approach described here and the individual project evaluation procedure described in Chapter 14 (using the positive net present value criterion) employ discounting of net benefits in the capital budgeting decision. In both procedures, an interest rate is needed for each time period for discounting purposes. However, in the programming approach, capital outlays in each period are discounted at interest rates determined endogenously or within the programming solution. Since the constraints on the amount of investment undertaken are expressed in terms of the size of the budget, the opportunity cost of capital can be determined endogenously. If, for example, the subset of projects selected exhausts budgets in some but not all years, the opportunity cost of capital is zero in those years in which some budgeted funds remain available.

The opportunity cost in years in which the budget is completely expended, however, is positive, and is determined by the rate of return on the marginal project which would have to be forgone if that particular year's budget were reduced. The interest rate reflecting the opportunity cost of capital in any year will thus depend on the relative scarcity of funds in that year, but this scarcity will only become evident as various sets of feasible projects are considered.

Budget limits may be more or less flexible. Fortunately, programming techniques are sufficiently adaptable that several different capital budgeting formulations can be developed for a variety of capital budgeting environments. The objective function can also be extended to include choice among risky alternatives, with both the mean and variance of project outcomes taken into account, though at the expense of increasing computational complexity. While the programming format is designed to treat financial interdependencies, it can be extended to include a limited number of the more important interdependencies arising from cost, performance, and demand effects as well. In practice, the choice of procedures will depend on the nature of the budgeting process, on the nature of planners' preferences, and on their ability to handle the necessary computational requirements.

Maximizing Expected Net Benefits: Linear Programming Models

The most likely framework for the budgeting problem is that of choosing those projects for which net benefits are maximized, subject to fixed budget constraints for several years. These constraints would presumably be prescribed by government budget planners, though they might also arise from legislative earmarking of certain user receipts. The constraints may, of course, be changed over time. Estimates for the immediate future will usually be relatively accurate. Constraints in the more distant future will be harder to forecast, but also less significant for present planning since there is more time for adjustment of public taxing or budgeting if the present estimates of these constraints turn out to be inappropriate. Most proposed projects under current consideration will entail large current capital outlays and yield benefits for some time to come. Time-staging considerations, however, often result in projects funded over many years, so that it will be useful to include budget constraints in the planning process for several years.

The choice of projects that maximize the discounted present value of benefits under fixed budget constraints is a simple linear programming problem.[1] It can be stated formally as follows: let b_{jt} be the net benefits of project j in year t, where b_{jt} includes financial as well as social benefits. Let c_{jt} be the net outlay required for project j in year t which is drawn from, or if positive adds to, the allocated budgets. Let C_t be the budget constraint in year t. Let x_j be the fraction of the project undertaken. Finally, let r_t be the discount rate in time period t for discounting net benefits.

---

1. Abraham Charnes, William W. Cooper, and M. H. Miller ([G3], pp. 229–58) first developed a linear programming model for analyzing physical and financial flows in the firm and the implications of these flows for budgeting decisions.

This rate is taken to be the subjective valuation of the utility of an additional dollar of benefits in any particular time period, which may or may not be well approximated by the market rate of interest and which need not be the same rate at which capital outlays are discounted.[2]

Initially, assume projects to be independent. The discounted present value of net benefits of accepted projects, subject to a budget constraint in each time period, can then be expressed as follows:[3]

Maximize
$$\sum_{j}^{n} x_j \sum_{t=1}^{T} \frac{b_{jt}}{1 + r_t},$$

subject to

(a)
$$\sum_{j=1}^{m} c_{jt} x_j \leq C_t \qquad \text{for } t = 1, \ldots, T,$$

(b)
$$0 \leq x_j \leq 1 \qquad \text{for } j = 1, \ldots, n.$$

If
$$\bar{b}_j = \sum_{t=1}^{\infty} \frac{b_{jt}}{1 + r_t}$$

is the present value of discounted benefits, the objective is to maximize
$$\sum_{j}^{n} \bar{b}_j x_j.$$

A variety of capital constraints can be readily incorporated into this model, as, for example, for foreign exchange funds, for external loans, and so on. These funds must, of course, be available for all projects being contemplated. They may warrant different interest rates, all of which will be determined endogenously. Nonfinancial constraints may be relevant and can also be included.

For all such programming problems there exists a complementary problem of the same mathematical form, the so-called dual, which incorporates the same information but in a form which has an important economic interpretation. A set of dual variables is defined, one for each constraint

2. William J. Baumol and Richard E. Quandt ([I3], pp. 317–29) point out this distinction between an objective rate of discount, the internal rate for discounting costs resulting from the capital constraints, and a subjective rate, the valuation of benefits given by the utility function. The ratio of the discount rates for net benefits in two periods is the slope of Fisher's willingness curves in his classic treatment of investment.

3. The basic development of the linear programming models of this section was done by H. Martin Weingartner [I39] in his examination of capital budgeting for the firm.

in the original problem (called the primal). The objective function in the dual minimizes the sum of these dual variables, each weighted by the value of the upper bound of the constraint it represents. This objective function is minimized subject to linear constraints which are a weighted sum of the dual variables, where the weights are elements of the transpose of the matrix of the original constraints and where the lower limits are the values of the coefficients in the original objective function.

The dual of the above programming problem would be to find the dual variables, d_t and e_j, which minimize

$$\sum_{t=1}^{T} d_t C_t + \sum_{j=1}^{n} e_j,$$

subject to
$$\sum_{t=1}^{T} d_t c_{jt} + e_j \geq \overline{b}_j \qquad \text{for } j = 1, \ldots, n,$$

$$d_t, e_j \geq 0 \qquad \text{for all } t, n.$$

This dual programming problem will always have a solution if the primal does, and the value of their objective functions will be equal.[4]

The motivation for examining the dual problem lies in the economic interpretation given the dual variables as shadow prices for each constraint. The dual variable corresponding to any particular constraint in the primal will have a nonzero value if that constraint is effective and a zero value if it is not. The economic interpretation of these shadow prices is that they assume zero values in the solution of the dual when the resource is a free good, that is, is not an effective constraint when solving the maximization problem. Since the dual and primal objective functions have the same solution, this means that all the maximized value is attributed to the scarce resources in the problem.

In the above problem, the shadow prices, d_t, for the budget constraints in each period will be nonzero if the budget constraints are effective. A nonzero value, d_t^*, can be interpreted as the net present value of another dollar added to the budget in year t if optimal budget allocations are assumed.[5] This may be useful information in the consideration of adjustments in both the size of the budget constraints and the social discount rates which were prescribed to discount net benefits. As suggested earlier, net benefits and current capital outlays will be related, though often admittedly imperfectly, via the capital markets. If the imputed interest

4. This is one of the basic theorems of linear programming. See Robert Dorfman, Paul A. Samuelson, and Robert Solow [113], pp. 100–04.

5. An asterisk denotes the actual values of the shadow prices in the programming solution.

rates on capital budgets seem low relative to alternative marginal returns on capital, either the interest rates prescribed for discounting net benefits are too low or the capital budgets allocated to this program are excessive. This sort of interpretation will be further discussed below.

Similarly, the shadow prices, e_j, will be positive if a project is chosen, zero otherwise. If a project is chosen, the corresponding dual restriction,

$$e_j^* \geq \bar{b}_j - \sum_t^T d_t^* c_{jt},$$

is met exactly, and hence e_j is the excess present value of the net benefits of an accepted project, discounted at the predetermined rate of interest, over the sum of discounted costs, the latter discounted at the endogenously determined opportunity cost of funds. Rejected projects have a negative net present value, that is,

$$\bar{b}_j < \sum_t^T d_t^* c_{jt}.$$

The shadow prices, e_j, and their equivalent for rejected projects,

$$f_i = \sum_t^T d_t^* c_{it} - \bar{b}_i,$$

suggest a way of ranking projects; this ranking will, in general, be different from a simple project-by-project present value ranking because the effects of budget constraints in the choice of a set of optimal projects are not included in the individual project approach. The programming ranking may be useful if an acceptable project is suddenly unavailable and a decision on project selection must be made without calculating a new solution to the entire budgeting problem. When such a change in the total program is small, the existing ranking of rejected projects will be a useful first approximation for selecting new projects to include, without reprogramming the entire budget.

This basic linear programming model can be extended to include some alternative capital budgeting arrangements, each of which introduces additional flexibility into the interpretation of the budget constraints. One particular sort of budget relationship which may be useful in a transportation context is that of budget deferrals, where funds not used in one period are available in the next. This is often a realistic representation of public budget allocation. For example, public trust funds created by earmarking certain user taxes as available only for specific purposes are quite common devices for transport financing. Such financing may, in fact, be a useful assurance to planners that they need not search too enthusiastically for ways of expending budgeted funds in any given year.

A simple change in the constraints in the preceding programming format yields a model for handling this type of deferral or funding arrangement. Defining S_t as the slack funds or unspent budgeted funds in budget year t, the program becomes:[6]

Maximize
$$\sum_{j=1}^{n} \bar{b}_j x_j,$$

subject to

(a)
$$\sum_{j=1}^{n} c_{jt} \cdot x_j + S_1 = C_1,$$

(b)
$$\sum_{j=1}^{n} c_{jt} x_j + S_t - S_{t-1} = C_t \qquad \text{for } t = 2, \dots, n$$

where

$$0 \le x_j \le 1 \qquad \text{for } j = 1, \dots, n.$$
$$S_t \ge 0$$

Unspent funds are thus available in future periods, although they will not have appreciated since it is assumed that they are not invested in the capital market in the interim.

Another potentially useful extension would be the introduction of an integer programming format. That is, by constraining the x_j in the solution to be either 0 or 1, essentially a yes or no decision can be made on each project. This eliminates the problem of interpreting fractional projects when there are significant project indivisibilities or other dependencies.[7] As noted in Chapter 15, an integer programming format can be used only at some computational cost. The available algorithms often converge to a solution only after many iterations, even in small problems.

The above discussion has focused on project dependencies that arise from the nature of the capital allocation process. It is conceptually straightforward to include other project dependencies as well, especially if an integer programming format is employed. There may, for example, be situations where a subset of feasible projects is composed of mutually exclusive projects, so that only one of the projects in the set can be under-

6. Weingartner [I39], pp. 123–25.
7. The number of fractional projects which will be included in the optimal set will have as an upper bound the number of time periods for which there exist budget constraints. Weingartner [I39], pp. 32–34.

taken. An additional constraint must be added for each set of mutually exclusive projects of the type

$$\sum_{j\in J} x_j \leq 1$$

where j is defined over all projects in the set, J, of mutually exclusive projects.[8] As before, accepted projects in the set will have a positive value at given interest rates. Rejected projects may also have a positive value but less than the accepted ones.[9]

In addition, it may be desirable to include contingency relationships among projects; if project m is desirable only if project k is accepted, the additional constraint can be included as $x_m \leq x_k$. Inclusion of project dependencies in the constraint set further complicates the integer solution. Contingency relationships can be represented in the integer format by quadratic constraints, but computational procedures for quadratic integer programming are not available.[10]

Difficulties in implementing integer programming, however, need not be taken too seriously. Customarily, an integer solution can be fairly closely approximated by using a linear programming procedure wherein the programming is conducted over groupings of projects (and a common mean and variance is the usual basis for determining the groupings). If the recommended set of investments includes a fractional part of a project group, any divisibility within each group created by the aggregation of projects can be useful in implementing the solution to the programming problem. At the same time, computational simplicity would be achieved since the number of alternative investments is reduced by aggregation.

Maximizing Benefits under Risk Averse Preferences: Quadratic Programming

An example of a decision-making problem under uncertainty was described earlier in the context of project design. The principles of decision

8. Weingartner [139], pp. 37–38.

9. It would be possible to introduce demand dependencies by this procedure; mutually exclusive projects might be the same project defined for alternative configurations of the adjacent part of the transport system.

10. Reiter has initiated efforts at obtaining computational procedures for integer programming in which all pairs of projects have positive interactions. Stanley Reiter [133], pp. 32–36, and Stanley Reiter and Gordon B. Sherman [134]. H. Martin Weingartner ([138], pp. 485–516) has summarized progress to date and formulated the interdependencies problem as a quadratic integer programming problem.

theory and subjective probability theory apply in a straightforward fashion to the capital budgeting decision as well. The assumed objective is to maximize expected utility, using a cardinal utility index, where the arguments of the utility function are the net benefits of possible projects and where the stochastic nature of outcomes is represented by a subjective probability distribution.

As noted, if the decision maker maximizes expected utility and has a linear function, the simple linear programming model is directly applicable. The variance and all higher moments of the probability distributions can be ignored in these circumstances. Such disregard for the variance and higher moments may not be unrealistic in a transportation capital budgeting context. If the transportation budget is only a small fraction of the total government budget, the variance of outcomes may be relatively unimportant to public planners. Also, the variance of the group of projects comprising the total transport budget will usually be low compared to the variances of individual projects. While generalizing is difficult, public officials may well be willing to assume some risk, especially in the less developed countries, and especially if the time stream of benefits at stake is in accordance with their (likely) high valuation of more immediate time periods. In many practical applications of public budget planning, this will be as sophisticated as one need be. The linear programming formulation can be straightforwardly applied, with the use of expected values rather than point estimates for the benefits and costs.

There may be cases, however, where attention to higher moments of the probability distribution of outcomes is useful. The data and programming requirements can become substantial when higher moments are considered. A particularly important case is that in which the means and variances of the probability distribution of outcomes is used to rank alternative budget allocations. This has been labeled the certainty equivalence model, in which decision makers describe their preferences for uncertain outcomes in the form of indifference curves between the mean, μ, and variance, σ^2. Illustrative indifference curves of this type appear in Figure 16-1; their shapes reflect different aversions to risk. This representation of choices among uncertain outcomes has considerable intuitive appeal and also is amenable to an uncomplicated programming solution.

The basis for a decision maker's choosing among alternative sets of projects by reference to the mean and variance of total benefits lies in simplifying assumptions about either the underlying utility function or the subjective probability distributions. If no restrictions are placed on the

FIGURE 16-1. *Illustrative Indifference Curves: Certainty Equivalence Representation*

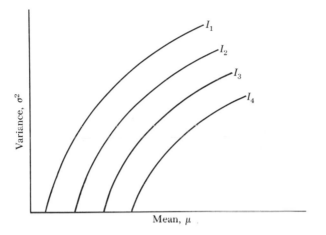

probability distributions but the utility function is quadratic, expected utility depends only on the mean and variance of outcomes.[11] Alternatively, regardless of the utility function, for any two-parameter family of subjective probability distributions the mean and variance of total benefits will be sufficient to rank order the alternative sets of projects.[12] One important special case is where the unknown outcomes are jointly normally distributed, in which case the indifference curves will be increasing and concave

---

11. Perhaps the simplest case, attributable to Markowitz's pioneering work, is where the utility function is quadratic:

$$U = aR + bR^2$$

where U is utility, R is return, a is a positive constant, and b less than zero, the latter implying risk aversion. Expected utility is

$$E(U) = aE(R) + b[E(R)]^2 + b\sigma^2$$

where σ^2 is the variance of the return R. Expected utility thus depends on the expectation and variance of the return. Harry Markowitz [I29], especially Chap. 13.

That a quadratic utility function is not appealing derives from the property that risk aversion increases with income, that is, as income rises the decision maker must receive an ever increasing addition to his expected return to compensate him for a given increase in the variance. John W. Pratt [H12], pp. 122–36.

12. Donald E. Farrar [I15], pp. 19–26. Farrar has shown that if the utility function is expanded in a Taylor series about the mean and if terms in the expansion beyond the quadratic are dropped, expected utility maximization is the same as reaching the highest indifference curve with a certainty equivalence model.

downward in the μ, σ plane.[13] The procedure outlined below follows this latter course, assuming normality.

A convenient representation of preferences which has considerable intuitive appeal for application in practical decision problems is the negative exponential;[14] if x denotes income and U utility, then

$$U(x) = 1 - e^{-cx}.$$

This function implies that the decision maker's cash equivalent or selling price at which he values any set of uncertain circumstances is invariant to changes in his asset position. In a capital budgeting context, this means that changes in the level of the budget do not affect one's valuation of any given set of possible outcomes, a considerable simplification for the analysis. The function has diminishing marginal utility of income and is bounded from above. In addition, the function is strictly risk averse, that is, the cash equivalent of any set of uncertain outcomes is less than the expected monetary value of the outcomes.[15] Such preferences can be represented by straight line indifference curves in the μ, σ^2 plane (hence concave downward using μ, σ axes), with constant slope $2/c(\mu - 2/c\sigma^2)$ where c is a constant. This slope is a measure of risk aversion, indicating how much of a reduction in the mean would be traded for a reduction in the variance. A high value of risk aversion results in flat indifference curves, which implies that a low expected value would be accepted to achieve a low variance. Conversely, with low risk aversion or steep indifference curves, a high variance will be accepted in conjunction with a higher expected value. Finally, a zero slope implies that the variance of outcomes will be disregarded. These alternatives are illustrated in Figure 16-2.

Thus, under the assumption of normality, the decision maker's valuation of any uncertain consequence is completely described by reference to the vector of means and the variance-covariance matrix of outcomes. The returns on the set of proposed projects distributed jointly normally will describe a feasible region in the μ, σ^2 plane which will be convex and of the general shape illustrated in Figure 16-2. Utility maximization will yield a best or preferred point, the location of which will depend on the decision

13. Martin S. Feldstein [I16] has recently pointed out that the assumptions of risk aversion and a two-parameter subjective probability distribution need not imply that indifference curves are convex. Normality does assure convexity.

14. This utility function was first used by Rudolf J. Freund ([I19], pp. 253–63), who saw its relevance in a capital budgeting framework.

15. The properties and desirability of a negative exponential utility function are discussed at length in John W. Pratt, Howard Raiffa, and Robert O. Schlaifer [H13], Chap. 4.

FIGURE 16-2. *Indifference Curves: Negative Exponential Utility Function*[a]

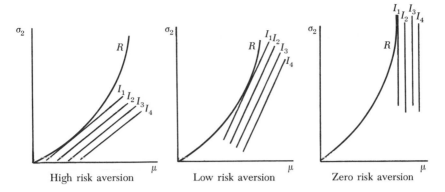

| High risk aversion | Low risk aversion | Zero risk aversion |

a. R denotes the feasible set; I, the indifference curve.

maker's attitude toward risk, which is represented by the coefficient in the negative exponential function.[16] The decision maker must specify this parameter. If presented with an approximation to the feasible region, the decision maker should with a little introspection be able to determine reasonably closely his trade-off between the mean and variance implicit in various degress of risk aversion.

Specifically, let projects have net benefits (financial outlays and other benefits) that have a joint normal distribution, with means μ_{jt}, variances v_{jt}, and covariances σ_{ijt} in year t. Let maximization of expected utility[17] be expressed as:

Maximize $\quad \sum_{j}^{n} x_j \sum_{t=1}^{\infty} \frac{\mu_{jt}}{1 + r_t} - c/2 \sum_{i}^{n} \sum_{j}^{n} x_j \left[\sum_{t=1}^{T} \frac{\sigma_{ijt}}{1 + r_t} \right] x_j.$

16. If $\tilde{x}$ is a normally distributed random variable with mean μ and variance σ^2, the cash equivalent of the lottery yielding the outcome $\tilde{x}$, is

$$S \equiv e^{-S/c} = E\,[1 - e^{-c\tilde{x}}] = \int_{-\infty}^{+\infty} (1 - e^{-c\tilde{x}}) \frac{1}{\sqrt{2\pi\sigma^2}} e^{-1/2 \frac{x - \mu^2}{\sigma^2}}\, dx$$

$$= -e^{-c\mu} + (2/c^2)\,\sigma^2$$

and hence $S = \mu - (c/2)\sigma^2$.

Maximizing the cash equivalent, S, with respect to x is equivalent to reaching the highest indifference curve.

17. Farrar [I15], pp. 26–28. Farrar formulated the programming solution for a single time period. For a nonmathematical formulation of the capital budgeting decision with risky alternatives, see James Van Horne [I37], pp. B84–B92.

The first term is the mean, the second the variance of the set of projects chosen. If the mean and variance are discounted to the present at the prescribed social rates of discount, and these discounted variables are designated by a bar $(-)$ over the variable, the programming problem becomes:

Maximize

$$\sum_{j}^{n} x_j \bar{u}_j - c/2 \sum_{i}^{n} \sum_{j}^{n} x_i \bar{\sigma}_{ij} x_j$$

subject to

(a)
$$\sum_{j=1}^{n} c_{jt} x_j \leq C_t \qquad \text{for } t = 1, \ldots, T$$

(b)
$$0 \leq x_j \leq 1 \qquad \text{for } j = 1, \ldots, n.$$

While the net benefits are stochastic (described by a density or probability distribution), project financial outlays, c_{jt}, in this model are assumed certain, so that constraints in each period can be met exactly. If the c_{jt} are stochastic as well, the constraints will not be met exactly. One possibility is to add to the program additional constraints which reflect the cost of exceeding a financial constraint (perhaps the interest cost of additional short-term financing to rectify the imbalance). Another possibility is to state the financial constraints in probabilistic terms, in which only projects for which the expectation of meeting the financial constraints exceeds a certain level are selected. This is a chance-constrained programming problem.[18] Constraints might be defined in terms of higher moments of the distributions as well. These extensions are probably not of great practical significance.

---

18. For a good exposition of chance-constrained programming, see Abraham Charnes and William W. Cooper [16], pp. 73–79. Application of these techniques in a capital budgeting context has been done by Bertil Näslund [I31], pp. 257–71.

In this application, the constraints

$$\sum_{j=1}^{n} c_{jt} x_j \leq C_t$$

can now be expressed as

$$Pr\left[C_t - \sum_{j=1}^{n} c_{jt} x_j \right] \geq \alpha.$$

Specification of the levels, α, is necessary. Solving the dual to the programming problem will provide the decision maker with estimates of how a change in α will affect the objective function. See Bertil Näslund and Andrew Whinston [I32], pp. 184–200. Solution, however, in general involves a nonlinear programming problem with inequality constraints. The Kuhn-Tucker conditions can be used to characterize the solution, but numerical solutions are not easily achieved. See Näslund [I31], pp. 268–71.

Financial outlays can often be forecast rather accurately relative to the probability distribution of net benefits. In addition, if the distributions of expenditures have finite second moments, recourse to the central limit theorem will assure that the planned budget allocations will be reasonably closely approximated by necessary outlays in most circumstances.

The quadratic programming problem, as described above, is not much more difficult computationally than most linear programming problems. Wolfe has developed what is probably the most efficient computational algorithm to date.[19] The solution will be unique as long as the matrix with elements $\bar{\sigma}_{ij}$ is nonsingular. Generally, more than one project will be chosen. This is because the nonzero covariance among two or more projects will result in a reduction of the variance for the set of projects, at little cost in terms of the expected value.

The quadratic programming model has a dual which is defined analogously to the dual in the linear programming model.[20] If λ_1 and λ_2 are

19. Philip Wolfe [140], pp. 282–98. Wolfe developed a computational procedure for solving problems of the form:

Minimize $\qquad\qquad Z = p^t w + \frac{1}{2} w^t Q w$

subject to $\qquad\qquad Aw \le K,$
$\qquad\qquad\qquad\quad w \ge 0.$

It is necessary that Q be positive semidefinite, which ensures that a local minimum in the numerical solution also is a global maximum. In the above capital budgeting problem, the maximization problem is an application of Wolfe. The matrix with elements $c\bar{\sigma}_{ij}$ must be negative semidefinite; this will be true since $\bar{\sigma}_{ij}$ are elements of the variance covariance matrix of projects, and the utility function assumed is risk averse.

20. The appropriate dual is suggested by reference to the Kuhn-Tucker conditions for solving nonlinear programming problems. Kuhn and Tucker develop conditions for solving the general programming problem of maximizing a differentiable function $g(x)$, subject to $F(x) \ge 0$. A new function is defined $\phi = g(x) + \lambda F(x)$, where λ is a vector with as many dimensions as constraints, F; and ϕ assumes the same form as the familiar Lagrangean maximization problem, but with the ability to include inequalities as constraints. Nonnegative x and λ are sought so as to satisfy the following conditions:

$$\phi(x,\lambda^0) \le \phi(x^0,\lambda^0) \qquad\qquad \text{for } x \ge 0$$
$$\phi(x^0,\lambda) \ge \phi(x^0,\lambda^0) \qquad\qquad \text{for } \lambda \ge 0.$$

This corresponds to finding a "saddle point" in x and λ for ϕ. This vector x will be a solution to the maximization problem. See H. W. Kuhn and A. W. Tucker [125].

In the capital budgeting under uncertainty problem, max $Z = cx + x'Dx$ subject to $Ax = b, x \ge 0$ can be solved by defining $\phi(x,\lambda) = cx + x'Dx - \lambda'[b - Ax]$, and then finding x and λ which meet the Kuhn-Tucker conditions for a saddle point. The dual is:

Minimize $\qquad\qquad Z' = -xDx + \lambda'b,$

subject to $\qquad\qquad -2Dx + A'\lambda \ge c', \qquad\qquad\qquad\qquad \lambda \ge 0.$

vectors of nonnegative shadow prices for the budget constraints and the size of projects, respectively, a dual can be defined, where λ_1 will be $1 \times T$, for T years, and λ_2 will be $1 \times n$, for n projects. Thus,

Minimize $\qquad Z = c/2 \sum_i^n \sum_j^n x_i \bar{\sigma}_{ij} x_j + \sum_t^T \lambda_1^t C_t + \sum_{j=1}^n \lambda_2^j$

subject to

(a) $\qquad\qquad c \sum_i^n x_i \bar{\sigma}_{ij} + \sum_t^T c_{jt} \lambda_1^t + \lambda_2^j \geq \mu_j \qquad$ for $j = 1, \ldots, n$

(b) $\qquad\qquad\qquad\qquad x_j \geq 0 \qquad\qquad\qquad$ for $j = 1, \ldots, n$

(c) $\qquad\qquad\qquad\qquad \lambda_1^t, \lambda_2^j \geq 0 \qquad\qquad\quad$ for $j = 1, \ldots, n$
$\qquad\qquad\qquad\qquad\qquad\qquad\qquad\qquad\qquad\qquad\quad t = 1, \ldots, T.$

If the original quadratic programming problem has a solution x^*, then there exist vectors x^* and λ^* which are a solution to the above dual.

The dual variables λ_1^t, for the $t = 1, \ldots, T$ budget constraints are interpreted as before, a positive value indicating the present value of expected utility of another dollar added to the budget in year t. The dual variables λ_2^j corresponding to the jth project, however, have a new interpretation. Each λ_2^j appears in one of the n constraints of the dual:

$$c \sum_i^n x_i \bar{\sigma}_{ij} + \sum_t^T c_{jt} \lambda_1^{t*} + \lambda_2^{j*} \geq \mu_j \quad \text{for all } j = 1, \ldots, n.$$

For accepted projects, λ_2^j will be positive, and for rejected projects, λ_2^j will be zero. The expression for the jth such shadow price, corresponding to the jth project, becomes:

$$\lambda_2^{j*} \geq \bar{\mu}_j - \sum_t^T \lambda_1^{t*} c_{jt} - c[x_1^* \bar{\sigma}_{1j} + x_2^* \bar{\sigma}_{2j} + \cdots + x_n^* \bar{\sigma}_{nj}].$$

The first part of the expression, $\bar{\mu}_j - \sum^T \lambda_1^{t*} c_{jt}$, is the present value of expected benefits less the project cost, the latter discounted at the discount rates determined endogenously by the solution to the opportunity cost of each year's capital budget,

$$\lambda_1^{t*} = \frac{1}{1 + r_t^*}.$$

The latter part of the right-hand side of the λ_2^{j*} inequality is a constant times the discounted change in the variance of expected returns for the entire mix of projects if project j were included. Thus the worth of including the jth project in the budget is defined by the effects on both the mean and the variance of outcomes of the entire budget.

This expression for λ_2^j* can be given a certainty equivalence interpretation. If, for the jth project, $\lambda_2^j* > 0$, then

$$\bar{\mu}_j - \frac{c}{2}[x_1^*\bar{\sigma}_{1j} + x_2^*\bar{\sigma}_{2j} + \cdots + x_n^*\bar{\sigma}_{nj}] >$$

$$\sum_{t=1}^{T} c_{jt}\lambda_1^t* - \frac{c}{2}[x_1^*\bar{\sigma}_{1j} + x_2^*\bar{\sigma}_{2j} + \cdots + x_n^*\bar{\sigma}_{nj}].$$

The left-hand term in the inequality is the increase in the expected value of discounted benefits less the increase in the variance of outcomes resulting from including project j in the budget. The slope of the certainty equivalence curves, $c/2$, provides the "numeraire" in this expression for weighting these changes in the mean and variance. The right-hand term is the "cost" of including project j, expressed in terms of benefits of forgone projects—their expected return, represented in the expression by the summation of project j's cost discounted at the endogenously determined interest rates, less the increase in the variance of outcomes of the entire budget implied by a marginal change in all projects. This certainty equivalence interpretation of the trade-off at the margin between an accepted project and alternatives forgone becomes precise if the feasible region is smooth and if projects are divisible.

Implications of the Programming Approach

A major advantage of the programming approach to budgeting is that it serves as a useful focal point for coordinating policy decisions in the areas of benefit measurement, subsidy, and pricing. Decisions with regard to capital expenditures and the pricing of public infrastructure will usually require the resolution of many divergent interests and attitudes. If the capital budgeting decision is made in a programming context, it is possible to introduce some simple systems effects and interdependencies among projects into planning and policy formation.

The discussion in Part 3 indicated the complex interrelationships among the sort of benefits to be counted, the amount of subsidy to be borne, and the appropriate degree of price discrimination to recoup benefits; it also indicated the nature of the many trade-offs in these decisions and the means by which they might be better incorporated into individual project evaluations. The discussion was, however, somewhat incomplete in its explanation of how these trade-offs should be reviewed in a broader context. Above all, these decisions are closely related in their implications for the use of available budgets.

The most important decisions in project evaluation center around the definition of project benefits, the pricing procedures employed, and public subsidies. It is through pricing policies that social benefits or social profitability are related to financial returns. The choice of a pricing policy will be conditioned by pricing procedures followed elsewhere in the economy (as described in detail in Part 1) and by the size of transport budgets. Thus, price discrimination may be deemed necessary to reduce public investment costs; or, conceivably, surplus funds might produce a search for more projects, based on a more liberal interpretation of benefits. Either way, the extent to which financial subsidies or a particular form of user pricing are justified should be reconsidered as the implications of budget constraints on transport investment decisions become more obvious or explicit.

Government must also be prepared to review transport projects relative to other uses of public funds. Decisions about pricing, subsidy, and project acceptance in the transport sector must ultimately be considered from a broader perspective. This need is heightened by the fact that transport budgets are often a large portion of the total public budget. Even individual projects may so affect the total budget, especially in the less developed countries, that the possible effects of different criteria for transport pricing or project acceptance on the total public budget can be significant.

A major advantage of budget programming is its usefulness in such an overall review. An examination of the imputed returns and shadow prices of transport projects and budgets relative to those of projects and budgets in other areas is a direct means of pursuing the objective of a rational total budget. Interpretation of any computed shadow prices or returns depends, of course, on what is counted as a benefit. To the extent that the benefit estimates are meaningful, especially in comparison to such returns for other public projects, these can be useful in deciding whether the number of transport projects as determined by the size of transport budgets needs to be expanded or contracted relative to other public investments. For example, if nearly all transport budget constraints are effective and if the rates of return on accepted projects seem excessive compared to other government projects, the proportion of public investment in transportation might well be increased.

Similarly, with the potential marginal benefits resulting from additions to any year's budget made explicit in the programming approach, important financial or budget constraints can be identified. If the implied opportunity cost of additional funds seems high relative to the availability of funds in either domestic or foreign capital markets, or to the availability of tax revenues, a change in capital budgets by borrowing or taxing may be recommended. The shadow prices of the constraints in the programming solution can be useful in this context. Shadow prices on foreign exchange constraints or domestic capital budgets in various time periods may suggest which budget constraints to relax in order to achieve the largest payoffs.

The use of programming procedures in capital budgeting or in network staging (as discussed in Chapter 15) are, in sum, important first steps in introducing systems effects into the project planning process. In the capital budgeting case, these procedures provide a flexible format for handling the dependencies arising from financial constraints. But other important systems effects, such as dependencies among projects arising from either demand characteristics or the performance of the system, are still not taken into account. While some of these dependencies might be included as sets of constraints in the capital budgeting algorithms, this adaptation is limited by computational capacity. Indeed, as noted earlier, the determination of net benefits for any individual project is almost always a vast oversimplification. An account of all of the net benefits of each project (regarded as a single input datum in the programming format for capital budgeting) is probably as complex a problem as the budgeting problem itself.

Similarly, the network-staging program also considers certain project dependencies explicitly (those arising from demand choices in an interdependent network). However, it does not include budget dependencies or any of the feedback effects of demand on the system's performance, and the economic feedback of the transport system, for example, on location decisions.

The programming techniques discussed in these last two chapters are thus only a first step to the systems viewpoint taken in Volume 2. In concentrating on system interdependencies, the analysis in Volume 2 draws in a complementary fashion on much of the discussion of pricing, benefits, and welfare theory developed in detail in this volume, although in an individual project context. From a practical standpoint, project and systems analyses are both essential tools for modern transport planning.

Appendixes

APPENDIX A

An Evaluation of Gravity and Linear Programming Transportation Models for Predicting Interregional Commodity Flows

THIS APPENDIX EVALUATES alternative techniques for predicting interregional commodity flows when supplies and demands are given for every region: the linear programming (L.P.) transportation model and the gravity model. In the gravity model, supply is distributed to receiving regions in proportion to the demand and in inverse proportion to the transportation cost.[1] All supplying nodes consider shipment to all demand points simultaneously. With the L.P. model the total transportation cost is minimized.[2] The assumption that the supply and demand of each region are given implies that production cost would not affect the optimal flow pattern even if the objective function were to minimize the aggregate cost of production and transportation.[3]

1. See Chapter 7, note 8, and Chapter 8, note 32.
2. See Chapter 7, note 9.
3. This is intuitively obvious because the amount of supply in any region cannot be increased or decreased even if the production cost there is substantially lower or higher than elsewhere (Robert Dorfman, Paul A. Samuelson, and Robert Solow [113], Chap. 5). However, the allocation of flows according to the L.P. transportation model yields as dual variables the relative profitability of the production of alternative supply regions, which, in turn, can be used as a guide for planning the future supply in every region (see Chapter 15).

As is indicated in Chapter 10, the characteristics of the two models are such that it is reasonable to suppose that the L.P. model simulates inter-regional flows better than the gravity model for fairly homogeneous commodities, while the gravity model does better for highly aggregated commodities. This study recommends a means for evaluating the two modeling techniques. The basic procedure is to calibrate each model to best fit the interzonal commodity flow data, and then to examine how well it fits.

The Data

The data used for testing the alternative techniques are interdistrict shipments on the Pakistan West Railroad during March 1962.[4] Because monthly data are used, little of the crosshauling caused by seasonal changes in supply-demand relationships is reflected. West Pakistan was divided into twelve geographical regions whose size varies: the average is about 140 by 140 miles, the largest 73 by 1,000 miles, the smallest 8.4 by 1,000 miles. The average distance from the center of one region to the center of the next region is nearly 200 miles.

Since rail transport is only one of several available modes, the data do not represent all interregional commodity flows or any uniform proportion thereof. The major spine of West Pakistan, the Indus River, is not navigable and consequently there is little barge transport. The rail data therefore represent most long-distance transport activities within West Pakistan. However, most short-distance hauls will not be recorded in the data, because they are largely carried out by trucks.

This data limitation is insignificant in applying the L.P. model, which can be used to represent commodity flows irrespective of total production. The L.P. model tests the rationality of the commodity flows within the framework of given supply and demand characteristics and transportation costs. Such a comparison of the derived with the observed data is not disturbed by the lack of data for other modes and home consumption.

The gravity model, however, is susceptible to this data limitation. It postulates flows as a function of the total production at the origin (including home consumption, shipment by truck, shipment by rail, and so on) and the total consumption at the destination. Therefore, the lack of data for home consumption and truck shipments will affect the results of the tests

4. These data are described in Brian V. Martin and Paul O. Roberts [F28].

FIGURE A-1. *Effect on Gravity Transportation Model of Limited Data for Home Consumption and Local Truck Shipments of Commodities*

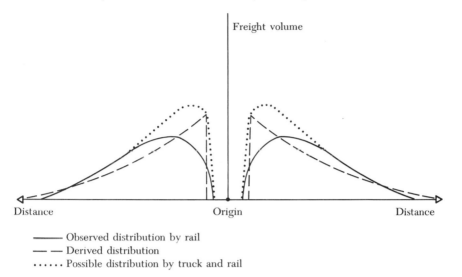

—————— Observed distribution by rail
— — Derived distribution
• • • • • • Possible distribution by truck and rail

of the two models. This specification problem in using the gravity model to fit the rail data is illustrated in Figure A-1. While the rail data fall off precipitously as the distance from the origin decreases, the distribution of commodity flows may continue to rise. The exponent derived by best fitting a curve to the data is thus likely to be too small,[5] the fit itself less good, particularly for short hauls, and the overall percentage error of estimation raised.

The extent of commodity aggregation and its relevance to modeling procedures is one of the major issues of this appendix. As noted, if a commodity contains heterogeneous elements, crosshauling is likely to take place, which cannot be explained by the L.P. model. Therefore, as the commodity is aggregated, the explanatory power of the L.P. model diminishes. In order to evaluate the effect of commodity aggregation, three types of commodity groups are identified and examined in the Pakistan West Railroad data.

5. Truck shipments are generally hauled shorter distances than rail shipments, even within the short-distance range. If regions are sufficiently small to differentiate short-distance hauls by different distance classes, the derived distribution pattern is not necessarily biased in one direction. If this is the case, the best exponent is not necessarily larger than the one derived from the rail data.

They are (1) homogeneous commodities, including rice, domestic wheat,[6] cement; (2) diversified commodities, including agricultural products (wheat, cotton, perishable fruit, vegetables, rice), all other agricultural products, textiles; and (3) mixed commodities, including fertilizers. The first group includes relatively homogeneous commodities. Imported wheat is excluded from the wheat category because of known quality differences. Each commodity in the second group consists of a great many different subcommodities. In the third group, each commodity is composed of a few distinct subcommodities. Fertilizers in West Pakistan include primarily two different subcommodities, one domestically produced and the other imported.

Interregional transportation costs were estimated from tonnage transportation charge data on rice and wheat, which were chosen because they are fairly homogeneous commodities and the transportation charge per ton of either one is considered to be more or less proportional to the transportation charge for all other commodities, if station-to-station charges are compared. Also, when data for rice and wheat were compared, no significant difference was found between the absolute mean values of transportation charges for either of them.[7] The final transportation charge table was made from data on rice and wheat whenever available, and from data on other commodities such as cotton and "all other agricultural products" if rice and wheat data were missing.

It should be noted that the transportation charge data are from railroad stations to railroad stations, not from representative points in the regions to representative points in other regions. Therefore, if either supply or demand locations differ for particular commodities, the resultant transportation charge from one region to another region varies. By averaging all the tonnage data and charge data from stations to stations within the regions, a representative transportation charge figure based on the present pattern of commodity flows is obtained. Since the locations of major production and consumption centers are not likely to change rapidly, the figures yielded by this method are considered more appropriate than those derived by assuming hypothetical production and consumption points within regions.

These transportation cost data were used for testing all the commodities considered. It is obvious from the above discussion that since the transpor-

6. West Pakistan imports a large amount of wheat. Since its port of entry is Karachi, which has only a small amount of cultivated land, all the wheat supplied from Karachi is assumed to be imported and is therefore eliminated from the calculations.

7. The mean charges differed by less than 2 percent.

tation charge table is primarily based on rice and wheat, it would represent the actual interregional transportation charges on rice and wheat very well but might not represent those on other commodities. Ideally, a separate transportation charge table should have been compiled for each commodity, but data and time limitations prevented this.

Criteria for Evaluation and Results

Three criteria were used in determining the goodness of fit of the data. The deviation of the derived flow from i to j, $\hat{q}_{ij}$, from the observed flow, q_{ij}, is the basis for two of the comparisons. One criterion is the ratio of the summation of the absolute deviations to the total quantity of the commodity moved:

$$d = \frac{\sum\limits_{\substack{i,j \\ i \neq j}} \hat{q}_{ij} - q_{ij}}{\sum\limits_{\substack{i,j \\ i \neq j}} q_{ij}} .$$

This index expressed as a percentage may be called the overall percentage error of prediction. It is sensitive to the accuracy of the origins of a commodity received by a region.

This index is not sensitive to the relative accuracy of the derived flow between any particular origin and destination pair, because each deviation is summed up before it is compared to the observed flow between the pair. If the relative accuracy of prediction for each pair is important, as, for example, when the purpose of flow prediction is to identify transportation bottlenecks, another index must be developed.[8] An alternate measure, the relative accuracy of the derived flow for each origin and destination pair, can be expressed by a ratio:

$$r_{ij} = \hat{q}_{ij}/q_{ij},$$

and the accuracy of a class of predicted flows can be expressed as a frequency distribution of these ratios:

8. When the commodity under consideration is the composite commodity of all the transportable goods, or is a major component in the total transportation demand, the result of flow prediction can be used for transport bottleneck identification. When the commodity is a minor component, the index under consideration does not have much significance.

Class of predicted flows	Relative accuracy of derived flow, r_{ij}	
I	0	2^{-2}
II	2^{-2}	$2^{-1/2}$
III	$2^{-1/2}$	$2^{1/2}$
IV	$2^{1/2}$	2^2
V	2^2	∞

A third criterion is the comparison of derived and observed total resource requirements in transportation. This requirement can be measured by the total ton-miles hauled or, more properly, by the total transport cost expended. In the empirical analysis below, total revenue is used as a proxy for the total transport cost because of the lack of cost data. Since the total transport cost is the minimand in the L.P. model, this model always yields a lower bound for, and, in actuality, an underestimate of, the usage of transport resources.[9] On the other hand, the gravity model implies varying degrees of transport utilization since, depending on the exponent used, the average distance of shipments will be larger or smaller.

The results of tests based on the overall percentage error of prediction are summarized in Table A-1 together with the percentages of crosshauls in the observed flows. In general, a pattern of commodity flows that is well explained by one model is also well explained by the other model. This is primarily because when the number of supply and demand regions is limited there is little difference between the flow patterns derived by alternative models. In the case of rice, both supply and demand regions are limited: two regions supply 84 percent of the total shipments and one region demands nearly 88 percent of the total receipts. Cotton, which is not tested here, is an extreme case: Karachi alone demands 91 percent of the total receipts (due to exports). In such cases, the choice between alternative techniques is trivial because every technique gives a good fit. Two commodities that are involved in a number of significant supply and demand regions are domestic wheat and cement. Although neither model simulates the real flow pattern well, the gravity model performs better for both commodities.

Within the category of diversified commodities, there is a distinct differ-

9. Conversely, by comparing the observed flow matrix to the one derived by the L.P. model, the degree of inefficiency or irrationality of the observed flow matrix can be determined. This is the approach taken by James M. Henderson [I22].

TABLE A-1. *Percentage Error of Gravity and Linear Programming Transportation Models in Predicting Interregional Commodity Flows, and Percentage of Crosshauls, by Commodity Groups, West Pakistan March 1962*

	Overall percentage error of prediction										
	Gravity model									Linear programming model	Percentage of crosshauls
Commodity group	Impedance parameter, α										
	0	0.1	0.3	0.5	1	3	5	7	10		
Short hauls included											
Homogeneous											
Domestic wheat	—	60.6	59.6	58.5	55.5	43.9	38.5	37.0	27.1	54.8	4.2
Rice	—	13.7	13.4	12.8	11.3	10.3	9.6	9.2	9.5	12.0	6.4
Cement	—	50.2	47.4	44.6	38.0	22.7	20.0	20.5	22.8	27.4	5.5
Diversified											
Agricultural products[a]	—	38.9	39.1	39.0	38.1	33.3	35.0	37.8	41.1	45.4	33.9
All other agricultural products	—	41.9	39.9	37.9	32.8	18.9	20.6	25.7	29.5	36.5	23.2
Textiles	36.2	37.3	39.3	41.1	48.3	43.7	46.0	54.0	—	49.8	43.8
Mixed											
Fertilizers	46.8	47.2	47.6	48.2	49.9	55.3	57.7	59.2	—	63.2	6.9
Short hauls omitted											
Homogeneous											
Rice	—	—	—	—	—	—	8.5	—	—	—	—
Diversified											
Agricultural products	—	—	—	—	18.0	14.9	—	—	—	—	—
All other agricultural products	—	—	—	—	—	—	—	—	—	—	—

a. Wheat, cotton, perishable fruit, vegetables, and rice.

303

ence between the performances of the two models. As expected, the gravity model produces flow patterns that are much closer to the observed ones, as seen in the case of agricultural products and all other agricultural products. In the case of textiles also, the gravity model gives a better fit.[10]

The mixed commodities category, as illustrated by fertilizer flows, is a case in which both models perform very poorly. Generally, however, it may be concluded that the gravity model gives a better fit than the linear programming model through calibration with the exponent. To the extent that there are different subcommodities in a mixed commodity, such as fertilizers, every one of which exhibits distinct performance characteristics, these separate elements are best treated as different commodities.

For rice, agricultural products, and all other agricultural products, another type of testing, with shorthauls omitted, was conducted for the gravity model. In the hope of eliminating the bias in estimating the optimal exponent, which is caused by trucks as well as trains having been used for short hauls, transportation within any single region was omitted from the data, thereby reducing the percentage error for every commodity. This improvement implies that there is a greater proportion of short hauls in the observed data than the gravity model indicates and that the L.P. distribution is better as far as the prediction of intraregional flows is concerned. Furthermore, it is interesting to note that the optimal value of the exponent obtained by the tests with short hauls omitted is slightly smaller than the one obtained by the first or unrestricted tests.[11]

It is reasonable, therefore, to conclude that the optimal distribution behaves more like the L.P. model for short hauls and more like the gravity model for long hauls. Graphically, the relationship between the observed and the derived distributions of flows would be as shown in Figure A-2. Thus, a modified gravity model that accommodates a greater proportion of short-distance hauls may fit the observed distribution better. Such a function is, for example, as follows:[12]

---

10. It should be noted that the best assumption for predicting the flow distribution of textiles is that the transportation cost has nothing to do with distribution ($\alpha = 0$).

11. Table A-1 does not give relevant figures for comparison, but numerical comparison of the three commodities shows that the optimal exponent is smaller than that obtained by the first test by roughly one.

12. This function, however, crucially depends on the absolute scale of the transportation cost or distance measurement, for example, if the cost is measured by dollars or rupees. In this sense, the modified gravity model is more realistic, but as a general model it has the drawback that this absolute scale must be determined case by case until a general empirical rule for the measurement is found.

$$q_{ij} = \frac{D_j/\alpha^{t_{ij}}}{\displaystyle\sum_{k=1}^{N} D_k/\alpha^{t_{ik}}}$$

where q_{ij} is the predicted amount of flow from region i to *region j*

  D_j or D_k is the demand in region j or k respectively

  t_{ij} or t_{ik} is the distance (or transportation cost) from region i to region j or region k respectively

  α is a constant empirically determined

For every individual flow space, such as a flow from region i to region j, the degree of accuracy of the model can be determined by taking a ratio of the amount of flow derived to the amount of flow observed. The ratios thus derived from all the flow spaces were classified according to their values.

The results of tests with this criterion are shown in Table A-2. The following conclusions can be established from the results: (1) For homogeneous commodities such as domestic wheat, rice, and cement, linear programming gives a superior simulation of the real commodity flows in terms of distribution of relative accuracy. (2) For diversified commodities the

FIGURE A-2. *Relationship between Observed and Derived Distributions of Interregional Commodity Flows*

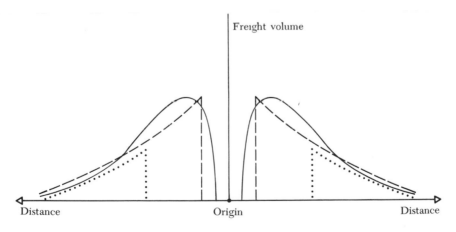

— Observed distribution
– – Gravity distribution
· · · · · Gravity distribution with short hauls omitted

TABLE A-2. *Relative Accuracy of Gravity and Linear Programming Models in Describing Individual Commodity Flows, West Pakistan, March 1962*

Commodity group	Type of model	Frequency distribution of relative accuracy of derived flow, $r_{ij} = \hat{q}_{ij}/q_{ij}$, by class of predicted flow[a]					
		Class I	Class II	Class III	Class IV	Class V	Total
Homogeneous							
Domestic wheat {	Gravity (5)[b]	10	8	49	5	72	144
	Linear programming	33	1	100	1	9	144
Rice {	Gravity (4)	19	8	59	9	49	144
	Linear programming	39	1	88	3	13	144
Cement {	Gravity (4)	11	12	25	8	88	144
	Linear programming	31	1	102	4	6	144
Diversified							
Agricultural products[c] {	Gravity (4)	26	24	31	20	43	144
	Linear programming	100	0	28	7	9	144
All other agricultural products {	Gravity (4)	33	18	34	27	32	144
	Linear programming	104	2	21	12	5	144
Textiles {	Gravity (1)	7	25	12	28	72	144
	Linear programming	88	5	42	1	8	144
Mixed							
Fertilizers {	Gravity (1)	4	11	67	2	60	144
	Linear programming	19	0	116	1	8	144

a. See p. 302.
b. Numbers in parentheses are the values of gravity model impedance parameter, α.
c. Wheat, cotton, perishable fruit, vegetables, and rice.

gravity model generally performs better. But in the case of textiles, the two models perform about equally well. (3) For the mixed commodity, fertilizers, the linear programming model provides a better simulation than the gravity model. (4) The L.P. model simulates the real interregional flow patterns better in terms of the distribution of relative accuracy for individual flow spaces when the number of positive entries in the observed flow spaces is small. This is because the maximum number of positive entries in an L.P. flow table is $2N - 1$, where N stands for the number of regions.

There is a maximum of N entries for intraregional flows and a maximum of $N - 1$ entries for interregional flows. In the case of West Pakistan, there are 23 positive entries in the table. In the cases analyzed, the number of positive entries in the table are as follows:

Domestic wheat	49
Rice	55
Cement	49
Agricultural products[13]	123
All other agricultural products	128
Textiles	108
Fertilizers	29

Since the homogeneity of commodities can be roughly represented by the number of positive entries in the observed table, it follows that, if the number of positive entries is relatively small, the L.P. model yields better predictions, and, conversely, if the positive entries are relatively large, the gravity model does better.

The total transportation cost for the derived interregional flows gives an indication of how much the total transportation system is used. The closeness of the derived intensity of transportation system use to the observed one is a necessary criterion to evaluate the alternative distribution techniques; the gross amount of investment for the transport sector in the optimal plan would be an important variable to be determined through the model. However, since the transportation cost table is based on data for wheat and rice, no comparison of the total transportation costs for other commodities could be made, though a tentative finding was derived from an examination of the data for wheat and rice. This comparison of estimated with actual may still be of some value, because homogeneous commodities are of primary interest when using the L.P. model, and rice and wheat are significant elements in the homogeneous commodity category. The results are summarized in Table A-3.

From the nature of the linear programming concepts, the linear programming model necessarily gives smaller total transportation costs than

13. The number of entries in agricultural products should be larger than that in all other agricultural products. The contradictory finding above is due to truncation involved in using different units of weight.

TABLE A-3. *Transportation Costs Derived from Gravity and Linear Programming Models as a Percentage of Costs Calculated for Observed Flows, Wheat and Rice, West Pakistan, March 1962*

Commodity	Gravity model						Linear programming model
	Impedance parameter, α						
	1	2	3	4	5	7	
Domestic wheat	114.3	108.3	103.6	101.0	99.1	97.1	95.0
Rice	102.0	100.4	99.7	98.7	98.8	98.3	98.0

the observed costs, as shown in the table. It should be noted that the gravity model also gives a smaller total transportation cost if the exponent is chosen optimally with respect to the first criterion and the total derived transportation costs of the alternative models do not differ too markedly. This result is consistent with the idea that prompted modification of the gravity model.

Time Discounting
Procedures for
Capital Budgeting

Several time discounting procedures are commonly employed in certain circumstances as an alternative to discounted present value as described in Chapter 12.[1] These can be classified into four broad types:

1. The benefit cost ratio, B/C, is the sum of the weighted (by time discounting) gross benefits over the sum of the weighted costs. The same notations as in Chapter 12, note 2, are used:

$$B/C = \frac{\sum\limits_{i=0}^{n} w_i GB_i}{\sum\limits_{i=0}^{n} w_i C_i}.$$

Projects are ranked by the ratio and accepted until the capital budget is exhausted.

2. The internal rate of return, r, is defined as the interest rate that makes

---

1. Several extensive discussions of these techniques exist. For example, G. David Quirin [G18], especially Chap. 3, or Harold Bierman, Jr., and Seymour Smidt [G2], Chaps. 2 and 3.

the sum of the weighted net benefits equal to zero. Thus, r is the value in the following equation:

$$\sum_{i=0}^{n} \frac{GB_i - C_i}{(1 + r)^i} = 0.$$

Projects are ranked by the internal rate of return and accepted until the capital budget is exhausted.

3. The payback period, P, is usually defined as the number of years after the initial year it takes to cumulate sufficient net benefits to cover the initial year's cost, C_0, of the project. That is, the payback period is P in the following equation:

$$\sum_{i=1}^{P}(GB_i - C_i) = C_0.$$

Sometimes the payoff period is translated into a percentage, which may be called the approximate rate of return, by dividing 100 percent by the payoff period. Thus, a project having a payoff period of five years is said to have an approximate rate of return of 20 percent. Projects are then ranked either by the reciprocal of the payoff period or by the approximate rate of return.

4. The average annual total cost is the constant payment that will cover all costs of the project during its life, including capital amortization and interest. If the initial year's costs are C_0, the constant annual payment that would amortize and pay the interest on a debt of this size over n years at interest rate r is

$$C_0 \left[\frac{r(1 + r)^n}{(1 + r)^n - 1} \right].$$

The figure in brackets in the above expression is called the capital recovery factor. It has been conveniently tabulated for various interest rates and time periods. When the constant annual payment is added to the average annual operating costs of a project, the average annual total cost of the project is defined. On the assumption that the gross benefits of every alternative project are the same in every year, the best project is the one that has the lowest costs. The capital recovery factor is really a simplification which arises from the net present value formula in the special case where one uses a constant discount rate over time and the net benefits of the project are zero in any prior time period and some constant amount in each of n succeeding time periods; under such circumstances, the present value formula reduces to[2]

$$PV = (GB - C) \frac{(1 + r)^n - 1}{r(1 + r)^n}.$$

Evaluation and Comparison

Discounted present value is the best of the alternatives because of its more general applicability. Its use will enable the analyst to select the appropriate project whenever the other more conventional measures will allow it and often when the other measures will not.

The average annual cost method is advocated by some because of its simplicity and because it seems to be better understood by most laymen than discounted present value. Grant and Ireson conclude:

For most economy studies . . . annual cost comparisons [are preferred] to present worth comparisons. The most important advantage is that, generally speaking, people seem to understand annual costs better than they understand present worths.[3]

Strictly speaking, average annual cost can be used only when it is assumed that the gross benefits of all relevant alternatives are equal in each year. In some transport problems, such as the consideration of alternative designs or the time staging of a project, this assumption can be useful, but in reviewing less homogeneous sets of projects it will almost always be unavoidably unrealistic. The average annual cost also requires the analyst to use the same interest rate throughout the entire time period, which may not always be reasonable.

2. In this special case,

$$\text{present value} = 0 + \frac{NB}{1 + r} + \cdots + \frac{NB}{(1 + r)^{n-1}} + \frac{NB}{(1 + r)^n}$$

$$= \frac{NB(1 + r)^{n-1} + \cdots + NB(1 + r) + NB}{(1 + r)^n}$$

$$= \frac{NB\dfrac{1 - (1 + r)^n}{1 - (1 + r)}}{(1 + r)^n} = NB\frac{(1 + r)^{n-1}}{r(1 + r)^n}$$

where NB is net benefits.

3. Eugene L. Grant and W. Grant Ireson [G8], p. 103.

The principal objections to using the payoff period criterion to rank projects are (1) that all net benefits occurring after the payoff period are ignored and (2) that equal weight is given to annual net benefits within the payoff period regardless of when they occur. The first objection can be illustrated as follows: Suppose two projects, A and B, each requires an expenditure of $100 next year. Project A will generate net benefits of $20 for each of the next five years and zero net benefits thereafter. Project B will generate annual net benefits of $19 over each of the next six years and $100 of annual benefits for years 7 through 50. Project A has a payoff period of 5 years, while Project B has a payoff period of 5.26 years. Yet Project B is preferable at any reasonable rate of interest.

The second objection can be illustrated as follows: Suppose each of two projects requires an expenditure of $100 the first year. Project A generates $90 of net benefits in year 2 and $10 of net benefits in year 3. Project B has $10 of net benefits in year 2 and $90 of net benefits in year 3. (Assume that both projects have equal benefits after year 3.) Both projects would have a payoff period of two years, but Project A should be preferred because the heavy returns, $90, are realized earlier.

It has been pointed out that under special conditions the rate of return implied by the payoff period closely approximates the internal rate of return. This special case occurs when the net benefits are the same in every year after the first year and the project is long-lived and has a salvage value of zero.[4]

Actually, the internal rate of return is itself appropriate only under

---

4. Let C_0 = costs in first period and NB = net benefits in each of the succeeding periods. Then the rate of return equals NB/C_0. In this special case, the internal rate of return, r, is found by solving the following equation:

$$C_0 = \sum_{i=1}^{n} \frac{NB}{(1+r)^i}.$$

So,

$$C_0 = \frac{NB}{r} - \frac{NB}{r(1-r)^n}.$$

It follows that

$$r = \frac{NB}{C_0} - \frac{NB}{C_0(1+r)^n}.$$

See Myron J. Gordon [G7], pp. 48–55.

certain conditions. Computational difficulties can present problems in applying it. The equation which is solved to find the internal rate of return is a polynomial of degree $n - 1$, where n is the number of years in the project's life. Solving this polynomial directly may be difficult. By contrast, computing the discounted present value only requires taking the sum of n multiplications. There may also be more than one real solution to the internal rate of return equation.[5] In this case it is not always obvious which solution should be regarded as *the* internal rate of return. Some authors have suggested that the appropriate answer for project evaluation purposes is the rate where the present value of net benefits is falling as r increases,[6] or that only the highest rate of return is relevant.[7] However, these distinctions among rates are ill chosen; the appropriate question is whether the project has a positive present value at the discount rate (or set of rates) regarded as the opportunity cost of funds expended or made available in different time periods.[8]

Another disadvantage of using either the internal rate of return or the rate of return over cost as an investment criterion is that both require weighting net benefits in year t by $1/(1 + r)^t$, where r is always the same number. This involves the implicit assumption that the opportunity cost or yield of project expenditures or receipts in any year can be evaluated by the single interest rate, r.[9] The discounted present value computation is more flexible in that it allows the analyst to use different values for the discount rate in different years. This flexibility can be important, since a project can have a positive present value with varying discount rates even while having a zero or negative present value at any constant discount rate.[10]

Even if a unique internal rate of return could be computed for each project, ranking projects by this criterion might lead to incorrect selection when they are mutually exclusive—for example, a single-lane road versus a double-lane road—or when there is an absolute shortage of investment funds. Consider the following example involving two two-year projects:

5. James H. Lorie and Leonard J. Savage [G13], pp. 62–65. Also see Ed Renshaw [G19], pp. 86–88.

6. John G. McLean [G14], p. 59.

7. J. F. Wright [G25], p. 125.

8. See Quirin [G18], pp. 34–55.

9. Ezra Solomon [G23], pp. 74–79.

10. Jack Hirshleifer [G10], pp. 224–25.

	Project A		Project B	
Benefits and costs	*Year 0*	*Year 1*	*Year 0*	*Year 1*
Gross benefits	$ 0	$150	$ 0	$150
Costs	100	2	90	15
Net benefits	− 100	148	− 90	135

Discount rate	*Present value of net benefits*	
(percent)	*Project A*	*Project B*
0	$48.0	$45.0
10	34.5	32.7
20	23.3	22.5
30	13.8	13.8
40	5.7	6.4

Though Project B has the higher internal rate of return (50 percent as compared to Project A's 48 percent), its net benefits have a higher discounted present value only for discount rates above 30 percent. If the analyst must choose between the two projects, he should select Project A if the discount rate is below 30 percent, even though Project A has the lower internal rate of return.

Of course, any project that has a positive discounted present value of its net benefits at some discount rate will also have an internal rate of return greater than its discount rate. Therefore, if the government has sufficient investment funds and all projects have equal lives, undertaking all projects with positive discounted present values at some specified discount rate will lead to the same set of projects as undertaking all projects with an internal rate of return greater than the same specified discount rate.

A variant of the internal rate of return criterion, and one subject to more or less the same limitations, is the discount rate that equates the discounted present value of the net benefit streams of two projects, called the rate of return over cost. Thus, the rate of return over cost for Projects A and B would be 30 percent. When the gross benefits of each project are assumed equal in each year, then the rate of return over cost is also the discount rate that equates the discounted cost streams of two projects. At a discount rate below 30 percent, Project A is the cheaper alternative; at a discount rate above 30 percent, Project B is cheaper.[11] Like the internal rate of return, the equation for the rate of return over cost may be difficult to solve and may give multiple answers.

11. For a more detailed discussion of this point, see Armen Alchian [G1], pp. 61–71, and Romney Robinson [G21], pp. 72–73.

The benefit–cost ratio avoids the difficulty of multiple rates of return, but it too can produce incorrect results when a choice must be made among projects whose benefit–cost ratios are greater than one, but where a choice is necessary because of budget constraints or because the projects are mutually exclusive. Consider the following example:

	Project A		Project B	
	Year 1	Year 2	Year 1	Year 2
Gross benefits	$ 0	$200	$ 0	$15
Costs	100	90	10	1
Net benefits	−100	110	−10	14
Ratio of gross benefits to costs, year 1		2.22		15
Ratio of gross benefits to costs, years 1 and 2	1.05		1.36	

If the ratio of gross benefits to operating costs is used as the criterion, Project B seems better. In year 2, however, Project A generates $110 and Project B only $14 of net benefits. Thus Project B is superior to Project A only if the $90 extra not invested in Project A in year 1 can generate at least $96 ($110 − $14) of net benefits in year 2 when used elsewhere in the economy.[12] Implicit, therefore, in the rankings are assumptions about alternative uses of the resources.

Problems in applying the benefit cost ratio can also arise when deciding whether a project consequence is treated as a gross benefit or a reduction in cost. For example, some analysts treat a reduction in vehicle operating and maintenance cost of a transport investment as an increase in gross benefits, while others include it as a reduction in costs associated with the project. The numerical value of the ratio of benefit to cost will depend on this treatment, whereas net benefits will be unaffected. Again, these numerical differences in the benefit–cost ratio will matter mainly if budget constraints are such that all projects cannot be undertaken and the benefit–cost ratio rank ordering is employed as a means of project selection.

Use of a simple alternative, such as the payoff period, is sometimes defended on the grounds that use of a more complicated criterion does not pay when the estimates of gross benefits and costs are themselves unreliable. However a criterion should be chosen because it is appropriate to the circumstances, not because it is easy to apply. Moreover, the implications for the choice of a discounting procedure because of uncertainty

12. See Roland N. McKean [F25], pp. 108–18.

in measuring net benefits are not obvious, nor is the appropriateness of the adjustments for uncertainty implicit in choosing different time evaluation criteria. For example, it is not clear that the best way to treat uncertain future net benefits is to neglect them by using an evaluation criterion that focuses only on benefits and costs in the immediate future, such as the payback period. Also, estimates of the net benefits of some projects will be more reliable than estimates for others. In short, instead of the investment criterion being made to compensate for the unreliability of the net benefit estimates, this reliability should be handled directly by improving the estimates of gross benefits and costs.

Bibliography

A. Costs

A1 Alchian, Armen. "Costs and Outputs," in Moses Abramovitz and others, eds., *The Allocation of Economic Resources*, Essays in Honor of Bernard Francis Haley. Stanford: Stanford University Press, 1959.

A2 Ferguson, Allen R. "A Marginal Cost Function for Highway Construction and Operation," American Economic Association, *Papers and Proceedings of the Seventieth Annual Meeting, 1957 (American Economic Review, Vol. 48, May 1958)*.

A3 Johnston, John. *Statistical Cost Analysis*. New York: McGraw-Hill, 1960.

A4 Meyer, John R. "Some Methodological Aspects of Statistical Costing as Illustrated by the Determination of Rail Passenger Costs," American Economic Association, *Papers and Proceedings of the Seventieth Annual Meeting, 1957 (American Economic Review, Vol. 48, May 1958)*.

A5 Meyer, John R., John F. Kain, and Martin Wohl. *The Urban Transportation Problem*. Cambridge: Harvard University Press, 1965.

A6 Meyer, John R., and Gerald Kraft. "The Evaluation of Statistical Costing Techniques as Applied in the Transportation Industry," American Economic Association, *Papers and Proceedings of the Seventy-third Annual Meeting, 1960 (American Economic Review, Vol. 51, May 1961)*.

A7 Meyer, John R., Merton J. Peck, John Stenason, and Charles Zwick. *The Economics of Competition in the Transportation Industries*. Cambridge: Harvard University Press, 1959.

A8 Soberman, Richard M. "A Railway Performance Model," Harvard Transportation and Economic Development Seminar, Discussion Paper 45. Processed. Cambridge: Harvard Transport Research Program, August 1965.

317

A9 Soberman, Richard M. *Transport Technology for Developing Regions: A Study of Road Transportation in Venezuela.* Cambridge: M.I.T. Press, 1966.

A10 Stigler, George. "Production and Distribution in the Short Run," *Journal of Political Economy,* Vol. 47 (June 1939).

A11 Straszheim, Mahlon R. *The International Airline Industry.* Washington: Brookings Institution, 1969.

A12 Walters, Alan A. "The Allocation of Joint Costs with Demands as Probability Distributions," *American Economic Review,* Vol. 50 (June 1960).

A13 Walters, Alan A. "Production and Cost Functions: An Econometric Survey," *Econometrica,* Vol. 31 (January–April 1963).

B. Pricing and Price Theory

B1 Adams, Walter, and Joel B. Dirlam. "Big Steel, Invention, and Innovation," *Quarterly Journal of Economics,* Vol. 80 (May 1966).

B2 Allais, Maurice. "Le Problème de la Coordination des Transports et la Théorie Économique," *Bulletin du P.C.M.* (October 1947). Reprinted in *Revue d'Économie Politique,* No. 2 (March–April 1948).

B3 Baumol, William J., and others. "The Role of Cost in the Minimum Pricing of Railroad Services," *Journal of Business,* Vol. 35 (October 1962).

B4 Boiteux, Marcel. "Peak-Load Pricing," in James R. Nelson, ed., *Marginal Cost Pricing in Practice.* Englewood Cliffs, N.J.: Prentice-Hall, 1964.

B5 Boiteux, Marcel. "La Tarification au Coût Marginal et les Demandes Aléatoires," *Cahiers du Séminaire d'Économétrie,* No. 1 (1951).

B6 Bonbright, James C. "Public Utility Rate Control in a Period of Price Inflation," *Land Economics,* Vol. 27 (February 1951).

B7 Brozen, Yale. "Welfare Theory, Technological Change and Public Utility Investment," *Land Economics,* Vol. 27 (February and May 1951).

B8 Buchanan, James M. "Peak Loads and Efficient Pricing: Comment," *Quarterly Journal of Economics,* Vol. 80 (August 1966).

B9 Chamberlin, Edward H. *The Theory of Monopolistic Competition: A Re-Orientation of the Theory of Value.* 8th ed. Cambridge: Harvard University Press, 1963.

B10 Drèze, Jacques H. "Some Postwar Contributions of French Economists to Theory and Public Policy, with Special Emphasis on Problems of Resource Allocation," *American Economic Review,* Vol. 54, Supplement (June 1964).

B11 Fishlow, Albert, and Paul A. David. "Optimal Resource Allocation in an Imperfect Market Setting," *Journal of Political Economy,* Vol. 69 (December 1961).

B12 Hershey, J. W. "The Rest of the Story on 'The Role of Cost in the Minimum Pricing of Railroad Services,'" *Journal of Business*, Vol. 36 (July 1963).

B13 Hirshleifer, Jack. "Peak Loads and Efficient Pricing: Comment," *Quarterly Journal of Economics*, Vol. 72 (August 1958).

B14 Leibenstein, Harvey. "Allocative Efficiency vs. 'X-Efficiency,'" *American Economic Review*, Vol. 56 (June 1966).

B15 Lerner, Abba P. "The Concept of Monopoly and the Measurement of Monopoly Power," *Review of Economic Studies*, Vol. 1, No. 3 (June 1934).

B16 Lipsey, R. G., and Kelvin Lancaster. "The General Theory of Second Best," *Review of Economic Studies*, Vol. 24, No. 1 (1956–57).

B17 Locklin, D. Philip. *Report on International Freight Rates*. H. Doc. 303, 78 Cong. 1 sess. (1943).

B18 Mason, Edward S. *Economic Concentration and the Monopoly Problem*. Cambridge: Harvard University Press, 1957.

B19 Mills, Edwin S. *Price, Output, and Inventory Policy: A Study in the Economics of the Firm and Industry*. New York: Wiley, 1962.

B20 Mohring, Herbert. "Relation Between Optimum Congestion Tolls and Present Highway User Charges," in *Traffic Congestion as a Factor in Road-User Taxation*. Highway Research Record 47. Washington: Highway Research Board, 1964.

B21 Nelson, James C. "The Pricing of Highway, Waterway, and Airway Facilities," American Economic Association, *Papers and Proceedings of the Seventy-fourth Annual Meeting, 1961* (*American Economic Review*, Vol. 52, May 1962).

B22 Nelson, James R. "Practical Applications of Marginal Cost Pricing in the Public Utility Field," American Economic Association, *Papers and Proceedings of the Seventy-fifth Annual Meeting, 1962* (*American Economic Review*, Vol. 53, May 1963).

B23 Nelson, James R. "Pricing Transport Services," in Gary Fromm, ed., *Transport Investment and Economic Development*. Washington: Brookings Institution, 1965.

B24 Peck, Merton J., and John R. Meyer. "The Determination of a Fair Return on Investment for Regulated Industries," in *Transportation Economics*. New York: Columbia University Press for the National Bureau of Economic Research, 1965.

B25 Roberts, Merrill J. "Transport Costs, Pricing, and Regulation," in *Transportation Economics*. New York: Columbia University Press for the National Bureau of Economic Research, 1965.

B26 Rose, Joseph R. "The Role of Cost in the Minimum Pricing of Railroad Services: A Comment," *Journal of Business*, Vol. 36 (July 1963).

B27 Ruggles, Nancy. "The Welfare Basis of the Marginal Cost Pricing Principle," *Review of Economic Studies*, Vol. 17, No. 1 (1949–50).

B28 Ruggles, Nancy. "Recent Developments in the Theory of Marginal Cost Pricing," *Review of Economic Studies*, Vol. 17, No. 2 (1949–50).

B29 Sharfman, Isaiah L. *The Interstate Commerce Commission: A Study In Administrative Law and Procedure*, Part Three, Volume B. New York: Oxford University Press, 1936.

B30 Steiner, Peter O. "Peak Loads and Efficient Pricing," *Quarterly Journal of Economics*, Vol. 71 (November 1957).

B31 Strotz, Robert H. "Urban Transportation Parables," in Julius Margolis, ed., *The Public Economy of Urban Communities*. Baltimore: Johns Hopkins Press for Resources for the Future, 1965.

B32 Vickrey, William. "Pricing as a Tool in Coordination of Local Transportation," in *Transportation Economics*. New York: Columbia University Press for the National Bureau of Economic Research, 1965.

B33 Walters, Alan A. "The Theory and Measurement of Private and Social Cost of Highway Congestion," *Econometrica*, Vol. 29 (October 1961).

B34 Westfield, Fred M. "Practicing Marginal-Cost Pricing—A Review," *Journal of Business*, Vol. 39 (January 1966).

B35 Wilson, George W. *Essays on Some Unsettled Questions in the Economics of Transportation*. Bloomington: Indiana University Library, 1962.

C. Location Theory and Location Decisions

C1 Alonso, William. "A Reformulation of Classical Location Theory and Its Relation to Rent Theory," in Morgan D. Thomas, ed., *Papers, The St. Louis Meeting, November, 1966*, Vol. 19, Regional Science Association, 1967.

C2 Borts, George H. "A Theory of Long-Run International Capital Movements," *Journal of Political Economy*, Vol. 72 (August 1964).

C3 Borts, George H., and Jerome L. Stein. *Economic Growth in a Free Market*. New York: Columbia University Press, 1964.

C4 Chenery, Hollis B. "Regional Analysis," in Hollis B. Chenery and Paul Clark, eds., *The Structure and Growth of the Italian Economy*. Rome: U.S. Mutual Security Agency, 1953.

C5 Creamer, Daniel. *Changing Location of Manufacturing Employment, Pt. 1: Changes by Type of Location, 1947–1961*. New York: National Industrial Conference Board, 1963.

C6 Fuchs, Victor R. *Changes in the Location of Manufacturing in the United States since 1929*. New Haven: Yale University Press, 1962.

C7 Hoover, Edgar M. *The Location of Economic Activity*. New York: McGraw-Hill, 1948.

C8   Isard, Walter. *Location and Space-Economy; A General Theory Relating to Industrial Location, Market Areas, Land Use, Trade, and Urban Structure.* Cambridge: M.I.T. Press, 1956.

C9   Isard, Walter. *Methods of Regional Analysis: An Introduction to Regional Science.* Cambridge: M.I.T. Press, 1960.

C10 Leontief, Wassily W. *The Structure of the American Economy, 1919–1939.* 2d ed. New York: Oxford University Press, 1951.

C11 Leontief, Wassily W., Alison Morgan, Karen R. Polenske, David Simpson, and Edward Tower. "The Economic Impact—Industrial and Re-gional—of an Arms Cut," *Review of Economics and Statistics,* Vol. 47 (August 1965).

C12 Meyer, John R. "Regional Economics: A Survey," *American Economic Review,* Vol. 53 (March 1963).

C13 Mueller, Eva, Arnold Wilken, and Margaret Wood. *Location Decisions and Industrial Mobility in Michigan, 1961.* Ann Arbor: University of Michi-gan, Survey Research Center, 1961.

C14 Olsson, Gunnar. "Central Place Systems, Spatial Interaction, and Stochastic Processes," *Regional Science Association Papers, Volume XVIII, 1967. European Congress, Vienna, 1966.* Philadelphia: Regional Science Asso-ciation and Wharton School, University of Pennsylvania, 1967.

C15 Perloff, Harvey S., Edgar S. Dunn, Jr., Eric E. Lampard, and Richard F. Muth. *Regions, Resources, and Economic Growth.* Baltimore: Johns Hopkins Press for Resources for the Future, 1960.

C16 Stewart, John Q. "Demographic Gravitation: Evidence and Applications," *Sociometry,* Vol. 2 (February and May 1948).

C17 Vernon, Raymond. *Metropolis 1985.* Cambridge: Harvard University Press, 1960.

C18 Weber, Alfred. *Theory of the Location of Industries.* Chicago: University of Chicago Press, 1929.

D. Urban Transportation Demand and Planning Techniques

D1   Barnes, Charles F., Jr. "Integrating Land Use and Traffic Forecasting," in *Forecasting Highway Trips.* Highway Research Bulletin 297. Washington: Highway Research Board, 1961.

D2   Black, Alan. "Comparison of Three Parameters of Nonresidential Trip Generation," in *Origin and Destination: Methods and Evaluation.* High-way Research Record 114. Washington: Highway Research Board, 1966.

D3   Bouchard, Richard J., and Clyde E. Pyers. "Use of Gravity Model for Describing Urban Travel: An Analysis and Critique," in *Travel Patterns.*

Highway Research Record 88. Washington: Highway Research Board, 1965.

D4   Brand, Daniel, Brian Barber, and Michael Jacobs. "Technique for Relating Transportation Improvements and Urban Development Patterns," in *Urban Land Use: Concepts and Models*. Highway Research Record 207. Washington: Highway Research Board, 1967.

D5   Carroll, J. Douglas, Jr., and Howard W. Bevis. "Predicting Local Travel in Urban Regions," in Gerald A. P. Carrothers and William Alonso, eds., *Papers and Proceedings of the Regional Science Association*, Vol. 3 (1957).

D6   Caswell, W. Stearns. "Effect of Zone Size on Zonal Interchange Calculations Based on the Opportunity Model in a Homogeneous Region," in *Origin and Destination: Advances in Transportation Planning*. Highway Research Record 165. Washington: Highway Research Board, 1967.

D7   Chapin, F. Stuart, Jr., and Shirley F. Weiss. *Factors Influencing Land Development*. Chapel Hill: University of North Carolina Press, 1962.

D8   Charles River Associates. "A Model of Urban Passenger Travel Demand in the San Francisco Metropolitan Area," Report 117-1. Processed. Cambridge: Charles River Associates, 1967.

D9   Cleveland, Donald E., and Edward A. Mueller. "Traffic Characteristics at Regional Shopping Centers." Processed. New Haven: Yale University, Bureau of Highway Traffic, 1961.

D10 Deen, Thomas B., William L. Mertz, and Neal A. Irwin. "Application of a Modal Split Model to Travel Estimates for the Washington Area," in *Travel Forecasting*. Highway Research Record 38. Washington: Highway Research Board, 1963.

D11 Domencich, Thomas A., Gerald Kraft, and Jean-Paul Valette. "Estimation of Urban Passenger Travel Behavior: An Economic Demand Model," in *Transportation System Evaluation*. Highway Research Record 238. Washington: Highway Research Board, 1968.

D12 Fertal, Martin J., and others. *Modal Split: Documentation of Nine Methods for Estimating Transit Usage*. U.S. Bureau of Public Roads. Washington: Government Printing Office, December 1966.

D13 Fitch, Lyle C., and Associates. *Urban Transportation and Public Policy*. San Francisco: Chandler Publishing Co., 1964.

D14 Fratar, Thomas J. "Forecasting Distribution of Interzonal Vehicular Trips by Successive Approximations," in *Proceedings of the Thirty-third Annual Meeting, January 1954*, Vol. 33. Washington: Highway Research Board, 1954.

D15 Gorman, David A., and Stedman Hitchcock. "Characteristics of Traffic Entering and Leaving the Central Business District," *Public Roads*, Vol. 30 (August 1959).

D16 Hansen, Walter G. "Evaluation of Gravity Model Trip Distribution Procedures," in *Trip Characteristics and Traffic Assignment*. Highway Research Bulletin 347. Washington: Highway Research Board, 1962.

D17 Hansen, Walter G. "How Accessibility Shapes Land Use," *Journal of the American Institute of Planners*, Vol. 25 (May 1959).

D18 Hansen, Walter G. "Land Use Forecasting for Transportation Planning," in *Traffic Origin-and-Destination Studies: Appraisal of Methods*. Highway Research Bulletin 253. Washington: Highway Research Board, 1960.

D19 Harper, B. C. S., and H. M. Edwards. "Generation of Person Trips by Areas Within the Central Business District," in *Traffic Origin-and-Destination Studies: Appraisal of Methods*. Highway Research Bulletin 253. Washington: Highway Research Board, 1960.

D20 Harris, Britton. "Experiments in Projection of Transportation and Land Use," *Traffic Quarterly*, Vol. 16 (April 1962).

D21 Harris, Britton. "Linear Programming and the Projection of Land Uses," PJ Paper 20. Processed. Philadelphia: Penn-Jersey Transportation Study (November 1962).

D22 Heanue, Kevin E., and Clyde F. Pyers. "A Comparative Evaluation of Trip Distribution Procedures," in *Origin and Destination: Methods and Evaluation*. Highway Research Record 114. Washington: Highway Research Board, 1966.

D23 Herbert, John D., and Benjamin H. Stevens. "A Model for the Distribution of Residential Activity in Urban Areas," *Journal of Regional Science*, Vol. 2 (Fall 1960).

D24 Hill, Donald M. "A Growth Allocation Model for the Boston Region," *Journal of the American Institute of Planners*, Vol. 31 (May 1965).

D25 Holmes, Edward H. "Highway Transportation," in *U.S. Transportation Resources, Performance, and Problems*. Publication 841-S. Washington: National Academy of Sciences–National Research Council (1961).

D26 Huff, David L. "A Probabilistic Analysis of Shopping Center Trade Areas," *Land Economics*, Vol. 39 (1963).

D27 Illinois Department of Public Works and Buildings. *Chicago Area Transportation Study, Final Report*, Vol. 2: *Data Projections*. Chicago, July 1960.

D28 Irwin, Neal A., and Daniel Brand. "Planning and Forecasting Metropolitan Development," *Traffic Quarterly*, Vol. 19 (October 1965).

D29 Kain, John F. "A Contribution to the Urban Transportation Debate: An Econometric Model of Urban Residential and Travel Behavior," *Review of Economics and Statistics*, Vol. 46 (February 1964).

D30 Kain, John F., and John R. Meyer. "Computer Simulations, Physio-economic Systems, and Intraregional Models," American Economic Association, *Papers and Proceedings of the Eightieth Annual Meeting, 1967* (*American Economic Review*, Vol. 58, May 1968).

D31   Kain, John F., and John R. Meyer. *A First Approximation to a RAND Model for Study of Urban Transportation*. RM-2878-FF. Santa Monica, Calif.: RAND Corporation, 1961.

D32   Kraft, Gerald, and Martin Wohl. "Special Survey Paper: New Directions for Passenger Demand Analysis and Forecasting," *Transportation Research*, Vol. 1 (November 1967).

D33   Kuhn, Tillo E. "The Economics of Transportation Planning in Urban Areas," in *Transportation Economics*. New York: Columbia University Press for the National Bureau of Economic Research, 1965.

D34   Lakshmanan, T. R., and Walter G. Hansen. "A Retail Market Potential Model," *Journal of the American Institute of Planners*, Vol. 31 (May 1965).

D35   Lathrop, George T., and John R. Hamburg. "An Opportunity-Accessibility Model for Allocating Regional Growth," *Journal of the American Institute of Planners*, Vol. 31 (May 1965).

D36   Levinson, Herbert S., and F. Houston Wynn. "Some Aspects of Future Transportation in Urban Areas," in *Urban Transportation: Demand and Coordination*. Highway Research Bulletin 326. Washington: Highway Research Board, 1962.

D37   Lowry, Ira S. *Model of Metropolis*. RM-4035-RC. Santa Monica, Calif.: RAND Corporation, 1964.

D38   Martin, Brian V., and Marvin L. Manheim. "A Research Program for Comparison of Traffic Assignment Techniques," in *Travel Patterns*. Highway Research Record 88. Washington: Highway Research Board, 1965.

D39   Mertz, William L. "Review and Evaluation of Electronic Computer Traffic Assignment Programs," in *Forecasting Highway Trips*. Highway Research Bulletin 297. Washington: Highway Research Board, 1961.

D40   Mertz, William L., and Lamelle B. Hamner. "A Study of Factors Related to Urban Travel," *Public Roads*, Vol. 29 (April 1957).

D41   Michigan State Highway Department. *Detroit Metropolitan Area Traffic Study*. Lansing, 1955.

D42   Oi, Walter Y., and Paul W. Shuldiner. *An Analysis of Urban Travel Demands*. Evanston: Northwestern University Press, 1962.

D43   Ruiter, Earl R. "Improvements in Understanding, Calibrating, and Applying the Opportunity Model," in *Origin and Destination: Advances in Transportation Planning*. Highway Research Record 165. Washington: Highway Research Board, 1967.

D44   Sharpe, Gordon B., Walter G. Hansen, and Lamelle B. Hamner. "Factors Affecting Trip Generation of Residential Land-Use Areas," *Public Roads*, Vol. 30 (October 1958).

D45   Shuldiner, Paul W. "Land Use, Activity, and Non-Residential Trip Generation," in *Origin and Destination: Methods and Evaluation.* Highway Research Record 114. Washington: Highway Research Board, 1966.

D46 Silver, Jacob. "Trends in Travel to the Central Business District by Residents of the Washington, D.C., Metropolitan Area, 1948 and 1955," *Public Roads,* Vol. 30 (April 1959).

D47 Soltman, Theodore J. "Effects of Alternate Loading Sequences on Results from Chicago Trip Distribution and Assignment Model," in *Origin and Destination: Methods and Evaluation.* Highway Research Record 114. Washington: Highway Research Board, 1966.

D48 Sosslau, Arthur B., Kevin E. Heanue, and Arthur J. Balek. "Evaluation of a New Modal Split Procedure," *Public Roads,* Vol. 33 (April 1964), pp. 5–19. This article also appears, in slightly abbreviated form, in *Travel Patterns* (pp. 44–68). Highway Research Record 88. Washington: Highway Research Board, 1965.

D49 Southeastern Wisconsin Regional Planning Commission, "Land Use-Transportation Study: Forecasts and Alternative Plans, 1990," in *Planning Report No. 7,* Vol. 2. Waukesha, June 1966.

D50 Steger, William A. "The Pittsburgh Urban Renewal Simulation Model," *Journal of the American Institute of Planners,* Vol. 31 (May 1965).

D51 U.S. Bureau of Public Roads. *Calibrating and Testing a Gravity Model for Any Size Urban Area.* Washington: Government Printing Office, July 1963.

D52 U.S. Bureau of Public Roads. *Calibrating and Testing a Gravity Model with a Small Computer.* Washington: Government Printing Office, October 1963.

D53 U.S. Bureau of Public Roads. *Pittsburgh Area Transportation Study,* Vol. 2: *Forecasts and Plans.* Washington: Government Printing Office, 1963.

D54 Voorhees, Alan M. "Forecasting Peak Hours of Travel," in *Travel Characteristics in Urban Areas.* Highway Research Bulletin 203. Washington: Highway Research Board, 1958.

D55 Voorhees, Alan M. "A General Theory of Traffic Movement," in *1955 Proceedings of the Institute of Traffic Engineers.* New Haven, 1955.

D56 Voorhees, Alan M., Charles F. Barnes, Jr., and Frances E. Coleman, "Traffic Patterns and Land-Use Alternatives," in *Trip Characteristics and Traffic Assignment.* Highway Research Bulletin 347. Washington: Highway Research Board, 1962.

D57 Walker, John R., and Gary R. Cowan. "Comparisons of Previous Seattle and Tacoma Origin and Destination Surveys with 1961 Puget Sound Regional Transportation Study Data." Staff Report 3 (rev.). Processed. Seattle: Puget Sound Regional Transportation Study, March 1964.

D58 Wright, Paul H. "Relationship of Traffic and Floor Space Use in Central Business District," in *Origin and Destination: Methods and Evaluation.*

Highway Research Record 114. Washington: Highway Research Board, 1966.

D59 Zettel, Richard M., and Richard R. Carll. *Summary Review of Major Metropolitan Area Transportation Studies in the United States*. Institute of Transportation and Traffic Engineering, Special Report. Berkeley: University of California, November 1962.

E. Intercity Transportation Demand

E1 Alcaly, Roger E. "Aggregation and Gravity Models: Some Empirical Evidence," *Journal of Regional Science*, Vol. 7 (Summer 1967).

E2 Belmont, Daniel M. "A Study of Airline Interstation Traffic," *Journal of Air Law and Commerce*, Vol. 25 (1958).

E3 Blackburn, Anthony J. "A Non-Linear Model of Passenger Demand," in *Studies in Travel Demand*, Vol. 2. Princeton: Mathematica, 1966.

E4 Blackburn, Anthony J. "A Test of a Generalized Gravity Model with Competitive Terms," in *Studies in Travel Demand*, Vol. 3. Princeton: Mathematica, 1967.

E5 Brown, Samuel L., and Wayne S. Watkins. "The Demand for Air Travel: A Regression Study of Time-Series and Cross-Sectional Data in the U.S. Domestic Market." Paper given at the 47th Annual Meeting of the Highway Research Board, January 16, 1968.

E6 Carrothers, Gerald A. P. "An Historical Review of the Gravity and Potential Concepts of Human Interaction," *Journal of the American Institute of Planners*, Vol. 22 (1956).

E7 CONSAD Research Corporation. "Design for Impact Studies." Northeast Corridor Transportation Project. Processed. Washington: CONSAD Research Corporation, 1965.

E8 Hammer, Carl, and Fred C. Ikle. "Intercity Telephone and Airline Traffic Related to Distance and the 'Propensity to Interact,'" *Sociometry*, Vol. 20 (December 1957).

E9 Ikle, Fred C. "Sociological Relationship of Traffic to Population and Distance," *Traffic Quarterly*, Vol. 8 (April 1954).

E10 Kent, Malcolm F. "Intercity Freight Haulage, by Commodity, Shipping Density and Type of Transport, 1960," in *Freight Transportation*. Highway Research Record 82. Washington: Highway Research Board, 1965.

E11 Lago, Armando M. "Intercity Highway Transportation Cost Functions in Underdeveloped Countries." Ph.D. dissertation, Harvard University, 1967.

E12 Lansing, John B., Jung-Chao Liu, and Daniel B. Suits. "An Analysis of Interurban Air Travel," *Quarterly Journal of Economics*, Vol. 75 (February 1961).

E13 Monsod, Solita. "A Cross-Sectional Model of the Demand for Rail Passenger Service in the Northeast Corridor," in *Studies in Travel Demand*, Vol. 2. Princeton: Mathematica, 1966.

E14 Morrill, R. L., and W. L. Garrison. "Projections of Interregional Patterns of Trade in Wheat and Flour," *Economic Geography*, Vol. 36 (1960).

E15 Moses, Leon N. "The Stability of Interregional Trading Patterns and Input-Output Analysis," *American Economic Review*, Vol. 45 (December 1955).

E16 Perle, Eugene D. *The Demand for Transportation: Regional and Commodity Studies in the United States*. Chicago: University of Chicago, Department of Geography, 1964.

E17 Polenske, Karen R. "A Case Study of Transportation Models Used in Multiregional Analysis." Ph.D. dissertation, Harvard University, 1966.

E18 Polenske, Karen R. "The Study of Transportation Requirements Using National and Multiregional Input-Output Techniques." Prepared for U.S. Department of Transportation. Processed. Springfield, Va.: Clearinghouse for Federal, Scientific and Technical Information, Report No. PB 174742 (April 1967).

E19 Putman, Stephen H. "Modeling and Evaluating the Indirect Impacts of Alternative Northeast Corridor Transportation Systems," in *Transportation System Analysis and Calculation of Alternate Plans*. Highway Research Record 180. Washington: Highway Research Board, 1967.

E20 Quandt, Richard E. "Tests of the Abstract Mode Model," in *Studies in Travel Demand*, Vol. 2. Princeton: Mathematica, 1966.

E21 Quandt, Richard E., and William J. Baumol. "The Abstract Mode Model: Theory and Measurement," in *Studies in Travel Demand*, Vol. 2. Princeton: Mathematica, 1967.

E22 Quandt, Richard E., and William J. Baumol. "The Demand for Abstract Transport Modes: Theory and Measurement," *Journal of Regional Science*, Vol. 6 (Winter 1966).

E23 Quandt, Richard E., and Kan Hua Young. "Cross-Sectional Travel Demand Models: Estimates and Tests," in *Studies in Travel Demand*, Vol. 3. Princeton: Mathematica, 1967.

E24 Richmond, Samuel B. "Interspatial Relationships Affecting Air Travel," *Land Economics*, Vol. 33 (February 1957).

E25 Rose, Mark L. "Some Problems and Prospects in Collecting Data on Travel Demand," in *Studies in Travel Demand*, Vol. 2. Princeton: Mathematica, 1966.

E26 *Studies in Travel Demand*, 3 vols. Princeton: Mathematica, 1966, 1967.

E27 Systems Analysis and Research Corporation. *Demand for Intercity Passenger Travel in the Washington-Boston Corridor*. Cambridge: SARC, 1963.

E28 U.S. Civil Aeronautics Board. "Measuring the Elasticity of Air Passenger Demand: A Cross-Section Study of Air Travel and Its Determinants in

300 City-Pairs in 1960 and 1964." Processed. Washington, December 1966.

E29 U.S. Civil Aeronautics Board. "Measuring the Elasticity of Air Passenger Demand: A Study of Changes Over Time from 1953–1964." Processed. Washington, February 1966.

E30 U.S. Civil Aeronautics Board. "Traffic, Fares, and Competition, Los Angeles-San Francisco Air Traffic Corridor." Staff Research Report 4. Processed. Washington, August 1965.

E31 Young, Kan Hua. "Testing the Adequacy of the Linear Abstract Mode Model," in *Studies in Travel Demand*, Vol. 3. Princeton: Mathematica, 1967.

E32 Zipf, George K. "The P_1P_2/D Hypothesis: On the Intercity Movement of Persons," *American Sociological Review*, Vol. 11 (December 1946).

F. Benefit Measurement and Resource Allocation

F1   American Association of State Highway Officials. *Road-User Benefit Analysis for Highway Improvements*. Washington, 1960.

F2   Baumol, William J. *Welfare Economics and the Theory of the State*. Cambridge: Harvard University Press, 1952.

F3   Brown, Robert T. "The 'Railroad Decision' in Chile," in Gary Fromm, ed., *Transport Investment and Economic Development*. Washington: Brookings Institution, 1965.

F4   Dorfman, Robert, ed. *Measuring Benefits of Government Investments*. Washington: Brookings Institution, 1965.

F5   Eckstein, Otto. "A Survey of the Theory of Public Expenditure Criteria," in *Public Finances: Needs, Sources, and Utilization*. Princeton: Princeton University Press for the National Bureau of Economic Research, 1961.

F6   Feldstein, Martin S. "Net Social Benefit Calculations and the Public Investment Decision," *Oxford Economic Papers*, Vol. 16 (March 1964).

F7   Graaff, J. de V. *Theoretical Welfare Economics*. London: Cambridge University Press, 1957.

F8   Harral, Clell G. "Preparation and Appraisal of Transport Projects." Washington: Brookings Institution, 1965, processed. Published by U.S. Department of Transportation, 1968.

F9   Harral, Clell G., and Tillo E. Kuhn. "Transport Planning in Developing Countries." Processed. Washington: Brookings Institution, June 1965.

F10 Henderson, Alexander. "Consumer's Surplus and the Compensating Variation," *Review of Economic Studies*, Vol. 8, No. 2 (February 1941).

F11 Henderson, James M., and Richard E. Quandt. *Microeconomic Theory: A Mathematical Approach*. New York: McGraw-Hill, 1958.

F12 Hicks, J. R. "The Generalised Theory of Consumer's Surplus," *Review of Economic Studies*, Vol. 13, No. 2 (1945–46).

F13 Hicks, J. R. *A Revision of Demand Theory.* Oxford: Clarendon Press, 1956.

F14 Hicks, J. R. *Value and Capital.* Oxford: Clarendon Press, 1939.

F15 Higgins, Benjamin H. *Economic Development: Principles, Problems, and Policies.* New York: Norton, 1959.

F16 Higgins, Benjamin H. "The 'Dualistic Theory' of Underdeveloped Areas," *Economic Development and Cultural Change*, Vol. 4 (January 1956).

F17 Hirschman, Albert O. *The Strategy of Economic Development.* New Haven: Yale University Press, 1958.

F18 Hufschmidt, Maynard M., John V. Krutilla, and Julius Margolis, with the assistance of Stephen A. Marglin. *Standards and Criteria for Formulating and Evaluating Federal Water Resources Developments.* Report of the Panel of Consultants to the Bureau of the Budget, 1961.

F19 Kaldor, Nicholas. "Welfare Propositions in Economics and Inter-Personal Comparisons of Utility," *Economic Journal*, Vol. 49 (September 1939).

F20 Knight, Frank H. "Some Fallacies in the Interpretation of Social Cost," *Quarterly Journal of Economics*, Vol. 38 (August 1924).

F21 Krutilla, John V., and Otto Eckstein. *Multiple Purpose River Development: Studies in Applied Economic Analysis.* Baltimore: Johns Hopkins Press, 1958.

F22 Kuhn, Tillo E. *Public Enterprise Economics and Transport Problems.* Berkeley: University of California Press, 1962.

F23 Little, Ian M. D. *A Critique of Welfare Economics.* 2d ed. Oxford: Clarendon Press, 1957.

F24 Maass, Arthur, and others. *Design of Water-Resource Systems.* Cambridge: Harvard University Press, 1962.

F25 McKean, Roland N. *Efficiency in Government through Systems Analysis, with Emphasis on Water Resources Development.* New York: Wiley, 1958.

F26 Marglin, Stephen A. *Public Investment Criteria.* Cambridge: M.I.T. Press, 1967.

F27 Marshall, Alfred. *Principles of Economics.* 8th ed. New York: Macmillan, 1920.

F28 Martin, Brian V., and Paul O. Roberts. "The Development of a Model for the Transport Sector," Harvard Transportation and Economic Development Seminar, Discussion Paper 18. Processed. Cambridge: Harvard Transport Research Program, 1965.

F29 Mera, Koichi. "Tradeoff Between Aggregate Efficiency and Interregional Equity: A Static Analysis," *Quarterly Journal of Economics*, Vol. 81 (November 1967).

F30 Mishan, E. J. "Realism and Relevance in Consumer's Surplus," *Review of Economic Studies*, Vol. 15, No. 1 (1947–48).

F31 Mishan, E. J. "A Survey of Welfare Economics, 1939–59," *Economic Journal*, Vol. 70 (June 1960).

F32 Mohring, Herbert. "Urban Highway Investments," in Robert Dorfman, ed., *Measuring Benefits of Government Investments*. Washington: Brookings Institution, 1965.

F33 Mohring, Herbert, and Mitchell Harwitz. *Highway Benefits, An Analytic Framework*. Evanston: Northwestern University Press, 1962.

F34 Myint, Hla. *Theories of Welfare Economics*. London: Longmans, 1948.

F35 Novick, David, ed. *Program Budgeting: Program Analysis and the Federal Budget*. Cambridge: Harvard University Press, 1966.

F36 Oglesby, Clarkson H., and Laurence I. Hewes. *Highway Engineering*. 2d ed. New York: Wiley, 1963.

F37 Pareto, Vilfredo. *Cours d'économie politique professé à l'Université de Lausanne*, Vol. 1. Lausanne: F. Rouge, 1896.

F38 Pigou, Arthur C. *The Economics of Welfare*. London: Macmillan, 1920.

F39 Prest, A. R., and R. Turvey. "Cost-Benefit Analysis: A Survey," *Economic Journal*, Vol. 75 (December 1965).

F40 Samuelson, Paul A. "Evaluation of Real National Income," *Oxford Economic Papers*, Vol. 2, New Series (1950).

F41 Samuelson, Paul A. "Social Indifference Curves," *Quarterly Journal of Economics*, Vol. 70 (February 1956).

F42 Schumpeter, Joseph A. *Capitalism, Socialism, and Democracy*. New York: Harper, 1942.

F43 van der Kroef, Justus M. "Economic Development in Indonesia: Some Social and Cultural Impediments," *Economic Development and Cultural Change*, Vol. 4 (January 1956).

F44 Weisbrod, Burton A. "Collective-Consumption Services of Individual-Consumption Goods," *Quarterly Journal of Economics*, Vol. 78 (August 1964).

F45 Weisskoff, Richard. "Transportation in Colombia: A Case Study of the Economics and Politics of Resource Allocation," Harvard Transportation and Economic Development Seminar, Discussion Paper 5. Processed. Cambridge: Harvard Transport Research Program, June 1964.

F46 Wildavsky, Aaron. "The Political Economy of Efficiency," *The Public Interest*, No. 8 (Summer 1967).

F47 Winch, David M. *The Economics of Highway Planning*. Toronto: University of Toronto Press, 1963.

G. Time Discounting

G1 Alchian, Armen. "The Rate of Interest, Fisher's Rate of Return Over Costs and Keynes' Internal Rate of Return," in Ezra Solomon, ed., *The Management of Corporate Capital*. Chicago: Free Press of Glencoe, 1959.

G2 Bierman, Harold, Jr., and Seymour Smidt. *The Capital Budgeting Decision: Economic Analysis and Financing of Investment Projects.* 2d ed. New York: Macmillan, 1966.

G3 Charnes, Abraham, William W. Cooper, and M. H. Miller. "Application of Linear Programming to Financial Budgeting and the Costing of Funds," in Ezra Solomon, ed., *The Management of Corporate Capital.* Chicago: Free Press of Glencoe, 1959.

G4 Farrar, Donald E. *The Investment Decision Under Uncertainty.* Englewood Cliffs, N.J.: Prentice-Hall, 1962.

G5 Feldstein, Martin S. "Opportunity Cost Calculations in Cost-Benefit Analysis," *Public Finance,* Vol. 19 (June 1964).

G6 Fisher, Irving. *Theory of Interest.* New York: Macmillan, 1930

G7 Gordon, Myron J. "The Payoff Period and the Rate of Profit," in Ezra Solomon, ed., *The Management of Corporate Capital.* Chicago: Free Press of Glencoe, 1959.

G8 Grant, Eugene L., and W. Grant Ireson. *Principles of Engineering Economy.* New York: Ronald Press, 1930.

G9 Hirshleifer, Jack. "Efficient Allocation of Capital in an Uncertain World," *American Economic Review,* Vol. 54 (May 1964).

G10 Hirshleifer, Jack. "On the Theory of Optimal Investment Decision," in Ezra Solomon, ed., *The Management of Corporate Capital.* Chicago: Free Press of Glencoe, 1959. Also in *Journal of Political Economy,* Vol. 66 (August 1958).

G11 Hirshleifer, Jack, James C. de Haven, and Jerome W. Milliman. *Water Supply: Economics, Technology, and Policy.* Chicago: University of Chicago Press, 1960.

G12 Lind, Robert C. "The Social Rate of Discount and the Optimal Rate of Investment: Further Comment," *Quarterly Journal of Economics,* Vol. 78 (May 1964).

G13 Lorie, James H., and Leonard J. Savage. "Three Problems in Rationing Capital," in Ezra Solomon, ed., *The Management of Corporate Capital.* Chicago: Free Press of Glencoe, 1959.

G14 McLean, John G. "How to Evaluate New Capital Investments," *Harvard Business Review,* Vol. 36 (November 1958).

G15 Marglin, Stephen A. "The Opportunity Costs of Public Investment," *Quarterly Journal of Economics,* Vol. 77 (May 1963).

G16 Marglin, Stephen A. "The Social Rate of Discount and the Optimal Rate of Investment," *Quarterly Journal of Economics,* Vol. 77 (February 1963).

G17 Mishan, E. J. "Criteria for Public Investment: Some Simplifying Suggestions," *Journal of Political Economy,* Vol. 75 (April 1967).

G18 Quirin, G. David. *The Capital Expenditure Decision.* Homewood, Ill.: Irwin, 1967.

G19 Renshaw, Ed. "A Note on the Arithmetic of Capital Budgeting Decisions," in Ezra Solomon, ed., *The Management of Corporate Capital*. Chicago: Free Press of Glencoe, 1959.

G20 Reuber, G. L., and R. J. Wonnacott. *The Cost of Capital in Canada—With Special Reference to Public Development of the Columbia River*. Washington: Resources for the Future, 1961.

G21 Robinson, Romney. "The Rate of Interest, Fisher's Rate of Return over Costs and Keynes' Internal Rate of Return: Comment," in Ezra Solomon, ed., *The Management of Corporate Capital*. Chicago: Free Press of Glencoe, 1959.

G22 Samuelson, Paul A. "Discussion," *American Economic Review*, Vol. 54 (May 1964).

G23 Solomon, Ezra. "The Arithmetic of Capital-Budgeting Decisions," in Ezra Solomon, ed., *The Management of Corporate Capital*. Chicago: Free Press of Glencoe, 1959.

G24 Tullock, Gordon. "The Social Rate of Discount and the Optimal Rate of Investment: Comment," *Quarterly Journal of Economics*, Vol. 78 (May 1964).

G25 Wright, J. F. "Notes on the Marginal Efficiency of Capital," *Oxford Economic Papers*, Vol. 15, New Series (July 1963).

H. Uncertainty, Probability Theory and Statistical Estimation, and Decision Theory

H1 Ackoff, Russell L. (with Shiv K. Gupta and J. Sayer Minas). *Scientific Method: Optimizing Applied Research Decisions*. New York: Wiley, 1962.

H2 Ellsberg, Daniel. "Risk, Ambiguity, and the Savage Axioms," *Quarterly Journal of Economics*, Vol. 75 (November 1961).

H3 Farrar, Donald E., and Robert R. Glauber. "Multicollinearity in Regression Analysis: The Problem Revisited," *Review of Economics and Statistics*, Vol. 49 (February 1967).

H4 Fellner, William. "Distortion of Subjective Probabilities as a Reaction to Uncertainty," *Quarterly Journal of Economics*, Vol. 75 (November 1961).

H5 Hirshleifer, Jack. "The Bayesian Approach to Statistical Decision: An Exposition," *Journal of Business*, Vol. 34 (October 1961).

H6 Johnston, John. *Econometric Methods*. New York: McGraw-Hill, 1963.

H7 Kuh, Edwin, and John R. Meyer. "How Extraneous Are Extraneous Estimates?" *Review of Economics and Statistics*, Vol. 39 (November 1957).

H8 Liu, Ta-Chung. "Underidentification, Structural Estimation, and Forecasting," *Econometrica*, Vol. 28 (October 1960).

H9 Luce, R. Duncan, and Howard Raiffa. *Games and Decisions*. New York: Wiley, 1957.

H10 Marquardt, Donald W. "An Algorithm for Least-Squares Estimation of Nonlinear Parameters," *Journal of the Society for Industrial and Applied Mathematics*, Vol. 11 (June 1963).

H11 Meyer, John R., and Robert R. Glauber. *Investment Decisions, Economic Forecasting, and Public Policy.* Boston: Harvard University, Graduate School of Business Administration, Division of Research, 1964.

H12 Pratt, John W. "Risk Aversion in the Small and in the Large," *Econometrica*, Vol. 32 (January–April 1964).

H13 Pratt, John W., Howard Raiffa, and Robert O. Schlaifer. *Introduction to Statistical Decision Theory.* New York: McGraw-Hill, 1965.

H14 Raiffa, Howard. *Decision Analysis.* Reading, Mass.: Addison-Wesley, 1968.

H15 Raiffa, Howard. "Risk, Ambiguity, and the Savage Axioms: Comment," *Quarterly Journal of Economics*, Vol. 75 (November 1961).

H16 Raiffa, Howard, and Robert O. Schlaifer. *Applied Statistical Decision Theory.* Boston: Harvard University, Graduate School of Business Administration, Division of Research, 1961.

H17 Savage, Leonard J. *The Foundations of Statistics.* New York: Wiley, 1954.

H18 Schlaifer, Robert O. *Probability and Statistics for Business Decisions.* New York: McGraw-Hill, 1959.

H19 Stone, Richard, and others. *The Measurement of Consumers' Expenditure and Behaviour in the United Kingdom, 1920–1938.* 2 Vols. London: Cambridge University Press, 1954.

H20 Tobin, James. "A Statistical Demand Function for Food in the U.S.A.," *Journal of the Royal Statistical Society*, Series A, Vol. 113 (1950).

II21 Wadsworth, George P., and Joseph G. Bryan. *Introduction to Probability and Random Variables.* New York: McGraw-Hill, 1960.

I. Programming Techniques

I1 Agin, Norman. "Optimum Seeking with Branch and Bound," *Management Science*, Vol. 13 (December 1966).

I2 Balinski, M. L. "Integer Programming: Methods, Uses, Computation," *Management Science*, Vol. 12 (November 1965).

I3 Baumol, William J., and Richard E. Quandt. "Investment and Discount Rates Under Capital Rationing—A Programming Approach," *Economic Journal*, Vol. 75 (June 1965).

I4 Bellman, Richard. "Notes on the Theory of Dynamic Programming—Transportation Models," *Management Science*, Vol. 5 (January 1958).

I5 Charnes, Abraham. *Introduction to Linear Programming, Part 2: Lectures on the Mathematical Theory of Linear Programming.* New York: Wiley, 1953.

I6 Charnes, Abraham, and William W. Cooper. "Chance-Constrained Programming," *Management Science*, Vol. 6 (October 1959).

I7 Charnes, Abraham, and William W. Cooper. "Networks and Models of
Incidence Type," in their *Management Models and Industrial Applications.* New York: Wiley, 1961.

I8 Clasen, R. J. "The MFOR Program." Processed. Santa Monica, Calif.:
RAND Corporation, 1962.

I9 Cooper, William W., and Alexander Henderson. *Introduction to Linear
Programming,* Part 1: *An Economic Introduction to Linear Programming.*
New York: Wiley, 1953.

I10 Dantzig, George B. "Application of the Simplex Method to a Transportation
Problem," in Tjalling C. Koopmans, ed., *Activity Analysis of Production
and Allocation.* New York: Wiley, 1951.

I11 Dantzig, George B. "The Shortest Route Problem," *Operations Research,*
Vol. 5 (1957).

I12 Davis, Ronald E., David A. Kendrick, and Martin Weitzman. "A Branch
and Bound Algorithm for Zero–One Mixed Integer Programming Problems." Project for Quantitative Research in Economic Development,
Report 69. Processed. Cambridge: Harvard University, Center for International Affairs, October 1967.

I13 Dorfman, Robert, Paul A. Samuelson, and Robert Solow. *Linear Programming and Economic Analysis.* New York: McGraw-Hill, 1958.

I14 Driebeek, Norman J. "An Algorithm for the Solution of Mixed Integer
Programming Problems," *Management Science,* Vol. 12 (March 1966).

I15 Farrar, Donald E. *The Investment Decision Under Uncertainty.* Englewood
Cliffs, N.J.: Prentice-Hall, 1962.

I16 Feldstein, Martin S. "Mean-Variance Analysis in the Theory of Liquidity
Preference and Portfolio Selection." Discussion Paper 6. Processed.
Cambridge: Harvard University Institute of Economic Research, No-
vember 1967.

I17 Ford, L. R., Jr., and D. R. Fulkerson. "Solving the Transportation Problem,"
Management Science, Vol. 3 (1956).

I18 Fox, Karl A. "A Spatial Equilibrium Model of the Livestock-Feed Economy
in the United States," *Econometrica,* Vol. 21 (October 1953).

I19 Freund, Rudolf J. "The Introduction of Risk into a Programming Model,"
Econometrica, Vol. 24 (July 1956).

I20 Funk, Monroe L., and Paul O. Roberts. "Toward Optimum Methods of
Link Addition in Transportation Networks." Processed. Evanston:
Northwestern University, September 1964.

I21 Healy, W. C., Jr. "Multiple Choice Programming (A Procedure for Linear
Programming with Zero–One Variables)," *Operations Research,* Vol. 12
(January–February 1964).

122 Henderson, James M. *The Efficiency of the Coal Industry: An Application of Linear Programming*. Cambridge: Harvard University Press, 1958.

123 Hershdorfer, Alan Martin. "Optimal Routing of Urban Traffic." Ph.D. dissertation, Massachusetts Institute of Technology, 1965.

124 Hitchcock, Frank L. "The Distribution of a Product from Several Sources to Numerous Localities," *Journal of Mathematics and Physics*, Vol. 20 (1941).

125 Kuhn, H. W., and A. W. Tucker. "Non-Linear Programming," in *Proceedings of the Second Berkeley Symposium on Mathematical Statistics and Probability*. Berkeley: University of California Press, 1951.

126 Land, A. H., and A. G. Doig. "An Automatic Method of Solving Discrete Programming Problems," *Econometrica*, Vol. 28 (July 1960).

127 Lawler, E. L., and D. E. Wood. "Branch-and-Bound Methods: A Survey," *Operations Research*, Vol. 14 (July–August 1966).

128 Marglin, Stephen A. *Approaches to Dynamic Investment Planning*. Amsterdam: North-Holland, 1963.

129 Markowitz, Harry. *Portfolio Selection*. New York: Wiley, 1959.

130 Moore, Edward F. "The Shortest Path Through a Maze." Paper presented at the International Symposium on Theory of Switching, Harvard University, 1957. (Reproduced as Bell Telephone System, Technical Publications Monograph 3523.)

131 Näslund, Bertil. "A Model of Capital Budgeting under Risk," *Journal of Business*, Vol. 39 (April 1966).

132 Näslund, Bertil, and Andrew Whinston. "A Model of Multi-period Investment Under Uncertainty," *Management Science*, Vol. 8 (January 1962).

133 Reiter, Stanley. "Choosing an Investment Program Among Interdependent Projects," *Review of Economic Studies*, Vol. 30 (February 1963).

134 Reiter, Stanley, and Gordon R. Sherman. "Discrete Optimizing," Institute for Quantitative Research in Economics and Management, Paper 37. Processed. Lafayette, Ind.: Purdue University, Krannert Graduate School of Industrial Administration, 1963.

135 Roberts, Paul O., P. N. Taborga, and Robert E. Burns. "A Model for the Formulation of Transport Alternatives." Paper presented to the American Society of Civil Engineers Conference, Miami, Florida, January 1966.

136 Taborga, P. N., and Paul O. Roberts. "Modelo Matemático, Para la Determinación de un Sistema de Transporte Óptimo en Chile," Inter-American Program Report. Processed. Cambridge: Massachusetts Institute of Technology, September 1965.

137 Van Horne, James. "Capital-Budgeting Decisions Involving Combinations of Risky Investments," *Management Science*, Vol. 13 (October 1966).

138 Weingartner, H. Martin. "Capital Budgeting of Interrelated Projects: Survey and Synthesis," *Management Science*, Vol. 12 (March 1966).

I39 Weingartner, H. Martin. *Mathematical Programming and the Analysis of Capital Budgeting Problems.* Englewood Cliffs, N.J.: Prentice-Hall, 1963.
I40 Wolfe, Philip. "The Simplex Method for Quadratic Programming," *Econometrica,* Vol. 27 (July 1959).

J. The Colombian Economy and Transport System

J1 Burns, Robert E. "An Applied Systems Approach for the Development of Regional and National Highway Systems in Underdeveloped Countries." Master's thesis, Massachusetts Institute of Technology, 1966.
J2 Haefele, Edwin T., ed. *Transport and National Goals.* Washington: Brookings Institution, 1969.
J3 Parsons, Brinckerhoff, Quade, and Douglas. "Plan for Improvements in National Transportation, Republic of Colombia." Processed. New York: Parsons, Brinckerhoff, Quade, and Douglas, 1961.

Index

337